Acting**Out**

Acting Out

Maladaptive Behavior in Confinement

Hans Toch and Kenneth Adams
with J. Douglas Grant and Elaine Lord

AMERICAN PSYCHOLOGICAL ASSOCIATION, WASHINGTON, DC

Published by
American Psychological Association
750 First Street, NE
Washington, DC 20002
www.apa.org

To order	Tel: (800) 374-2721, Direct: (202) 336-5510
APA Order Department	Fax: (202) 336-5502, TDD/TTY: (202) 336-6123
P.O. Box 92984	Online: www.apa.org/books/
Washington, DC 20090-2984	E-mail: order@apa.org

In the U.K., Europe, Africa, and the Middle East, copies may be ordered from
American Psychological Association
3 Henrietta Street
Covent Garden, London
WC2E 8LU England

Typeset in Palatino by EPS Group Inc., Easton, MD

Printer: Sheridan Books, Ann Arbor, MI
Cover designer: Naylor Design, Washington, DC
Technical/Production Editor: Jennifer Powers

The opinions and statements published are the responsibility of the authors,
and such opinions and statements do not necessarily represent the policies
of the American Psychological Association.

Library of Congress Cataloging-in-Publication Data
Toch, Hans.
    Acting out : maladaptive behavior in confinement / Hans Toch and
  Kenneth Adams, with J. Douglas Grant and Elaine Lord
      p. cm.
    Rev. ed. of: Coping, maladaptation in prisons. ©1989.
    Includes bibliographical references and index.
    ISBN 1-55798-880-3 (softcover : alk. paper)
      1. Prisoners—New York (State)—Longitudinal studies.
  2. Prisoners—New York (State)—Mental health.
  3. Prison psychology.   4. Adjustment (Psychology)
  5. Deviant behavior.   I. Adams, Kenneth, 1953–   II. Grant, James
  Douglas, 1917–   III. Lord, Elaine.   IV. Toch, Hans. Coping,
  maladaptation in prisons.   V. Title.

    HV9475.N7
    365'.6'019—dc21   2002001986

British Library Cataloguing-in-Publication Data
A CIP record is available from the British Library.

Printed in the United States of America
First Edition

To the memory of
Lawrence Holbrook,
epitome of the Renaissance man.

Contents

Preface

Revised books have been compared to suits with refash-ioned lapels, and such may indeed hold where books are unimprovable, and it takes nothing more than a nip here and a tuck there and a brief mention of the inexorable passage of time.

Acting Out is a reincarnation of a book called *Coping*. In its retailored edition, this book has been fully revamped, al-though we are not ashamed of the study the original edition reported. We have, however, ourselves changed in the past 15 years, and so has the world of prisons. The problems of disturbed inmates that posed dilemmas at the time of our research efforts have now reached crisis proportions. Solu-tions to these problems are no closer at hand now than they were then. The situation may be to some measure due to changes in the makeup of institutionalized populations, which show increased admixtures of multiproblem individ-uals, many of who tend to experience impaired mental health. As a confluence, however, responses to behavioral manifestations of psychological problems in detention facili-ties have become less tolerant, more risk aversive, and more punitive. Nowadays, disturbed individuals whose difficulties express themselves in abrasive or destructive ways are mostly apt to languish in settings calculated to perpetuate or worsen their condition.

Many observers of prisons complacently point out that conditions of confinement have steadily improved across the board, because the overpopulation of jails and prisons is no longer at emergency levels. And with regard to the specific subject of our concern, mental health services appear to have become more widely available, and due-process considera-tions seem to be more salient where inmates are subject to punitive dispositions.

Such developments, however, have been overwhelmed by obsessive concerns with custodial objectives, and some fo-rensic mental health workers have adjusted to the overarching perspective by viewing clients who act out with undiluted trepidation, cynicism, and pessimism. As for enhanced commitment to due process, this has frequently translated into bureaucratic formalities governing the dispensation of ever-more draconian dispositions.

The clients of punitive ministrations have often enacted the self-fulfillment of assigned prophecies. Diagnosed character deficiencies have reliably asserted themselves, sequestered troublemakers have made scheduled trouble, and earmarked rebels have duly rebelled. As the upshot, isolation cells have proliferated, occupied by men lost in anesthetizing sleep, pacing endlessly with restless boredom, nurturing bitterness and rage, and cementing the unregenerate violence-proneness that was their foreordained fate.

Some prison managers fortunately have had second thoughts about the human impact of prevailing custodialism. Across the United States, moves are tentatively under way to ameliorate the most extreme sensorily depriving conditions of incarceration, and prisons have begun to attend to the prevalence of mental illness among those who are punitively confined. Litigation may provide a spur, but much concern is proactive and genuinely humane.

In reappraising our work, we mourn the loss of a member of our team, J. Douglas Grant, a close friend and long-term mentor. We have represented, as best we can, Doug's contributions to our communal endeavor. We have expanded on Doug's cherished ideas of differential treatment, the involvement of clients in self-appraisal and self-reform, and the participation of frontline workers in therapeutic interventions.

We have concomitantly added a new valued member to our team to supplement our substantive coverage and enrich our perspective. We have enlisted the partnership of Superintendent Elaine Lord, a redoubtable innovator and veteran manager of a pioneering women's prison. With Elaine's involvement, we have filled a gap in our study and hopefully broadened the generalizability of our inferences.

Finally, we have tried to highlight and sharpen those themes in our analysis that we think have stood the test of time and appear congruent with the findings of other researchers, including observers working in different settings with different populations. We have also fleshed out, as best we could, some notions about what could be done to ameliorate the problems we have described. We hope that our book has thus gained in substance as well as timeliness, although we see no problem ourselves with stylishly refashioned lapels.

Acknowledgments

The book reflects experience accumulated in a research enterprise that spanned several years. This enterprise was underwritten by a grant (R01-MH39573) from the Center for Studies of Antisocial and Violent Behavior of the National Institute of Mental Health. Our hosts—who extended themselves to permit the work to be done—were the New York State Department of Correctional Services and the New York Office of Mental Health. We owe particular debts of gratitude in this connection to Raymond Broaddus and Frank Tracy of the Department of Correctional Services and to Joel Dvoskin and Ronald Greene of the Office of Mental Health.

We are most grateful to our associates, Gail Flint and Mary Finn, for long hours organizing data collection, coding records, and supervising research assistants. We also owe thanks to Timothy Flanagan, Cornelius Stockman, and Alan Lizotte for helpful suggestions, and we could not have operated without repeated accommodations made by Donna Mackay and her staff to allow for our protracted searches through inmate records. Finally, Sally Spring worked many months transcribing case histories and typing and retyping text. Her patience, sense of humor, and attention to detail eased the more onerous aspects of our effort.

The original version of this book, which was called *Coping*, was put out by Transaction Publishers in 1989 and issued in paperback in 1991. We are indebted to Irving Louis Horowitz for publishing *Coping* and for deaccessing the book to enable us to prepare a new, revised edition.

As for the present volume, which updates and revises our thinking on the subject, it would not have come about without the support and persistence of Mary Lynn Skutley of APA Books and her colleagues. Judy Nemes and Jennifer Powers guided the development and production of the manuscript and Karen Silinsky heroically gave it shape. David Lovell was a source of ever-helpful suggestions, and we are grateful for his wise counsel.

Our thanks to Kluwer Academic Publishers for republication of extracts from "Effective Treatment for Disturbed Violent Prisoners?" which appeared in S. Hodgins (Ed.), *Violence Among the Mentally Ill* (2000). Also, thanks go to Sage Publications for an excerpt from "The Future of Supermax Confinement" published September 2001 in *The Prison Journal, 81*, 375–387. Other material is reprinted with permission from Harry H. Vorrath and Larry K. Brendtro, *Positive Peer Culture* (2nd ed., New York: Aldine de Gruyter). Copyright 1985 Harry H. Vorrath and Larry K. Brendtro.

Acting Out

1

Introduction: Studying Maladaptive Behavior in Confinement

In this book, we combine a concern with personal destructiveness and an interest in mental health problems, and describe what we see as the overlap. Our focus is on the perspectives and motives of people who repetitively act out. This differs from more familiar research questions that have to do with violence propensities, if any, of patients diagnosed with a serious mental illness. A redoubtable literature has sprung up about this subject, covering efforts to predict the chances of patients behaving violently[1] to rosters of prescriptions for the prevention and treatment of violence among mentally ill offenders.[2]

This literature responds appropriately to public concerns and apprehensions. Accentuating dangerousness, however, can lead to intrusive interventions based on inflated assessments of risk. Overselling the notion that the link between mental illness and violence is somehow distinct also makes it more difficult to discover common denominators in the dynamics of violence or destructive behavior. We ourselves believe that if one wishes to intersect and interrupt destructive careers, one has to make sense of them, no matter where individuals fall on a diagnostic spectrum or how much damage they do. What we need to this end are concepts that highlight both uniqueness and commonality among motives for destructiveness.

We confined our own study to descriptions of prison behavior of convicted offenders who have acted out in confinement settings. Some of these individuals will have been diagnosed as emotionally disturbed, others will have been described as intellectually limited or inept, as callous and amoral, as culturally constrained or malformed. The behavior we review, which involves repeated acting out, will invariably be viewed (although not by the individuals themselves) as maladaptive.

Maladaptive Behavior

The criteria that are customarily used when observers classify behavior as maladaptive imply notions of the person consistently failing to accomplish goals; arranging for self-destructive or self-injurious contingencies; demonstrating deficits of perceptiveness, skill, or acumen; and, finally, creating problems for the environment and other people in the environment.[3] It is reasonable to assume that any and all of these criteria could denote maladaptation, with the proviso that "all" is more convincing than "any" in adjudging behavior maladaptive.

If we take our four criteria in combination, it means that people who manifest patterned maladaptation must demonstrate consistent failures of accomplishment or self-defeating behavior, manifest clumsiness and other deficits in efforts to negotiate their environment, and produce problems for others around them.

Combinations that fall short of this formula might be considered less serious or more specialized. A disturbed student who is disruptive and academically deficient might thus be considered a more serious problem than a student who is disruptive but who academically excels; however, a student who regularly assaults vulnerable classmates could qualify as a very serious problem even if the student is academically proficient and gets an exemplary bill of mental health.

Maladaptive behavior is almost invariably pathologically tinged, in the sense that conventional conceptions of mentally healthy behavior fit uneasily when we use them to describe patterns of maladaptation. Maladaptive involvements reflect distorted appraisals, skewed perspectives, and specialized motives, impervious to experiences of failure. When we say of a maladaptive person "he (or she) cannot be diagnosed as emotionally disturbed," it is a far cry from providing the person a clean bill of mental health.

In practice, we prefer to think of the actions of disruptive individuals as resulting from unencumbered exercises of rational choice. We especially prefer it when these individuals engage in the habitual use of violence or aggression. A pattern of repeated acting out invites reactions to the harm the person does and the fact that he or she keeps doing it. In responding this way, we are not tempted to uncover psychological states or traits, short of pathology, that may underlie a person's acting-out behavior.

In a recent court proceeding that illustrates how this issue arises, an obstreperous defendant named David Mooney had threatened to kill the president of the United States. The judge in the case (*United States v. Mooney*, 123 F Supp.2d 442 [ND Ill. 2000]) recalled that

> This Court made some evidentiary rulings against the prosecution and other evidentiary rulings against the defense. At the conclusion of the day Mooney reacted with extreme and frightening violence in direct consequence of the adverse rulings, even though his counsel had apparently told him that they believed things were going quite well in substantive terms.

The judge directed that the defendant, Mr. Mooney, be hospitalized for a mental health examination to determine his competence to stand trial. The examiner's report, when submitted, included a status summary describing the examinee's behavior while confined in the hospital. The summary included the following details:

He reportedly pulled a toilet seat off the wall, stating: "I'll kill anyone that comes near me . . . He received several additional incident reports during the first week of his stay at FMC [Federal Medical Center] Rochester. He remained in the locked unit for his entire stay, due to extremely disruptive and threatening behaviors at various times throughout the evaluation period . . . The following morning he apologized to the Officer and asked for a pen and paper to write apologies to all the staff members he had offended. He was observed by staff to be calm, articulate, lucid, and coherent during interactions that day.

Three days later, however, Mr. Mooney refused to put on leg irons for his physical examination. Despite being informed of the reasons for the leg irons, Mr. Mooney became irate, loud, and argumentative, and he was not redirectable. Similarly, on August 3, 1999, he requested Tylenol for tooth pain and, when he was told he could not have a larger dose than that which was ordered, he became verbally abusive and demanding. Finally, after receiving an order for more medications, the nurse noted that he controlled his behavior for several minutes to enable her to open the trap door. She reported that once the trap door was opened, he slapped the medications and water off the trap door. She reported that he stated, "next time you reach your arm over here, I will f—ing pull it off. Write me up for that, f—ing bitch." . . . He began banging and pounding on his cell wall and door and would not respond to redirection. The next day he was observed by staff trying to remove his desk from its bolts in the floor and wall. He reportedly made threats to harm staff with the desk. He succeeded in pulling the desk out of its floor bolts, continuing to make threatening comments toward staff. He hid under the bed so he could not be effectively monitored. He also threw food around his cell on occasion and pounded on the wall of his cell, yelling at the inmate next door. When the defendant returned from his (dental) appointment, he demanded pain medication and when this was not delivered promptly, he flooded the toilet in his cell while laughing and swearing at the staff. In total, Mr. Mooney received incident reports for making verbal threats, refusing to obey orders, 2 counts of destruction of property, and multiple counts of insolence.

The examiner in his report concluded that Mr. Mooney's acting out was not a product of a mental disease or defect subsumable under standard *Diagnostic and Statistical Manual of Mental Disorders* (4th ed., *DSM–IV*) diagnostic categories. He wrote in part,

> The majority of his behavioral outbursts appeared to be in response to clear precipitating factors, often involving his requests and demands not being immediately gratified. He exhibited no apparent psychotic symptomatology during the course of his evaluation. He demonstrated no confusion or disorganization of thought and consistently denied auditory and visual hallucinations. He slept well and ate well, he was active, and he displayed no problems with concentration and memory.
>
> While he has evidenced some disruptive and destructive behavior while at FMC Rochester, these behaviors appeared volitional and seemed to be a reaction to specific precursors. This contrasts with what one would expect of an individual in a manic state. Mr. Mooney's behavior during his stay at FMC Rochester suggests he has a severe personality disorder that includes antisocial and borderline (psychotic) personality traits, although the defendant does not appear to meet full diagnostic criteria for either personality disorder.

A second expert later testified for the defense and disagreed with the assessment. He wrote that

> There would be no logical, conscious, adult reason why anyone would act so badly while in prison. What would Mr. Mooney have to gain in a logical adult sense? . . . The FMC admits that he reacts severely to known precipitants. I strongly believe that it is naïve and unsophisticated of FMC to state, "these behaviors appeared volitional." . . . It would make no adult, logical sense at

all for anyone to react in this way, especially with the consistency as Mr. Mooney did.

To underline the consistency he had alluded to, the expert added that

> Today I received a (collect) call from David Mooney. He stated that he had read my report, given to him by his attorney, and was going to "tear it up and throw it into the toilet." His voice was loud and angry . . . He used much profanity.

The judge, who had been on the receiving end of Mr. Mooney's acting-out behavior in the courtroom, was not about to be appeased by the assertion that Mr. Mooney "did not fit into any of the categories of mental diseases identified in the *DSM–IV*" or the argument that his "'personality disorder' . . . does not meet the statutory standard of 'mental disease or defect.'" The judge resoundingly rejected the implicit presumption of normalcy of Mr. Mooney's behavior. He wrote

> Indeed, [the] conclusion that Mooney's explosive manifestations of rage represent "volitional behavior" is totally unrealistic and is flat-out rejected by this Court . . . [The examiner] has not observed, as this court has on two separate occasions, the totally out-of-control violent behavior by Mooney that has manifested itself in the specific environment of trial and other legal proceedings.

As for the insignificance of the alleged residual diagnoses, the judge wrote

> I conclude that a personality disorder such as that suffered by Appellant is much more than a mere quirk. It is a systemic, enduring, and severe condition resulting in an extremely abnormal perception of and reaction to everyday events . . . It is an enduring pattern of behavior and inner experience which can affect cognition (i.e., ways of perceiving and understanding) and affectivity

(emotional reactions). Therefore, it can be said to be "mental." In addition, it does not just manifest itself now and again in response to a particular set of circumstances; it is pervasive and inflexible. It is not just one part of a person's personality which is annoying, distasteful, or rude; it is a trait or group of traits which dominates the person's mental state to the point where they experience significant functional impairment or subjective stress. Thus, it comports with the general connotation of a "disease or defect" in that it is neither a temporary condition nor a chosen way of responding but rather a systemic, impairing psychiatric abnormality.

The judge also took the opportunity to unburden himself of a "parenthetical observation" relating to what he called a "tyranny of labels" and the "total reliance" on "*DSM–IV* pigeon holes." He observed that

> Anyone who had had occasion to address problems in the field of mental health (or its absence) has to be conscious of some fundamental difficulties with the *DSM–IV* definitions, which will sometimes provide (for example) that someone who exhibits four of seven specified characteristics fits a defined category of mental disease, while someone who exhibits only three of the seven does not. Even apart from the problems inherent in seeking to establish bright-line rules for exploring the arcane mysteries of the human mind, the just-described approach necessarily treats all of the characteristics at issue as somehow fungible and of equal weight, thus ascribing no significance to the subtle differences and gradations that exist in this most difficult field of diagnosis (wholly unlike the objective medical determination whether, for example, a patient has suffered a fracture).

Diagnostic lines of the sort alluded to in this sidebar comment are admittedly hard to draw and sometimes are mechanically drawn by insensitively ignoring the "subtle differences and gradations" cited by the judge. Once drawn, however, diagnostic lines have ineluctable consequences.

One such consequence in this case was that of downgrading Mr. Mooney's pattern of maladaptiveness and underselling its complexity. The judge's reaction to the examiner may have been partly prompted by the desire not to have to deal with Mr. Mooney in the courtroom should he be adjudged competent. More to the point, however, the judge had personally experienced the indignant rage sparked in Mr. Mooney by innocuous actions he had somehow defined as threatening, rejecting, or belittling him. The judge had become aware of the consuming nature of the self-doubt and suspiciousness that impelled Mr. Mooney to act out as he did. The judge appropriately concluded that he could not conceive of the behavior he had witnessed as falling within the pale of normal behavior. He was consequently appreciative when a second expert highlighted the complexity of Mr. Mooney's motivations and their deviation from normalcy.

The case is unusual because of the personal experience of the judge and his recognition of its implications. But the incidents in the hospital record are not unusual. We review several such institutional careers later in this book and describe their patterning and consistency. We shall have occasion to cite many instances in which behavior similar to Mr. Mooney's was deemed not to qualify for diagnoses of mental illness. Such failures to qualify for a diagnosis must not be taken to mean that the maladaptive inmates at issue were mentally healthy.

The outcome of the Mooney case illustrates both the dilemma posed by maladaptive behavior and its refractory nature. The judge ended his dictum by expressing

> deep concern that Mooney may well face long-term (even lifetime) commitment for a charged offense as to which he has not been found guilty and that, even if he *were* convicted, would not call for anything remotely approaching such a result.

We shall see that there are also careers similar to that of Mr. Mooney's which mature out or go into remission or become attenuated over time. Other such patterns of maladaptation, however, continue for long periods and there is often no resolution in sight.

Mr. Mooney's prospects were partly uninviting because he posed a continuing risk, not only in the courtroom but also elsewhere. An expert's report said of Mr. Mooney, "the precipitants, frequency and intensity of his rages are unpredictable. During them, he would most likely be very dangerous." Mr. Mooney had exploded when he had felt put upon, and he had felt provoked with disquieting frequency. Given the redundancy with which Mr. Mooney had acted out, it was reasonable to assume he would keep doing so.

One can respond to dilemmas such as those presented by Mr. Mooney with efforts to incapacitate the individual by escalating the penalties for violent acts he might commit. Because Mr. Mooney had not in fact committed a violent act, an alternative option would be to involuntarily confine him to a hospital, where the disorder that presumably underlay his threatening behavior could be hypothetically addressed. Failing this, Mr. Mooney could be held indefinitely, as long as he remained diagnosably disturbed and presumably dangerous.

But the strategy of confining Mr. Mooney only relegates the problem he poses to the setting in which he has been confined. By extension, this induces the setting to confine him even further. We note that the hospital report records that "he remained in the locked unit for his entire stay." The confinement within confinement was not buttressed by diagnostic considerations but was a response to Mr. Mooney's acting-out behavior. Mr. Mooney was thus imprisoned within the hospital for posing a perceived danger to its staff. Should he act out more seriously—such as by physically assaulting a staff member—he could be arrested, charged, convicted, and imprisoned. He would presumably then get to act out in the prison, probably end up on long-term segregation status, and qualify as a subject for our study.

One needs to react to what Mr. Mooney is doing as long as he is doing it. But if one were to be alarmed or put off by Mr. Mooney's disruptiveness to the point of becoming over-cautious, one might be reacting to risk where it no longer exists. We could create the risk we predict if our security measures struck Mr. Mooney as unfair, demeaning, and arbitrary, calling for an angry (and thus risk-aversive) response. This sort of process can escalate, with Mr. Mooney ending up sequestered in a supermax cell nurturing a towering and impotent rage.

The Disturbed–Disruptive Syndrome

People who act out arrive disproportionately in prisons, where they continue to act out, to the discomfiture of officials who administer prisons. Not least among sources of discomfiture is the fact that the prisoners who act out frequently defy stereotypical preconceptions, which draw watertight distinctions between cold, premeditated troublemaking and clear-cut mental illness.

Contrasting images are reinforced by the research literature, which describes chronic prison infractors as young, criminally sophisticated offenders who serve short sentences but arrive with extensive apprenticeships in jungle warfare from exposure to juvenile facilities and other prisonlike settings.[4] By contrast, the inmates we see as having trouble surviving in prison are depicted as personally nonresilient and disadvantaged individuals with subculturally unsophisticated backgrounds and histories of mental health problems, who follow a retreatist path in the prison and are victimized by more sophisticated peers.[5]

The contrast between these two types is inviting on several grounds. First, it helps us make a distinction between mad and bad people, which is conceptually reassuring, particularly because "madness" can be attributed to personal limitations whereas "badness" can be blamed on exercises of volition. Second, the two types of people appear to call for different institutional responses, which in one case means punitive (or at best, corrective) measures, and in the other case consists of protective, supportive, and therapeutic services. And finally, the two types of people are ideal-type participants in stereotyped transactions in which transgressors are victimizers and the "weak" provide a pool of invitingly help-less victims.[6]

Considerations such as these account for the fact that the literature contains little information that points to the eva-nescence of the distinction between intransigence and non-resilience. This failure to consider mad (weak)/bad (tough) combinations holds particularly for offender populations, who consequently bluff us (despite evidence of neuroticism, for instance) with well-rehearsed veneers of toughness or re-gale us with rosters of symptoms in mitigation of shame-lessly predatory behavior.

Occasional indicators exist, to be sure, that raise questions for us about the airtightness of customary dichotomies, par-ticularly in settings such as prison where we have client be-havior under close scrutiny. Settings created for particularly troublesome inmates, for example, are redolent with obvious mental health problems,[7] whereas diagnosed inmate–patients, when they are not medicated into a stupor, can be troublesome to their keepers. The latter fact has enabled us to describe a subpopulation of *disturbed–disruptive inmates* who do a great deal of shuttling between disciplinary seg-regation and mental health settings.[8] This group often causes conflicts among staff in the prison around the question of who is a "legitimate mental health problem" as opposed to a management problem masquerading as a patient.[9]

Our presumption is that the disturbed–disruptive combi-nation is the tip of an iceberg whose dimensions may be sub-stantial. This would mean that an unknown proportion of people who *are* problems (prove troublesome to settings in which they function) also *have* problems (demonstrate psy-chological and social deficits when they are subjected to closer scrutiny).

In making this assumption, we recognize that definitional problems are overwhelming. The latter consideration partic-ularly applies to nonresilience, which lacks criterion mea-sures that are agreed on and reliable.

Mental health staff in prisons who could call attention to the complexity of motives for maladaptation have a disin-centive for doing so. Staff could be hypothetically swamped with uninviting clients if they contended that chronicity of misbehavior denotes complexity of motive and that the persistent infractor has implicit mental health problems.[10] They gain most freedom by asserting that typical infractors are of no interest to clinical professionals in that they at worst have a characterological defect that is unresponsive to therapeutic ministrations.[11]

Disciplinary or custodial personnel sometimes press a differentiated view, in that they can raise the issue of whether an inmate is disturbed or nondisturbed; however, the question they cannot pose has to do with the appropriateness, congruence, or fit between the inmate's behavior and the prison's response to the behavior. This question arises because the prison's response—which is mostly punitive—implicitly presupposes that the inmate's behavior is in fact volitional and susceptible to deterrence. This means that disciplinary sanctions would be particularly appropriate where the inmate does what he or she does because he or she wants to (and would do it again) but would be less appropriate where the inmate's motives are actually complex and his or her basic problem or disposition remains predictably unaddressed by the sanctions to which the inmate must be subjected.

The point was well captured by Vernon Fox 30 years ago when he wrote that

> The traditional prison summary court, which places prisoners in solitary confinement for misconduct, operates on the assumption that the offender is a free moral agent who chooses to violate rules and can be "conditioned" to behave otherwise . . . The increased demand on the emotionally immature individual or the psychopath actually intensifies his problem, setting up the recidivism cycles and resulting in repeated misconduct of the same general type without the ability to appraise himself.
>
> For those people, there is a need for a moratorium on the system of rewards and punishments to permit emotional maturation to occur in a controlled environment . . . Consequently, the custodial personnel who attempt to maintain discipline in a prison must be prepared to

> understand human behavior, rather than trying to judge
> the amount of pressure necessary to keep a man in line.[12]

It appears obvious that when prison staff themselves show sophistication by raising questions, or when they contend that questions relating to the inmate's motivation or limitations could be raised if a forum for raising such questions existed, we ought to assume that the inmate's pattern of maladaptation deserves scrutiny even though mental health staff may maintain that the inmate is clinically nondisturbed. This does not mean that the line between "routine" chronic misbehavior and more complex patterns of maladaptiveness is easy to draw. It does mean, however, that any attempt to draw this line by exploring the complexity of inmate motives can render a service both to the inmate and to those who must deal with him or her.

This issue is not confined to prisons and their inmates. Disruptive students in school settings raise similar questions, and they keep raising them as they move from classrooms to alternative classrooms to reformatories, jails, and prisons. In the case of some such unimpressive careers, dossiers contain diagnoses such as "childhood schizophrenia" and "extreme learning disability" while simultaneously listing a "conduct disorder" transmuting into an "antisocial personality." At the same time, they describe the person with characterizations such as "hedonistic," "callous," "predatory," "explosive," and "manipulative" but abound with references to low self-esteem, bouts of anxiety, and traumatic injuries sustained by falling off trees.

Confusing biographies not only reflect checkered careers but also reveal unsuccessful efforts by observers to make sense of them. To help improve understanding, we would have to accommodate added complexity by recognizing that conceptually disparate traits (including vulnerabilities and antisocial propensities) can coexist, and different labels can address different features of the same person or traits that emerge at different points in time. We would also have to acknowledge that observers will talk past each other as long as they reflect different concerns (a concern with disruptiveness, for instance, or a concern with pathology) and are un-willing to relinquish these concerns. It is obvious, moreover, that some concepts are inhospitable to integrated perspec-tives because they preempt, while at the same time they maintain distance from the data to be explained, which are the person's specific acts. It may be sophisticated to postulate that a person's misbehavior has neurological origins, for in-stance, but this hypothesis does not help us to understand why the person does what he or she does.

The word *understand*, in this context is crucial. In trying to explain maladaptation to any setting, we need information that people who run the setting can use in making sense of behavior. We also need concepts the maladaptive person himself or herself can use in trying to get a handle on his or her behavior, which excludes concepts that are needlessly pe-jorative, intangible, or obtuse.

Concepts that are most useful in this regard must describe patterns of behavior; they must accommodate change while acknowledging continuity. Characterizations must be careful not to follow individuals beyond their point of applicability or presuppose qualitative shifts where change is a mixed bag. The phrase *schizophrenia, recovered, in remission,* for example, sounds as if it describes a person who was ill but is now well; but what matters most about many individuals de-scribed in this way is that they are neither ill nor well, usually have a great deal of difficulty adjusting to life situations, and can be driven over the edge by overwhelming demands.

It is important to be aware of where the person stands in relation to his or her short-term and long-term career, as is a sense of how the person relates to his or her environment. In this regard, it is crucial that clinicians and others who deal with a person have intimate knowledge of the setting in which the person functions (a school psychologist, for ex-ample, is advantaged in dealing with a maladaptive student), and this includes researchers such as ourselves who are con-cerned with studying adaptation or maladaptation. In this sense, any study of prison adaptation must be based on knowledge of the prison, and the reader of such a study probably is likely to encounter more detail than he or she wishes to about life in the prison.

The Subject of Our Study

The content of this book can be described with varying degrees of pretentiousness. At minimum, we can claim to present highlights of a research study in which we follow problem prisoners over a period of years, with attention to the sequence in which their problems arise. We focus on mental health and behavioral problems and center on combinations of the two.

We study inmates over time because we are interested in personal change. We presume that being in prison represents a phase of a *career*, in the same sense as does a term in school or a period of employment. And just as scholastic averages often increase or decrease and work performance improves or declines, we expect change to occur in the behavior of people who happen to be sequestered and confined. This notion may seem obvious, but it is not, in that most citizens see prisons as places of storage.[13] As for prisoners, their goal of "doing time" implies that survival is an occupation, with a concomitant suspension of development. This perspective is unfortunate given the relative youthfulness of most prison inmates, and the fact that much of the conduct for which offenders are imprisoned suggests that they could usefully acknowledge that there is room for personal improvement.

Putting aside the question of whether prisons can be designed to promote constructive change, there is the far-from-hypothetical question of whether any environment can *avoid* contributing to changes among people who are exposed to it. And if we assume that prisons must contribute to positive or negative changes among inmates whether one likes it or not,[14] it follows that we ought to be able to describe these changes.[15]

The idea of studying change in prisoners during their terms of incarceration is by no means novel. Studies involving opinion inventories administered to inmates at varying stages of their sentence once enjoyed considerable popularity, and the results of such surveys reinforced the concern with "prisonization" that then dominated the prison literature. This concept came to refer to a presumed process whereby prisoners increasingly subscribed to antisocial, antistaff, or antiauthoritarian values, which were said to peak midway during prison sentences and to decrease in salience (in an inverted U curve) with the proximity of release.[16] In explaining this process, its authors assumed that heavy peer influence (the "inmate culture") was operating to subvert the behavior-modifying efforts of prison staff. The same experts, under the spell of what became known as *functional analysis* in sociology, argued that prisoners' recalcitrance in prison represented a compensatory adjustment to the travails of confinement. This view of prisoner behavior originated with Richard Sykes and with Donald Clemmer, who coined the term *prisonization*. Clemmer's version of prisonization, however, had to be tempered by the discovery that the way individuals adjust to confinement occurs differently for offenders who bring different outlooks and attitudes into the prison. This differentiated conception began with studies that reported variations in modes of prison adjustment, such as differences in the adaptive behavior of men and women.[17]

It also became obvious that no environments—even imprisoning environments—ordain what people do, even if the uniformity of their behavior suggests this. Where people behave similarly, they could arrive at similar solutions to similar problems, which is a far cry from following prescriptions for adaptation. The same point applies where we find commonalities among people who maladapt in the same way to a given environment.[18]

In our inquiry, we relied on prison records that describe behavior that strikes staff as noteworthy. In this sense, we must see inmates through the eyes of staff, although we know that staff are not only acute observers of prison life but also participants in inmate–staff encounters. There arguably may be some virtue to this contamination, however, given the staff's responsibility to act as custodians of the prison environment, whose perspective governs the way the system reacts to behavior.

We can use prison staff judgments as a criterion measure of "good" (effective) and "bad" (ineffective) adjustment by recognizing that staff are sources of favorable and unfavorable consequences of behavior. This means, among other things, that an unfavorable assessment by staff brings an adverse reaction of staff, representing unwelcome feedback from the environment to the inmate's behavior. This does not imply, of course, that the inmate's acts are intrinsically unhealthy or noxious or undesirable, but it does mean that the inmate who has invited problems with staff has at minimum not advanced the cause of his or her getting along in the setting in which he or she must function.

At extremes, a relativistic approach to adaptation is obviously untenable, in that it adjudges as maladaptive whatever "sane" (or legitimately rebellious) behavior we find in "insane" (or illegitimately authoritarian) places.[19] However, in a moderately civilized prison, we can reject as implausible the notion that a penchant for getting into trouble can in any sense be equated with a pattern of heroic, principled resistance. Moreover, where destructive transactions between an inhabitant and a custodian of an environment occur—as they do when an inmate and a guard both lose their equanimity and escalate a minor confrontation—we would not adjudge the result to be an example of effective coping by anyone but rather as an instance of compounded maladaptiveness.

We do not deny that there are junctures at which prison inmates are cavalierly dealt with, unfairly punished, individually discriminated against, or even harassed. But except for settings such as supermax confinement (which we describe in chapter 16), such instances are circumscribed and are unlikely to underlie trends in behavior rates and patterns of incidents, with which our study deals. And even when the prisoner is a victim of abuse, we can assume that some reactions to being victimized are more constructive or effective than others. We also know that in the absence of "objective" information or observations of staff–inmate confrontations, a prisoner's self-portrait can be adjudged no less self-serving than the staff's view of the inmate.

Ultimately, however, all such arguments are academic, in that we must stipulate limitations and liabilities of settings in which people must function. If we ask whether a student adjusts to a school, we must be concerned with his or her academic performance, and we must use criteria such as level of attendance or truancy and the presence or absence of behavior problems. In viewing adjustment in this way, we may know that the school's grading methods are imperfect, that the educational experiences provided may be less than inspiring, and that "real learning" is a rare (if attainable) commodity. The need to compromise is ineluctable because the only way in which we can pose the question "How well (or poorly) does a person adapt?" is with regard to the imperfect world in which the person, and the rest of us, must function.

Gauging Maladaptive Behavior in Prison

The most obvious criterion of maladaptation in the prison is that of disciplinary infractions. Infractions are charges lodged by officers (and, on occasion, by other staff) against inmates that bring penalties ranging from the suspension of minor privileges to extended periods of formal segregation and the loss of good-time credit that shortens an inmate's sentence.[20] Infractions are thus acts that are officially deemed objectionable and result in adverse repercussions to the actor.

By the same token, occasional prison infractions can be accorded no significance whatsoever. Given the omnipresence in prison of rules and rule enforcement, only a saint or an isolate can live an infraction-free prison existence. Moreover, one must allow for the sometimes imperfect exercise of adverse discretion by prison staff who are the arbiters of misbehavior.

Despite such considerations, high infractions rates can be reliable measures of behavior. Records of infraction are exhaustively maintained, sources of judgments are spread among staff members, and behavior descriptions are more or less governed by definitions in prison rule books. The validity of infraction measures as behavior descriptions is enhanced by the requirement that charges be documented, particularly where a charge is serious, and by the fact that the level of visibility of behavior for which inmates are written up is usually high. None of this, of course, bears on whether the behavior is maladaptive.

The issue of whether prison violations can be classed as maladaptive arises unavoidably because many prison rules gratuitously circumscribe the behavior of prisoners. Moreover, prisons are pressure cookers. A correctional institution is either a place of corrosive solitude or a closed social milieu in which people face 24-hour-a-day enforced contact and cohabitation. One attribute is shared by the latter type of prison and other closed congregate environments—such as military installations, boarding schools, monasteries, and hospitals— and it is that each person's behavior can significantly affect the experience of other people and can enhance or contaminate their quality of life. Prisons are among settings that challenge the capacity of people to constructively (or nondestructively) coexist and to deal with the adversities of enforced cohabitation.

The corrections officers who assess the adequacy of the inmates' behavior are prominently wielders of power, and it is this fact that has impressed most observers of prisons.[21] The jurisdiction of officers permits unimpeded inquiry into almost any aspect of the lives of inmates.[22] More seriously, officers are able to define their own personal conflicts as maladaptive transactions, in that disobeying guards' orders and showing them disrespect places inmates at risk of being penalized.

However, prison guards often claim that they are subject to more circumscription than the inmates they supervise.[23] If one sets this overblown assertion aside, guard power has to be limited by the need to secure inmate cooperation, which means that there must be some give-and-take between prisoners and officers. Observers have also noted that most guards want to be seen as fair and dispassionate[24] and that they assert that the respect of inmates must be earned by the way authority is exercised rather than by entitlement.[25] Most importantly, the officers know that full enforcement of prison rules is not possible, that a routine practice of "writing up" every inmate who could be charged would paralyze the prison disciplinary system and that disciplining many inmates would make guards, rather than inmates, be adjudged maladaptive.[26]

The discretionary element in rule enforcement varies, to be sure, with attributes of the inmate's prison offense. Acts that are committed in private are less apt to bring sanctions than those that are designed for ostentatious display, and persistent offenses that follow repeated admonitions reliably invite formal dispositions. Violations that are nondiscretionary and invariably result in formal charges include assaultive, predatory, and violent behavior, the destruction of prison property (for which repayment is exacted), drug and alcohol involvement, and threats to physical order maintenance, which covers behavior ranging from arson to the instigation of prison riots.

A fact of relevance here which prison administrators cite is that the least leeway for discretion and the heaviest penalties mostly accrue to acts of physical violence that are obviously acts that threaten the personal safety of individuals in the prison, which in most instances means other inmates. What this implies is that characterizations of the codified disciplinary system as arbitrarily regulating behavior in subservience to order as an end in itself, or as a manifestation of paranoia or nitpicking, apply with lesser cogency to the most severely sanctioned offenses.

Another point that is not obvious is that prison regulations are heavily publicized, and violations in ignorance or by happenstance are correspondingly rare. Every inmate who arrives in prison is handed a rule book, whose content is regarded as the core of the induction process. Prisons are also legalistically oriented, particularly in processing serious violations that carry serious penalties.[27] Despite such considerations, we must accommodate the fact that prisons are more authoritarian than they need to be and rely excessively on the enforcement of disciplinary codes that regulate inmate behavior in excessive detail.

Agenda of This Book

This book begins with a statistical section that describes comprehensive patterns of behavior incidents, moving from cross-sectional pictures to sequential ones and from unidimensional to multidimensional views. We next examine detailed accounts of the behavior of prisoners over time, grouped in terms of the content of their behavior. Finally, we outline a regenerative enterprise that we believe uses some of our methods and findings.

The first part of the book (chapters 2–5) is quantitative, in that we report the results of efforts to find statistical patterns among incidents in which prisoners were involved. Our analysis—especially of patterns of involvement of disturbed and disruptive inmates over time—is facilitated by our access to many prisoner files containing incident-related data. The second part of the book (chapters 6–13) contains case studies of prison careers. The emphasis is still on incident patterns—in this case, of patterns that reveal underlying psychological dispositions. Here, we examine chronological patterns of maladaptive behavior for what they might tell us about the perspectives and motives of maladaptive personalities.

Parts I and II of the book are interdependent. The first part of the book provides a map, and in Part II we view high points of the terrain in that the individuals selected for review in depth stand out in terms of the nature and magnitude of the problems they pose. In both parts of the book, we group individuals who resemble each other, although we ask different questions about the types that emerge.

Chapter 2 describes data collection procedures and our approach to the analysis of incident patterns. The study we report took place 15 years ago, in collaboration with a large prison system. This system—that of New York State—has since grown in population, but the problem behavior we describe remains undiminished in volume and salience. Today, roughly 8% of New York's prisoners are segregated or locked in for disciplinary reasons. Mental health services and mental health staff ranks have expanded. Concomitantly, the time served by New York prisoners has increased (contributing to population increments) by virtue of sentencing "reforms."

Although our research may be topical, it is hard to envisage the study being assiduously replicated. Prison files have become computerized, but descriptive detail of the sort we focus on—especially in tracking careers of prisoners—has become less accessible. Changes in available data sources foreclose the transition from aggregate statistical analysis to in-depth reviews of careers.

In chapter 3, the most distinctive feature of our analysis is a typological approach that permits us to distinguish junctures at which problems develop for prisoners of different age levels serving sentences varying in duration. We focus on previously reported correlations between age and acting-out behavior and on the assumed stability of careers of long-termers and lifers. We also focus on the issue of timing (including chronicity) of maladaptation.

Chapter 4 deals in similar ways with mental health problems. Using our typological approach on incidents symptomatic of mental health problems, we locate along varying career paths the manifestations of mental illness and treatment efforts that respond to them.

In chapter 5, we juxtapose patterns of disruptive and symptomatic behavior and inquire into the relationship between disruptiveness and mental illness, including disturbed–disruptive behavior. Our concern in this chapter is with the disproportion of maladaptive behavior involving mental health problems. We are also interested in chronological manifestations of problems.

Chapter 6 introduces a typology that differentiates patterns of maladaptation in terms of purposes, motives, or perspectives. The taxonomy is based on content analysis of behavior descriptions and encompasses five types, with varying numbers of subtypes. The types differentiate behavior that appeared to subserve the purposes of (a) gratifying impulses, (b) defending esteem, (c) pursuing autonomy, (d) seeking refuge, and (e) maintaining sanity. Chapters 7–11 define and illustrate these five career types.

Chapter 7 deals with aggression that is reflexive, governed

by short-term sentiments, and self-defeating. In chapter 8, we review patterns of acting out that represent efforts to cement self-esteem by building reputations or defending against perceived affronts. In chapter 9, we are concerned with people who react maladaptively in situations they see as incursions on their autonomy, who act out to reinforce dependency bids, or both. Chapter 10 describes patterns of escape or retreat associated with unsuccessful or clumsy acting-out behavior.

In chapter 11, we discuss the disruptive behavior of prisoners who are seriously emotionally disturbed. These patterns have fight–flight attributes and reflect recurrent unsuccessful struggles against loss of control or idiosyncratic reinterpretations of environmental impingements. The behavior poses the most troubling dilemmas for prison administrations and raises formal interface issues for custodial and mental health staff.

Chapter 12 discusses the application of our taxonomy and its use as a tool for enhancing understanding of the dynamics of maladaptive behavior. The issues dealt with relate to interventions (fleshed out in chapter 16) for use of behavioral taxonomies to promote self-study and encourage the expansion of behavioral repertoires.

Chapter 13 describes patterns featuring behavioral improvements and discontinuance of maladaptive behavior. In this chapter, we focus on the process of behavior change and on the role of prison staff in promoting and supporting personal reform, suggesting a potential for interventions in the careers of disruptive offenders.

Chapter 14 summarizes conclusions drawn from our study, and chapter 15 supplements these conclusions as they relate to disruptive women in prison. Chapter 16 outlines treatment approaches, including a model that capitalizes on our analysis, deploying a therapeutic community to promote the study and self-study of patterns of maladaptive behavior.

Notes

1. Monahan, J. M., Steadman, H. J., Silver, E., Appelbaum, P. S., Robbins, P. B., Mulvey, E. P., Roth, L. H., Grisso, T., & Banks, S. (2001). *Rethink-*

ing risk assessment. New York: Oxford University Press; Quinsey, V. L., Harris, G. T., Rice, M. E., & Cormier, C. (1998). *Violent offenders: Appraising and managing risk*. Washington, DC: American Psychological Association.

2. Hodgins, S., & Mueller-Isberner, R. (Eds.). (2000). *Violence, crime and mentally disordered offenders: Concepts and methods for effective treatment and prevention*. Chichester, England: Wiley; Hodgins, S. (Ed.). (2000). *Violence among the mentally ill: Effective treatments and management strategies*. Dordrecht, The Netherlands: Kluwer Academic; Hodgins, S. (Ed.). (1993). *Mental disorder and crime*. Newbury Park, CA: Sage.

3. In most maladaptation, there is a tendency for the ineffective behavior to persist or to escalate despite feedback of ineffectiveness. In discussing the careers of chronic disciplinary violators in the prison, for example, Vernon Fox (1958, p. 325) spoke of a "recidivism cycle," which he described as follows: "The progression begins with (1) the situation in the institution with which the prisoner cannot cope, (2) failure to solve the problem, followed by (3) replacement of realistic efforts by substitute regressive behavior, (4) an intensification of the original problem by failure of substitute methods, (5) repeatedly grasping for an answer, any answer and, finally (6) the compulsive repetition of the one answer he has found whether it works or not" (Fox, V. [1958]. Analysis of prison disciplinary problems. *Journal of Criminal Law, Criminology and Police Science, 49*, 321–326).

   Another point made in the literature is that maladaptive individuals seek reinforcement from other maladaptive individuals, whereas good copers have recourse to individuals who can assist them in trying to solve their problems (Mechanic, D. [1962]. *Students under stress: A study in the social psychology of adaptation*. New York: Free Press).

4. Flanagan, T. (1983). Correlates of institutional misconduct among state prisoners. *Criminology, 21*, 29–39.

5. Toch, H. (1992). *Mosaic of despair: Human breakdowns in confinement*. Washington, DC: American Psychological Association.

6. Bowker, L. H. (1980). *Prison victimization*. New York: Elsevier; Lockwood, D. (1980). *Prison sexual violence*. New York: Elsevier; Bartollas, C., Miller, S., & Dinitz, S. (1976). *Juvenile victimization: The institutional paradox*. New York: Wiley.

7. Studies of disruptiveness in mental hospitals also show that chronic patterns are heavily concentrated among a minority of patients. One study cited by Smith (1979, p. 529) found that "2 percent of patients accounted for 55 percent of all violent incidents" (Smith, A. C. [1979]. Violence. *British Journal of Psychiatry, 134*, 524, 529). A Canadian team surveyed 198 patient assaults and discovered that "13% ($N = 18$) of the patients committed 61% of the assaults" (Quinsey, V. L. [1977]. Studies in the reduction of assaults in a maximum security psychiatric institution. *Canada's Mental Health, 25*, 21–23, p. 21). For more recent documentation, see Bjoerkly, S. (1999). A ten-year study of aggression

in a special secure unit for dangerous patients. *Scandinavian Journal of Psychology, 40,* 57–63.

8. Toch, H. (1982). The disturbed disruptive inmate: Where does the bus stop? *Journal of Psychiatry and Law, 10,* 327–349. The shuttling procedure is called *bus therapy,* and it reveals pressures to make the "bus stops" as brief as decency permits. Wilson (1980, p. 8) noted that "Correctional administrators, wanting to get rid of their bad apples, will ship them off to mental health. And the mental health administrators don't want to monkey around with acting-out clients, so they send them back" (Wilson, R. [1980]. Who will care for the 'mad and bad'? *Corrections Magazine, 6,* 5–17).

   Freeman, Dinitz, and Conrad (1977, p. 30) concluded that "neither mental hospitals nor prisons welcome the disturbed and dangerous inmate . . . The resulting 'bus therapy' expresses the reluctance which both kinds of institutions feel in contemplation of the burden of this kind of inmate. Until courts and administrators can establish rules to govern the disposition of such inmates, their programming will be punctuated by bus movements which are clearly not intended for their benefit" (Freeman, R. A., Dinitz, S., & Conrad, J. P. [1977, January–February]. A look at the dangerous offender and society's efforts to control him. *American Journal of Correction,* 25–31).

9. Wilson, "Mad and bad" (note 8, supra) pointed out that "a common criticism by psychiatrists of prison administrators is that they want the doctors to handle the problem cases, which are not always psychiatric problems" (p. 14). Vicki Agee (1981, p. 2), by contrast, recalled that "we drove our disturbed delinquents there—they beat us back —with the diagnosis of 'manipulation' . . . (We) tried to outplay Mental Health at the 'Name Game.' They won, of course—you can't help but win when you hold all the cards . . . Most of the games revolve around the Psychotic versus Character Disorder (diagnoses) . . . Character disorders (which I think means anybody who intimidates, messes over, or hurts people) particularly do not belong in hospitals, because they are untreatable" (Agee, V. L. [1981, September 10]. *The closed adolescent treatment center.* Paper presented at the Utah Correctional Association Annual Conference, Salt Lake City, UT). The same point is made in Toch, H. (1998). Psychopathy and antisocial behavior in forensic settings. In T. Millon, E. Simonson, M. Birket-Smith, & R. D. Davis (Eds.), *Psychopathy: Antisocial criminal, and violent behavior* (pp. 144–158). New York: Guilford Press.

10. This is the position reflected by Vernon Fox (note 3, supra). One forensic clinician suggests a delivery modality he calls "The Bum of the Month Club" to which wardens would be invited to send obstreperous inmates.

11. See Reveron, D. (1982, March). Mentally ill—And behind bars. *APA Monitor,* pp. 10–11. The "characterological defect" view is often expressed by diagnosing inmates as suffering from "antisocial person-

ality disturbance." This category, as defined in the *DSM*, could be applied to most inmates but is in practice reserved for those who manifest behavior problems. (See Toch, note 8, supra.)

12. Fox, *Prison Disciplinary Problems* (note 3, supra), p. 326.

13. This statement holds to the extent to which the public gives the matter any thought, though to be fair, the public is more concerned about keeping violent offenders off the street than about the content of prison programs.

14. We noted elsewhere that "we can, of course, carelessly leave the environment's impact to chance by running warehouses where we unwittingly let negative influences predominate. Or, we can consciously try to maximize constructive and positive forces available to us even in the last-resort prisons" (Toch, H. [1981]. Classification for programming and survival. In D. A. Ward & K. F. Schoen [Eds.], *Confinement in maximum custody* [p. 40]. Lexington, MA: Lexington Books). See also Toch, H. (1992). *Living in prison.* Washington, DC: American Psychological Association.

15. This distinction is explicitly drawn by Norval Morris (1974), who wrote that "'rehabilitation,' whatever it means and whatever the programs that allegedly give it meaning, must cease to be the purpose of the prison sanction. This does *not* mean that the various developed prison programs within the prison need to be abandoned; quite the contrary, they need expansion. But it does mean that they must not be seen as *purposive* in the sense that criminals are to be sent to prison *for* treatment" (Morris, N. [1974]. *The future of imprisonment.* Chicago: University of Chicago Press, pp. 14–15). According to this position, rehabilitative programs can be justified because the prison can thus meet the needs of disadvantaged people in prisons who stand in need of remedial services (Morris, N., & Hawkins, G. [1977]. *Letter to the President on crime control.* Chicago: University of Chicago Press). The alternative is to let people deteriorate in confinement. In the words of another author (Rotman, 1986, p. 1028), "Rehabilitation in this sense means a state effort to prevent and neutralize the unwanted harmful side effects of its own punitive intervention, as well as to respond to the human challenge posed by the extremely socially deprived offenders" (Rotman, E. [1986]. Do criminal offenders have a constitutional right to rehabilitation? *Journal of Criminal Law and Criminology, 77,* 1023–1068).

16. Donald Clemmer (1965, p. 299) wrote, "we may use the term *prisonization* to indicate the taking on in greater or less degree of the folkways, mores, customs, and general culture of the penitentiary. Prisonization is similar to assimilation" (Clemmer, D. [1965]. *The prison community.* New York: Holt, Rinehart & Winston). Clemmer distinguished between "universal factors of prisonization," which have to do with inmates accepting their inmate status and making a home of the prison, and long-term prisonization, which embues inmates with

"the criminalistic ideology in the prison community." Clemmer's scheme suggests that the longer the inmate stays in the prison, the more antisocial the inmate will become.

The first of the questionnaire studies that showed the inverted U curve was reported by Stanton Wheeler (Wheeler, S. [1961]. Socialization in correctional communities. *American Sociological Review, 26,* 697–712). Wheeler's is a cross-sectional study, but he suggested reinterviewing inmates in future studies. Wheeler also anticipated that the liberalization of prison conditions "may be able to strengthen tendencies toward positive change in attitude during the late phases of imprisonment." Wheeler's study has been repeatedly replicated. One successful large-scale replication is that of Peter Garabedian (Garabedian, P. [1963]. Social role and processes of socialization in the prison community. *Social Problems, 11,* 140–152).

17. The best study contrasting adjustment modes of male and female prisoners was Giallombardo, R. (1966). *Society of women: A study of a women's prison.* New York: Wiley. Giallombardo contrasted her findings about female prisoner adjustment with the description of male prisoner adaptation by Sykes, G. (1958). *The society of captives: A study of a maximum security prison.* Princeton: Princeton University Press. A more recent study of female prisoner adaptation is Owen, B. (1998). *"In the mix": Struggle and survival in a women's prison.* Albany: State University of New York Press.

18. Zamble, E., & Porporino, F. J. (1988). *Coping, behaviour and adaptation in prison inmates.* New York: Springer.

19. Rosenhan, D. (1993). On being sane in insane places. *Science, 179,* 250–258; *180,* 365–369.

20. Good-time credit is subject to restoration if the inmate's behavior improves and the improvement is sustained over time.

21. For a comprehensive discussion of the exercise of power by correction officers, see Sykes, *The society of captives* (note 17, supra).

22. This relationship between custodians and inmates has been described by Erving Goffman, whose observations, however, derive from contacts between hospital attendants and psychiatric patients. See Goffman, E. (1961). On the characteristics of total institutions. In *Asylums: Essays on the social situation of mental patients and other inmates* (pp. 1–124). Garden City, NY: Doubleday (Anchor).

23. Among the studies which describe the feeling of powerlessness of guards are Poole, E. D., & Regoli, R. M. (1981). Alienation in prison: An examination of the work relations of prison guards. *Criminology, 19,* 251–270; and Toch, H., & Klofas, J. (1982). Alienation and desire for job enrichment among correction officers. *Federal Probation, 46,* 35–44.

24. Sykes, *The society of captives* (note 17, supra). Also see Mathiesen, T. (1965). *The defences of the weak: A sociological study of a Norwegian correctional institution.* London: Tavistock.

25. Lombardo, L. X. (1981). *Guards imprisoned: Correctional officers at work.* New York: Elsevier.
26. Sykes, *The society of captives* (note 17, supra); Lombardo, *Guards Imprisoned* (note 25).
27. Due process in disciplinary hearings has resulted from court interventions and the threat of further interventions, and it includes such elements as the disclosing of charges, the calling of witnesses at the inmate's request, expeditious processing, the availability of appeals, the maintenance of stenographic records, and the presence of a staff member representing the inmate's interests.

I

Aggregate Patterns

2

Data Collection and Analysis

Complex research projects require many decisions pertaining to research design and data analysis. These decisions
involve crucial issues, such as how the sample will be drawn,
as well as more mundane questions, such as how variables
will be labeled and formatted. Because many of the choices
that researchers make directly affect the integrity of the research enterprise, it becomes important to document this aspect of the research process, particularly with regard to difficulties that researchers inevitably encounter along the way.
Thus, in this chapter, we describe our research site, introduce
our approaches to the use of aggregate statistics, review the
data collection procedures, and discuss several of the problems we face in a project of this type.

We conducted our study in the New York State prison system. In September 1986, this system housed 38,000 inmates
in 50 correctional institutions that employed 21,000 prison
staff.[1] By 2001, the system had grown to include roughly
70,000 inmates in 70 facilities, thus reflecting nationwide
trends in the growth of correctional systems.[2] Not only was
and is the system cosmopolitan and substantial (the fifth largest in the United States[3]), but prison administrators also had
identified our subject matter as an area of concern to them,
as had the providers of mental health services to the system.

This interest was critical in gaining the cooperation of agency officials particularly with regard to accessing the large number and variety of prison and mental health records we needed.

Strong support of our project can be partly traced to a tradition of concern in New York State for locating inmates with "special needs" and providing services for such inmates. This tradition of concern is reflected in the fact that Thomas Coughlin, the commissioner of the Department of Correctional Services from 1979 to 1994, had been the first commissioner of the Office of Mental Retardation and Developmental Difficulties.[4] Around the time of our project, New York's top correctional official declared,

> During my tenure as Commissioner, DOCS [the Department of Correctional Services, New York's prison system] has steadily expanded and improved the programs available to inmates with developmental disabilities and other handicapping conditions. I also recognize that we need to do more. And, we are willing to do more.
>
> At reception, inmates who are identified as being most in need of special services are referred to the extended classification program. Here, a more in-depth evaluation is performed and the individual's behavior will continue to be observed and assessed. Special assessment instruments are administered to these inmates. These instruments are then scored and evaluated.
>
> Inmates who go through extended classification will be held at reception until an appropriate placement can be made, taking into consideration . . . the safety and individual needs of the inmate . . . In order to establish appropriate work and treatment programs for such inmates, it is absolutely necessary that DOCS be able to identify and fully assess all inmates suspected of having handicapping conditions.[5]

New York also has a longstanding tradition of care for inmates who need mental health services. The system once contained two large hybrid institutions (combined prison and psychiatric hospitals), which had widely recognized progressive features. However, these institutions retained some inmates for protracted periods of time, leading to a series of court decisions on commitment and discharge procedures and treatment resources.[6] The state eventually responded to this situation by completely overhauling the prison mental health system. Along with the transfer of responsibility for the treatment of inmates with mental illnesses to a different agency, the Office of Mental Health, a new service delivery system was set in place, including an accredited acute care hospital facility—Central New York Psychiatric Center (CNYPC) that in 2000 had a capacity of 191 beds.[7]

This new system was organized around a community mental health model that has as one of its goals reducing the time patients spend in hospital settings.[8] The system was designed to be both effective and cost efficient.[9] Administrators realized that if inmates with mental illnesses were going to spend more time in their "community" (i.e., prison), they would have to be provided with a variety of supportive services. Recognition of this fact led to the development of a network of prison outpatient clinics. These clinics, described as "satellites units" of the hospital, are located at major prisons scattered throughout the state. Each satellite unit is staffed by a complement of psychiatrists, psychologists, social workers, and nurses and comes equipped with provisions for short-term observation and residential treatment. Several satellite units offer longer term residential programs (intermediate care units), operated jointly with the prison system. These programs are designed to house inmates who have serious difficulties adjusting to prison life but who do not require hospitalization. In 2000, the range of nonhospital treatment resources included 21 clinic treatment programs, 131 crisis residence beds, and 513 program beds for inmates with serious mental health problems. Furthermore, service plans for the fiscal year 2000–2001 call for the addition of 82 staff members that will focus, among other things, on inmates in disciplinary housing units and on discharge planning.[10]

Inmates come to the attention of mental health staff in a variety of ways. During the reception and classification process, an inmate's behavior is closely watched and his or her social and medical history is reviewed. In 2000, roughly 4 out of 5 state confinement facilities reported that they screen inmates for mental health problems at intake.[11] Furthermore, roughly 10% of state inmates reported, when asked, that they have a mental or emotional condition, and almost 11% indicated that they had been admitted to a hospital for a mental or emotional problem.[12] On the basis of inmate reports and staff observations, inmates may be referred immediately to mental health staff or they may be assigned to a prison and placed on caseload. Throughout the correctional system, moreover, any staff member can refer an inmate to the mental health unit. Many, if not most, referrals come from security staff, most of whom are in a position to observe the inmate's daily behavior in a variety of social settings. Finally, inmates have the option of making a self-referral to mental health staff.

These developments in the prison mental health system held several implications for our project. Most significantly, the involvement of the Office of Mental Health in delivering psychiatric services to prison inmates created a division of responsibilities across agency lines, and issues surfaced where lines proved difficult to draw clearly. One such issue has to do with the sorts of inmates who are of interest to us, and particularly the inmates with mental disorders who disrupt prison routines. Both corrections and mental health staff expressed concerns that the problems of many such inmates were not fully understood and were not being dealt with adequately.

Especially promising was the fact that the involvement of the Office of Mental Health led to a substantial improvement in clinical recordkeeping, and the emphasis on outpatient treatment meant that inmates with mental illnesses would be spending as much time as possible in the prison, where prison records could uninterruptedly track their careers. From a research point of view, these developments pointed to the availability of relatively reliable and complete data sources about inmate mental health problems in the prison. In our experience, the availability of such data is not common.

As we have noted, we are interested in manifestations of symptomatic and disruptive behavior over the course of an inmate's prison term. We are especially interested in the more extreme ends of these behavioral spectrums. This agenda poses several methodological issues relating to sampling, sources and coding of data, and the description of sequences of events over time.

Sampling

Inmates who are highly disruptive or who are seriously emotionally disturbed admittedly constitute a minority within prison populations. Research on the prevalence of mental illness among New York State inmates suggested that 5% of these prisoners can be regarded as severely psychiatrically disturbed and 10% as significantly disturbed and in need of services.[13] Likewise in New York State, 6% of inmates are in special settings, such as special housing units or super-maximum security institutions, as a result of disruptive or violent behavior.[14] The relatively few inmates who are the primary focus of this study pose the first research design problem.

To ensure reliability in statistical analyses, one needs an adequate number of participants. When simple random sampling procedures are applied to the study of infrequent events, large sample sizes with correspondingly large expenditures of resources are necessary to identify an adequate number of individuals. A way of dealing with this problem is to make the sampling procedure more efficient by using a stratified design. This design involves a two-step process that first divides the population into strata or groups and then randomly samples at different ratios across the strata. The advantage of a stratified design is that it allows one to "oversample" participants of greatest interest and "undersample" participants of least interest.[15] For this reason, we chose to use a stratified sampling procedure.

Our sampling frame, or the population from which we selected our sample, is a cohort of inmates released from the

New York State prison system between July 30, 1982, and September 1, 1983. During this 15-month period, 10,534 inmates were released to the community. Prison mental health experience and rate of disciplinary infractions are the variables that we used to stratify the sampling frame.[16]

In New York, inmate disciplinary records were stored at the last facility of confinement, so there was no central source to tap for this information. This meant that before we could stratify the cohort, we had to collect the disciplinary record of each inmate from the prison from which he was released. With the cooperation of the Department of Corrections, we were able to collect disciplinary records for 9,103 inmates. We then tabulated the number of disciplinary incidents and used this information in conjunction with admission and release dates to identify inmates with high and low infraction rates.

Our next step was to cross-reference the names and birthdates of inmates in our release cohort against computerized client records maintained by the Office of Mental Health. This matching procedure allowed us to identify inmates who were hospitalized during incarceration or who had received outpatient services.

These procedures allowed us to cross-classify the cohort of inmates in terms of mental health experience and disciplinary history. We then proceeded to oversample inmates with histories of serious mental health problems and inmates with extensive disciplinary records. The stratification categories and the sampling ratios we used are displayed in Table 2.1. We included in the sample all inmates who were hospitalized during their prison term as well as all inmates with disciplinary rates above the 95th percentile.

To compensate for selection biases introduced through stratification, we must use an inverse weighting procedure in the statistical analyses. For example, cases drawn from strata with a sampling ratio of one half are multiplied by two during statistical analyses, cases with a sampling ratio of one eighth are multiplied by eight and so on. Cases with a sampling ratio of one (i.e., hospitalized inmates) are unaffected by inverse weighting. The weighting procedure yields numerical estimates for the entire release cohort, and for this

Table 2.1

Details of Stratified Random Sampling Design

Disciplinary experience			No service (n = 7,565)		Prison mental health experience			
					Outpatient (n = 1,368)		Hospitalized (n = 170)	
Group name	Annual rate	Percentile range	Sampling ratio	N cases	Sampling ratio	N cases	Sampling ratio	N cases
Low	0–2.5	0–50	1:10	480	1:2	328	1:1	56
Medium	2.6–4.9	51–75	1:8	209	1:2	163	1:1	48
High	5.0–9.9	76–92	1:5	188	1:1	218	1:1	26
Special interest	10.0+	93–100	1:1	565	1:1	174	1:1	41

reason the number of cases reported in tables exceeds the number of cases we sampled.

Sources of Data

Our primary source for disciplinary information was the warden's record card. This document follows an inmate as he moves through the correctional system and lists the date, charges, and disposition of each prison rule violation. The warden's card also serves as a record of institutional transfers. Our major source of information for mental health–related behavior was the treatment files maintained by mental health staff. These files also follow inmates as they move through the correctional system and contain all clinically relevant information.

Prison and mental health files can be seen as documenting a series of events over the course of a prison term, and we approached the coding task from this framework. For each relevant entry in an inmate's record, we coded the date of the event and the associated event descriptions. For example, when reviewing disciplinary records, we coded the date of the infraction, the disciplinary behavior, and the disposition. Similarly, when reviewing mental health files, we coded the date of the observation and the behavior that was described. Although we developed separate coding schemes for disruptive and symptomatic behavior, use of behavioral codes was not constrained by the source of information. Thus, if disruptive acts were noted in the mental health files, they were coded along with symptoms that were described. In addition to observations of the inmate's behavior, we coded dates and destinations of prison transfers, including commitments to the psychiatric hospital and placement in special therapeutic correctional programs.

The event framework allows us to combine prison and mental health information into a single file and to arrange the data in chronological order. This means that we can locate incidents in time over the course of an inmate's prison term and describe temporal sequences of events.

The Department of Correctional Services tapped their computerized recordkeeping system to provide us with background information on inmates in the sample. Additional information, including preprison mental health experience, was collected from the inmate's central office folder. Our main sources for this information were the presentence report, which accompanies an inmate into prison, and his prison classification documents. We also used central office files to supplement the warden's card in situations in which disciplinary information was missing or incomplete.

Mental health files are retained at the last treatment facility, and the Office of Mental Health arranged for our access to these records by having them shipped to their central office. Despite such cooperation, we were unable to locate files for 256 outpatients in our sample after canvassing all prison treatment facilities.[17] These inmates were admitted to outpatient service, but no record could be found concerning the nature of their problems. We were, however, able to consult computerized service delivery records. We found that service delivery contacts for these inmates were very infrequent and in many cases limited to only one contact. Although we cannot be certain about the precise nature of these inmates' problems, it appears unlikely that the problems at issue were serious.[18]

Prison Careers

We have indicated that we approach the description and analysis of an inmate's prison experiences as a delimited portion of a career. The *American Heritage Dictionary* defines a "career" as, among other things, a path or course, and more specifically as "the general course or progression of one's life."[19] Our use of the term is more or less consistent with this definition, which does not require that the term refer to occupational or professional advancement. Within the social sciences, there is well-established precedent for using the career concept quite broadly. Career studies have included descriptions of the socialization of medical students,[20] the lives of drug addicts over time,[21] and the predations of persistent thieves.[22] Studied in this way, a career involves

> an activity or sequence of activities with a natural history that is seen without particular regard to high or low points but rather to changes over time that are common to participants. In this sense careers such as pool hustler, felon, hippie, mental patient, and alcoholic can be approached in the same way as those of lawyer, doctor, businessman, pop star, and so forth.[23]

The career framework has been applied to the study of the difficulties and successes of mental patients as they move from hospital to community.[24] In these studies, as in the present study, one focus is on sequences of experiences marked by significant transitions from one social context to the next. The career framework also has been applied to the study of criminal behavior among offenders.[25] In this context, researchers concentrate on the onset or start of criminal behavior, its persistence over time, with special emphasis on chronic offending, and its desistance or termination. Variations in criminal careers are studied over the life course, and developmental theories are used to explain these variations.[26]

Because we are interested in prison experiences, we circumscribe an inmate's career as time spent between admission and release, and we then examine an inmate's experiences chronologically. When we find it useful to refer to parts of an inmate's prison career, we refer to such periods as career segments or stages. Our descriptions of inmate careers begins with an inventory of changes in rates of behavior in the aggregate. We then disaggregate the careers statistically based on patterns of change into career types. The supplementation of these career types with individual career patterns derived through the use of the case study method integrates quantitative and qualitative approaches and nomothetic and ideographic modes of analyses.[27]

Because we are interested in temporal changes, we define our rates in terms of the number of observations per unit of time. Selecting an appropriate time unit (e.g., day, week, month, or year) for computing the rates is an important de-cision because it can influence the way we perceive changes in rates. For example, using a small time unit (e.g., day) will generate many data points, and there will be considerable "noise" or instability in the time curve that can make the curve difficult to interpret. Conversely, a large time unit (e.g., year) will generate a small number of data points and will produce a smoother curve, but important variation may be masked.

In related fashion, we need to deal with the fact that in-mates serve widely varying amounts of time in prison, from as little as 1 year to as many as 10 or more years. Time plots need to be made comparable across inmates with different prison terms if the data are to be analyzed in aggregate form. Prison terms can be divided on the basis of absolute time units (such as days, weeks, or months) or proportional time units (such as halves, thirds, or quarters). As we pointed out in Chapter 1, early prisonization studies generally trisected the inmate's career, and they did this by dividing the prison term into the first 6 months, a variable middle phase, and the last 6 months.[28] More recent research on inmate behavior has used proportional time measures. For example, one study investigated disciplinary infraction rates over time by divid-ing an inmate's prison terms into four equal units (quar-ters).[29]

A proportional time model has the virtue of simplicity be-cause each inmate, regardless of length of prison term, has the same number of time-served units. However, under a proportional model, the amount of time represented by each unit becomes smaller or larger as the prison term becomes shorter or longer. For example, one quarter of an 8-year prison term represents twice as much time as one quarter of a 4-year term. The absolute time model avoids this problem but produces unequal numbers of time units across prison terms of varying lengths. If we were to compute rates over successive 3-month periods, an inmate serving 18 months will have 6 data points, an inmate serving 21 months will have 7 data points, and so on. Because we can combine in-mates only with the same number of data points into an aggregate time curve, this would mean that we would have to conduct as many analyses as there are unique numbers of data points and present each separately.

The following example based on hypothetical data illustrates some of the issues that are involved. Let us assume that we have 3 inmates serving prison terms of 15, 21, and 27 months. Let us also assume that the monthly number of disciplinary involvements for each inmate remains at one for the first 3 months, increases by one each month for the next 3 months, remains constant at four for the next 3 months, declines by one each month for the next 3 months, and remains constant at one until the end of the prison term. These data are displayed in Figure 2.1. We can see that the infraction pattern is essentially the same for all 3 inmates; the distinguishing factor among the curves is the length of the "tail" or the segment representing the period beyond 12 months.

Figure 2.2 displays the infraction rates for the same 3 hypothetical inmates when the prison term is divided into thirds. We find that for the first inmate the curve shows a sharp rise and fall consistent with the pattern in Figure 2.1. In contrast, the curve for the second inmate indicates steady disciplinary involvement followed by a decline, whereas the curve for the third inmate shows a consistent decline in disciplinary involvement. The reason why the proportional model produces such different patterns becomes clear if we divide the curves in Figure 2.1 into three equal segments. Because the proportional time segments for each inmate vary in length (i.e., 5, 7, and 9 months), they intersect the monthly plots at different points, thereby obscuring common features of the original curves.

The curves we have presented are hypothetical and therefore present a neater picture than we might expect to find in the real world. However, the data illustrate a plausible scenario of prison adjustment, which may be characterized by a sharp period of transition taking place early in the sentence and covering a relatively fixed period of time (i.e., the length of the transition period may be independent of the length of the prison term). An absolute time model would confirm this

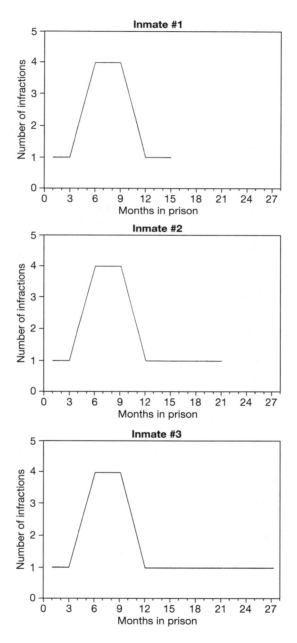

Figure 2.1. Monthly rate of disciplinary infractions for 3 hypothetical inmates.

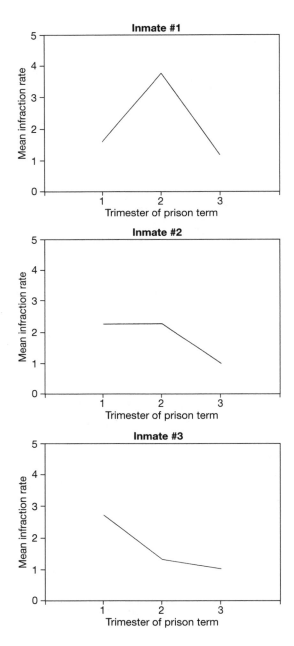

Figure 2.2.   Mean rate of disciplinary infractions by time-served trimester for 3 hypothetical inmates.

hypothesis using our hypothetical data, but a proportional time model would lead us to the opposite conclusion.

In sum, when computing rates over time, we need to keep in mind the following. First, the time period should be small enough so as to be sensitive to important short-term variations but not so small as to highlight fluctuations that contribute little to our understanding of the problem. And, second, time periods should be comparable across inmates so as to allow for aggregate analyses and should not vary greatly in absolute amount of time.

We approached the problem of selecting a time period for computing rates inductively and began with a trial-and-error process. After computing rates over a number of time periods, it appeared that a 3-month interval captured the important features of the distribution while reducing excessive noise in temporal variations. This decision, however, leaves unresolved issues relating to proportional and absolute time models. Our strategy was to develop a hybrid model that retained the advantages of each pure model. We divided the sample into four time-served groups and then divided the prison terms for each group into equal segments. The number of segments was selected so as to yield an average value of approximately 3 months across inmates within a group. This produced a model in which the number of segments was the same within the time-served groups but different across the groups.

The four time-served groups we created are short term (8 to 18 month), low-average term (19 to 30 months), high-average term (31 to 48 months), and long term (49 months and more). Descriptive statistics on the distribution of cases and on the length of time segments across groups are displayed in Table 2.2. This table shows that 27% of the sample falls into Group 1, 41% into Group 2, 19% into Group 3, and 13% into Group 4. We also note that the mean career segment length, or the time period used for computing rates, is 84 days for Group 1, 79 days for Group 2, 93 days for Group 3, and 92 days for Group 4.

Given that the number of career segments varies by time-served groups, data are presented separately for each group

Table 2.2
Number and Length of Prison Term Segments by Time Served

Time served group	No. of segments	Length of segments (days) M	SD
Short term, 8–18 months (*n* = 2,379)	6	84	15
Low-average term, 19–30 months (*n* = 3,653)	9	79	11
High-average term, 31–48 months (*n* = 1,665)	12	93	12
Long term, 49+ months (*n* = 1,206)	24	92	34

when necessary. In addition, because the length of time segments is similar but not identical across inmates, we must standardize rates to avoid introducing error into the statistical analyses. We therefore present annual or yearly rates throughout.

Notes

1. New York State Department of Correctional Services. (1986, September). *Annual Report—1986* [Mimeograph]. Albany: Author.
2. Retrieved January 1, 2002 from http://www.docs.state.ny.us
3. Beck, A. J., & Harrison, P. M. (2001). *Prisoners in 2000* (NCJ 188207). Washington, DC: U.S. Government Printing Office.
4. New York State Department of Correctional Services (August 24, 2001). Press release. Retrieved January 1, 2001 from http://www.docs.state.ny.us/PressRel/coughlinpr2.html
5. Testimony of Thomas A. Coughlin before Assembly Standing Committees on Correction and Mental Health, Mental Retardation and Developmental Disabilities (1987, December 9). *Public Hearing on Persons With Developmental Disabilities and the Criminal Justice System,* pp. 1–3.
6. For a discussion of the early history of inmate mental health services in New York, see Association of the Bar of New York City. (1968). *Mental illness due process and the criminal defendant.* New York: Fordham

University Press. For a commentary on the legal issues that resulted in changes in the New York State forensic system, see Morris, G. (1968). The confusion of confinement syndrome: An analysis of the confinement of mentally ill criminals and ex-criminals by the Department of Corrections of the State of New York. *Buffalo Law Review, 17,* 561–599.

7. New York State Office of Mental Health. (2001). *Statewide comprehensive plan for mental health services, 2001–2005.* Albany, NY: Author.

8. An outline of concepts underlying the organization of New York State prison mental health services can be found in the following documents: Abreu, D. (2001). Quality outpatient mental health services in a correctional environment—The Central New York Psychiatric Center model. In G. Landsberg & A. Smiley (Eds.), *Forensic mental health: Working with offenders with mental illness* (pp. 20-1–20-6). Kingston, NJ: Civic Research Institute; Condelli, W. S., Dvoskin, J. A., & Holanchock, H. (1994). Intermediate care programs for inmates with psychiatric disorders. *Bulletin of the American Academy of Psychiatry and the Law, 22,* 63–70; Dvoskin, J. A., & Steadman, H. J. (1989). Chronically mentally ill inmates: The wrong concept for the right services. *International Journal of Psychiatry and Law, 12,* 203–210; New York State Office of Mental Health. (undated). *CNYPC—Psychiatric services for convicted persons: A community approach* (mimeograph). Albany: Author.

A more general discussion of models for inmate mental health service delivery can be found in Maier, G. J. & Miller, R. D. (1997). Models of mental health service delivery to correctional institutions. *Journal of Forensic Sciences, 32,* 225–232.

In most states, 24-hour mental health care is made available through a combination of psychiatric and prison hospital settings (Morrissey, J., Swanson, J. W., Goldstrom, I., Rudolph, L., et al. [1993]. *Overview of mental health services provided by state adult correctional facilities, United States, 1988* [Mental Health Statistical Note No. 207]. Rockville, MD: U.S. Department of Health and Human Services, Public Health Service, Substance Abuse and Mental Health Administration). When the Department of Corrections funds 24-hour hospital mental health care, it also tends to fund all inmate mental health services. However, when the Department of Mental Health funds 24-hour hospital mental health care, funding sources for all types of prison mental health treatment tended to be mixed (Swanson, J. W., Morrissey, J. P., Goldstrom, I., Rudolph, L., et al. [1993]. *Funding, expenditure, and staffing of mental health services in state adult correctional facilities, United States, 1988* [Mental Health Statistical Note No. 208]. Rockville, MD: U.S. Department of Health and Human Services, Public Health Service, Substance Abuse and Mental Health Administration).

9. There is considerable variability in spending on inmate mental health services. A national survey on expenditures found that total annual funding per inmate ranged from $5.67 to $3,159.41 (Swanson, J. W., Morrissey, J. P., Goldstrom, I., Rudolph, L., et al., 1993).

10. Supra, note 7.
11. Beck, A., & Marushak, L. (2001). *Mental health treatment in state prisons, 2000* (NCJ 188215). Washington, DC: U.S. Government Printing Office.
12. Ditton, P. M. (1999). *Mental health treatment of inmates and probationers* [NCJ 174463]. Washington, DC: U.S. Government Printing Office.
13. Steadman, H. J., Holohean, E., & Dvoskin, J. L. (1991). Estimating mental health needs and service utilization among prison inmates. *Bulletin of the American Academy of Psychiatry and Law, 19,* 287–307. The NYS Office of Mental Health uses these figures in their most recent service delivery plan (supra, notes 2–7). Also, these figures are in line with a recent national estimate that places the proportion of mentally ill prison inmates at 16.2%, or 283,800 inmates nationwide (supra, notes 2–10).
14. Goord, G. S. (2000). *Commissioner's policy paper on prison safety and inmate programming.* Albany, NY: Department of Correctional Services. The percentage does not include inmates who are on keeplock status in their own cells. The combined rate of disciplinary segregation is 79 per 1000 prisoners.
15. A discussion of the technical aspects of stratified sampling can be found in Levy, P. S., & Lameshow, S. (1999). *Sampling of populations: Methods and applications.* New York: Wiley; and Ackoff, R. (1953). *The design of social research.* Chicago: University of Chicago Press.
16. For practical reasons, we limited our sample to males. Among inmates for whom we were able to locate disciplinary records, only 4% ($n = 367$) are women. This low proportion reflects the fact that relatively few women are sent to prison. In addition, we found that female inmates are less likely to exhibit the types of behavior of interest to us. Female inmates had a lower (about 30%) mean infraction rate, and only 2 women were hospitalized. However, a substantial proportion (37%) were placed on outpatient caseloads. Elaine Lord has dealt with the problem of disturbed and disruptive female inmates in New York State. The results of her inquiry are found in chapter 15, this volume.
17. Demographic comparisons between outpatients for whom we were able to locate treatment files and other outpatients reveal the following differences: Outpatients with treatment files are less likely to be high school graduates (23% vs. 29%), less likely to be employed at conviction (64% vs. 75%), and more likely to admit to drug use (65% vs. 58%). On the average, outpatients are also younger (25.4 years vs. 27.0 years), are first arrested at an earlier age (17.3 years vs. 18.3 years), and are first institutionalized at an earlier age (20.2 years vs. 21.7 years). There are no statistically significant differences between the two groups on mental health history variables.
18. A nationwide study of inmates receiving mental health services, which found that personality disorders predominated among outpatients, supports this view. Swanson, J. W., Morrissey, J. P., Goldstrom, I., Rudolph, L., et al. (1993). *Demographic and diagnostic characteristics*

of inmates receiving mental health service in state adult correctional facilities, United States, 1988 [Mental Health Statistical Note No. 209]. Rockville, MD: U.S. Department of Health and Human Services, Public Health Service, Substance Abuse and Mental Health Administration.

19. *The American Heritage Dictionary, Second Edition* (1985). Boston: Houghton Mifflin Company.

20. Hall, O. (1948). The stages of a medical career. *American Journal of Sociology, 53*, 327–336.

21. Waldorf, D. (1973). *Careers in dope.* Englewood Cliffs, NJ: Prentice Hall.

22. Shover, N. (1996). *Great pretenders: Pursuits and careers of persistent thieves.* Boulder, CO: Westview.

23. Waldorf (note 21, supra), p. 10. Similarly, Goffman (chapter 1, note 22) wrote: "Traditionally the term 'career' has been reserved for those who expect to enjoy the rises laid out within a respectable profession. The term is coming to be used, however, in a broadened sense to refer to any social strand of any person's course through life. The perspective of natural history is taken: unique outcomes are neglected in favor of such changes over time as are basic and common to the members of a social category, although occurring independently to each of them. Such a career is not a thing that can be brilliant or disappointing; it can no more be a success than a failure" (p. 125).

24. Steadman, H., & Cocozza, J. (1974). *Careers of the criminally insane.* Lexington, MA: DC Heath.

25. Blumstein, A., Cohen, I., Roth, J. A., & Vischer, C. A. (Eds.). (1986). *Criminal careers and "career criminals"* (Vols. I and II). Washington, DC: National Academy Press; Farrington, D. P., Ohlin, L. E., & Wilson, J. Q. (1986). *Understanding and controlling crime: Towards a new research strategy.* New York: Springer-Verlag; Tonry, M., Ohlin, L. E., & Farrington, D. P. (1991). *Human development and criminal behavior: New ways of advancing knowledge.* New York: Springer-Verlag.

26. See generally, Thornberry, T. (1977). *Developmental theories of crime and delinquency: Advances in criminological theory* (Vol. 7). New Brunswick, NJ: Transaction Press; Sampson, R. J. & Laub, J. H. (1993). *Crime in the making: Pathways and turning points through life.* Cambridge, MA: Harvard University Press.

27. For a discussion of the advantages of this combined methodological approach to research and related recommendations for innovative methods of data analysis, see: Maltz, M. D., & Mullany, J. M. (2000). Visualizing lives: New pathways for analyzing life course trajectories. *Journal of Quantitative Criminology, 16*, 255–281.

28. See Wheeler (chapter 1, note 16) and Garabedian (chapter 1, note 16).

29. Flanagan, T. (1980). Time served and institutional misconduct: Patterns of involvement in disciplinary infractions among long-term and short-term inmates. *Journal of Criminal Justice, 8*, 357–367.

Chapter

3

Patterns of Prison Misbehavior

In this chapter we are concerned with disruptive behavior, as reflected in disciplinary infraction rates, across the prison term. We identify the social and criminal history correlates of prison misbehavior and describe patterns of disruptiveness over the course of institutional life. Finally, we develop a career typology that distinguishes among patterns of highly disruptive behaviors, and we investigate the characteristics of inmates who display different patterns.

We begin by looking at the overall infraction rate for inmates in our sample. Among the entire release cohort, the average disciplinary rate is 3.6 infractions per year. Infraction rates do not vary much across time-served groups with the exception of long-term inmates, who have a substantially lower rate than do other inmates (2.6 per annum).

Table 3.1 summarizes the results of a multiple regression analysis exploring the relationship of criminal and social history variables to overall infraction rates. The analysis indicates that age and preconviction employment status are the variables most predictive of disciplinary rates. In general, younger inmates and unemployed inmates are likely to have higher levels of disciplinary involvement. We also find other variables to be modestly predictive of infraction rates. A history of prior arrest for violent crime and race (low rates in

Table 3.1

Results of Stepwise Multiple Regression Analysis of Disciplinary Infraction Rates

Step	Variable	β	Significance	R Square
1	Age[a]	−.26	.000	.170
2	Employment[b]	−.20	.000	.213
3	Prior violent offense	.09	.000	.225
4	Education[c]	−.07	.000	.231
5	Marital status[d]	−.08	.000	.235
6	Race[e]	.07	.000	.239
7	Murder[f]	−.07	.000	.243
8	Burglary[f]	.03	.000	.244
9	Rape[f]	−.04	.000	.245
10	Assault[f]	−.03	.001	.246
11	Drug[f]	−.03	.001	.247

Note. [a]At prison entry. [b]Not employed (low), employed (high) at conviction. [c]High school graduate: no (low), yes (high). [d]Single (low), married (high). [e]White (low), non-White (high). [f]Conviction offense.

the case of White inmates, high for non-White inmates) show a positive correlation, whereas education level shows a negative correlation. We also find that type of offense is a very weak predictor of infraction rates. In the analysis, dummy variables were created for each crime type with the exception of robbery, and results are to be interpreted in relation to this crime category. We find that people convicted of murder, rape, assault, and drug offenses have lower infraction rates, whereas those convicted of burglary have higher infraction rates. The strongest relationship is for murder, although taken as whole, conviction offense information increases the amount of explained variance only by about 1%.[1]

Prior research shows age to be a consistent correlate of prison infractions, and our data confirm that young inmates are much more likely to engage in prison misbehavior than older inmates.[2] Previous research has also shown marital status and work history to be fairly consistently associated with infraction rates, and we find similar associations. Although we did not find strong effects for conviction offense, those who commit murder have been reported to have lower prison infraction rates, and our data are consistent with this finding. Finally, we confirm that employment history is associated with infraction rates. Most other studies do not report this relationship.

Our results indicate that single, unemployed, and uneducated inmates have higher infraction rates. These findings insinuate a picture suggesting psychological continuity, in that offenders with marginal lifestyles in the community appear to have greater difficulty adjusting to prison. The fact that prior violence emerges as an important correlate of prison infractions also suggests a continuity of misbehavior from community to institution. However, the influence of preinstitutional offense behavior appears restricted, because prior criminal record did not emerge as significant in the analysis.[3]

Timing of Disciplinary Infractions

We now examine issues regarding the timing of disciplinary involvement. In general, we find that the later the onset of misbehavior, the lower the overall infraction rate. For example, inmates who commit their first violation within 30 days of admission show a rate of 7.3 infractions as compared with a rate of 1.8 infractions for inmates who commit their first violation more than 150 days into their sentence. Inmates who begin violating rules early in their prison sentence tend to accumulate more substantial disciplinary records than other inmates over the course of the prison term.

Mean annual infraction rates over career segments are displayed in Figure 3.1. In general, we see that the overall pattern of misbehavior is relatively similar across time-served groups. Infraction rates are highest at the beginning of prison terms and lowest at their end. Early portions of sentences are

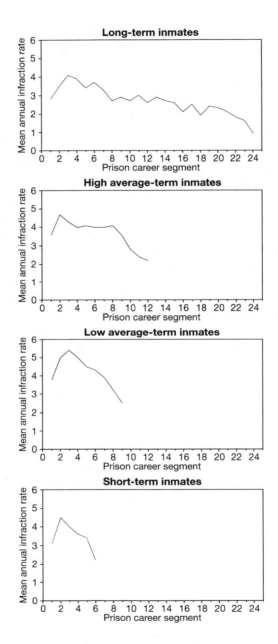

Figure 3.1. Mean annual disciplinary infraction rates by time served.

characterized by a sharp rise and fall in disciplinary rates, after which disciplinary rates show a consistent downward trend. The rate of decline is related to the length of the sentence, with short-term inmates showing the steepest drop and long-term inmates displaying the most gradual decline.

This statistical pattern pertains to the "average" inmate, and we might expect that the depiction is more appropriate for some inmates than others. We have seen that criminal and social history variables are related to infraction rates, and this leads us to ask whether these variables influence the *pattern* of infraction rates over time. Age is of particular interest, because this variable has been often reported as a strong correlate of antisocial behavior. Figure 3.2 displays mean infraction rates over career segments by age categories.

The data indicate that young inmates consistently have higher infraction rates at all points in a prison term. We also observe that young inmates exhibit the most dramatic changes in misbehavior rates over time. Misbehavior by these inmates rises sharply in the early stages of the prison career and then steadily declines over the remainder of the sentence. In contrast, we find that older inmates have lower infraction rates that remain fairly stable from admission to release. Thus, the infraction rate curve for older inmates appears relatively flat and does not exhibit any substantial fluctuations over time. These age-related patterns hold across all time-served categories.

In sum, we find a consistent pattern of inmate disciplinary rates over the course of prison terms. Rates of disciplinary involvement rise and fall early in the sentence and then continue to decline until the end of the prison term. The overall pattern holds for all the time-served groups but varies considerably by age, being most characteristic of younger inmates. Younger inmates exhibit the sharpest changes in misbehavior rates, whereas rates for older inmates are relatively constant over time. In addition, we find that younger inmates reliably show higher infraction rates at all points in their sentence. Thus, overall higher infraction rates for young inmates are not just the result of short periods of intense disciplinary

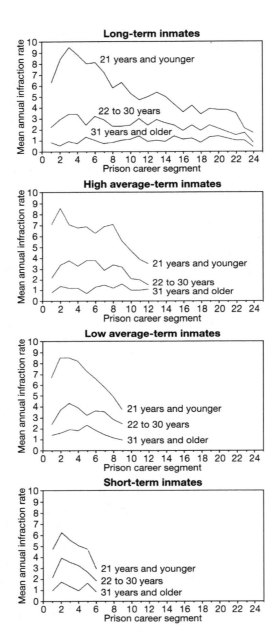

Figure 3.2.   Mean annual disciplinary infraction rates by age and time served.

involvement. Rather, a greater propensity for disruptiveness is manifest across the entire prison sentence of these inmates.

A strong inverse relation between age and rates of antisocial behavior ranks as the most consistent finding in criminological research. Explaining this association, however, has not been easy because "when attention shifts to the meaning or implications of the relationship between age and crime, that relation easily qualifies as the most difficult fact in the field."[4]

In an attempt to explain the age–crime relationship, some scholars have emphasized the variety of social and psychological changes that accompany the aging process.[5] These changes can include developments in areas of marriage, family, and employment that lead to greater attachments to others and stronger community ties.[6] Changes can also include broad psychological developments (as discussed in chapter 14, this volume), such as replacement of hedonistic values with more abstract and principled normative systems, and shifts in time perspectives from a concern with the here-and-now to concern with the longer term consequences of behavior.[7]

The data we have presented so far suggest an undiluted aging effect, because as inmates become more prosocial over time they also grow older (or vice versa), raising the possibility that changes in disciplinary involvement may simply be the result of increasing chronological age. By implication, however, if chronological age is the operative factor, prison experiences should contribute little to the decline in infraction rates. Therefore, we can expect to find equivalent infraction rates across inmates of the same age at different points in their sentences. To address this issue, we computed infraction rates for age-equivalent groups at various points in the prison term. We especially examined the time surrounding admission and release, because these periods encompass the greatest difference in behavior.

The data in Table 3.2 suggest that prison experiences *do* temper inmate misbehavior. Infraction rates are lower at the end of prison sentences than at the beginning, allowing for the fact that inmates grow older while incarcerated. The ef-

Table 3.2

*Mean Annual Disciplinary Infraction Rates During Early and
Late Segments of Prison Terms for Inmates of the Same Age*

Age (in years)	First 6 months	Last 6 months	First 9 months	Last 9 months
18	9.0	5.6	9.1	9.0
19	7.6	5.6	8.4	7.2
20	6.2	4.4	6.8	5.5
21	5.6	4.8	6.3	5.3
22	4.6	4.0	4.8	4.4
23	4.0	3.2	4.4	3.5
24	4.6	2.8	4.7	3.5
25	3.0	2.6	3.0	2.9
26	2.8	2.8	2.8	2.8
27	2.2	2.4	2.5	2.4
28	2.8	2.6	3.1	2.4
29	2.0	1.8	2.1	1.9
30	2.2	1.8	2.1	2.3
31	3.0	1.8	3.2	2.3
32	1.4	2.0	1.3	1.7
33	2.0	2.0	2.5	1.6
34	1.0	1.4	0.9	1.6
35	1.8	0.6	2.1	0.8

Note. Age categories are based on age at admission for the first 6-
and 9-month segments and age at release for the last 6- and 9-
month segments.

fect, however, is conditioned on chronological age such that
only inmates age 25 or younger show a consistent decrease.
We also notice that chronological age has a stronger effect on
infraction rates than stage of sentence, given that reductions
are more substantial across age categories holding location in
sentence constant.

These data support the argument that aging per se does
not provide a complete explanation of why misbehavior decreases as inmates complete their sentences. Although chron-

ological age is strongly related to rates of disruptive behavior, experiential factors emerge as important added considerations, particularly for young offenders. The simple passing of time may serve to reduce antisocial propensities, but what happens while time passes is not completely irrelevant.

The experience-based changes we infer from the data are interesting because of where and for whom they occur. Prisons stand outside the context of normal social arrangements. They provide a highly structured environment with opportunities for education and job training more assertively available than in the community. For example, inmates follow a strict schedule that dictates when to wake up, when to eat, and when to go to bed, and they often are required to work or attend school even if they are not so inclined. Young inmates, who are presumably more rambunctious and less mature than older inmates, appear to derive some benefit from this forced-choice environment. We assume that learning, the association of positive and negative consequences with behaviors, plays a role in fostering changes. We also show (in chapter 13, this volume) that meaningful participation in conventional activities can turn attitudes in a prosocial direction, and we argue that maturational advances at the lower end of the spectrum can have substantial influence on behavior. It is perhaps both surprising and encouraging to find that prison inmates who are initially most resistant to restrictions on their personal liberty demonstrate increasing levels of conformity over time.

Given that antistaff values find expression in prison rules violations, our data hold implications for theories of prisonization.[8] We recall that early perspectives implied that prisonization might be a functional adjustment to confinement, which means that it would increase as a function of time served. This framework is clearly not supported by the data.[9] Not only do infraction rates show a consistent nonlinear pattern early in the prison term, but the overall direction of change is opposite of that predicted.

We have also noted that more recent perspectives view prisonization as a nonlinear function of time and often describe this in terms of an inverted-U pattern.[10] This framework predicts that the degree of prisonization will rise and then fall over the course of a sentence and be greatest in the middle of the sentence when inmates are most removed in time from community influences.[11] The data indicate that disciplinary rates rise and then fall as predicted, but the fit of the inverted-U pattern appears to vary by sentence length. The careers of short-term inmates fit the pattern best, but inflection points for longer term inmates occur much earlier than at midsentence. We might be inclined to interpret the curves as evidence for the differential appropriateness of the inverted-U pattern by sentence length except that disciplinary rates for all sentenced groups peak during the second or third career segment. It seems to us that the more important finding is that disciplinary rates peak for all inmates somewhere between the first 6 to 9 months of incarceration. That this point happens to be closer to midsentence for short-termers than for other inmates can distract us from the consistency in the data.

We also do not find strong evidence for an *anticipatory resocialization* effect, which is an important part of the inverted-U theory of prisonization.[12] Rates of antisocial behavior do not decrease just prior to release but instead seem to reflect a steady decline. Because this conclusion is based on visual inspection of the graphs, we attempted to investigate the anticipatory resocialization issue more directly. The concept predicts that levels of conformity increase in preparation for return to the community, and key factors in this equation are proximity and certainty of release date. Events that clearly signal impending return to the community should therefore produce noticeable changes in behavior. We examined infraction rates at 1- and 2-month intervals before and after the last parole hearing, in which the inmate learns of his impending release, and found the rates to be nearly identical. We also compared disciplinary rates between penultimate and release facilities and found no difference.

We interpret the pattern of changes in disciplinary rates as evidence that prison entry presents a difficult period of adjustment. Incarceration seems to involve an experience of "transition shock" as reflected in a consistent rise in disciplinary rates early in the sentence. Adjustment difficulties are most substantial among younger inmates, in that they have the highest infraction rates and show dramatic changes in behavior. In contrast, disciplinary rates for older inmates are low to begin with and fail to show any remarkable changes. However, we find that early periods of incarceration generally stand out as a critical stage characterized by the highest levels of nonconformity. We also find that young inmates continue to have the greatest problems adjusting but, following initial adjustment difficulties, the overall trend is that of consistent improvement in behavior over time.

Our findings bear on issues regarding differences in adjustment patterns between short-term and long-term inmates. Prior research reports that long-term inmates consistently have lower infraction rates than other inmates, even across age categories.[13] We have not found this observation to be replicable. In fact, we find that among the younger inmates, infraction rates for long-term inmates at their peak are higher than for other inmate groups. Changes in sentencing practices, producing corresponding shifts in inmate populations, may help to account for the different findings. In recent years, prison administrators have maintained that changes in laws dealing with violent and repeat felons have created a new breed of long-term inmates who are more difficult to manage.[14] It is possible that our data reflect this development among young inmates serving long sentences.

Prior studies have also found that infraction rates of long-term inmates are fairly stable over time, leading to the conclusion that, unlike other inmates, long-termers do not undergo critical stages of adjustment. In contrast, we find that differences in adjustment patterns are more a function of age than of sentence length. The adjustment patterns of long-term inmates resemble those of other inmates across comparable age groups. Some researchers have also observed that compared with other prisoners, long-term inmates demonstrate a more settled and mature attitude, are more accepting of their situation, are more likely to recognize the need to get along with prison staff and peers, and tend to view their prison activities in the context of more extended time perspectives. It would appear that these perspectives are typical of older inmates, a group that is overrepresented among long-termers.

Types of Infractions

A variety of rules, ranging in degree of seriousness and in purpose, govern inmate behavior. Some prison rules find analogues in the outside community, other rules are common to institutional settings, and yet still other rules are unique to prisons. We now examine the frequency of rule violations across categories. We then investigate differences in types of infractions across inmates.

Overall, we find that the most common disciplinary charge is refusing orders (45%), followed by failure to follow posted facility rules (35%).[15] Other frequent charges relate to inmate movement (28%) and interference with or harassment of prison staff (23%). The incidence of violence is relatively high (17%) and is on par with charges of creating a disturbance (17%) and contraband violations (14%). Violations involving the destruction of property are relatively infrequent (6%), as are violations of fire, health, and safety rules (4%); riots, strikes, or escapes (2%); and sexual misbehavior (0.5%). Self-injuries (0.2%) and victimizations (0.2%) written up as disciplinary incidents characterize a very small proportion of violations.

When we examine types of violations by age of inmate, modest differences surface. Young (age 21 or younger) inmates are more likely to be charged with violent behavior than older (age 30 or older) inmates (18% vs. 13%). In contrast, older inmates are more likely to be involved with contraband violations (18% vs. 11%) and riots, strikes, or escapes (4% vs. 2%).

Violent behavior is of particular interest because normative prohibitions against such acts transcend institutional settings. We find individual rates of violent and nonviolent infractions to be correlated at about the .50 level. This association carries several implications. To begin with, we can infer that violent inmates are not highly specialized and lead relatively extensive and checkered disciplinary careers.[16] In addition, we can infer that highly disruptive inmates show a greater propensity toward violence. This suggests that rules peculiar to prison settings are not the exclusive source of problems for inmates with serious adjustment difficulties.

When we examine rates of violent infractions over time, we find that the general pattern parallels that of overall infraction rates. For all time-served groups, rates of violence peak in the early stages of the prison term and then rapidly fall off. Violence rates show more variability than overall disciplinary rates, but this may be a function of scale and of low base rates.

Career Typology

Up to this point, our analyses have focused on central tendencies (i.e., mean infraction rates) and on differences between groups of inmates (such as young and old, short term and long term). Patterns of human behavior that encompass a great deal of variation at the aggregate level invite further disaggregation because distinctive attributes of groups cannot be taken for granted as being descriptive at the individual level. We now turn our attention to the individual level of analysis and develop a behavioral typology of inmate disciplinary careers. The main purpose of the typology is to describe the individual patterns of adaptation that occur in prisons. In addition, the typology will lay the groundwork for investigating questions relating to chronic disciplinary violators.

Our typology is constructed around sequences of highly disruptive behavior throughout the course of prison sentences. We begin with our basic framework of career segments and designate a segment as "disruptive" if the annualized rate of infractions is greater than 12. This criterion corresponds to the 95th percentile in the distribution of overall infraction rates.

By simply designating career segments as disruptive or

nondisruptive, we can identify 64 different patterns for short-term inmates and 16,777,216 different patterns for long-term inmates. It is unlikely, of course, that every pattern will be represented in our data, but the need for simplification should be obvious. We therefore labeled career segments as part of early, middle, or late career stages, with particular designations contingent on sentence length. Short-term inmates would have only early and late career stages. Both low-average and high-average-term inmates would have only one middle stage, and long-term inmates, two middle career stages.[17] These divisions are based on our data, which indicate that infraction rates of short-term inmates are in abrupt decline over most of the sentence, whereas rates of long-term inmates show a much more gradual decline.

As the next step in constructing our typology, we designated the early, middle, and late career stages as either disruptive or nondisruptive. To screen out unusually brief periods of disruptive activity, we require that at least two thirds of the career segments in a given career stage be labeled disruptive for the career stage to be classified as disruptive. This requirement ensures chronicity in the identification of disruptive career stages. Thus, our classification scheme is built around three career stages (early, middle, and late), which are characterized as disruptive or nondisruptive. This scheme leads to a total of eight adjustment patterns. We describe the patterns as follows: conforming (low, low, low), late bloomer (low, low, high), inverted U-shape (low, high, low), mid-bloomer (low, high, high), early starter (high, low, low), U-shaped (high, low, high), late reformer (high, high, low), and chronic (high, high, high).[18]

Table 3.3 contains the overall distribution of disciplinary careers and the distribution by time-served group. We find that three quarters of the inmates (75.3%) can be classified as conformers in that they fail to exhibit any period of highly disruptive behavior. Thus, the majority of inmates are relatively well behaved and do not encounter substantial problems adjusting to prison rules.[19]

The most common pattern of disruptiveness is the early starter (6.9%). This pattern is followed in frequency by in-

Table 3.3

Percentage Distribution of Disciplinary Career Patterns by Time Served

Disciplinary career pattern	% Total (N = 9,428)	Time-served group			
		% Short term (n = 2,914)	% Low average term (n = 3,653)	% High average term (n = 1,655)	% Long term (n = 1,206)
Nondisruptive (low, low, low)	75.3	78.0	72.0	69.7	86.6
Early starter (high, low, low)	6.9	10.9	5.6	4.3	4.6
Inverted-U (low, high, low)	4.6	—	6.6	9.5	3.2
Late bloomer (low, low, high)	2.8	5.4	2.1	1.5	0.2
Late reformer (high, high, low)	3.5	—	4.4	7.4	3.5
U-shape (high, low, high)	2.5	—	1.1	0.9	0.6
Mid-bloomer (low, high, high)	1.5	—	2.4	3.0	0.4
Chronic (high, high, high)	3.0	5.8	5.8	3.6	0.9

Note. Dashes indicate no data.

verted U-shape (4.6%) and late reformer (3.5%) careers. Less frequent career patterns are chronic (3.0%), U-shape (2.5%), and mid-bloomer (1.5%).

The distribution of disruptive patterns varies across time-served groups. In particular, the early starter pattern is most common among the short-termers; the low-average-term inmates are characterized by early-starter, inverted-U, and chronic patterns; the chronic pattern is least frequent among long-term inmates. This latter finding is consistent with the fact that long-termers have a lower overall infraction rate and probably reflects the difficulty of maintaining a high level of antisocial behavior over a very long period of time.

The career typology we have developed is an individual-level classification that illustrates the variety of ways in which inmates adjust or fail to adjust to their environment. In this respect, the career typology takes us beyond aggregate descriptions of adjustment patterns. Yet, we find that the early starter, the pattern that best resembles the overall distribution of infraction rates, is the most frequent of the disruptive patterns. We also note the low proportion of chronic infractors. This finding indicates that relatively few inmates present serious disciplinary problems over most of their sentence.

Our typology comprises all the logical combinations of patterns within the definitions we have set, and intuitively we might suspect that some disruptive patterns are more significant or important than others. One way of approaching this issue is to examine the relative frequency of each subtype as we just have done. From this perspective, subtypes that rarely occur can be viewed as relatively minor constituents of the typological scheme. Another strategy is to examine whether subtypes differ in terms of features, such as social and criminal history, that are not constituent parts of the typology. The latter approach moves us beyond consideration of typologies as a useful tool for describing behavior patterns and leads us to ask if patterns of behaviors correspond with personal attributes. Subtypes that simply describe behavior tend to be less useful than subtypes that also distinguish types of people. This is because relationships between personal attributes and behavior patterns can provide insight

into motivations, and these insights in turn can lead to explanations. Thus, having described the *what* of our typology,
we now try to identify the corresponding *who*, which will
put us in a position to speculate about the *why*.

We begin our investigation with a discriminant function
analysis. As the name suggests, this technique allows us to
determine whether we can "discriminate" across career
types.[20] Independent variables are grouped into functions,
and the results tell us how the functions relate to categories
of the dependent variable. If the functions are discriminating,
our ability to correctly classify individuals by career type
should be high.

At the outset, we attempted to distinguish across all the
career patterns, and we imposed no restriction on the number
of functions. After several trials, it became obvious that only
a few functions were statistically significant and that we
could classify accurately only three career types. These patterns are the nondisruptive, the early starter, and the chronic.
On the basis of these first findings, the remaining career types
were then combined into a single category, and the analysis
was repeated.

The final analysis generated three statistically significant
functions that are displayed in Table 3.4. The asterisk iden-
tifies the function for which the loading of a variable is largest. The first function describes inmates with the following
characteristics: older at admission, did not receive mental
health services in prison, high school graduates, and no prior
record of criminal hospitalization. The second function describes employed, non-White, drug offenders with longer
prison terms and with prior prison experience who are
younger when first arrested and older when first institutionalized. The third function describes inmates with no prior
record of violent offense, with varied conviction offenses (assault, rape, burglary, robbery, and murder),[21] who are un-
married, admitted drug users, and without a record of civil
hospitalization. In general, the first function describes older
inmates with no record of mental health involvement, the
second function describes criminalized minority group drug

Table 3.4

Description of Functions Produced by Discriminant Analysis

Variable	Function 1	Function 2	Function 3
Age at prison entry	.82*	−.20	−.11
Prison mental health experience	−.32*	.00	.17
Education (high school graduate)	.19*	.05	−.09
Prior criminal hospitalization	−.14*	.07	.01
Employment (at conviction)	.08	.54*	.25
Age at first institutionalization	−.37	.48*	.44
Time served	−.28	.45*	−.11
Prior prison experience	−.30	.43*	.07
Age at first arrest	.30	−.36*	.32
Race (non-White)	−.02	−.25*	.09
Drug use	−.15	.23*	.05
Prior violent offense	.04	.17	.64*
Assault[a]	.01	.02	.52*
Rape[a]	.13	−.10	.51*
Burglary[a]	.04	−.13	.47*
Robbery[a]	−.03	.13	.26*
Murder[a]	.17	.02	.24*
Marital status (married)	.19	.09	−.23*
Prior civil hospitalization	−.04	.05	−.16*
Drug offender[a]	.04	.03	.14*
Percent of explained variance in variables			
Before rotation	90	7	3
After rotation	48	47	5

Note. *Highest loading factor; [a]conviction offense.

offenders, and the third function describes the majority of the inmate population (at least in terms of commitment offense).

The proportional contribution of each function to the total amount of explained variance in the variables is 90% for the first function, 7% for the second function, and 3% for the third function. After a varimax rotation is performed, which optimizes the fit of the functions to the variables, the percentages for each function become 48%, 47%, and 5%, respectively. The first two functions share most of the explained variance, whereas the last function contributes very little. This finding indicates that the third function is relatively unimportant, which is not surprising given the variables that compose this function.

Table 3.5 displays the relationships of the functions to career categories. Function 1 shows a positive relationship to the nondisruptive group and negative relationships to the other groups, the strongest of which is for the chronic career type. Function 2 shows relationships that are very similar to Function 1, whereas Function 3 is positively related to the early-starter pattern and marginally related to the other groups. The strongest relationships in the table indicate that nondisruptive inmates are more likely to resemble older inmates with no mental health involvement or criminalized drug offenders, whereas chronically disruptive inmates are less likely to resemble these inmate groups. To a lesser extent, we find that the early starters resemble the typical offender at least in terms of commitment offense (Function 3).

The classification results of the discriminant analysis are dis-

Table 3.5

Relationship of Discriminant Functions to Career Categories

Career category	Function 1	Function 2	Function 3
Nondisruptive	0.48	0.41	−0.03
Catchall[a]	−1.36	−0.87	−0.06
Early starter	−1.34	−1.47	0.47
Chronic	−1.98	−1.94	−0.04

[a]Includes inverted-U, late bloomer, late reformer, U-shape, and mid-bloomer.

Table 3.6

Classification Results (in Percentages) From Discriminant Analysis

Actual group membership	Predicted group membership			
	% Nondisruptive	% Catchall[a]	% Early starter	% Chronic
Nondisruptive	77 (n = 5,146)	8 (n = 559)	6 (n = 381)	9 (n = 592)
Catchall[a]	41 (n = 471)	24 (n = 274)	7 (n = 84)	28 (n = 320)
Early starter	33 (n = 202)	11 (n = 66)	23 (n = 139)	33 (n = 203)
Chronic	26 (n = 129)	12 (n = 57)	10 (n = 50)	52 (n = 251)

Note. The percentage of "grouped" cases correctly classified is 65%. [a]Includes inverted-U, late bloomer, late reformer, U-shape, and mid-bloomer.

played in Table 3.6. Overall, we are able to classify correctly 65% of the inmates, which represents a significant achievement. The proportion of correct classifications is adjusted for the actual distribution of the data, thereby imposing a more stringent criterion. Accuracy of classification varies across career types and is greatest for the nondisruptive pattern. We are able to classify correctly 77% of the nondisruptives, with misclassifications distributed evenly across remaining categories. Classification results for the chronic career type are good in that we can accurately classify 52% of these inmates. Errors in classification for the chronic pattern concentrate in the nondisruptive group.

The discriminant analysis performs less well in predicting the early-starter pattern or the catchall group of patterns.

Among the early-starter inmates, 23% are correctly classified, with errors evenly balanced between nondisruptive and chronic patterns. The classification results for the catchall group are very similar, although more classification errors involve the nondisruptive group.

Discriminant analysis examines relationships of independent variables grouped as functions across all categories of the dependent variable. The format interposes an intermediary element in the interpretation of effects (i.e., a function) and does not allow us to examine differences between some categories, excluding consideration of other categories. The technique, for example, does not readily lend itself to answering questions such as, How do early starters differ from chronics?

To investigate these questions, we performed logistic regression analysis between pairs of the career types that emerged as significant from the discriminant analysis. Logistic regression operates on a modification of standard regression procedures to provide estimates of how independent variables affect the log-likelihood that a given case will fall into either category of the dependent variables.[22] The results of the analyses are presented in Table 3.7. The interpretation of effects derives from the direction and relative magnitude of coefficients.

We find that, when compared with nondisruptive inmates, the early starters are younger; less educated; more likely to be non-White, single, and unemployed; and less likely to have been in prison before. The early starters are also more likely to have a history of criminal psychiatric hospitalization; serve shorter prison terms; and have greater chances of being sentenced for assault, rape, and burglary. Most of these differences also emerge in a comparison of chronics with nondisruptives, but the magnitude of effects tends to be greater. Additional differences are that chronic disruptives start their criminal careers later but are institutionalized earlier. This paradox may be partly explained by the finding that chronic disruptives are more likely to have a history of violent crime, because early institutionalization may reflect shorter, more serious criminal careers. Chronic disruptives

Table 3.7

*Results of Logistic Regression Analyses Between Types of
Disciplinary Careers*

Variable	Nondisruptive vs. Early starter	Nondisruptive vs. Chronic	Early starter vs. Chronic
Social history			
Age at prison entry	−0.66	−1.04	
Age at first arrest		0.96	
Age at first institution-alization		−1.44	−1.17
Race (non-White)	0.69	0.73	
Education (high school graduate)	−0.55	−0.69	
Employment (at conviction)	−0.56	−1.07	−0.59
Marital status (married)	−0.86	−0.39	
Criminal history			
Prior prison experience	−0.49	−0.59	
Prior violent offense		0.95	0.85
Mental health history			
Prior civil hospitalization		0.71	0.60
Prior criminal hospitalization	0.52	0.93	0.40
Conviction offense			
Murder		−2.01	−2.34
Assault	0.72	0.80	−1.52
Rape	1.02	−2.06	−0.36
Burglary	0.75		−0.72
Robbery			−0.49
Time served	−0.34	0.14	0.23
Constant	1.44	0.08	1.91
Goodness-of-fit χ^2	1,035	1,244*	599*
df	1,006	586	243
Hosmer statistic	25*	35*	8
df	8	8	8

Note. p < .05.

are also more likely to have a history of civil psychiatric hospitalization and less likely to be sentenced for murder, assault, and rape in their current prison term. When we compare early starters with chronics, we find that only a few personal characteristics distinguish among career types, including age of first institutionalization, employment, violent offense history, and mental health experience.

In summary, the data indicate that we can distinguish three main career types—nondisruptive, early starter, and chronic —in terms of inmate attributes. We also find that our ability to classify inmate behavior patterns by personal attribute is greatest at the extremes and otherwise relatively weak. The discriminant analysis classifies best the nondisruptives and the chronics, and the logistic regression equation fits best (as indicated by the Hosmer statistic) when we compare these two groups. These findings lead us to conclude that nondisruptive and chronically disruptive careers involve very different inmates, whereas other careers encompass less distinctive inmates.

Chronically disruptive inmates differ from nondisruptive inmates in several ways that not surprisingly include being younger. We also note that inmates who present chronic disciplinary problems are relative newcomers to crime, as evidenced by tendencies to begin criminal involvement at a later age and to arrive at prison with no prior incarceration experience. However, against this relatively modest framework of criminal achievement, we find that the chronics are more likely to have a track record of violence, and their chances of having been in a psychiatric hospital are greater. The salience of both civil and criminal hospitalizations is noteworthy because of differences in the reasons for commitment. Criminal hospitalizations are predicated on manifestations of pathology and antisocial behavior, leaving open the possibility that one may be interpreted as the other. Civil hospitalizations present a less ambiguous symptomatic picture, which makes a stronger argument for a link between a history of pathology and prison disruptiveness. Our ability to predict with a fair degree of accuracy which inmates will become chronic violators, coupled with their brief but violent and pathologically tinged community track record, suggests the utility of targeting these inmates for intensive therapeutic interventions. The multivariate analyses confirm that chronically disruptive inmates differ from other inmates in ways that transcend the behavior at issue. Differences in background characteristics can provide clues as to the nature of the maladaptive process, and the fact that psychiatric hospitalization is a predictor of chronic disruptiveness suggests that serious psychological deficits may be at work. The modal pattern of increasing conformity over time indicates that initially high rates of prison misbehavior do not signal impending chronicity. This means that inmates must be given the opportunity to work out transitional adjustment problems, and only when misbehavior persists beyond the point when most inmates begin to adapt to their situation should remedial intervention strategies be considered.

Those who commit murder and rape are more likely to be nondisruptive than chronically disruptive, whereas those who commit assault and burglary are more likely to be early starters than nondisruptive or chronic. Common offense behaviors (such as assault and burglary) thus are associated with typical disruptiveness patterns. The tendency for murderers to be well-behaved inmates has been noted by others, and our results confirm this finding.

Prior violence discriminates chronics from nondisruptives and early starters, establishing a continuity of serious antisocial behavior. Most of the factors that distinguish between nondisruptive and typically disruptive inmates (such as the early starters) distinguish even better between nondisruptives and chronic inmates. These findings suggest that as we move across degrees of disruptiveness, the same factors discriminate between groups of inmates with few new variables entering the picture, and contrasts become increasingly sharper as we approach extremes. Differences between early starters and chronics relate mostly to prior violence and to mental health experiences, again suggesting that extreme disruptiveness is presaged by serious antisocial behavior and may be influenced by pathology.

System Costs Associated With Chronic Disruptiveness

We suggest later in chapter 16 that therapeutic programs targeted at chronically disruptive inmates may be both appropriate and advantageous. This suggestion is supported by our findings that chronic disruptives tend to have histories of emotional disorder and violent behavior. Another consideration is the disproportionate amount of prison resources that chronically disruptive inmates consume. These resources involve the administrative processing of infractions as well as the imposition of punitive measures. We have seen that chronically disruptive inmates constitute 3% of our release cohort, but this small group accounts for 12% of adjudicated disciplinary infractions, 13% of time spent in keeplock,[23] and 9% of time spent in special housing disciplinary units.[24] Our data thus confirm what most prison administrators have probably come to suspect through experience: A small group of recalcitrantly disruptive inmates consumes a disproportionately large share of prison resources. This small group represents a substantial portion of the workload of disciplinary committees and more frequently invites placement in high-security disciplinary settings. These facts lead us to assume that there is payoff in developing intervention programs that can intercept cycles of chronic misbehavior for inmates who are unresponsive to disciplinary actions based on traditional notions of punishment and deterrence.

Notes

1. The *R*-square statistic indicates that age accounts for most of the explained variance in disciplinary infraction rates. Most of the other variables in the equation (i.e., education through drug conviction offense) account for less than 1% of explained variance. These variables, although statistically significant in the context of a large sample size, are relatively unimportant from a substantive point of view.
2. Adams, K. (1993). Adjusting to prison life. In M. Tonry (Ed.), *Crime and justice: A review of research* (Vol. 16, pp. 275–359). Chicago: University of Chicago Press.

3. Zamble and Porporino (chapter 1, note 18) have documented the continuity and consistency of intramural and extramural coping deficits.
4. Hirschi, T., & Gottfredson, M. R. (1983). Age and the explanation of crime. *American Journal of Sociology, 89,* 552–584, p. 552.
5. Wilson, J., & Hernstein, R. (1986). *Crime and human behavior.* New York: Simon & Schuster.
6. Sampson and Laub (chapter 2, note 26).
7. Adams, K. (1977). Developmental aspects of adult crime. In T. Thornberry (Ed.), *Developmental theories of crime and delinquency: Advances in criminological theory* (Vol. 7, pp. 309–342). New Brunswick, NJ: Transaction Press.
8. Prisonization involves a complex socialization process that includes, but is not limited to, the adoption of antistaff values. Wheeler (chapter 1, note 16) wrote: "Conformity to staff expectations obviously taps only part of the phenomena referred to as prisonization by Clemmer and others. It does seem to get at a central core: the acceptance or rejection of norms and role definitions applied to inmates by the prison staff" (p. 700). Because prison rules represent a formal normative code of staff expectations of inmate behaviors, we can expect that as antistaff values increase, behaviors that indicate a rejection of this code will also increase.
9. Clemmer (chapter 1, note 16) suggested that length of exposure to prison was directly related to degree of prisonization. In other words, Clemmer viewed prisonization as a linear function of time served.
10. Wheeler (chapter 1, note 16) emphasized the importance of inmate time perspectives in relation to prison admission and release, leading him to develop a model of prison careers with early, middle, and late stages. Wheeler also emphasized the competition between the value systems of prison and society. His research led him to conclude that "Inmates who have been in the broader community and inmates who are to return to that community are more frequently oriented in terms of conventional value systems. Inmates conform least to conventional standards during the middle phase of their institutional career. These inmates appear to shed the prison culture before they leave it, such that there are almost as many conforming inmates at the time of release as at the time of entrance into the system" (p. 706). This pattern of prisonization is often described as an inverted-U (low, high, low), implying that prisonization is a nonlinear function of time served.
11. Wheeler (chapter 1, note 16) stated that "we might expect that the [prison] culture would exert its major impact on inmates during the middle of their stay, at the point in time where an inmate is farthest removed from the outside world" (p. 709).
12. Wheeler (chapter 1, note 16) described the concept of *anticipatory resocialization* as "the preparatory responses that frequently precede an actual change in group membership, such as the movement from prison to the broader community" (p. 698). He went on to elaborate

that "as time for release approaches, the problems deriving from imprisonment recede relative to prospective adjustment problems on parole. Such a shift in reference should also give rise to a resocialization process beginning just prior to release" (p. 709).

13. Although Flanagan (chapter 1, note 4) found strong effects for age, he also found that long-term inmates have lower infraction rates across all age categories and across amount of sentence served.

14. See, for example, Innes, C. (1997). Patterns of misconduct in the federal prison system. *Criminal Justice Review, 22,* 157–174.

15. Because a disciplinary incident (estimated $N = 79,435$) can involve more that one rule violation, percentages sum to greater than 100.

16. The issue of offense specialization has received much attention in the criminological literature. See, for example, Wolfgang, M., Figlio, R., & Sellin, T. (1972). *Delinquency in a birth cohort.* Chicago: University of Chicago Press. To pursue the issue further, we examined the correlation between pairs of sequential disciplinary infractions, which were categorized as violence, disturbance, refusing orders, movement, property/contraband, and other. Almost all the correlations were statistically significant given the large number of pairs ($n = 70,906$). Most of the correlations (30 out of 36) were less than 0.05. The strongest correlation observed was 0.09. These findings do not argue for offense specialization in disciplinary careers. However, the analysis has several limitations because, first, degree of consistency may increase if we view events from a broader perspective (e.g., entire careers); second, gross categories of behavior may fail to indicate consistency operating at a different level (e.g., motivational or situational consistency); and, finally, aggregate analyses can mask consistency at the individual level, especially if most offenders are jacks of all (criminal) trades and only a small proportion are specialized.

17. We designated time-served segments (1 up to 24) in terms of career stages (early, middle, late) as follows. Short-term inmates: early = 1 to 3, late = 4 to 6; low-average-term inmates: early = 1 to 3, middle = 4 to 6, late = 7 to 9; high-average-term inmates: early = 1 to 4, middle = 5 to 8, late = 9 to 12; and long-term inmates: early = 1 to 6, early middle = 7 to 12, late middle = 13 to 18, late = 19 to 24.

18. Our classification of disciplinary patterns builds on the fourfold scheme—accidental, early starter, late bloomer, and chronic—developed by Simon Dinitz and his colleagues in prison studies done as part of the monumental Dangerous Offender Research Project conducted at the Academy for Contemporary Problems, Ohio State University, Columbus, Ohio.

19. An issue we might pursue is whether the observed distribution of career types differs from that which can be expected to occur by chance. Our major interests, however, lie not in the proportion of inmates with a given career type but in identifying differences in personal attributes among groups of inmates with various patterns of

maladjustment. The typology of disciplinary careers is a vehicle that moves us toward this end by allowing us to disaggregate patterns of disruptiveness, and later on we use multivariate statistical techniques to examine differences between groups of inmates.

20. For a technical discussion of discriminant analysis, see Johnston, J. (1972). *Econometric methods* (2nd ed.). New York: McGraw-Hill; and Bibb, R., & Roncek, D. (1976). Investigating group differences: An explication of the sociological potential of discriminant analysis. *Sociological Methods and Research, 4*, 349–379. Discriminant analysis is a statistical technique that appears to be uniquely suited to our investigation. Bibb and Roncek noted that a useful application of the technique is that of "testing preexisting typologies for empirical adequacy." They went on to say, "Once data are grouped into cells of the typology, discriminant analysis can be used to measure the power of the schema . . . it is also possible to identify precisely those variables which are most crucial in contributing to differences among cells" (p. 372). Discriminant analysis assumes interval-level data, statistically independent and normally distributed variables, and equal variance–covariance matrices between groups (p. 364). Although the technique is fairly robust with regard to violations of these assumptions, particularly with large samples, we use logistic regression analysis (which does not require these assumptions) to confirm our results.

21. Sodomy, larceny, drug, and "other" are the only offense categories not included in this function.

22. For a technical discussion of log-linear techniques, see Bishop, Y. E., Feinberg, S. E., & Holland, P. W. (1975). *Discrete multivariate analysis: Theory and practice.* Cambridge, MA: MIT Press. In logistic regression analysis, the chi-square statistic is used to judge the fit of the model to the data. A low chi-square value (with a correspondingly probability value) indicates small differences between observed and predicted values. By this criterion, our logistic regression models do not fit very well, a situation that can be attributed, in part, to a low ratio of cases to unique combinations of independent variables. We could improve the fit of the models by recoding variables into fewer categories or by deleting variables from the analysis. However, because the discriminant analysis deals directly with the issue of predictive ability, and because we are primarily interested in identifying which of many possible factors distinguish between groups of inmates, we chose not to optimize the chi-square statistic.

23. Keeplock is when inmates are confined to their cells as punishment for misconduct.

24. The relative proportions of sanctions via segregation have changed since the time of our study, and today less use is made of keeplock, and much greater use of special housing arrangements that involve total separation from the prison population. Chronicity of infractions can become a criterion for assignment to segregated housing.

Chapter

4

Patterns of Pathology

In the preceding chapter, we examined one manifestation of maladaptive behavior: repeated violations of prison rules. In this chapter, we examine behavior that suggests another form of maladaptation: that produced by emotional disorder. We describe the personal attributes that are associated with emotional problems and ascertain the timing of symptomatic events. We particularly focus our attention on inmates who require hospitalization, because these inmates are the most seriously disturbed mental health clients.

We begin by examining the background characteristics of inmates who require mental health services. Table 4.1, which displays social and criminal history information, shows that hospitalized inmates are older at admission to prison, less likely to be married, and more likely to have been living alone at time of conviction. These inmates are also more likely to have a record of violent criminal behavior prior to their current conviction, and to have been in prison before. These differences help to account for the fact that hospitalized inmates serve longer prison terms, nearly twice as long, compared with inmates who do not require mental health services.

We also find that outpatients comprise the highest proportion of White inmates, are younger at admission to prison,

Table 4.1

Social and Criminal History by Prison Mental Health Experience, in Percentages

Variable	% No service (n = 8,012)	% Outpatient (n = 682)	% Hospitalized (n = 145)
Social history			
Race (non-White)	73	62	71
Education (high school graduate)	26	23	28
Employment (at conviction)	67	64	77
Drug use	61	65	50
Marital status (married)	32	31	15
Living arrangements at conviction (alone, institution)	14	18	39
Age at prison admission (mean years)	26.2	25.4	28.6
Criminal history			
Prior prison experience	26	29	38
Prior violent offense	53	62	72
Age at first arrest (mean years)	18.2	17.3	18.7
Age at first institutionalization (mean years)	21.4	20.2	21.7
Conviction offense			
Murder	6	10	11
Rape	2	5	7
Sodomy	2	6	6
Robbery	35	33	37
Assault	6	7	9
Burglary	19	21	15
Larceny	3	2	3
Drug	19	9	6
Other	9	9	6
Time served (mean months)	28.2	35.1	51.0

Table 4.2

Preprison Mental Health History by Prison Mental Health Experience

Mental health history	Prison mental health experience		
	No service (*n* = 8,012)	% Outpatient (*n* = 682)	% Hospitalized (*n* = 145)
Prior psychiatric hospitalization	7	16	61
Prior civil hospitalization	4	10	33
Prior criminal hospitalization	4	10	42
I.Q. at prison admission (mean)	99.3	96.8	89.3
Years between last hospitaliza-tion and prison admission (mean)	8.6	5.8	3.9

and show lower levels of educational achievement. They are also least likely to have held a job at conviction and most likely to have a history of drug abuse. In addition, they are most likely to stand convicted of burglary, and they begin their criminal involvement at an earlier age.[1]

Inmates who did not receive mental health services are more likely to be convicted of drug offenses. They are also less likely to be convicted of serious violent offenses, such as murder, rape, and sodomy, in comparison to inmates who received mental health services, either as an outpatient or as a hospital patient. Finally, they also demonstrate a lower probability of having been in prison before and of having a record of violent crime prior to their last offense.

Table 4.2 compares the preprison mental health experiences of patients and nonpatients. We find that inmates who were hospitalized during their current prison term are substantially more likely to have a record of prior hospitalization. Overall, 61% of hospitalized inmates show a history of psychiatric commitment on admission to prison. Experiences of forensic hospitalization are more common, although the difference in the incidence of criminal and civil commitments is not large (42% vs. 33%). Hospitalized inmates also disproportionately fall into the lower IQ range. We also find that the proportion of outpatients with a preprison history of psychiatric hospitalization is more than twice that of inmates who do not receive mental health services (16% vs. 7%).

When we examine inmates with a preprison history of psychiatric commitment, we find that the mean time between the last hospitalization and prison admission is shortest for inmates who are subsequently hospitalized (3.9 years) and longest for inmates who do not receive mental health services (8.6 years).

The general picture that emerges of hospitalized inmates is one of persons with multiple social and psychological deficits. These inmates are unlikely to have established significant interpersonal attachments or stable domestic arrangements prior to entering prison. The majority have already spent time in psychiatric hospitals, both criminal and civil, and their measured intellectual ability is below that of other inmates. Both the experience and recency of preincarceration psychiatric commitment emerge as major risk factors in prison hospitalization. Inmates who are unsuccessful at negotiating the prison environment are likely to have demonstrated similar coping problems in the community. These findings point to a continuity of psychiatric disability from one setting to the next, at least within a limited time frame. Finally, hospitalized inmates evidence a propensity toward violence in terms of current and prior offenses, which makes it unsurprising that many of these inmates have been in prison before and that, as a group, they serve prison terms that are much longer than average.

The average demographic profile of outpatients is that of a social dropout who turns to crime possibly as a "vocation." These inmates, who tend to be disproportionately White, find it difficult to stay in high school or to hold a job, and begin their criminal careers early in life. Burglary and drug abuse are common activities, pointing to a combination of economic and escapist motivations to crime. These inmates also show preincarceration involvement with the mental health system.

Although the findings are more compelling for hospitalized inmates, these data are consistent with the argument that a history of emotional disorder predicts future emotional disorder.

Descriptions of Inmate Behavior

Having described the characteristics of inmates who receive mental health services, we can now describe the nature of their emotional problems. We begin by examining the behavior of inmate patients in Table 4.3. For hospitalized inmates, we list hospital and prison experiences separately. We also note that the data are presented in a multiple-response format, which indicates the proportion of observations that contain descriptions of various behaviors. Because more than one piece of behavior may be described in a single observation, the percentages sum to greater than unity.

The most frequently reported symptoms for hospital patients are thought disturbances typical of psychoses—hallucinations and delusions—appearing in at least one of three observation reports. The second most frequent symptomatic behavior, also characteristic of psychotic disorders, is confused, disorganized, and irrelevant speech. Other common observations describe anxious or excited moods, withdrawn behavior, and hyperactivity. As we might anticipate, the symptomatic picture for outpatients differs substantially from that of hospital patients. Clinical notes for outpatients are most likely to describe anxious and depressed moods and sleep disturbances. Yet we note a substantial reporting of withdrawn behavior and of serious thought disturbances among the outpatients, although levels do not reach those of hospitalized inmates.

Differences in disturbed behavior are observed across settings. For hospital patients, reports of hallucinations, delusions, and self-injury are more common in prison, and these observations may well be precipitating events for psychiatric commitment. Reports of anxious or depressed moods are also more common in prison, and this may be a function of dif-

Table 4.3

Percentage of Mental Health Observations by Categories of Behaviors

Variable	Hospital patient		% Outpatient (*n* = 3,379)
	% Hospital (*n* = 10,258)	% Prison (*n* = 8,554)	
Thought disturbance			
Delusions, hallucinations	32	41	13
Disoriented (time, place, or person)	2	3	0.6
Confused, disorganized	19	24	10
No insight, poor judgment	13	4	4
Other	4	8	4
Self-injury	4	9	6
Affect, mood disturbance			
Flat, inappropriate affect	13	12	7
Depressed	9	16	18
Anxious, excited	16	27	39
Angry, hostile, suspicious	17	13	8
Other	2	2	1
Social behavior			
Withdrawn behaviors	26	30	19
Refusing medication	12	12	5
Poor hygiene	4	6	2
Malingering, manipulative	4	2	3
Other	0.2	0.3	0
Psychomotor behaviors			
Sleep disturbance	5	4	15
Hyperactive	11	12	5
Hypoactive	7	4	2
Motor tension	1	2	2
Somatic complaints	16	6	4
Eating disorder	2	4	2
Other	2	12	5

Note. Because a symptomatic observation can involve more than one behavior, percentages sum to greater than 100.

ferences in treatment regimens or in environment stimuli. In contrast, notations that patients lack insight or adequate judgment and that patients appear to be manipulative or are malingering are more likely to appear in hospital records. Patients are also more likely to voice somatic complaints while hospitalized, a finding that may be related to changes in medication regimens or that may reflect greater attentiveness to physical maladies by patient and clinician. Finally, we note that medication refusal does not vary between prison and hospital, even though forced medication is an option that is available in hospital settings, and we assume that patients must be aware of this fact.

In general, the data confirm the obvious fact that most observations of hospitalized inmates describe major psychiatric disorders. Outpatients are much less likely to demonstrate serious symptomatology, and those who do exhibit serious symptoms illustrate the point that mental disorders can be treated in prison settings. These findings suggest that levels of intervention can be geared to problem seriousness as is consistent with the community mental health model we described in chapter 2.

We find that the recorded picture becomes less alarming as the same patients move from prison to hospital. This difference is important because it indicates that clinicians do not always see the same problem as the treatment responsibility transfers from one staff member to the next. In this case, differences in symptomatic behavior may result from environmental changes as patients move from prison to hospital. However, the fact that hospital staff are more likely to characterize patients as malingering or manipulative indicates that these differences may be perceptual, which can create friction between prison and hospital treatment staff.

Symptom Rates Over Time

Having described the overall distribution of disturbed behavior, we can now turn to changes in the rates of these behaviors over time. Figure 4.1 displays mean annual symp-

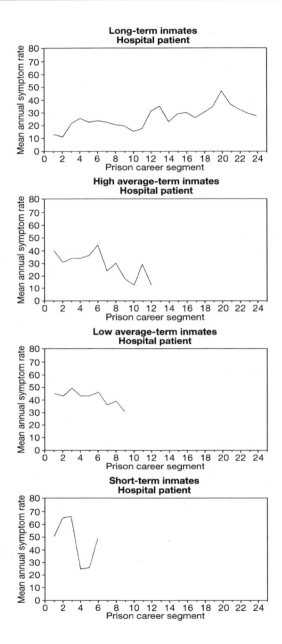

Figure 4.1. Mean annual symptom rates for hospital patients by time served.

tom rates for hospitalized inmates over the course of their prison term. The data include observations made during hospitalization and therefore represent a comprehensive picture of inmate experiences.

Looking at the graph, we find that short-term inmates show a dramatic oscillation in symptom rates. Symptomatology is very high at admission, drops substantially about halfway through the sentence, and then rises sharply just prior to release. In addition, we find that short-term inmates display the highest level of recorded symptoms, peaking at a mean rate of 65 per year. The trend for both low-average-term and high-average-term inmates is very similar. Symptom rates reach their highest point early in the prison term and show a relatively steady decline over time. The situation for very long-term inmates, however, is substantially different. For this inmate group, symptom rates start off at a relatively low level and increase steadily throughout the prison term.

A common feature across time-served groups of hospitalized inmates is that their difficulties briefly increase toward the end of the prison term. Both the high-average and the long-term inmates show a small "spike" in symptom rates in roughly the last quarter of the prison term. The increase, however, is most noticeable for short-term inmates who enter and leave the prison with nearly equal rates of symptomatic behavior.

Figure 4.2 charts rates of symptomatic behavior for outpatients. The first item we notice is that, compared with hospitalized inmates, outpatient symptom rates are relatively low, reaching a high of only 6.7 per year. Looking at the overall trends, we find that inmates serving shorter sentences enter prison with relatively high levels of disturbed behavior that drop off very sharply over time. In comparison, symptom rates for longer term inmates show less variability. However, high-average-term inmates evidence mildly declining symptom rates, whereas long-term inmates show an opposite trend. For outpatients, displays of recorded symptoms tend to be brief. If we divide the prison term into early, middle, and late stages, we find that only one fourth (23.2%) of out-

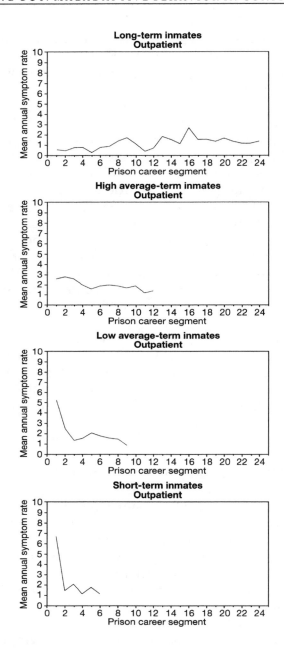

Figure 4.2.   Mean annual symptom rates for outpatients by time served.

patients display symptomatic behaviors at a nonzero rate for more than one career stage.

Symptom rate patterns reveal fair consistency between hospitalized inmates and outpatients but differ substantially across time-served groups. Short-term inmates consistently show the most unstable levels of pathology. However, hospital inmates demonstrate a cyclic rise-and-fall pattern, whereas outpatients evidence a declining trend. For both classes of patients, decreasing levels of pathology are characteristic of average-term inmates, whereas long-term inmates show steadily increasing pathology levels. In general, it seems that disturbed behavior tends to subside over time for most inmates. The exception is the long-term inmates, who appear to demonstrate increasing pathology levels.[2]

The observation that symptom rates for hospital patients show a brief increase prior to discharge from prison is interesting, because the pattern suggests that anxiety levels for severely disturbed inmates rise in anticipation of return to the community. The findings thus depict an *anticipatory release* phenomenon, the nature of which is quite different from that discussed in the prisonization literature. Severely disturbed inmates may view the transition from prison to community as a particularly stressful experience, thereby resuscitating dormant symptomatology. This scenario implies the utility of prerelease preparation and the coordination of treatment plans between prison and community service providers for inmates with serious emotional disorders. As mentioned in Chapter 2, the NYS Office of Mental Health has recognized this issue and plans to address it with the addition of new staff.

Timing of Hospitalizations

Figure 4.3 displays the cumulative percentage distribution of months between prison admission and initial hospitalization. We see that first commitments occur very early in the prison term and that men with a preprison psychiatric history are hospitalized earlier than other inmates. Among hospitalized

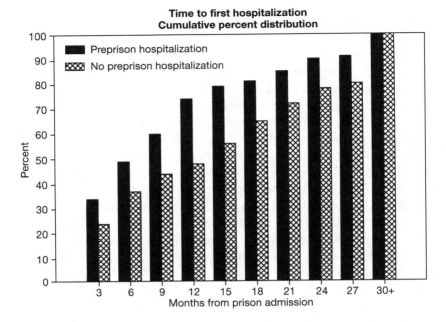

Figure 4.3.　Cumulative percentage distribution of time to first hospitalization by preprison mental health experience.

patients, half of those with a prior record of hospitalization and almost two-fifths of other inmates were committed within 6 months of prison entry. These data suggest that early portions of a prison term represent a critical period during which there is a tendency for serious disturbed behavior to make an appearance. This tendency is exacerbated if an inmate has a preincarceration history of psychiatric hospitalization.

　　Several factors, which may be working together, can help to account for our findings. One possibility is that early hospitalizations reflect situations wherein inmates who are seriously emotionally disturbed at sentencing continue the course of their illness on admission to prison. We can add to this the facts that the activities of prison inmates are scrutinized daily, thereby lessening the chances that eccentric behavior will go unnoticed, and that prisons generally have ready access to mental health staff, which affords greater opportunities for diagnosis. This interpretation receives some support from the data in that 8.3% of the hospitalized inmates, as compared with less than one half of 1% of other inmates, were found incompetent to stand trial prior to conviction on their current offense. Although incompetency findings are predicated on criteria that go beyond the simple presence of mental disorder, the data confirm that at least some inmates who require hospitalization in prison were suspected of having a serious emotional disorder following arrest.[3]

Another possibility is that prison admission is a stressful experience that can strain coping resources to debilitating levels for some inmates, and this effect becomes amplified for inmates with a history of emotional problems. We have already discussed the notion of transition shock with regard to our analysis of disciplinary rates, and the data on psychiatric hospitalization provide additional evidence for this type of process.[4] We find the confluence of findings to be significant. The early months of incarceration appear to be a critical transition period during which problems of adjustment are greatest and maladaptive behaviors come to the fore. Although inmates can manifest their coping difficulties in a variety of ways, certain personal characteristics seem to increase the likelihood that certain maladaptive behavior will manifest itself. Young inmates are more likely to "act out" or rebel against institutional rules, whereas inmates with a history of emotional problems are more likely to decompensate to a point at which hospitalization becomes necessary. In this regard, our data confirm that there are different risk factors associated with various avenues of maladaptation.

Multiple Hospitalizations

Thus far, our analysis has dealt only with initial hospitalizations. We can expect that some inmates will end their careers as hospital patients after one commitment and that others will recidivate. This leads us to examine the issue of

Table 4.4

*Percentage of Hospitalized Inmates With Multiple
Hospitalizations by Time to First Hospitalization and by
Time Served*

| | | Type of hospital patient | |
Variable	n	Single hospitalization	Multiple hospitalization
Time to first (single) hospitalization			
2 months or less	40	50	50
3 to 8 months	37	57	43
8 to 16 months	30	37	63
17 months or more	40	50	50
Time served on current sentence			
18 months or less	14	64*	36*
19 to 30 months	45	62*	38*
31 to 48 months	35	51*	49*
49 months or more	53	32*	68*

*$p < .05$.

multiple hospitalizations. In our sample, nearly half (49%) of
the hospitalized inmates were committed once, one quarter
(25%) were committed twice, and one quarter (26%) were
committed three or more times.

In Table 4.4, we find the proportion of multiply hospitalized inmates by time to first hospitalization and by length of
incarceration. The data indicate that the timing of the initial
hospitalization does not affect the chances of rehospitalization. Inmates who are first hospitalized very early in their
prison term have the same probability of being rehospitalized
as inmates who are first hospitalized later in their sentence.
In contrast, we notice that length of incarceration is related
to the chances of rehospitalization, in that inmates serving
long prison terms are more likely to be hospitalized more

than once. Specifically, the chances of rehospitalization among long-term inmates are more than double those of short-term inmates.

Juxtaposed against this relationship, we find that the proportion of time inmates spend in hospitals in relation to length of prison term is fairly constant across time-served groups. The proportions are 20% for short-term inmates, 18% for low-average term inmates, 15% for high-average term inmates, and 18% for long-term inmates. This finding indicates that while long-term inmates are hospitalized more often, their relative amount of hospital time is comparable with that of inmates with shorter sentences.

As we already noted, hospitalized inmates in our sample have a 50–50 chance of rehospitalization. However, the probability of recommitment is related to the number of prior commitments. Conditional probabilities for second thru sixth hospitalizations are .51, .51, .58, .64, and .71. By the time an inmate has been hospitalized seven times, the chances are four out of five (.80) that rehospitalization will be necessary. Thus, the probability of recommitment increases as the number of prior commitments increases.

We have identified two factors that play an important role in rehospitalization. The first is the length of time that an inmate is in custody of the system. In general, the longer disturbed inmates are incarcerated, the greater the chances they will require rehospitalization. This relationship may be interpreted simply as a reflection of time at risk, because the length of an inmate's sentence circumscribes the prison's responsibility for providing treatment. A second and competing explanation derives from the assumption that prison environments aggravate psychiatric disorders among highly vulnerable inmates. Thus, our findings can be interpreted as supporting the principle that continued exposure to pathogenic stimuli increases the probability of rehospitalization.

By extending our investigation into the community, we could evaluate competing explanations by asking whether short-term inmates have comparable rates of rehospitalization over a standardized follow-up period. In so doing, however, we would have to allow for differences between prisons and the community in both formal and informal commitment practices. On the basis of the available data, we feel that our findings on multiple hospitalization are best interpreted taking a "time at risk" perspective. The fact that the proportion of time inmates spend hospitalized is the same across time-served groups suggests that need for hospitalization is relatively constant adjusting for sentence length. Furthermore, although long-term inmates do show higher symptom rates over time, the increase is modest.

We have also seen that the chances of rehospitalization increase as an inmate builds up a track record of psychiatric commitments and that beyond a certain point the probability of recommitment begins to approach certainty. This finding indicates that a small number of inmates have emotional problems that are both serious and chronic, raising the question of whether periodic hospitalization supplemented by outpatient services is the most appropriate treatment model for this group. Repeated "shuttling" of patients between prison and hospital can aggravate an inmate's condition and can unduly strain working relationships between custody and treatment staff.

Our findings on rehospitalization hold several implications for mental health service delivery. The most obvious implication is that treatment planning should allow for length of incarceration. An inmate's availability for services, which is fundamentally related to the likelihood of achieving treatment goals, is circumscribed by legal decisions made at sentencing. By definition, inmates with short prison terms cannot be long-term clients of a prison mental health system. In the case of such inmates, service delivery must be geared toward reaching shorter term objectives, and treatment plans need to be organized around the coordination of services between prisons and community agencies. In contrast, inmates with extended prison terms have the opportunity to become longer term clients of a prison mental health system. Clinicians therefore have the opportunity to work toward more enduring or difficult-to-achieve treatment goals, and they are also in a better position to take advantage of prison resources by coordinating therapeutic and correctional programs.

Notes

1. Our findings that hospitalized inmates are older and that outpatients are younger and disproportionately White are consistent with the findings of a national study on inmate mental health services. Swanson et al., chapter 2, note 18.

2. A possible explanation for the increasing symptom rates of long-term inmates is changes in recordkeeping. In chapter 2 we noted that in 1975, the Office of Mental Health assumed responsibility for treatment services leading to improvements in clinical records. This transition occurred 7 to 8 years prior to the time period that defines our release cohort, and some inmate patients in our sample had served prison terms that span this period. For inmates serving 10 years in prison, the first five to seven career segments would fall under the old system. Although we did find and code mental health-related information prior to 1975 in both correctional and mental health files, our impression is that the frequency of observation notes, particularly in hospital settings, is greater under the new system.

3. One large-scale study of defendants found incompetent to stand trial reports that 41% of these defendants were eventually sentenced to incarceration. See Steadman, H. (1979). *Beating a rap?* Chicago: University of Chicago Press.

4. Zamble and Proporino (chapter 1, note 18) reached the same conclusion, based on their studies of prisoner careers in Canadian prisons.

Chapter

5

Disturbed–Disruptive Patterns

U p to this point, we have separately examined patterns of misbehavior and emotional problems, and we have seen two different pictures emerge. Disruptive behavior reveals a consistency that cuts across sentences of varying lengths. Rates of disciplinary infractions peak shortly after admission to prison and then steadily decline. The manifestation of symptoms, in contrast, shows greater variety, but the general pattern, especially among outpatients, is one of declining rates over time. There are also indications that for hospitalized inmates, prison admission and release are junctures that coincide with increased levels of personal difficulty.

We now explore how disturbed and disruptive behaviors relate to each other, and we focus on the concurrence and sequencing of these two types of behavior. After investigating these issues, we examine how prisons attempt to manage multifaceted behavior problems.

A number of prior studies report that mentally ill inmates have higher-than-average disciplinary rates.[1] Our data indicate that hospital patients have a mean annual rate of 5.1 infractions, whereas outpatients have a rate of 5.9 infractions, and no-service inmates have a rate of 3.7 infractions. The rate for hospital patients is adjusted for time spent outside of prison, and the outpatient group represents only those inmates who we could verify had received services. These differences in disciplinary rates are consistent with other research, and they suggest that within prison settings emotional disorder and disruptive behavior are interconnected. We also found that outpatients have higher infraction rates than hospital patients. We have more to say about this finding at a later point.[2]

Disciplinary records list incidents that are officially handled as violations of prison rules. Mental health files likewise record staff observations that are relevant to the diagnosis and treatment of emotional disorders. Types of records overlap with types of behavior, and the correspondence is not perfect. Disruptive acts can be described as aspects of mental health problems, whereas displays of symptoms can be noted in narratives of disciplinary incidents.

We found that 130 disciplinary incidents included descriptions of emotional problems. Of these incidents, 112 involved reports of self-injury. Descriptions of disruptive acts in mental health files present a different situation. Among hospitalized inmates, we find that 3.5% of symptomatic observations include assaultive behavior, 4.6% describe a serious disturbance (such as yelling, screaming, and shouting), 2.8% list refusing an order (e.g., will not come out of cell), 11.2% report refusing medication, and 7.4% characterize the patient as hostile, angry, or belligerent. Overall, 27.2% of prison mental health incidents (16% if we exclude refusing medication) involve disruptive behavior. Outpatients' records reveal similar findings, with 1.5% of prison mental health observations involving assaultive behavior, 1.5% describing a serious disturbance, 9.9% including refusing orders, 5.7% noting medication refusal, and 5.7% describing the patient as angry, hostile, or belligerent. Among symptom descriptions for outpatients, 25.9% (20.2% if we exclude refusing medication) report disruptive behavior.[3]

These data indicate that, whereas clear-cut descriptions of disturbed behavior rarely find their way into official disciplinary records, disruptive behavior is often recorded in mental health files. For both hospital patients and outpatients, about one quarter of clinical observations include descriptions of disruptive behavior. These findings show that disruptiveness is often part of the presenting symptomatic picture considered by prison clinicians, and the frequency of such notations in treatment files confirms that mental health staff view some disruptive behaviors as clinically relevant.

To a large extent, the one-sided overlap we observe between reports of disruptive and disturbed behaviors can be attributed to differences in the ways disciplinary and mental health files are kept. Most descriptions of disciplinary incidents are terse, usually listing the rules that are violated or giving a shorthand description of the person's behavior (such as out of place, refused an order). Although we coded as much detail as the records offered, the mental health files contained more extensive narrative accounts and provided more detailed descriptions of incidents. For these reasons, our data do not permit conclusions as to the extent to which disciplinary committees are made aware of behaviors that suggest an inmate is emotionally disordered, though at a later point we examine evidence that indicates that disciplinary committees are sensitive to the possible presence of mental illness among disruptive inmates.

The act of designating specific acts as symptoms of illness, as sanctionable violations of prison rules, or as both depends in part on judgments about an inmate's mental health status and about the relation of this status to the person's behavior in a given situation. In general, we might expect that the chances of disruptive behavior being referred for disciplinary action diminish in the presence of flagrant emotional problems. This would appear to be especially true for situations that combine minor infractions with evidence of serious pathology. Figure 5.1 examines this issue by comparing the pre- and posthospitalization experiences of inmates in terms of the proportion of inmates written up for disciplinary incidents and the proportion who exhibited disruptive symptoms of mental illness. The disruptive symptoms we refer to represent behaviors that are listed as prison rules violations and therefore present an opportunity for disciplinary action. The data clearly indicate that as hospitalization approaches, the reports of disciplinary violations decrease whereas re-

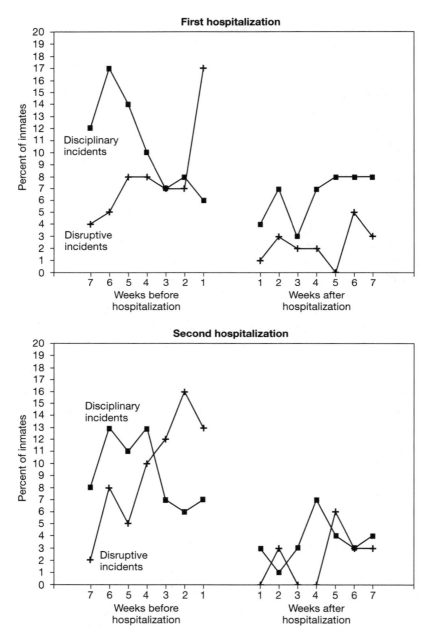

Figure 5.1. Percentage of inmates with disciplinary incidents and disruptive symptoms before and after hospitalization.

ports of disruptive symptoms increase. We also find that rates of both disciplinary incidents and disruptive symptoms are lower after hospitalization.

These findings suggest that a redefinition of disruptive behavior occurs in the presence of serious psychopathology. Behavior that otherwise might be regarded as a violation of prison rules becomes viewed as part of the overall symptomatic picture, and punitive responses come to be seen as less appropriate in light of impending hospitalization. One of the factors that helps to account for this change in perspective is that inmates who were suspected of being seriously mentally ill at the time of our study were usually placed in specialized therapeutic settings. By sequestering emotionally disordered inmates, the impact of disruptive behavior on institutional order is minimized. Thus, therapeutic interventions that become appropriate given displays of symptomatic behavior can help to reduce the pressure on custodial staff to react to the person's disruptive behavior. Placement in therapeutic settings also represents a professional judgment that an inmate may be mentally ill, thereby reinforcing the notion that a variety of unusual behaviors should be interpreted as manifestations of mental illness.

Disciplinary Careers of Inmate Patients

Do patterns of disciplinary involvement differ for inmates with emotional difficulties? Table 5.1 displays the distribution of disciplinary career types by mental health status. We find that nondisruptive careers are less frequent among mentally ill inmates. Overall, 67.6% of hospitalized inmates, 60.1% of outpatients, and 77.1% of no-service inmates show periods with no substantial disciplinary involvement. Looking at the distribution of other career types, we observe that hospitalized inmates are more likely to demonstrate late bloomer (low, low, high) and mid-bloomer (low, high, low) patterns, and they are less likely to show early starter (high, low, low), late reformer (high, high, low), and chronic patterns (high, high, high). In contrast, outpatients are overrepresented in

Table 5.1

Percentage Distribution of Disciplinary Career Patterns by Prison Mental Health Experience

Disciplinary career pattern	Prison mental health experience		
	No service (n = 7,634)	Outpatient (n = 435)	Hospitalized (n = 141)
Nondisruptive (low, low, low)	77.8	63.0	68.1
Early starter (high, low, low)	6.3	13.6	7.1
Inverted-U (low, high, low)	4.2	6.7	7.8
Late bloomer (low, low, high)	2.4	3.4	5.0
Late reformer (high, high, low)	3.0	4.4	2.8
U-shape (high, low, high)	2.3	2.1	2.8
Mid-bloomer (low, high, high)	1.4	1.6	2.8
Chronic (high, high, high)	2.5	5.3	3.5

late reformer (high, high, low) and chronic patterns (high, high, high) and underrepresented in the early starter (high, low, low) pattern.

In general, hospitalized inmates are less likely to show disruptiveness patterns that encompass early portions of the sentence, whereas outpatients are more likely to demonstrate patterns that span more than one career stage (i.e., semi-chronic and chronic patterns). Given that hospitalization tends to occur early in the prison term and that inmates are not at risk for disciplinary write-ups while hospitalized, disciplinary patterns for hospitalized inmates appear to be influenced by the timing of commitments. Hospitalization thus intersects disciplinary careers in ways such that prevalent patterns of disruptiveness (i.e., early starter) occur less often. In addition, the disciplinary careers of hospital patients suggest that a transition occurs from serious psychopathology to high levels of antisocial behavior. At a later point, we investigate the issue of behavior transitions more directly.

Career patterns for outpatients allow us to be more specific with regard to our finding that these inmates exhibit high infraction rates. Higher infraction rates do not result from brief periods of unusually intense disciplinary involvement but rather can be attributed to fairly chronic disruptiveness. Thus, outpatients generally accumulate substantial disciplinary records by persisting in rule violations over long periods of time.

Combined Disturbed and Disruptive Patterns

We now turn to examine questions regarding the concurrence of symptom-related and disruptive behaviors. One of the simplest analyses is a straightforward investigation of the correlation between rates of disciplinary incidents and symptomatology. In light of the findings reported in earlier chapters, however, we can find several problems with this approach. We have already noted that patients are not at risk for disciplinary actions while they are hospitalized. This means that there can be no relationship between symptom rates and infraction rates during hospital stays. We have just seen how these gaps influence disciplinary patterns, so characterizing disturbed–disruptive patterns over entire prison careers is difficult for hospital patients. Among outpatients, we have also seen that rates of symptomatic behavior are low and that individual manifestations of pathology tend to be relatively brief. In contrast, outpatient disciplinary rates are relatively high, and these individuals exhibit fairly chronic disruptiveness. On the basis of these findings, we can anticipate that periods of overlap between disturbed and disruptive behavior for outpatients will be relatively infrequent and brief.

Our analysis of disturbed–disruptive patterns builds on the concept of *episode*, which can be defined as a series of incidents that are proximate in time. The episode as a framework for analysis offers several advantages in that we can use the number and types of behaviors to describe and classify episodes. We can also examine transitions from one type of episode to the next as well as locate episodes within career segments.

A key decision to be made in the definition of an episode is the maximum time between successive incidents that qualifies the incidents as part of the same episode. Although selection of this criterion is in a sense arbitrary, the time frame should be such that we can view the behaviors as related manifestations of an inmate's coping difficulties. Our time requirement for defining incidents as part of the same episode is 10 days. Thus, two behaviors that occur within 10 days of each other represent the start of an episode, whereas a hiatus of 11 or more days between successive incidents signals the end of an episode. Given this criterion, we find that an average episode for hospitalized inmates lasts 13.4 days and contains 6.7 incidents, whereas outpatient episodes last 8.0 days and include 3.0 incidents. We also find that hospital patients average 7.3 episodes over the course of their prison term, whereas outpatients average 4.5 episodes.

We characterize episodes as disturbed, disruptive, or disturbed–disruptive on the basis of the presence of symptomatic and disciplinary behavior. For hospitalized inmates, 44% of episodes are classified as disturbed, 23% as disruptive, and 33% as disturbed–disruptive. If we describe episodes in terms of seriousness of behavior, we find that 47% are nonviolent–nonpsychotic, 35% are psychotic–nonviolent, 13% are nonpsychotic–violent, and 4% are psychotic–violent. The distribution of episode classifications for outpatients is 13% disturbed, 65% disruptive, and 22% disturbed–disruptive. Alternatively, outpatient episodes can be described as 68% nonpsychotic–nonviolent, 5% psychotic–nonviolent, 26% nonpsychotic–violent, and 1% psychotic–violent.

Looking more closely at the various types of episodes, we find that, on average, disturbed–disruptive episodes for hospitalized inmates last longest (18.5 days) and have the largest number of incidents (9.2). In contrast, disruptive episodes are shortest (6.8 days) and have the fewest number of incidents (2.6). Disturbed episodes fall in between, with an average length of 13.0 days and 8.4 incidents.

It is not surprising that disturbed episodes are the most common type of episode for hospitalized inmates, given the nature of this group. Yet, it is significant that compound disturbed–disruptive episodes (33%) are more common than pure disruptive episodes (23%).[4] This finding indicates that more often than not periods of high disciplinary involvement overlap with symptomatic behavior for seriously disturbed inmates. We also note that the most serious type of incident, violent–psychotic episodes, is very infrequent (4%), substantially less so in fact than the prevalence of nonpsychotic–violent episodes (13%). Our analysis identified 50 such episodes over the combined prison terms of 145 seriously disturbed inmates. The rarity of violent psychotic episodes is significant because this combination of behavior is central to stereotypic views of the "criminally insane."[5]

In contrast, we find that among outpatients disruptive episodes (65%) are most common, followed by disturbed–disruptive episodes (22%). Consistent with these findings, we note that outpatients are more prone to violent episodes than hospital patients (27% vs. 16%). Finally, we see that pure disturbed episodes among outpatients are relatively rare (13%). These data indicate that disruptiveness is the central feature of maladaptive patterns among outpatients. Although sometimes disruptiveness is linked with symptomatology, unadulterated manifestations of emotional disorder are unlikely to occur.

Table 5.2 examines transitions between types of episodes for hospitalized inmates. The data depict the distribution of classifications from prior to subsequent episodes. In looking at the table, we notice a strong consistency between successive episodes, as indicated by the high percentages along the diagonal. This means that our best prediction of the next type of episode is that it will be the same as the preceding one. Beyond this general observation, we find that disturbed episodes are likely both to precede and to follow hospitalization. Disturbed–disruptive episodes show an equal chance of being followed by a hospitalization or by a disturbed episode, whereas disruptive episodes are more likely to be followed by disturbed–disruptive episodes than by disturbed

Table 5.2

Percentage Distribution of Transitions Between Preceding and Subsequent Episodes for Hospital Patients

Preceding episode	Subsequent episode			
	Disturbed	Disruptive	Disturbed–disruptive	Hospital
Disturbed	42.7	2.5	18.8	36.0
	(n = 206)	(n = 12)	(n = 91)	(n = 483)
Disruptive	12.5	58.5	21.8	7.3
	(n = 31)	(n = 145)	(n = 54)	(n = 248)
Disturbed–disruptive	27.6	8.0	40.5	23.9
	(n = 103)	(n = 30)	(n = 151)	(n = 89)
Hospital	50.2	16.1	25.5	8.2
	(n = 134)	(n = 43)	(n = 68)	(n = 22)

episodes. We also find that 4 out of 10 hospitalizations (41.6%) are followed by episodes that involve disruptive behavior. Finally, we note that transitions from purely disturbed to purely disruptive episodes and vice versa are infrequent.

Data on transitions between episodes for outpatients are presented in Table 5.3. Again we find that transitions between episodes of the same type are common. However, unlike the pattern for hospitalized inmates, we find that transitions to purely disruptive episodes are more likely across the board. We also find that transitions to disturbed–disruptive episodes are less likely. These results are consistent with the statistical picture of lower symptom rates and higher infraction rates of outpatients.

We now consider the characteristics that differentiate between types of episodes, including inmate attributes and characteristics of preceding episodes. Table 5.4 contains the results of logistic regression analyses comparing one type of episode with all others for hospitalized inmates. Because we are interested in the influence of prior episodes, the first epi-

Table 5.3

Percentage Distribution of Transitions Between Preceding and Subsequent Episodes for Outpatients

Preceding episode	Subsequent episode		
	Disturbed	Disruptive	Disturbed–disruptive
Disturbed	45.9	23.2	30.9
	($n = 83$)	($n = 42$)	($n = 56$)
Disruptive	3.8	81.0	15.2
	($n = 42$)	($n = 893$)	($n = 167$)
Disturbed–disruptive	17.9	42.8	39.3
	($n = 62$)	($n = 148$)	($n = 136$)

sode in a series is not included as part of the dependent variable.

The results indicate that disturbed episodes are unlikely to be preceded by disruptive episodes or by disturbed–disruptive episodes. We also find that disturbed episodes occur later in the prison term and are more likely to involve inmates convicted of sodomy. In comparison, disruptive episodes occur earlier in the prison term and tend to be preceded by a disruptive episode shorter than the current episode. Disturbed–disruptive episodes are also likely to follow in sequence and tend to involve inmates who admit that they are drug users. It comes as no surprise that the number of symptoms in an episode that precedes hospitalization, especially psychotic symptoms, is positively related to hospitalization, whereas the number of disciplinary infractions is negatively related to hospital commitment. In addition, prior prison experience shows a positive relationship to hospitalization.

In general, the results of the multivariate analyses confirm what we observed in the transition matrix. There is continuity in maladaptation in that as inmates move from one

Table 5.4

Results of Logistic Regression Analyses Comparing One Type of Episode With All Others

| Variable | Type of episode | | | |
	Disturbed	Disruptive	Disturbed–disruptive	Hospital
Social history				
Drug use			1.88	
Criminal history				
Prior prison experience				1.05
Current prison experience				
Time-served (months)	−0.003			
Time-served (proportion)	1.14			
Sodomy conviction	0.71			
Prior episode				
Disruptive type	−2.41	2.15		
Disturbed–disruptive type	−0.78			
Duration		−0.08	−0.01	−0.06
No. of disciplinary infractions				−0.30
No. of symptoms				0.12
No. of psychotic symptoms				0.14
Current episode				
Timing				
#1 to #10		1.60		
#11 to #20		0.77		
Duration		−0.80		
Constant	−0.42	−2.35	−0.73	−4.62
Goodness-of-fit χ^2	1,078*	728	1,133	369
df	822	873	874	946
Hosmer statistic	3	10	5	26
df	8	8	8	8

Note. $*p < .05$.

episode to the next, they tend to repeat similar types of behavior. An interesting aspect of this continuity is what we do
not find to be significant. With the exception of hospitalization, the number and types of behavior in the preceding episode are unrelated to the type of subsequent episode. This
lack of findings suggest that a general pattern of escalation
or deescalation of behavior is not characteristic of episode
transitions.

With regard to admixtures of behavior, we find that simple
transitions from disturbed to disruptive or vice versa are rare.
Instead we find a tendency to move to or persist in "combination" episodes. The timing of episodes reveals that disruptive episodes occur early in the prison term and disturbed
episodes occur late.

In general, the findings suggest that disturbed–disruptive
inmates present a complex behavioral picture that remains
fairly constant over time. When changes are observed, the
short-term trend (between episodes) is that of moving from
simple to complex patterns, whereas the long-term trend
(across prison terms) is that of moving from disruptive to
disturbed behavior. In other words, inmates rarely oscillate
between disturbed and disruptive behavior. Rather, they tend
to specialize in one behavior or the other, or they repeatedly
manifest both types of behavior at about the same time.

These findings point to some encouraging and some difficult aspects of dealing with inmates who have serious adjustment problems. General types of maladaptation tend to
be consistent over time, suggesting that individual patterns
can be identified and that appropriate interventions can be
generated. Yet, we see that maladaptation cannot always be
described neatly because inmates often display compound
adjustment problems. Furthermore, when unidimensional
problems change direction, they tend to take on new features,
retaining the old. Thus, many seriously maladjusted inmates
present a complex behavioral picture, and changes in maladaptive patterns tend to acquire more complexity. The challenge then is to develop interventions that accommodate this
behavioral complexity and to interrupt cycles of develop-

ment early when problems are neater and possibly easier to address.

Our findings for hospital inmates underscore the limitations of viewing custodial and mental health problems as separate and discrete. Temporal coincidence does not necessarily imply causation in the sense that disciplinary problems are always the result of emotional disorders. It does suggest, however, that at some level, different manifestations of coping problems are interrelated. An integrated framework that posits relationships between emotional and interpersonal deficits would appear to be more useful than a paradigm that insists on artificially drawn boundaries. Human service professionals may gravitate toward neat definitions of their clientele, but our data suggest that problems of maladaptation are often complex, in that they include more than one problem area.

Administrative Responses

Disciplinary infractions for hospitalized inmates are roughly equally distributed across disruptive episodes, disturbed–disruptive episodes, and nonepisodic situations (31%, 31%, and 38%, respectively). For these inmates, infractions that are part of a disruptive episode are treated more seriously than are other infractions. About 15% of infractions in disruptive episodes result in an administrative procedure that often leads to the imposition of severe penalties, compared with about 10% of other infractions. In contrast, we find that about 15% of infractions in disturbed–disruptive episodes result in a mental health referral by the disciplinary committee compared with about 5% of other infractions. Thus, infractions that are part of a series of misbehaviors tend to be handled more seriously than other infractions, whereas infractions that coincide with symptom-related behavior are more likely to be viewed as possible manifestations of emotional disorder.[6]

Rates of disciplinary behaviors can be affected by therapeutic interventions. For hospitalized inmates, the mean annual rate prior to commitment is 8.3 infractions.[7] In the posthospitalization phase, the rate drops to 3.5 infractions. However, transfers to other therapeutic settings do not show similar effects. Prior to admission into special prison programs for such disturbed inmates, the mean annual infraction rate is 4.3 infractions. During program enrollment, the rate rises to 5.5 infractions, and after leaving the program, the rate drops back to 4.2 infractions. The increase in disciplinary violations while inmates are enrolled in these programs is curious and may result from greater surveillance that accompanies participation in these programs.

In reviewing correctional folders, we found that disruptiveness is often cited as a reason for institutional transfers, and many times a notation was added indicating that the inmate required a more secure custodial setting. For chronically disruptive inmates, who spend most of their prison careers in maximum-security facilities, justification for transfer occasionally invoked the argument, "We've had him long enough. Now it's some one else's turn." What we found to be most interesting were rationales postulating that inmate behavior may improve as a result of transfer.[8] A simple version of this rationale is based on the premise that changes in prison environment are disequilibrating and can interrupt the momentum of disruptive behavior. A more sophisticated version highlights situations in which interpersonal relationships have degenerated to a point at which improvement is effectively foreclosed. The opportunity for a "fresh start" at another institution is presumed to permit an inmate to extricate himself from what has become an entrenched cycle of disruptiveness. A still more sophisticated version of this strategy attempts to match inmates to environments in such a way as to turn the tide of disruptive tendencies. For example, inmate behavior may presumptively improve from relocation to a prison that has a different population mix. Transfers to prisons with specialized programming that can address an inmate's personal deficiencies or that might capture and sustain his interest are another version of this strategy.

Use of transfers as a means of curbing disruptive behavior implies a positive relationship between disciplinary and transfer rates. We therefore examined these correlations and found different patterns across time-served categories. For short-term inmates, disciplinary and transfer rates show negative correlations (in the order of $-.07$) toward the end (last three career segments) of prison careers. For inmates with low-average prison terms, we find few statistically significant correlations. High-average-term inmates show positive correlations (between .04 and .09) toward the end of their prison term, and long-term inmates shows relatively strong negative correlations (between $-.08$ and $-.17$) during the first half, and equally strong positive correlations (between .11 and .20) during the second half of their sentence.

These findings do not provide a straightforward confirmation of the hypothesis that inmates are transferred in response to behavior problems. The data point in opposite directions across prison terms of inmates with different sentence lengths. It is difficult to make sense of contradictory findings, and with this caveat in mind our interpretation of the data is as follows. For short-term inmates, there appears to be a preference for dealing with problems at the institution where problems become manifest. This preference may develop in response to the fact that short-term inmates enter and leave the prison system quickly, so there is less opportunity to solicit transfers. Long-term inmates present more opportunities for transfers. Yet, we find relationships in opposite directions between the beginning and end of long prison terms. This finding suggests an initial preference to deal with problems where they occur even for long-term inmates. It is only later in the sentence, perhaps after local attempts to deal with problems have failed, that the strategy of interrupting disruptive behavior through institutional transfers becomes deployed.

An example of a transfer predicated on the assumption that a change in population mix can reduce disruptive behavior is that of moving an inmate from a youth facility to an adult institution. The rationale is that older inmates are less inclined to act in ways that reinforce immature behavior and can serve as positive role models for young inmates. We find that such transfers are rare, but they do appear to have the effect of reducing misbehavior. Inmates transferred from youth facilities to mainline correctional settings show an average annual rate of 11.6 infractions before transfer compared with a rate of 7.9 infractions after transfer. In comparison, the mean infraction rates before and after transfers between maximum-security institutions are almost identical (5.5 pre; 5.4 post). It is of course possible that changes in disciplinary rates are the result of different disciplining thresholds between staff of different institutions.[9] Although we are not in a position to test this alternative explanation, the data do not require us to reject the hypothesis that actual changes in inmate behavior take place.

Disciplinary committees face a difficult situation when dealing with emotionally disordered inmates. Legalistic concerns dictate standardized case processing with equivalent punishments assigned to similar infractions. Yet, mentally ill inmates are often involved in nonroutine violations, and if disciplinary committees are to fulfill their "correctional" function, a more flexible, individualized posture seems warranted.

Our data indicate that disciplinary dispositions for seriously emotionally disturbed inmates often involve requests for mental health services, which shows that officers who assign penalties are concerned about their effects. Among hospitalized inmates, 1 in 10 disciplinary incidents result in referrals to clinicians as compared with a rate of about 1 in 50 incidents for other inmates. We also find that when a request for therapeutic services is made, disciplinary committees are less inclined to see a need for punitive action. Among incidents involving mental health referrals, 43% were given nonpunitive dispositions (such as counseling or suspended sentence) compared with 27% of other infractions. This tendency, to be sure, is affected by an inmate's status as patient, as evidenced by the finding that among hospitalized inmates 55% of incidents involving mental health referrals were unaccompanied by punitive sanctions.

When we compare disciplinary outcomes between inmate mental health clients and other inmates, we find the overall distributions to be nearly identical. If we disaggregate outcomes by type of incident, some differences emerge for violent infractions. Table 5.5 shows that violent infractions by hospitalized inmates are more likely to result in nonpunitive dispositions (such as counseling), and the proportion of such dispositions is almost twice as great for the hospitalized group as it is for the no-service group (16% vs. 9%). At the same time, however, we find that violent infractions by hospitalized inmates disproportionately invite the most serious penalties (28% vs. 19%) such as loss of good time or placement in special housing units. Before discussing the implications of these findings, we turn to examine disciplinary responses to other mental health-related behavior.

Some infractions can be described as peculiar or eccentric in that they lead us to ask questions about an inmate's mental condition. These infractions stand out not just because they are relatively infrequent but because the standard presumption of a rationally motivated offender seems inappropriate. How do disciplinary committees respond to such situations? To investigate this question, we classified infractions as "pe-

Table 5.5

Percentage Distribution of Disciplinary Dispositions by Type of Infraction and Prison Mental Health Experience

	Prison mental health experience		
Disposition	Hospital	Outpatient	No service
Nonviolent infractions			
Counseled	29.9	26.7	28.2
Loss of privileges	25.3	26.9	28.5
Keeplock	37.5	37.5	35.3
Special housing/loss of good time	4.0	4.0	3.4
Other	3.3	4.9	4.6
Violent infractions			
Counseled	15.7	11.2	8.8
Loss of privileges	9.1	11.5	13.9
Keeplock	46.2	52.9	57.1
Special housing/loss of good time	28.0	23.2	19.4
Other	1.0	1.2	0.8

culiar" if they suggested that the inmate manifested a highly unusual state of mind. Infractions such as self-injury, throwing feces, setting fire to one's cell, and poor personal hygiene were included in this category. Supporting our assumption that these behaviors are suggestive of unusual emotional states, we found that 12% of infractions for hospital patients fell in this category compared with 4% for outpatients and 3% for nonpatients.

We find that, in general, peculiar infractions are dealt with less severely than other infractions. For example, such incidents more commonly result in loss of privileges (33% vs. 27%) than in keeplock (29% vs. 38%). When we examine the dispositions of these infractions by level of seriousness (violent vs. nonviolent), however, we find that assaultive acts combined with behavior suggestive of emotional disorder are dealt with more seriously than other assaults. Among peculiar assaults, 36% thus resulted in loss of good time or placement in special housing compared with 20% of other assaultive infractions.

Some of our findings demonstrate the willingness of disciplinary committees to invoke the assistance of mental health professionals, though the attractiveness of the mental health option varied with the type of inmate and the type of behavior under consideration. Such outreach efforts are important because they represent attempts by disciplinary committees to understand reasons for infractions and to consider underlying causes of disruptiveness. They are also important because they imply that disciplinary committees worry about the impact of what they do, and they implicitly acknowledge a need to have available options that might ameliorate or supplement the usual punitive measures.

Our findings also highlight some of the tensions administrators face when dealing with problem inmates and the need to select between competing models of prison discipline. A *flexible-rules* model, which proposes that disciplinary responses be custom-tailored to individuals, holds out the possibility that underlying causes of antisocial behavior can be considerately or constructively addressed. In contrast, a *legalistic* model, which emphasizes consistency and fairness in procedures and outcomes, is a cornerstone of general deterrence strategies for maintaining institutional order.[10] The conflict is that actions that are beneficial to the person may be viewed as counterproductive from an institutional perspective and vice versa.

Given that over one quarter of all infractions invite nonpunitive or relatively minor dispositions, disciplinary committees cannot be accused of acting as if every violation of prison rules should result in punishment. Additionally, the fact that about half of the incidents in which hospitalized inmates are referred for mental health services are unaccompanied by sanctions indicates that disciplinary committees feel comfortable about suspending or mitigating punishment where they feel that it would serve no purpose. The other side of the coin is that in the remaining half of the incidents disciplinary committees saw a need to combine punishment with treatment.[11] These situations suggest that multiple goals are sometimes pursued by incorporating aspects of a flexible-rules approach into a legalistic model.[12] The differences we reported in how assaultive acts are responded to are relevant to this issue. Not every violent act is viewed as a serious threat to institutional order. However, assaultive acts coupled with disturbed behavior are punished more harshly than other assaults, indicating that these "mixed" incidents, which are often spontaneous and unpredictable, are viewed as more serious threats to the task of maintaining prison order. For us, this finding illustrates how issues pertaining to behavioral complexity, including assumptions about rationality and the effect of punishment on behavior, can become secondary considerations in situations in which perceived threat to institutional order is great, and the option of sanctioning is the only one available.

Notes

1. Adams, K. (1983). Former mental patients in a prison and parole system: A study of socially disruptive behavior. *Criminal Justice and Behavior, 10,* 358–384; Adams, K. (1986). The disciplinary experiences of

emotionally disordered inmates. *Criminal Justice and Behavior, 13,* 297–316; Toch, H., & Adams, K. (1986). Pathology and disruptiveness among prison inmates. *Journal of Research in Crime and Delinquency, 23,* 7–21.

2. Earlier (Toch and Adams, note 1, supra), we reported that outpatients had lower infraction rates than hospitalized inmates. This finding was based on an analysis that included outpatients for whom we subsequently were unable to locate treatment files.

3. Because mental health observations can include more than one disruptive behavior, the totals we report are less than the sum of individual behavior categories.

4. A study of mentally disordered prison inmates shows that among various indicators of psychiatric impairment, confusion and depression are most closely related to violent behavior. Baskin, D. R., Sommers, I., & Steadman, H. J. (1991). Assessing the impact of psychiatric impairment on prison violence. *Journal of Criminal Justice, 19,* 271–280.

5. The term *criminally insane* variously refers to persons with combined criminal justice and mental health involvement. The major categories are (a) inmates found incompetent to stand trial, (b) inmates adjudicated not guilty by reason of insanity, (c) mentally ill prison inmates, and (d) civil mental patients legally classified as dangerous. Both clinicians (see Thornberry, T., & Jacoby, J. [1979]. *The criminally insane.* Chicago: University of Chicago Press) and the general public (see Steadman, H., & Cocozza, J. [1977]. Selective reporting and the public's misconception of the criminally insane. *Public Opinion Quarterly, 41,* 523–533) view this group as being highly unpredictable and dangerous.

6. A possible explanation for this finding is that types of disciplinary infractions differ between single and episodic incidents. Another possible explanation is that evaluations of infractions as either serious or symptomatic are contingent on the context of other recent behaviors.

7. Disciplinary rates throughout the analysis of transfer effects are based on the entire period spent at sending and receiving institutions.

8. This perspective contrasts with others that view prison transfers as an unregulated form of punishment (see Broude, J. [1974]. The use of involuntary interprison transfer as sanction. *American Journal of Criminal Law, 3,* 117–164).

9. Another consideration is a statistical "regression effect," which refers to the fact that when people are selected on the basis of extreme scores, subsequent scores will gravitate back toward the mean score. Although we did not specifically choose inmates with high infraction rates for this analysis, the scenario we are investigating assumes that disproportionate disciplinary involvement is one reason behind transfers from youth facilities to maximum-security adult facilities.

10. Glaser is probably the leading proponent of the flexible-rules model (Glaser, D. [1964]. *The effectiveness of a prison and parole system.* Indian-

apolis: Bobbs-Merrill). He wrote, "The flexible-rule and constructive-penalty approach ... is more concerned with giving the deviant inmate new hope than with giving him new fears. ... It follows from any conception of rehabilitation as a change in a man's inner values that discipline rehabilitates inmates most in the long run of their lifetimes, and probably improves their behavior in prison as well, if the rules become internalized as their personal moral opinions. If rules are accepted only as part of the restrictions of the immediate environment to which one must learn to adjust in order to avoid penalties, there is no interest in following them when the environment changes, or whenever the risk of being caught and punished is considered negligible" (p. 181). In contrast, Fogel was among the first to argue for a legalistic model of prison discipline (Fogel, D. [1975]. "... *We are the living proof....*" Cincinnati, OH: Anderson). He wrote, "In the context of prison, justice-as-fairness means having clear rules, insuring their promulgation, and following a procedure for determining and punishing rules infractions rooted in due process safeguards" (p. 228).

11. A study of the disciplinary experiences of inmates receiving psychiatric services bears on this issue. Sometimes, inmates are sanctioned as part of a treatment strategy designed to reinforce a cause–effect relationship between behavior and punishment. Alternatively, staff is often aware of the treatment plans for inmates and may, for example, dismiss a rules violation if preceded by a change in medication. McShane, M. D. (1989). The bus stop revisited: Discipline and psychiatric patients in prison. *Journal of Psychiatry and Law, 17*, 413–433.

12. See Adams (note 1, supra, 1986) for additional evidence on this subject.

II

Individual Patterns

6

A Taxonomy of Maladaptation

To derive a better picture of maladaptation in prisons, we reviewed the careers of 239 men in our cohort in as much detail as possible. We selected as candidates for review four types of inmates: those with dense disciplinary dossiers that contained descriptions of eccentric violations; those on mental health caseloads with high disciplinary infraction rates; those with high infraction rates who had been clients of special programs; and those with low measured intelligence and high disciplinary infraction rates.

We screened the folders of all inmates drawn from these sources and discarded those that contained no detailed behavior descriptions. Because we do not know what factors influence data availability or relate to our selection criteria, we can record no claim of representativeness for our cases. What we claim is that the inmates we reviewed fall within the high range of maladaptive behavior that is of interest to us.

We extracted all behavior descriptions that the folders contained, arranged the data in chronological order, and prepared synopses or summaries of them. In each case we began by listing the inmate's offense and characterizing his official record of misbehavior. We then entered a step-by-step narrative of the inmate's career over time, starting with his first

123

prison sentence and ending with his reconfinement where it occurred. We followed this narrative with a short analytic statement, characterizing the behavior pattern with as much specificity as possible.

After the case histories were prepared, we reviewed a sub-sample of the accounts and drafted a roster of themes (with definitions) to cover the principal features of the behavior patterns. This roster was subsequently reorganized and shortened by consolidating themes.

Nature of the Pattern-Analytic Scheme

The taxonomic system we shall detail here evolved inductively. This means that we cannot contend that the classification is theory-based. The selection of themes, however, is congruent with firmly held preconceptions, and we can list some of these as constituting underlying assumptions.

1. *We assume that behavior is purposive, although some behaviors are more purposive than other behaviors.* We ask, "What is the person we review trying to achieve?" The question is often difficult to answer, and when we deal with maladaptive behavior, we are more frequently baffled because conventional conceptions of purpose are derived from, and associated with, adaptive behavior. This means that in defining purpose we must sometimes strain to accommodate idiosyncratic ends and improbable means–end relationships. The difficulty is most acute when we try to specify the goals of disturbed individuals, but it also applies to impulse-ridden individuals, whose peremptory approaches to goal achievement distract from goals that are pursued.
2. *We assume that behavior is guided by perspectives and that these perspectives can be consistent across behavior.* We ask, "How does the person define the situation to which he responds?" The task is to reconstruct the definitional scheme, putting aside the issue of how rational or irrational it may be. We assume that the only world one is in a position to respond to is the world that one

perceives, and that external definitions of stimuli are therefore not helpful. However, the difference between *objective* (externally defined) and *subjective* (individually perceived) situations can help us to explain seemingly cryptic conduct. This is particularly the case where distortions or reinterpretations occur repeatedly in different encounters, prompting consistently inappropriate reactions.

3. *We believe that nuances matter.* We ask, "What, precisely, does the person resonate to when he responds as he does?" We hold that if we want to differentiate maladaptive acts from each other, we must discriminate among equivalently dysfunctional behavior in terms of the differential quality of the perceptions that underlie it and of the feelings with which the behavior is imbued. It matters whether a person feels pushed, crowded, overwhelmed, or degraded and whether he explodes with anger, resentment, panic, or rage. The stimulus for differently motivated behavior may be identical (e.g., the person may be admonished), and the response may be indiscriminable (e.g., the person may lash out), but to advance understanding we center on subtle differences in the process that intervenes between stimulus and response.

4. *We believe that effective coping is problem solving and that maladaptiveness is not.* We ask, "How does the person approach problems so as to end up creating new problems for himself and other people?" There are two parts to this question. The first has to do with failures to achieve one's goals and with ways in which these come about. The issue is that of efficacy and competence, or lack thereof. The second concern is interpersonal and has to do with strategies and approaches to other people that end up creating resentment, disharmony, conflict, and suffering. The concern covers instance in which problems are "solved" at the expense of others, even when this is done "competently."

5. *We suspect that any failure to be instructed is in itself instructive.* We ask, "To what extent is the person unable to profit from experience?" The answer to this question helps us to see a link between coping failures. Most people occasionally fail but they learn from their mis-

takes and do not make comparable mistakes over and over. Where a person perseveres in demonstrating conduct that has untoward consequences, we define the person's maladaptation as patterned, even when his difficulties are at first glance disparate.

6. *We feel that a person's capacity for change must be acknowledged.* We ask, "Where, when, and how does the person improve his pattern of behavior?" Behavior patterns extend over time but rarely over lifetimes. The point of tracking careers is to define behavior in terms of its onset and decay, as well as in terms of increases and decreases in its level and quality.

Where changes in behavior are noted, we can try to assign the inception of change to the person or the setting or both. One question is whether we are witnessing a fundamental reorientation or the results of an intensification or diminution of pressures or temptations. Changes also sometimes provide clues about why the person originally behaved as he did, why he behaves differently now, and what it would take to regenerate him further.

7. *We regard settings as limiting behavior options but not as constraining them.* We ask, "To what extent is the person's behavior seemingly forced on him by circumstance?" Many people engage in less-than-effective behavior but describe themselves as unable to act otherwise. To the point to which they are correct they have postulated an alibi: A person cannot be adjudged to be a poor problem solver because he fails to solve an insolvable problem or because he fails to explore unavailable (or only remotely available) options. To assess adaptation, we must consider the constraints within which the person operates and gauge the quality of his solutions in terms of the adequacy of resources that are available to him. By the same token, we must recognize that perceiving behavior as constrained (e.g., assuming that a person must fight or flee) is a self-exonerating assumption subject to confirmation.

One corrective to buying into this premise where it is unjustified is to compare the person's behavior with that of others faced with comparable circumstances who have achieved different outcomes. Another strategy is to review the chronology of events, which can show that a person has helped to create the situation to which he feels "constrained" to respond. Many offenders thus cite addiction as a cause of crime, ignoring antecedent behavior (drug taking) in which they exercised more unconstrained options.

8. *We see setting attributes as unique, although they may comprise variations on common themes.* We ask, "To what extent does the person react to a setting as he would to other settings?" Adaptation can be at times setting-specific, and adapting to one setting (such as country life) can spoil a person for another setting (city life). One way to deal with this problem is to refrain from generalizing. We view the displaced farmer in the city and adjudge him to be a poor coper, admitting that he might be a better coper back home. This strategy is most appropriate when we are concerned with problems of adaptation to specific settings (in this case, the asphalt jungle) but it teaches us less than we want to know about the process of adaptation. A contrasting strategy is to center on a person moving across as many settings as possible. Using this approach, we may conclude that our farmer is resilient (effective in coping with changes of setting) although he remains a small-town person at heart.

Adaptation is always *to* something. To appreciate what coping with a setting means, we need to know detailed facts about the setting (whether the setting is a school, hospital, factory, foreign country, or prison tier) because these facts define the tasks with which the setting's inhabitants must deal and the difficulties they must negotiate.

It is true, of course, that *any* setting—no matter how exotic it may be—has attributes in common with other settings, but *no* setting contains shared attributes without skewing them in some fashion. In other words, there is no such thing as a *typical* setting, nor one that is completely *unique*.

We recognize that caution must be exercised in characterizing anyone's coping capacity on the basis of his behavior in one environment, such as a place of confinement, but we can generalize about coping if we consider attributes of the setting and think in terms of settings with comparable attributes. If a prison inmate takes unkindly to guards, we may expect that he will do equally badly in organizations in which he encounters guard equivalents (teachers or forepersons) who evoke the same resentments that prison guards evoke. By the same token, prisons do not gauge the person's capacity to negotiate some challenges (such as how to deal with people of the opposite sex) that are not among the attributes of the setting.

Goals of Classification

Our taxonomy is not designed as a diagnostic system but as an aid to thinking about maladaptive behavior in the prison and (to some extent) elsewhere. The purpose of the categories is not to fit people into types but to group behavior patterns so as to facilitate discussion of the psychological dispositions and motives they reflect. The scheme, in other words, is a behavior-related shorthand system. In using the system, we do not ask "Is the person a Type 1 or Type 2 person?" but "Does it make most sense to think of the person as engaging in Type 1 or Type 2 behavior?" and "How does it help us to think of the person's behavior in this way?"

Our assumption is that the *process* of using the system matters as much as its *substance*. We see such usage ideally as a group process, and we regard the concern with classification as a stimulus to group thinking and as a means of expediting clinical discourse. Instead of "going back to scratch" in a group's efforts to understand an individual, the taxonomy can help by taking the group part of the way, providing conceptual options and headings that the group can try on for size.

We do not regard the themes that we propose as mutually exclusive but as segments along continua of behavior. In drawing lines between such segments, we venture hypotheses about the dynamics of behavior and about the motives that behavior subserves. Alternative headings represent alternative (but often related) hypotheses, subject to documentation and verification. The point is to find the most plausible summary for a set of behavior incidents, and the plausibility of one summary or another can be a subject to spirited and sometimes enlightening debate.

Outline of the Classification System

We grouped patterns under five headings to describe the dominant goals the behavior patterns appeared intended to subserve. The goals we listed are those of (a) gratifying impulses, (b) seeking refuge, (c) enhancing esteem, (d) pursuing autonomy, and (e) maintaining sanity. These goals are not personality portraits but dispositions we assume are prepotent while the person is engaging in maladaptation.

We describe and illustrate our categories in the chapters that follow. At this point, we offer brief, preliminary characterizations of the five headings and definitions of the themes subsumed under each.

Gratifying Impulses

Under this heading, we describe difficulties that derive from an emphasis on immediate and short-term gratification, with limited regard for longer term consequences or interests of others. The categories we include under this heading are the following.

- □ *Unlicensed conduct:* This defines a person who operates at the level of infancy and who engages in repeated behavior designed to satisfy his needs in direct and primitive fashion. (This category represents the "purest" type under the heading.)
- □ *Predatory aggression:* The person regards others as objects of need satisfaction and uses violence or threats of violence to intimidate, extort, and expropriate or strong-arm those susceptible to intimidation.
- □ *Frustration to aggression:* When such a person is disappointed or obstructed in the pursuit of his goals, he be-

comes disgruntled and engages in explosive aggression, which mostly consists of expressions of blind anger and rage.

□ *Stress to aggression:* When situations close in on the person, he experiences panic and anxiety, and he tends to blow up under pressure with tantrums that express a sense of helplessness.

□ *Russian roulette:* The person takes unreasonable risks in pursuit of short-term goals and excitement and seemingly does not care that he gets into trouble, or at least does not draw lessons from the fact.

□ *Jailing:* In pursuit of his definition of the "good life"— which consists of accumulating illicit amenities—the person centers on sub rosa activities (which include hustling) and participates elsewhere as a sideline.

□ *Games that turn "sour":* The person engages in nonreflective, childlike, self-serving, casual, short-sighted, and irresponsible behavior that invariably generates adverse repercussions. When this occurs, the person indulges in self-pity.

Enhancing Esteem

Under this heading, we describe behavior designed to cement the person's sense of self-esteem, either by trying to build a reputation or by defending against feelings of low self-esteem through compensatory behavior. Most of the patterns described under this heading feature displays of violence or aggression.

□ *Advertising toughness:* The person engages in demonstrations of toughness in an attempt to achieve a reputation as a person to be admired by his peers.

□ *Conforming:* The person is a member of a violence-prone peer group who acts with and on behalf of his group and in defense of its values.

□ *Gladiating:* The person regards violence as a skill and a routine way to resolve disputes, and he engages in combat readily and casually to resolve interpersonal problems.

□ *Preempting unpopularity:* The person expects to be rejected and reacts with provocation and hostility in anticipation of rejection, thus documenting his assumptions.

- □ *Countering aspersions:* The person feels easily disparaged and affronted, and he reacts violently when he feels offended or slighted.
- □ *Standing fast:* The person feels unable to compromise or retreat from rigidly defined positions and equates this stance with defending his sense of worth.

Pursuing Autonomy

Under this heading, we describe behavior that is concerned with one's dependence on or independence from parental figures, such as people in authority. For men who engage in such behavior, the issue of dependence–autonomy is emotionally charged, because it relates to definitions of adulthood that include emancipation and loss of support.

- □ *Dependence:* The person expects and pursues "parental" intervention to help him arrange a congenial environment for himself.
- □ *Conditional dependence:* The person alternates between dependent and rebellious behavior, contingent on whether he feels his needs are met or frustrated.
- □ *Defying authority:* The person takes a systematically rebellious, defiant, and challenging stance toward those in authority.
- □ *Rejecting constraints:* The person feels that no one has a right to infringe his autonomy and to tell him what to do; he reacts angrily to infringements whose rationale he cannot accept. (Monitoring and punishment are irksome to such a person because these experiences are reminiscent of childhood.)

Seeking Refuge

Under this heading, we describe behavior in which the person retreats from a setting because he regards it as threatening. The issue for the person is safety, and his strategy is physical retreat. (This is different from psychological retreat or escape from reality, which we cover under our next heading.)

- *Sanctuary search:* The person has victim attributes or self-assigned victim attributes that place him in situations which inspire retreat into protective settings or the need to be placed in such settings.
- *Catch-22:* The person both seeks and rejects protective settings. He feels a need for sanctuary, but protective arrangements are uncongenial to him because they are circumscribing, or he regards protective settings as nonequivalent to other settings and feels that the choice matters.
- *Sheep's clothing:* The person seeks sanctuary, but with safety achieved, he changes his role from victim to aggressor and becomes assertive, manipulative, pugnacious, or predatory.
- *Bluff called:* The person starts with a stance of defiance and toughness but ends up declaring himself in need of protection.
- *Turned tables:* Exploiting others backfires, and the victimizer becomes a victim who feels he must retreat from perceived threats.
- *Earned rejection:* Clumsy interpersonal manipulations boomerang, and ineffective behavior invites ostracism, which requires the person to seek sanctuary to extricate himself from the consequences of his actions.
- *Stress avoidance:* The person seeks refuge from stress posed by the presence of others, which he cannot tolerate; he may also experience considerable anxiety, short of a break with reality, which causes him to retreat. (This subheading is transitional to the next heading.)

Maintaining Sanity

Under this heading, we describe behavior that is engaged in by disturbed individuals as they try to negotiate their social environments while grappling with the feelings, urges, and delusional assumptions that are products of their pathology. We speak of "maintaining sanity" because such individuals struggle (mostly unsuccessfully) against loss of control and of contact with reality.

- *Escaping reality:* The person withdraws from his surroundings, lives in a private world, and at extremes neglects his self-care and hygiene.
- *Flight–fight:* The person for the most part withdraws but on occasion explodes, attacks other people in his environment, or attempts self-destructive acts.
- *Paranoid aggression:* The person feels persecuted, explodes at people who he imagines wish him ill or want to harm him, and otherwise lives with suspicion and unease.
- *Tinged rebelliousness:* The person on occasion attacks or resists people in authority, but his protest and rebelliousness go hand in hand with feelings that are products of his disorder, such as fear, confusion, and the inability to cope with complexity.
- *Cryptic outbursts:* The person engages in seemingly unmotivated attacks on others or against himself; his motives for these outbursts are private, inaccessible, and related to his mental condition, including hallucinations, delusions, accumulating tension, anxiety, resentment, and self-hate.
- *Oscillating:* The person oscillates between being emotionally disturbed and nondisturbed, sometimes depending on contextual conditions, in other instances reflecting seemingly spontaneous change. Viewed over time, such a person shows marked contrasts between behavior deemed normal and disturbed.

Applying the Classification

The themes we have defined were devised as shorthand language for describing maladaptive behavior patterns in the prison, and our premise was that these themes are best used by groups (not excluding the subject of discussion) as a way of thinking about a person's behavior.

Given this view of the taxonomy and its use, it would make no sense for one typologist (worse, the originator of the taxonomy) to classify the 239 case histories we compiled on the presumption that his was the final judgment. However, if we constituted a small group to discuss the cases, we would lose the opportunity to assess the reliability of the hypotheses advanced as independent assessments. We compromised by having the code developer (Coder 1) independently arrive at preliminary assessments, then using a second coder (Coder 2) to arrive at a final classification.

We began by having Coder 2 independently classify subsamples of 10 to 15 protocols. After each subsample was completed, Coder 2's ratings were compared with those of Coder 1, and discrepancies between ratings were resolved through conference discussion. These discussions provided training in the classification system for Coder 2 and incidentally led to clarification and modification of the classification categories.

This procedure was continued until Coder 2 felt he had reasonable understanding of the categories. The subsamples covered included 103 protocols, leaving 136 protocols that were classified by Coder 2 without consultation with the initial coder. We can look at the reliability of classification of these 136 cases over the major categories, over subcategories within each of the major ones, and over the entire group of 31 subcategories.

For the 136 protocols, Coder 1 and Coder 2 agreed on classification in one of the five major categories in 91 cases, or 67% of the time (agreement expected by chance is 20%). There was variation in the ease with which categories could be clearly identified, ranging from 46% for seeking refuge to 88% for maintaining sanity. The figures are as follows:

Gratifying impulses 59%
Defending esteem 67%
Pursuing autonomy 59%
Seeking refuge 46%
Maintaining sanity 88%

Agreement was also calculated on classification into subcategories for those protocols in which there was agreement on the coding of the major category (disagreement on the latter would preclude agreement on the subcategory classification). For the 91 protocols on which such agreement occurred, Coder 2 agreed with Coder 1 in 48 cases, or 53% of the time (agreement expected by chance ranges from 14% to 20%, depending on the number of subcategories involved). Again, there were differences in the ease of classifying subcategories across the major categories (subcategories of disturbed behavior proved to be particularly obdurate, although the category is reliably distinctive). The proportions of agreement are as follows:

Gratifying impulses 62%
Defending esteem 79%
Pursuing autonomy 62%
Seeking refuge 64%
Maintaining sanity 32%

Finally, agreement was calculated across the entire range of 31 subcategories. For the 136 protocols, Coder 2 agreed with Coder 1 in 48 cases, or 35% of the time (agreement expected by chance is 3%).

We can conclude that the classification system has sufficient reliability for its didactic or analytic use, though it would invite further development as a formal typology. The classifications used in this report are somewhat more reliable than the percentages given above portray in that the conference agreement, identifying the primary theme in the protocol, was used to replace Coder 1 classification when there was a discrepancy between the two coders.

There is evidence that additional training of Coder 2 could have improved agreement. An analysis of the results of conference codings show that these were resolved in favor of Coder 1 in 71% of the cases and in favor of Coder 2 in 22% of the cases.[1] In the remaining cases (7%), the coders agreed to use a new category.

The most exciting result of the consensus codings was the enhancement arising from the discussion of disagreements in classification. By having each coder create a rationale for the (disagreed) code given by the other, each coder expanded his understanding of the pattern revealed in the protocol. It became clear that we were approaching consensus by integrating each other's perceptions into our combined perspective. The result of these shared approximations was a fuller understanding of what was being suggested by the individual inmate's protocol, and this in turn enriched our understanding of the kinds of behaviors manifested—simultaneously or sequentially—by the inmate.

In what follows, we give examples of these shared perspectives. In each case, there were differences in the classification of the protocol. The indented material is taken from the protocol and is intended to support either one or the other of the classifications. The commentary summarizes the understanding that emerged out of the discussion of the disagreement.

Gratifying Impulses: Russian Roulette Versus Defending Esteem—Advertising Toughness

The "Russian roulette" element has to do with going out of one's way to take chances:

> The defendant was raised in a decent religiously oriented environment but rejected this as being "too boring." The man seeks excitement by skirting danger or at least by taking risks at every turn. He admits that he finds it exciting to drive stolen cars. He accumulates stolen razor blades in his locker and carries marijuana cigarettes through detection equipment. He displays loaded guns and throws bars of soap at officers. He finds such games exciting.

But the man was also found to engage in demonstrations of toughness in an attempt to achieve a reputation as a person to be admired by his peers:

> He signs himself into protection after receiving threats. When he leaves protection he attacks another inmate, hitting him in the back with a broom. An officer who in-

vestigates this incident concludes, "I believe the inmate used this incident to avoid a reputation as a 'snitch.'"

It is easy to see a synthesis in which Russian roulette behavior is the dynamic used to advertise toughness to enhance esteem—not only in the eyes of the inmate's peers but also to handle the man's own anxieties concerning his self-image. Toughness can be projected by other than Russian roulette behavior, and Russian roulette behavior can in turn be used to handle impulse control anxieties without the need to impress peers.

There is justification in the protocol for each coder's perception of the inmate's pattern of behavior. Each coder can be considered to have some approximation to "the truth" about the inmate. Sharing of these approximations led to a new synthesis—an enhanced understanding in which the whole became more than the sum of the perceptions of the individual coders.

Pursuing Autonomy: Rejecting Constraints Versus Defending Esteem–Advertising Toughness

Consider the following two excerpts:

> You were given an order to move down a table and fill the last seat at supper meal in the mess hall and you refused to obey this order. At this time more inmates came to the table and they refused to move down. You then said to the other inmates, "You guys don't have to move down just because the officer says so." The officer asked you if you were the spokesman for the group, and you replied, "Yes, they are my home boys."

> * * *

> The man is a professional alcoholic and vagrant. However, both in prison and outside the prison he is a bum with pride, and some of his conflicts with officers reflect efforts to preserve his self-esteem and reputation.

We concluded that this man feels (and needs to feel with alcohol's help) that no one has a right to tell him what to do.

Hence he reacts angrily to infringements on his autonomy, whose rationale he cannot understand or accept.

Such a pattern is at least compounded by the "bum with pride" component. Rejecting constraints becomes a means to advertise toughness and to achieve a reputation as a person to be admired by his peers.

Incidentally, this pattern synthesis is relevant to the finding that the pattern of defying authority—in which the offender takes a systematically rebellious, defiant, and challenging stance toward any person in a position of authority—is seldom simple. The stereotype of an "authority problem" as the outstanding dynamic of chronic offenders does not hold up across the board. All authority problems are not alike, and complicated patterns underlie the stereotype.

Seeking Refuge: Bluff Called Versus Defending Esteem–Preempting Unpopularity

Sometimes the integration of patterns is sequential. In the following case, initial aggressiveness brings about bluff-calling and fearful requests for protection:

> The prison describes the man as "definitely not an asset." His first major incident at this prison begins after he concludes that he had been insulted by a fellow inmate and enters his enemy's housing unit armed with a shovel intent on "self-defense." It requires four officers to subdue the inmate, who complains that "other inmates threatened his life." After he is released from segregation, the man asks for protection, claiming that "he has many troubles with his peers," though a counselor suspects that he is attempting to control his outbursts by segregating himself so as to avoid rejection by the parole board.
>
> The next incident shows that the man's losses of temper in the prison are not confined to inmates. The charge reads: "On the above date and time the officer reports that you had extra rations of sausage on your tray and that he ordered you several times to put them back but

you refused . . . the officer reports that you assaulted him by hitting him in the face with a tray full of food and again assaulted him by hitting him in the face with your fist. [He] reports that you caused a disturbance in the mess hall by your actions of not following direct orders and by assaulting him while you were in line for breakfast." The inmate is not only punished for this incident but is transferred to administrative segregation (involuntary protection) "until such time as you are either released or transferred from this facility." This move is prompted by the fact that the inmate has succeeded in making a number of enemies who have taken to assaulting him whenever the opportunity arises.

The inmate is rescued from permanent segregation status through transfer to a maximum-security prison which has an older population and a notoriously strict regime. In this institution the inmate spends the remainder of his time without a single disciplinary incident.

We decided that this man's difficulties are twofold. First, he has a hair-trigger temper and explodes at the slightest provocation, thereby generating conflicts, punishments, and unequivocal unpopularity. Second, the man's peers regard him as a threat that must be neutralized. As a result, the man becomes afraid and must be protected, which to him is a fate indistinguishable from punishment. The irony is that the man reacts the way he does because he is easily hurt but arranges for himself to be more substantially hurt.

Again, each perceived pattern catches a significant component of what the inmate is doing, but integrating the perceptions of the two coders produces a more complete understanding of the inmate's behavior over time.

Seeking Refuge: Turned Tables Versus Gratifying Impulses–Jailing

Another example of enrichment through shared perceptions is the somewhat sequential merging of a pattern of exploiting others that backfires (gratifying impulses) and a pattern in which the victimizer becomes a victim, whose fear inspires retreat (seeking refuge). The shared perception begins with the inmate's pursuit of his definition of the "good life," which consists of accumulating illicit amenities through sub rosa activities (including hustling), while his participation in more approved activities is only a sideline (gratifying impulses: jailing).

The latter pattern misses the intrigue dynamic of the refuge seeking described below, but the refuge-seeking pattern leaves out, or at least shortchanges, the man's sophisticated engagement in and manipulation of correctional institution dynamics:

> The inmate is, however, not an unfortunate victim of his sexual preference, forced to spend years vegetating in the sterile backwaters of the prisons to which he is assigned. His pattern rather resembles that of a scorpion who darts out from under rocks, stings passing animals and then darts back again. He belongs to a subgroup of inmates who exploit each other for material gains and exploit others weaker than themselves, and who experience strongly felt rivalries which lead to no-holds-barred competition. This subgroup has members in every prison and outside the prison, so that their vendettas can be extended and can be carried over from one setting to another. The vendettas lead to aggressive acts which include physical altercations, threats, manipulation of others in rival cliques, and the manipulation of prison staff to serve the interests of one clique at the disservice of another. In this connection a favored strategy involves informing on any illegal activities of opponents, and manufacturing details of illegal acts where necessary to supplement the facts.
>
> In this game, prison staff are not in charge, but rather are pawns of inmate machinations, and are particularly susceptible to peremptory bids that capitalize on staff's responsibility to ensure that no inmates are harmed, to react to violation of rules, and to observe inmates' civil rights. This man presses all three of these buttons with recurrent claims that he is about to be knifed or burned alive, with submissions in which he identifies inmates engage in illegal acts, and with grievances and law suits.

In this case staff know what the inmate is about but are still obliged to move the inmate and/or his enemies around the chess board of the prison system until they literally run out of squares. In the meantime, the man's list of enemies cumulates, and the proportion of time he spends locked away in protection becomes increasingly substantial.

Pursuing Autonomy: Rejecting Constraints Versus Defending Esteem–Countering Aspersion

Another integration comes from the interaction of countering aspersion efforts with a volatile rejection of constraints:

> The man's unpredictability results from the fact that one does not know when he feels mortally affronted because one no more understands him than he understands those around him. The central issue often appears to be that the man feels himself treated like a child, and that his version of machismo holds that no man must be ordered about by another man and that it is demeaning and insulting to be told to do things, particularly when you explained why you do not wish to do them, or would have explained it if you could have.
>
> The issue of uniforms does not enter the equation because the man sees encounters between himself and officers as personal, and perceives custodial instructions as originating in whims and expressions of disdain or disrespect. When the man feels disdained or disrespected in this way he reacts at the first available opportunity, which may not coincide with the move that sparks the offense to which he reacts.
>
> In the first incident, for example, the officer does not know that the inmate is puzzled and enraged when an officer takes a plastic spoon the inmate thinks he will need for his meal. The officer also does not heed the inmate's expression of resentment, which consists of spitting on the floor, and an attack follows when the officer lectures the inmate about prison sanitation rules, which the inmate (who does not understand most of

this lecture) perceives as adding insult to injury. In the second incident an officer is similarly oblivious to the fact that the inmate is enraged because he has ordered one brand of cigarettes and has been mistakenly given another, an act the inmate regards as deliberate and contemptuous.

When the inmate must rely on officers to obtain what he needs (or thinks he needs) such as cigarettes, a sergeant or a psychiatrist, or permission to wash his clothes, he feels that this dependency in itself is demeaning. Thus, when his requests are not immediately responded to, the humiliation becomes more serious because not only has he had to ask for something, but those who have compromised his manliness by making him a mendicant now deny his requests, to show him who is boss. He also sees himself receiving arbitrary and demeaning messages when officers present him with forced-choice situations (such as "submit to the frisk or return to your cell") which do not include the option (go to the yard for exercise) the inmate elects to pursue. Since the officers want what they want and the inmate wants what he wants, there is nothing further to be said as he sees it, a fight ensues, and his subjection by (occasionally overwhelming) force reinforces his perspective. The fact that he keeps losing these fights because he is badly outnumbered has no bearing on the principle involved, which is that a man must fight when he must fight, and that it is better to fight and lose than to permit oneself to be belittled and emasculated by being ordered about like a child, having legitimate requests denied, or having somebody else's will prevail in a contest of will, which denotes childish subservience.

To be wrestled to the ground by vastly superior forces is not unmanly and is not a cause for shame, particularly if one can indicate, by spitting at one's retreating enemy or by otherwise declaring oneself inviolate ("You can't hurt me. Me tough.") that suppression is not tantamount to surrender.

It can be argued that pursuing autonomy (rejecting constraints) is the means whereby the man attempts to enhance his self-esteem (countering aspersions). He feels easily disparaged and affronted, and he reacts violently when he regards himself as offended or slighted, which occurs when there is some infringement on his autonomy.

These of course are only illustrative examples. The point we are making is that shared perceptions, using the patterns as a relevant frame of reference, can enrich individual perception. The empirically grounded framework of incident pattern analysis can facilitate both self- and self–other understanding.

Conclusion

There is sufficient independent coding agreement to warrant further development of the pattern-analytic scheme and use of the existing scheme for heuristic purposes. The process of sharing perceptions of patterning over incident reports is a promising procedure for building interest and competence in studying and understanding patterns. A pattern analyzer projects his or her own biases and understandings into his or her perception of incidents. This can precipitate concentration and motivation for understanding, particularly if it is one's own incidents one is observing. Sharing pattern perceptions further enriches and enhances the integrity of the approximations to "pattern truth."

The objective of pattern analysis we outline as a treatment modality in our last chapter (chapter 16) is to develop an understanding of the chronic offender's repetitious behavior that will make sense to the offender and for which he can construct a self-management strategy. We assume that such understanding must have enough group consensus for a group to be able to provide insights and support for the offender and to help him make sense of his own behavior. Pattern analysis of this kind requires intense study, and a group sharing of pattern analysis provides a concentrated introduction to participation in group problem solving addressed to the understanding of maladaptive behavior.

Note

1. There is reason to believe that something other than the persuasion of seniority determined the conference resolutions. Coder 1 and Coder 2 have worked together in developing classification systems over a series of correctional studies. They are very comfortable in disagreeing with one another, and in turn respect the other's opinions in resolving disagreements.

7

Gratifying Impulses

The maladaptive behavior patterns that unquestionably get the worst press are those in which adults govern their encounters in childlike ways, reacting to temptations and pressures the way infants do, by easily yielding to short-term opportunities and exploding under stress. As precocious young offenders, such men are considered better-than-average bets for careers that begin early and end (if ever) late. These delinquents have been labeled *unsocialized aggressives* by some observers because the key impulse that they express is aggression. Wattenberg described the manifestation of this disposition as follows:

> Lacking any security and confronting aggression, these children carry so heavy a load of hate that they cannot master it or their other impulses except for temporary delinquent purposes. In school, they are readily recognized even in primary grades. They cannot settle down to work; they are enraged by minor setbacks; they see the world as united against them; they are cruel to other children; they are foolhardy little daredevils bereft of a sense of consequences.
>
> Unless something is done, these violent and aggressive boys will develop into equally dangerous men. Through-

out their lives they will menace other people and themselves.[1]

The term *unsocialized* describes socialization failures that
have to do with defects in the mechanisms that mediate between impulses and the expression of impulses and that
modulate or suppress inappropriate urges.

Gratifying impulses is by definition a destructive enterprise,
because other people become objects of need satisfaction.
Less obviously, impulse gratification can be self-destructive,
because the reactions the person invites compound his or her
problems and can escalate into ugly, no-win confrontations.
Successful and rewarding careers of unlicensed conduct are
therefore rare (at least, in prisons). Moreover, in most patterns
of impulsivity, failures to profit from experience become an
increasingly obvious liability.

Predatory Aggression

It is easy to overlook the self-destructiveness of a person's
behavior pattern when the person himself is oblivious of
these consequences. It is even easier to ignore self-destructive
repercussions for the person when these seem deserved, as
they are among predatory aggressors who intimidate or
strong-arm weak or susceptible victims. An example of such
a pattern is that of a young man who had been convicted of
a mugging and serves a short but very variegated sentence.

As soon as the inmate enters the system, he alerts staff to
the fact that he expects a hostile reception from other inmates
because he has "hurt a lot of dudes out there" who might
"take revenge." He does become involved in fights but also
encounters problems for writing on walls, creating disturbances, violating the dress code, being out of place, using
abusive language, passing contraband, destroying property,
talking, playing his music loudly, delaying counts, harassing
officers, carrying weapons, and other offenses. Really serious
involvements have to do with a propensity the man develops
to make advances to female staff members. In one institution,

a nurse complains that he keeps appearing requesting that his genitalia be examined because he suffers "from too much masturbating." The nurse eventually reports:

> I had informed the doctor of the problem with the inmate the previous day, and he agreed to see him and treat the problem. The inmate refused to let the doctor touch him and requested that I hold him again. The doctor asked the inmate to immediately remove himself and noted the incident on the inmate chart. Again (during the next two days) the inmate reported to the medical building and I refused to even talk with him and he was instructed by the other nurse to leave. In the interest of my safety and due to total humiliation, I'm requesting that this inmate be so assigned that he will not have to associate with me.

In the next prison to which the inmate is sent, a female officer reports:

> He has been harassing me for a while now. I verbally warned him about touching me. One morning during the week (I don't remember the date) he passed by me a number of times and each time he touched me. He would either hit my arm with his arm, swing his hands back and forth, and hit my leg with his hand. When I told him about it he claimed he didn't know he was touching me. I told him from now on to walk around the table away from me but on [date] he started touching me again. He would sit at a table close by me and ask me personal questions, where I lived because he wants to see me when he gets out, what kind of car I drove, was I married, do I have any kids, did I ever go to bed with a black man, if I ever kissed a black man. I never answered any of his questions except to tell him to stop asking me about my personal life because it was none of his business. He said I was beautiful and he was in love with me.

One month after the inmate is paroled, he becomes involved in a series of holdups. Back in prison, he is caught stealing from fellow inmates, who are determined to exact retribution. He is locked in protective segregation, but someone reaches him there and throws "a mixture of hot water and hot baby oil" onto his chest, inflicting burns. The inmate promptly reveals the identity of his enemy and informs on other inmates, who happen to be members of his gang. As a result, he has now become a favored target of retribution from erstwhile companions.

In relation to staff, the prisoner continues to be insubordinate. In one incident, he agitates other inmates waiting for home telephone calls, informing them that "these fucking C.O.s [correctional officers] are always fucking everybody out of everything." He also keeps stealing, and on one occasion is apprehended wearing eyeglasses he has appropriated from another inmate. And after repeated transfers, the system is close to running out of institutions to which he can be sent, given the ill will he has generated.

This individual seems bent on illustrating the proposition that there is "no honor among thieves," and he lies and steals from companions and betrays them whenever it suits his short-term ends. The fact that he informs on others, however, does not make him an asset for staff because he is prone to lie and dissemble when he thinks lying and dissembling are advantageous to him. All people are objects to this man, and all people are targeted for exploitation and expropriation. Targets, of course, very much include women, and the fact that a woman may be a staff member or wearing a uniform is inconsequential as far as this predator is concerned.

It is obvious that this man plays his games casually as the mood or impulse strikes him. He is not following a serious strategy in that he is seemingly unconcerned (to the point of obliviousness) about consequences at the time that he acts. He continues to behave as he does even when adverse consequences are certain, as they are when he visits the infirmary for the seventh time demanding sexual contact with a nurse, publicly wears eyeglasses he has stolen from a fellow inmate, or continues stealing in situations in which he is the only plausible suspect. Understandably, as time goes on, the consequences of such behavior cumulate, and the man's career takes a turn for the worse. The man must now seek refuge to gain physical safety, but even this does not bring him face to face with realities he steadfastly continues to ignore. To the end, he antagonizes staff on whom he depends for survival and stirs up trouble among peers, adding to his roster of enemies. The prison's assigned role is to protect this man from himself, a goal with which he steadfastly fails to cooperate.

Such are the grounds for classing the man's behavior as maladaptive. The crucial point is that when this man acts in what he regards as his interest (which is most of the time), he reliably defeats his ends, and he is so constituted that he is unable to profit from the experience.

Frustration to Aggression

Not all impulsives, to be sure, go through life disregarding self-generated adversities, unfazed by the obstructions and untoward circumstances they encounter. A key attribute of core impulsivity (denoted by the concept of low frustration tolerance) leads us to expect that impulsives will not only act blindly to satisfy their needs but also react blindly when they do not achieve the satisfaction to which they feel entitled. Many such individuals feel outraged when they are stymied and will express their sense of outrage through acts of blind or indignant aggression. These frustration–aggression reactions are apt to generate cycles which exacerbate the adversities that prompt them.

An illustration of this pattern is furnished by a young inmate convicted of a burglary and an attempted robbery. This man had been mostly institutionalized since the age of 11, at which time he was diagnosed as hyperactive and sent to a reformatory. In a second juvenile institution, he manifested his diagnosed hyperactivity by assaulting a counselor and destroying furnishings. Transferred to yet another youth institution, he escaped 1 week before he became involved in the offenses for which he was sentenced.

In prison, the man receives high ratings as a kitchen

worker but has difficulties accommodating to the custodial regime. This combination—the fact that the inmate takes his work seriously but has trouble adjusting to supervision— produces a serious incident that earns him 3 months of segregation, some loss of good-time credit, and a psychological referral. An officer involved in this incident records the following:

> I went to the back sink to pick up a spatula that was needed on the serving line. As I started to walk away with the spatula, the inmate came up to me and said, "I need the spatula at the back sink to scrape the pans with." I then informed the inmate that we have a regular pan scraper for that job and that I would get it for him in about five minutes when I had someone to cover me on the line. I then walked to the serving line, set the spatula down, and turned around to walk back to my station on the line, and collided with the inmate who was directly behind me. He attempted to pick up the spatula when I again said, "no." I blocked his path of retrieval and ordered him out of the serving area. The inmate then walked out but turned and said, "don't push me no more, don't put your hands on me because I won't be fronting." The inmate was raising his hands in a menacing way the entire time that he said this. I then ordered the inmate to return to the back sink area. I again told the inmate that I would get him a pan scraper as soon as possible and ordered him to return to the area. The inmate then stated that if I came any closer that he would hurt me. I again ordered him to return to his area. In order to avoid a situation where someone could get injured, I left the confrontation and returned to the serving line.

The officer reports the incident to a sergeant, who attempts to lock the inmate in his cell. The sergeant recalls:

> I approached the inmate and told him that he had been keeplocked and I wanted him to come to reception with the officer and myself. The inmate refused to leave the

kitchen and said, "fuck that. I'm not leaving and nobody better put their mother-fucking hands on me." He was very anxious and nervous, in a fighting position and constantly moving around. The inmate picked up a can opener (approximately 24 inches long) and stated, "don't nobody come near me. I will hit you." He continued moving and again stated, "The state considers this a deadly weapon and I am going to use it as a deadly weapon. If any of you try to take me out of here, I'm going to use this weapon on you, you, and you."

Other inmates and myself tried to talk him into putting the weapon down and coming with the officer and myself. Finally, he gave the weapon to the inmate and I escorted him to reception without further incident.

The disciplinary board explains its penalty by reminding the inmate that "in your last twenty-two appearances . . . you have been extensively counseled regarding your unsatisfactory behavior." The board recalls that on occasions it has suspended the inmate's sentence to test his capacity to exert self-control. The board discusses the inmate's failure to respond to this treatment and adds that "hopefully he will understand that it is necessary to control his temper and not to resort to violence when frustrated by situations."

When the inmate is served with the charges resulting from the mess hall incident, he explodes, and when he is served with charges resulting from his explosion he explodes again, sets a fire, and refuses to permit himself to be transferred to an observation cell. A narrative history of the entire sequence reads as follows:

At approximately 4:57 p.m. you intentionally broke your lightbulb. . . . Approximately five minutes later you destroyed your cell bench and table by throwing said items around your cell and ramming your bed against your cell wall. At approximately 6:20 p.m., same date, it was discovered that you had caused your toilet bowl to separate from the wall, breaking the wall mounting section of same, and that you had dismantled your metal bed frame. At approximately 6:40 p.m. you refused to comply with orders given to you to effect your movement to an observation cell. . . . You instead threatened the sergeant stating, "if you come in after me I'm going to fuck one of you up." You then positioned yourself in the left rear corner of your cell wearing a pair of cloth workgloves . . . you raised both of your hands (gloved) and started swinging them about when the officers approached you. You continued to resist by swinging your hands and kicking your feet about wildly when (the officers were) removing you from your cell to effect the cell transfer. During said movement it was discovered that you had set fire to your mattress causing a section of the mattress cover approximately eight inches in diameter to burn before being extinguished.

The inmate attributes his actions to feelings of "hostility" and explains that he "refused to come out of his cell because he was upset about being charged with another incident and receiving a superintendent proceeding." The inmate also explains that "when the officers came and grabbed me I struggled to get their arms off me. I had no intention of striking anyone." He later writes:

I realize what I did was wrong but I meant no harm. I was just frustrated because I felt I was in the right and that no one would take time out to really investigate what really happened . . . I do not normally act this way. I was also frustrated because of family and girl problems and also because I have another year to serve after this sentence and I see my second (parole) board (in a few days) and I didn't want to go being in the box . . . I promise that my behavior will improve.

Three weeks later, however, the inmate sets fire to a large pile of shredded paper on his cell floor and is referred for psychiatric observation. The fire is described as an expression of the inmate's continued feeling of "frustration," and the staff adds that he "goes through periods of not caring what happens to him."

A few months after completing a term of parole, the man

is apprehended in the course of a burglary by two police officers, who arrest him. The officers report that when they "start to handcuff" the man he becomes acutely disturbed and pushes one officer into the path of an approaching car, which runs over the officer's foot. He then escapes and is chased by the other officer who apprehends him, after which the inmate is described as "resigned to his situation."

This man fairly reliably explodes when he feels cornered. Situations in which the man has a right to feel cornered arise frequently as a result of his actions, which he usually views as insufficiently serious to produce the consequences they produce. In retrospect, the man invariably regrets his explosions, but at the time he explodes the encompassing feeling he seems to experience is panic, rage, a sense of hopelessness, and a desire to escape the inevitable fate that looms before him. It appears as if he wants to reverse the course of history, wipe the slate clean, and destroy a game he has obviously lost. He wants to remove himself from the situation, but at some level he knows that he cannot, which makes him helplessly angry.

The man is probably correct when he claims that he does not mean to attack guards and other authority figures but sees them at times as menacing and as placing him in imminent physical danger. He reacts to the officer in the kitchen, for example, as if the officer was intending to beat him, and he similarly appears afraid of officers who intend to escort him to an observation cell. In both instances the guards represent inevitable consequences of actions the inmate has reflexively and unthinkingly taken, such as physically reclaiming a spatula or expressing his frustrations by setting fires or wrecking his cell.

Incidents represent chains of junctures in which frustration-induced rage has invited retributive consequences that he cannot accept or assimilate. When in an appeal he writes, "I meant no harm," he probably accurately describes his retrospective state of mind. Because he meant no harm, punishment represents the manifestation of an arbitrary, inhospitable fate that he finds too painful to face.

Stress to Aggression

The flavor of frustration-induced aggression is that it largely expresses blind—and sometimes retaliatory—rage. Other explosions, however, have a different flavor that is more evocative of panic and of a sense of helplessness. The issue for the people involved in such explosions is still frustration, but rather than feeling crossed or offended these people feel impotent or defeated.[2] These people do not see their environment as hostile but as overwhelming. Sensing no recourse as events inexorably close in on them, they throw tantrums that symbolize their despair.

People who explode in this way can be described as *stressed*, in that the challenges they encounter exceed their self-defined capacity to cope.[3] The reason impulsivity is also at issue (despite evidence of anxiety) is because of the helpless, out-of-control, reactive nature of the responses that stress inspires.

A case that illustrates the process is that of an inmate serving a prison sentence for burglary who becomes involved in a strange assortment of institutional rule violations in which the most frequent charge is "destruction of state property." There are additional incidents involving arson, fighting, an assault on an officer, and a suicide attempt. The inmate is also occasionally found out of place and is written up for refusing to work or for not reporting to assignments.

The man has a history of problems. At age 7, someone adjudged him "very possibly brain damaged." Seven years later, complaints about him were registered by the school system. Among other things, the boy allegedly destroyed the car of a teacher by setting it on fire in the school parking lot.

The inmate also became a problem for the community by setting expensive and life-threatening fires. He burned down one building because "he was angry at [a resident] for failure to return [some items] he had borrowed a number of months before." He narrowly missed burning down an office building because some employees working in this building "had teased him."

The man was placed in a psychiatric facility from which he promptly escaped. The staff report concluded:

> He was not in need of psychiatric treatment but rather of a supervised closed environment in which the chance of further incendiary acts could be precluded. Cognitive functioning is simplistic and concrete, with no evidence of major psychiatric disorder. Although constantly seeking attention and acceptance from peers and staff, the level of such interpersonal skills resulted in rejection and nonacceptance by the peer group . . . [The inmate] stated he would elope whenever given the opportunity . . . It became necessary to transfer him to a secure locked ward to prevent further incidents which threatened injury to self or others [including the real danger of incendiarism] . . . A transfer agent accompanied him to a developmental center for his admission, as ordered in a family court order.

The developmental facility was not pleased by the fact that its new resident "has frequently threatened to use physical force to attain his end." They also complained that he "cut through his window screen and left the grounds." Returned to the developmental center, the absconder broke into the administration building and set a fire, and it is this offense for which he was sent to prison. In the presentence report, the probation officer recommended an indeterminate sentence on the grounds that "the community needs to be protected from the defendant's inappropriate behavior *and because there is no viable alternative available*" [italics added].

When the man enters the prison, he at first "makes a favorable impression, and did not appear to be a particularly resistive or hostile sort, but may be given to using rather poor judgment." The inmate almost immediately embarks on a string of incidents that changes the "favorable impression" he has made. He does not like being locked up and makes a set of ropes out of bedsheets, and when these are confiscated he cuts his arms with a piece of glass. He also "burned his blankets, sheets, and pillowcases because he wanted out of his cell" and "threw bedding out of his window." Two weeks later he sets fire to his mattress, explaining that "he had just realized how much time he had to do, and that he did not have any visits." The man also refuses to come out of his cell and participate in programs. The staff explain that "this is a very disturbed resident as far as this facility is concerned, [who] is scared to death of the more mature population" and should "be transferred to a facility for younger men."

The inmate is, in fact, transferred to a youth prison, where an officer reports:

> The inmate never came out of his cell when the bells rang. When I went down to see what was the matter the inmate was laying on the bed. I asked him if he was going to program. He stated, "No, I'm not going to fucking program. I'm fucking sick." The inmate was given a Notice of Report.

The inmate explains that "he refused to come out of his cell because he fears other inmates and he won't ask for help because he fears retaliation." A psychiatrist writes:

> The inmate is on mental status observation in reception at present time because of an apparent outburst of uncontrollable aggressive behavior. He acknowledged with regret and spontaneously being in "deep trouble" and appears very distressed over his losing control of himself. However, he indicated "it wouldn't have happened if he was not provoked." He feels strongly that he will not be able to control himself and fears that he might do something "more serious" stating he will continue to fight if provoked.

By this time, the man has been written up for a variety of offenses, including fights, attempts at self-mutilation, and refusals to participate in programs, and he claims that inmates and officers "pick on him." There is validity to at least some of these complaints in that he has been removed from school "due to being picked on by other students." He understandably becomes increasingly disgruntled with his situation.

Early one morning, an officer reports that "the inmate crushed his eyeglasses by stepping on them, then handed them over to me and stated that he likes tickets." That same evening another officer reports:

> The inmate admitted that he did not have his keeplock tray to turn in because he had thrown it out the window. The inmate was questioned about his misbehavior. His retort was, "I'm not in jail anymore. I can do whatever I want to. The fact is I threw just about everything in my cell out the window." In checking the yard under his cell it was observed that several articles of clothing, bed linens, books, etc. were there. The inmate has been acting strangely of late. He appears to not care about anything.

A counselor interviews the inmate and reports:

> He admits destruction of state property (eyeglasses) by stepping on them. Claims he had too many problems, a fight in the center yard, harassment from several inmates on the company. After breaking his glasses he admitted cutting his left forearm. Later that evening he admits he threw his clothes, his coat, his books, his hat, bed linens, I.D. card, program card, church card, medication card, keeplock tray out the window. He claims he did this because he hopes to be released on appeal. He also claims he cannot take the harassment by inmates and [an officer]. He claims he has not listened to the adjustment committee because he cannot take the harassment any longer.
>
> The next night he banged on the wall and threw his bucket against the wall and started throwing things around in his cell. He presently claims that he has been "seeing images of his family." He also claims he has been hearing voices from his family to come home. He claims he then punched the radiator and yelled at the voices.

The distraught inmate next appears before the disciplinary board and remarks, "you tell your damn officers to leave me alone or next time someone is going to get hurt." He also explains that he "tries to be cool" but when he gets upset he "just goes off."

The man is then briefly hospitalized but otherwise continues to regularly appear before disciplinary panels for a variety of violations. He is finally transferred to a special protective unit, where he is accused of "self inflicted wounds in the cell block" which "caused the disruption in the smooth order of the facility." He explains that "he acted out because he had many problems on his mind."

Program staff write that the inmate "is a generally cooperative person; however, he does act impulsively." They point out, however, that despite several misbehavior reports, "it would appear there is some slow positive program adjustment within the [unit]."

The inmate completes his sentence in the program and is paroled with the provision that he be referred to a mental health setting, but he soon returns to prison convicted of attempted arson in satisfaction of a charge of arson, burglary, and attempted rape. According to the probation officer who prepares the presentence report:

> For about four weeks he had been living "on the streets" sleeping anywhere he could find. This consisted mainly of cardboard boxes outdoors. He also was drinking heavily and smoking marijuana every day. He further states that at the time of the crimes he didn't care what he did or what happened to him because his "life has been hell." On the day of the incident he was drinking all day in various downtown bars. He felt depressed and angry ... He states that there was no reason for picking [a specific] residence to start a fire. He states that he picked it because when it came over him to start the fire "it was the closest one." ... He set the fire in a store because he was upset because there was no money there for him. As he was leaving the store by way of the fire escape he noticed a young woman walking past. He states that he followed her hoping to have sexual relations with her. After following her for a while he ran up and grabbed her from behind ... He states that he didn't want to hurt the woman, just have sex with her. He states further that

he "doesn't care anymore what happens to me." He feels that he would rather spend the maximum amount of time on his sentence and not get out on parole.

After the inmate predictably returns to the prison, intake analysts write that

> he had been adjusting adequately at the reception center until just recently when he reacted to a situation by punching the wall and burning himself with a cigarette. He had previously expressed to the counselor that he was doing alright, but continually had feelings of anger and "felt like going off."

The man is returned to the protective program and there attempts to commit suicide by overdosing with dilantin. Three months later, he requests protective custody because he indicates another inmate had "stated he was going to stab him when he got the chance since he refuses [the other inmate's] sexual demands."

By then, he has been placed in a succession of settings with which he cannot cope and which cannot cope with him. When a setting overtaxes the man's capacity to adjust to it, his first reaction is to try to escape, and when escape is thwarted he sometimes explodes with frustration. Ironically, the inmate often discovers that the setting in which he next finds himself is even more frustrating, and this makes him nostalgic for settings in which he has failed to cope at earlier junctures. It is in this spirit that the man demands return to a developmental program from which he has eloped and where he subsequently sets a fire when the pressure again mounts. It is also in this spirit that he talks longingly (or at least resignedly) of prison when he is rejected by relatives and is relegated to living in discarded cardboard containers.

At earlier junctures in the inmate's career, some of his explosions have a vindictive, retaliatory flavor and are directed at perceived sources of frustration. Subsequently, his explosions become general expressions of frustration, and even become self-punitive, and they sometimes communicate that he is helplessly angry, though he paradoxically maintains "I don't give a damn anymore."

Some of the change in the man's outlook has to do with the fact that he increasingly feels that the cards (meaning life circumstances in general) are stacked against him, that no one likes him, and that everyone wishes him harm. This makes the man feel resourceless and tense, and he senses the tension in himself. He also concludes that at some juncture he must "go off," a circumstance that he—somewhat reluctantly—regards as a given. In other words, he sees himself as a pawn of his own runaway feelings, which he in turn ascribes to the overwhelming array of hostile forces that impinge on him. This view in part derives from the fact that he holds a low opinion of himself and that he has given up even the slightest tinge of hope of negotiating the challenges of his environment.

Russian Roulette

We have indicated that not all impulsivity reflects awareness of the repercussions that impulsivity invites. Where awareness of consequences exists, a person may regret his actions, but he may see himself as powerless to affect them. In such instances, the inability to profit from experience has to do with difficulties—or at least, perceived difficulties—in maintaining a resolve to reform or in translating this resolve into action. In other cases, however, the person may not care about the propensity he has to arrange adverse repercussions through impulsive acts.

One variant is the converse of the Protestant ethic, which prescribes that we defer short-term rewards to secure long-term benefits. Any impulsive person's sights are almost by definition set on the present, or at most on the short-term future. In some cases, this stance is accentuated, however, in that the person seems to go out of his way to take risks to defy probabilities of consequences and to value the defiance. The gain is not only short-term reward but also the excitement of obtaining this reward under inhospitable circumstances, which makes the enterprise a test of resilience or a game.

A case in point is a man who returned to prison following a conviction for fraudulently cashing other people's unemployment checks. He explains that he needed the money because he is "a real dope fiend." In prison, the man's offenses include such charges as refusing orders, loitering, creating disturbances, fighting, and lying.

This man is first assigned to a medium-security prison from which he is evicted after inciting other inmates to a mini-riot in the mess hall. In this incident the inmate, who at the time is a member of the institution's liaison committee, produces a paper alleging that "we can get all the food we want. The superintendent said so." According to a correction officer,

> He stopped at the line and demanded more food. I says, "you have to wait till almost everybody is served. If there is any left over you could possibly get more food." He started yelling and screaming in the line, "if we don't get more food, how would the cooks and officers like to be taken hostage over more food?" At that time I ordered him to go to the table. He stayed right there and kept yelling and screaming at us, "how would the officers and cooks like to be held hostage?" . . . All the inmate liaison committee paper stated is that all inmates should receive the same amount of food from the first inmate to the last inmate.

According to the man himself it was not he, but the officer, who had lost his cool. The inmate testifies,

> He tells me I don't know what you're talking about. What are you, crazy? He's the one that came out the side of his neck: I saw him getting all upset. I just took my tray and sat down. That was it . . . Nobody mouthed off at him. He's the one who started mouthing off. I just sat down. I saw the way he was getting.

The inmate is assigned to another prison, but the recipient institution turns him down based on his record as a ring leader of disturbances. The prison that initiated the transfer defends its recommendation based on the contention that "the incident was not quite as serious as officials first thought." Prison staff discover, however, that the mess hall disturbance was not an isolated event. In an incident weeks later, an officer reports:

> You ran to the big yard gate, and you were yelling, "come on, let's get the fuck out of here." At this time other inmates left the company with you but when ordered to come back, they did. The officer states you continued to run and attempted to incite others to join you.

In a third disturbance, the inmate has prolonged a telephone conversation after having been told that his time was up and is then cut off. The inmate remonstrates with the officer in charge, who reports:

> At this time there were approximately 15 inmates in the area and five complained that they did not have enough time. You had also told the inmates, "watch your time. He'll fuck you over."

The man receives a 30-day penalty for this incident, but his punishment is suspended and he is paroled. Three months later he returns, his parole having been violated "for continuing to use drugs and failure to make office reports." He serves 6 months additional time and is released on the expiration date of his sentence. Within 2 months, however, he is stopped by a police officer after he drives through a red light and cannot produce a license or registration. The police further report that "a gun, fully loaded, was discovered sticking out from under the driver's seat." The man thus returns to prison, where he accumulates a string of violations, all of which involve possessing marijuana, with occasional excursions into owning $10 bills or storing liquids with high alcohol content. At this time, the man resides in an institution for younger offenders from which he requests transfer, arguing that "I'm over the age of 18 and not an adolescent to be treated as one, and will not tolerate any harassments by the officials of this facility which are constantly disrespecting the adolescents that are in this facility."

This man appears to enjoy his practice of taking risks, or at least disregarding odds. His pattern of behavior can be described as brazen. He boasts about being a dope fiend and takes few pains to hide incriminating evidence such as being intoxicated during interviews, having marijuana cigarettes in his cell, and carrying loaded guns while driving unregistered cars. His lying is painfully transparent, and it seems more designed for show than for exoneration. The man appears to be full of the joy of life as he defines it. His protests are exuberant, and they suggest that he gets carried away whenever the opportunity arises to make a scene, particularly when he can get others to join in the excitement.

The inmate is probably right when he argues that it is officers who lose their cool and not he, because his dominant emotion is enthusiasm rather than anger. He uses drugs to get excitement and commits crimes that are visible and involve sufficient risk to make them exciting. He continues his sensation seeking in prison through participation in the prison underworld and through the games he plays with authority figures and the prison disciplinary machinery.

Deterrence is a concept that obviously does not apply to this man because the threat of punishment appears to be an incentive to him. Taking risks, as he sees it, can be the spice of life.

Jailing

When a person with a short-term perspective finds himself temporarily in any environment, the here-and-now setting is the one that becomes the world of consequence to him and the arena in which he seeks his rewards. In the prison, this stance is called *jailing*, a term that means "to cut yourself off from the outside world and to attempt to construct a life within the prison."[4] The impulse-dominated prisoner pursues impulse satisfactions by seeking the acquisition of prized illicit amenities. Life after prison has no tangible meaning to the person because it lies in the irrelevantly remote future; the "official" prison is only of interest to him insofar as it provides increments in privilege, and his program participation is at best perfunctory. Impulsive behavior patterns such as "hustling" are transplanted from the community to the prison, but many prisoners also "jail" as a career, and such people have often spent their lives in institutions. The perspective of an individual of this kind, according to John Irwin, can become specialized:

> The prison world is the only world with which he is familiar. He was raised in a world where "punks" and "queens" have replaced women, "bonaroos" are the only fashionable clothing, and cigarettes are money. This is a world where disputes are settled with a pipe or a knife, and the individual must form tight cliques for protection. His senses are attuned to iron doors banging, locks turning, shakedowns, and long lines of blue-clad convicts. He knows how to survive, in fact prosper, in this world, how to get a cell change and a good work assignment, how to score for nutmeg, cough syrup, or other narcotics. More important, he knows hundreds of youths like himself who grew up in the youth prisons and are now in the adult prisons.[5]

One example of a "jailer" is a man who commits unimpressive prison violations resulting in charges such as "the inmate went to the movies when he was supposed to be on bed rest," "wrestling with another inmate," "refused to lock in and kept talking with his friends," "carrying on a conversation with two inmates after the quiet bell," "stayed at the end of the company when his cell was opened for the evening mess," "came to my desk and said he didn't want to do his assignment, went to the men's room and did not return promptly," "during his cell frisk, I found contraband items including a tape deck belonging to another inmate," "during a frisk, I found a burnt soda can with a shoestring handle. He said he used it to heat water," "the inmate was told three times to stay away from another inmate who was taking a test," "he left the drafting class without permission, said he was looking for a cup," and "he threw a spoonful of macaroni, which hit several inmates sitting nearby."

The man enters the prison on crutches (he has had a leg amputated 9 years earlier) and is fitted with a prosthesis. Soon, he signs himself into protection, claiming that an inmate "had slapped him around and threatened him with a knife" and "wanted to perform sex on him." The other inmate explains indignantly that he "is not a homo chaser" but the man is transferred to a protective program. In this program, he secures his high school diploma but is not considered an asset. The program staff write that

> since entering [program], the inmate appears to have continued his unsatisfactory custodial adjustment of the past. Specifically he has been the subject of eighteen misbehavior reports during his fourteen months tenure with this program . . . The inmate seems to associate with only a few individuals at any given time. These relationships appear to be . . . limited to manipulation on the inmate's part to obtain commissary items and use of the other's personal belongings . . . The subject tends to avoid demonstrating this type of behavior with more aggressive inmates, which leads to the inference that he is an "opportunity predator" of sorts.

The man is eventually released to the community but returns to prison after he has held up a taxi driver at knifepoint. In prison he "reports that he had a $1,000 a day cocaine habit at the time of arrest," which seems an exaggeration. However, he adjusts well to confinement, is lauded for his "motivation, achievement, social behavior, and work habits," and is said to show "a cooperative spirit."

In fact, the man rather enjoys prison but—at least during his first term—makes it obvious that the prison world in which he operates is not the same prison system that is run and monitored by the staff. The man's world consists of illicit amenities and of routines and pastimes that involve extensive socializing, which includes exchanges of commodities and gossip, leading to the possibility of misunderstandings, which lead to the possibility of conflicts. It also becomes obvious that the man is not above exploiting those who are exploitable, because he is a career hustler, and hustling includes using other people to obtain goods and services whenever assertiveness and glibness can influence those who are less verbally skilled.

When the man leaves prison, he again commits a substantial offense, which, given that he also has an impressive crime on record, nets him a very long prison sentence, and he embarks on this sentence giving every indication of becoming an experienced old con who creates a congenial home for himself in the institutional environment.

Games Turn Sour

Although inmates such as our jailer are successes in their own eyes, there are other impulsives who experience setbacks that they find difficult to ignore. Admitting failure, however, usually climaxes a long history of setbacks, which are brushed off or blamed on adverse or inhospitable circumstance.

The turning point tends not to be one of insight and self-discovery but one of shock and self-pity. The person does not deduce that his childish games have boomeranged but discovers with chagrin that others reject him determinedly and consistently and that authorities throw the book at him.

A case in point is an inmate serving a long sentence for a small-time robbery. His incarceration includes a year in the jail and considerable time credit lost because of prison violations, which mostly consist of fights with other inmates. According to the probation officer, the man, when arrested, "lived in 'the street,' associated with other idle and disorderly youths and seemed adjusted to the values and mores of a criminal subculture." The probation officer also refers to the fact that the man had spent years being rounded up every few weeks for possessing marijuana, disorderly conduct, selling narcotics, promoting gambling, and petit larceny.

The inmate himself admits to intake analysts in the prison that he has engaged in "general hustling." He also boasts that he "generally sold marijuana but claimed that it was not actually marijuana but rolled up tea. He indicates that this was the familiar means of support for him."

After the man receives three misbehavior reports in rapid succession at the reception center, he is assigned to a youth prison where he accumulates 10 more misbehavior reports in a short time. These include 3 for fighting and 1 "for possession of a dangerous weapon (a razor blade melted into a toothbrush handle)." Six months later, the total has climbed to 18 reports, and 1 of these involves a fight in which the inmate assaults another inmate whom he thinks has stolen one of his shirts, and he breaks the other man's jaw. In response to the penalty this incident invites, the inmate writes to the commissioner of corrections, complaining, "I don't think this sentence is fair because I've seen a few inmates get seven days for breaking another inmate's jaw, and the staff here pay me no mind."

A few weeks later, he runs into additional difficulties. An officer reports:

> At about 7 p.m. in the special housing unit I smelled the odor of marijuana coming from the area of [the inmate's] cell. A cell frisk was conducted by [two officers]. They found a total of seven cigarettes believed to be a controlled substance of marijuana. The cigarettes were field tested by a sergeant with a field test kit and proved positive marijuana.

The inmate tells the sergeant that he has received the cigarettes from his stepfather during a visit, and the sergeant writes,

> I asked the inmate how he had gotten the marijuana back · to his cell and he stated he had swallowed a small bag of it in the visiting room, and after returning to his cell had coughed it back up.

The incident brings the inmate a 90-day extension of his segregation time and 3 additional months loss of good time.

After serving his segregation sentence, the man is released. However, after 6 months of minor property offenses his parole officer (to whom he has not been reporting) revokes his parole. He serves the remainder of his sentence without becoming involved in conflicts but is referred to the psychologist because he "appears disturbed," and at this time the staff record that "the inmate has a tendency to escape by becoming drowsy, in contrast to others who may 'act out.'"

There is an indication that the man's pattern of adjustment has been unfrozen at this point, toward the end of his career, which is a mixed blessing because his mood is now one of apathy and depression. Prior to this, the man has faced adversity by leading a happy-go-lucky existence, using whatever resources he finds at hand and relying on his peer group for support and sustenance. He leads this existence both inside and outside the prison, hustling and socializing in a fashion that makes the extramural and intramural enterprises difficult to distinguish. The man also relies on drugs for entertainment and to cheer him up, and he incurs frequent stays in jail, which to him is like a familiar motel room for a traveling salesman who spends a good deal of time on the road.

Some problems the man experiences in prison are similar to those he runs into on the street when police officers interrupt his card games or narcotics transactions, but prison disciplinary committees, unlike the courts, attend to *patterns* of minor transgressions and penalize the inmate for chronicity. Another problem the man encounters is that he settles disputes through fights; he has the particular misfortune that one of his peers has a glass jaw and that prison staff are therefore obligated to take at least one fight seriously, with painful consequences to the inmate.

Part of this man's pattern has been to do his best to ignore the physical presence of authority figures such as teachers, police officers, guards, and parole officers, whom he regards as unwelcome facts of life who at worst have some nuisance value. It is this premise that is ultimately exploded by the fact that prison authorities segregate the man for extended periods of time and lengthen his prison stay, and by the fact that parole officers whom he ignores return him to prison for ignoring them.

Notes

1. Wattenberg, W. (1964). Psychologists and juvenile delinquency. In H. Toch (Ed.), *Legal and criminal psychology*. New York: Holt, Rinehart & Winston. The concept of the *unsocialized aggressive* delinquent was first delineated by Hewitt, L. E., & Jenkins, R. L. (1946). *Fundamental patterns of maladjustment*. Springfield: State of Illinois. The latest version of the concept has been formulated by Terrie Moffitt in differentiating types of delinquent careers. See Moffitt, T. E. (1993). Adolescence-limited and life-course-persistent antisocial behavior: A developmental taxonomy. *Psychological Review, 100*, 674–701.

   The diagnostic categories currently in use that apply most directly to such youths are conduct disorder, undersocialized and aggressive types. Among the "associated features" the *Diagnostic and Statistical Manual of Mental Disorders* (4th ed.; *DSM–IV*) lists for conduct disorders are poor frustration tolerance, irritability, temper outbursts, and recklessness. *DSM–IV* notes that "typically, the most severe conduct problems (e.g., rape, theft while confronting a victim) tend to emerge last. However, there are wide differences among individuals, with some engaging in the more damaging behaviors at an early age" (American Psychiatric Association. [1994]. *Diagnostic and statistical manual of mental disorders* [4th ed., pp. 87–88]. Washington, DC: Author).

2. Both frustration–aggression and stress–aggression fall under the heading of *hostile* (impulse-related, angry, aversively stimulated, expressive, and irritable) as opposed to *instrumental* aggression. In the latter, the victim is harmed as a means to secure some ulterior end, such as dominance or material reward, whereas in the former, the medium (aggression) is the message. The distinction between the two categories of aggression was originally drawn by Buss, A. (1961). *The psychology of aggression*. New York: Wiley; and Feshbach, S. (1964). The function of aggression and the regulation of aggressive drive. *Psychological Review, 71*, 257–272.

   The frustration–aggression relationship as it is currently understood evolved out of psychoanalytic and learning perspectives. See Dollard, J., Doob, L., Miller, N., Mowrer, O., & Sears, R. (1939). *Frustration and aggression*. New Haven, CT: Yale University Press. The literature includes a book on the subject written 2,000 years ago by the teacher and philosopher Seneca, who noted that some persons are disproportionately angered by (among other things) exaggerating the import of trivia. Toch, H. (1983). The management of hostile aggression: Seneca as applied social psychologist. *American Psychologist*, 38, 1022–1026.

Susceptibility to stress-generated aggression can have its origin in a limited repertoire of coping options, or of self-defined coping options. A person who feels his verbal skills are circumscribed, for example, may turn a verbal conflict into a physical confrontation because he finds the situation overwhelming. Toch, H. (1992). *Violent men*. Washington, DC: American Psychological Association.

3. People who are clinically described as impulsives are presumed not to suffer from anxiety, but in practice impulsivity (including aggressive impulsivity) and pervasive anxiety often go hand in hand. See Redl, F., & Wineman, D. (1951). *Children who hate*. Glencoe, IL: Free Press.
4. Irwin, J. (1970). *The felon*. Englewood Cliffs, NJ: Prentice Hall (Spectrum), p. 68.
5. Irwin (1970), note 4, supra, p. 74.

8

Enhancing Esteem

Adaptive and maladaptive behavior frequently have the same psychological ends, and nowhere is this fact more apparent than with behavior that is designed to build reputation or cement self-esteem. Enhancing esteem is deemed a "basic" need by personality theorists.[1] This means that the need for esteem is a universal and irreducible human motive but that specific indices used as measures of esteem vary from culture to culture.

Differences in indices of esteem can be sources of problems where criteria of esteem applicable in one culture are inappropriately imported into another. Skill at headhunting, for instance, may have been valued in the hinterlands of New Guinea, but in New York or Melbourne demonstrations of headhunting skill would produce adverse repercussions.

In this connection, it is well to recall that "cultures"—in the sense of nonoverlapping values—are often found in geographical juxtaposition, particularly in pluralistic societies such as the United States. Definitions of valued behavior can thus vary in the same neighborhood or from classroom to classroom in the same school. Anthropologists speak of *sub-cultures* in discussing such differences, to confirm that an overall culture to which groups belong unites them to some measure, whereas deviations from the values of this culture separate them.[2] The existence of subcultural values, however, is not per se a problem, because it is accommodated to achieve coexistence, as in families with children who belong to the teenage subculture. In such cases we learn to tolerate differing criteria of esteem, such as prevailing indices of teenage popularity.

At times, subcultural differences become an asset. Business establishments that are culturally distinct, for example, may draw their clientele from members of other cultures. A culture may even adopt subcultural criteria of esteem, as in the admiration we accord to members of the "jock" subculture. Congeniality cannot be assumed, however. Conflicts arise where subcultural practices are not compatible with cultural criteria or those of other subcultures, though some deviant norms may be adjudged barely tolerable, such as the fact that some students pursue mediocrity to garner admiration. However, serious conflicts can arise when the behavior that is admired in a group is deemed noxious or harmful outside the group.

The most predictable problems are created by members of groups (called *contracultures*) that *make a point* of prescribing conduct that diverges from behavior that is valued in the culture at large. Where such norms are applied, they may earn an individual peer approval but bring him or her a jail sentence. This helps to explain the travails of teenage gang members.[3] A leading theorist, Albert Cohen, noted that preadolescents are invited by society at large to value themselves in terms of scholastic achievement, but that this is an enterprise at which many do not excel. The esteem needs of such youths would remain unmet if they valued education and thus accepted the usual criteria of success. Many youths consequently reject school as a proving ground and gain esteem through a group process that sees proficiency at violence as a measure of worth. This means that the youths can garner esteem through a willingness to engage in violent conduct, of which we disapprove.

Violence ranks high among subcultural themes that are deemed maladaptive by society-at-large. One study of subcultures (by Wolfgang and Ferracuti) places this theme center stage by talking of *subcultures of violence*, referring to members who are subculturally linked because they prize violent solutions for a wide range of situations.[4] Violence is said to predominate among indices of esteem because the proficiency that is required in exercising physical violence is commonly available among able-bodied males.[5] When we examine men who repeatedly engage in violence,[6] one type of pattern we encounter is a clear subculture of violence pattern, and it has to do with the conferred obligation to behave violently in support of subcultural goals in exchange for peer admiration.[7]

Subcultural norms, of course, must be translated into motives, then into behavior. Some subculture members are more violent than others because they respond more eagerly—or overeagerly—to prescriptions that place a premium on toughness or pugnaciousness. There are differences in the degree to which these individuals seek subcultural approval and in the extent to which they are attracted to the behavior (demonstrating toughness) that brings approval. The result is that overconformity to violence norms can rarely be ascribed to group norms but must usually be traced to personal dispositions. Such dispositions often represent an exaggerated need for approval as a way of gaining a sense of esteem the person cannot otherwise secure. Given strong enough needs for esteem, this pattern becomes counterproductive in that it inspires resentment, uneasiness, or fear rather than approval from one's audience.

Advertising Toughness

One reliably maladaptive pattern thus involves using violence to stage demonstrations of toughness that are designed to build or cement a reputation. This pattern may or may not secure approval, in that the audience may be real, imaginary, or nonexistent. In either case, the goal of the pattern is to enhance one's sense of esteem under the impression that the criterion one uses (demonstrated toughness) would be impressive to others.[8]

An example of this pattern is provided by a young man who has been involved in a gang war in the community in which one of his opponents is shot. The man's disciplinary record in prison includes many fights and a good deal of resistance to authority.

The first prison incident is another gang fight. In this incident, the inmate finds that he is on the losing end of the fight but refuses to be signed into protective custody. He not only defines himself as resilient but also as a leader of organized resistance. He rallies the troops on his cell gallery by yelling "kill the pigs" and throwing glass jars at officers. In another instance, he is handed a disciplinary notice, castigates the officers and tells them that they are faggots and that they cannot make him conform, and then challenges them to "send me to the box, I don't care." He also repeatedly accuses officers of harassment.

The man does not do better with his counselor. The counselor writes that during an interview, "the resident stood up, read the bulletin board, left to get a drink of water, and informed the counselor that he would be back." The inmate does not come back. In another interview, the inmate spends time "going to the window, looking at the secretaries, checking the wall, etc." and makes fun of the counselor when asked for his plans. He recites, "I want to get involved with the blind and exercise my concerns with the field of humanity, any jobs like that, dealing with the handicapped," adding "let's get down to the dirt, this part interests you the most," referring to his misbehavior record.

The man routinely challenges disciplinary dispositions to which he is subjected. In the last half of his sentence, he even manages to have several judgments rendered in his favor, and some decisions are expunged from his record. However, these victories do not appease him. Toward the end of his sentence, there is a communication in which he ventures the conclusion that the correction officers union is running the prisons and that their goal is the systematic harassment of inmates. He expresses his position by wearing Black Power jewelry. When officers show some interest in this jewelry, altercations result.

In a number of instances, this inmate refuses to appear before adjustment committees or rejects the conclusions of disciplinary panels and engages in argumentative disputes after the hearings. Once, he is transferred to a lower security facility from which he is returned as unsuitable after having staged a series of disciplinary violations. There is, however, also a period of progress that is associated with his attendance in a college program, and the prison sentence ends with a notation that "at the present time, the inmate's institutional behavior has shown marked improvement from the past. He has been counseled to continue this improvement." Another note says: "Contrary to his institutional behavior, he seems to function well in his school assignment, earned his high school diploma, and is involved in the college program."

After his release, the inmate is cited by his parole officer for failing to observe curfew and for changing his residence without permission. His first report in his new term of incarceration covers several months in which there are no disciplinary reports of any kind on file.

The inmate during his younger days had invested considerable effort to build an image designed to cement his reputation among peers. He also gained considerable satisfaction with the rehearsed routines of being a staff resistor, a troublemaker, and a defier of authority, a one-man challenge to the system. He appears to have been deflected from this cause toward the end of his sentence through involvement in education, but at first continues to combine the rewards of academic success with his stance as rebel. There is therefore some indication of a graduated transfer to legitimate opportunity structures as a means to garner esteem, neutralizing a heavy involvement in the illegitimate opportunity system that he had prized when he operated in the community.

West Side Story

We have noted above that in some instances, the link of the subculture to individual maladaptive behavior is direct, in that the person acts—or thinks that he acts—on behalf of his subculture or in defense of its interests.

A second of our "success" stories illustrates this pattern. The man at issue arrived in prison at age 16, after he was involved in gang conflicts in which he stabbed—on one occasion, fatally—members of the opposition. He had also participated in gang rapes and other assaultive offenses, lists his drugs of preference as "heroin, cocaine, marijuana, hashish, acid, pills, glue, and carbona," and confesses to "excessive" use of alcohol.

The man commits his prison violations in the early stages of his sentence. The violations include refusing to work, stealing food, getting drunk, attempting self-mutilation, fighting, "destroying cell equipment" (all of it), and an assault on officers, which earns the man 3 months of segregation and a year's loss of good time.

The assault climaxes a dramatic escalation that has relatively modest origins. An officer describes the incident as follows:

> When the inmate reported to work at approximately 9:10 a.m. I noticed that he had on contraband pants (ones which had been altered), and a headband (allowed only in the recreation areas), and a pair of gloves (leather) which had all of the fingers removed. I told the inmate that he was not allowed to wear these items in the laundry and then sent him by pass to the block to change his clothes. When the inmate appeared back in the laundry at approximately 9:30 a.m. I noticed that he was still wearing the headband and gloves. I then told him that he wouldn't be allowed to work in the laundry unless he was wearing only standard uniform items. At this point another inmate (whom he had brought back from the mess hall) appeared and told this officer that I could not tell the inmate what he could or could not wear. I then asked the other inmate who he was and what he

was doing in the laundry. He stated that it was none of my business who he was and then hollered to the other inmates (in Spanish). I then asked him for his I.D. card and he stated that he didn't have one. I then went to the phone and started to call the gate to get an escort to take the inmate to his cell. The other inmate then came to the phone and tried to rip the wire from it. He then went behind this officer and grabbed me around the neck in a "yoke" hold, then hollered to the inmate, "Hit him. Do you want to hit him? Hit him. Hit him." The inmate then picked up a broom and started toward this officer. I tried to get loose from the hold and another inmate came to help hold me. The inmates pulled me against the front counter of the laundry and the inmate started swinging the broom at me . . . (Reinforcements arrived and) the inmates then let go of me and headed into the laundry corridor . . . An unknown inmate was coming through the corridor and was carrying some broken metal chair pieces. The inmates grabbed the broken pieces of chair and headed toward us . . . They were stopped by other officers.

In explaining this incident, the inmate proclaims that "I have been here for a while, always wore the headband and gloves. No one told me to take them off except when going into mess hall." Eight months later, he becomes similarly indignant because his property has not been expeditiously delivered to him. The explosion that is sparked by his unhappiness results in a charge which reads:

On the above date and time an officer escorted your company to chow, but you refused to go. When the officer returned to the gallery, you had cut yourself and had broken your toilet, sink, chair, and broom which were all still in your cell.

At a later juncture, the inmate is overheard informing a friend, "I've got to take care of business. My two crimees turned states [state's evidence] and I am going to take care of it." This remark is interpreted as a threat, and he is placed in involuntary protective segregation. At some juncture thereafter, however, the inmate undergoes a transmutation, and spends 4 years in confinement with a record that—with one exception—is completely incident-free. The man's reform dates almost precisely to a wedding arranged for him at the prison by the Chaplain's Corps.

After the inmate is married in the prison, he is transferred to an institution where he can receive conjugal visits and take college courses. By this time, he has already obtained a high school certificate while in confinement and has declared that he "feels that he would like to change his previous methods of adjusting, and to change for the better."

The man is at one point referred to mental health staff, depressed because "his wife is having difficulty in the street." In assessing the inmate's psychological adjustment toward the end of this prison term, staff note that "the subject's threshold for control of anxiety appears lower than 'normal'" and that "while the subject shows progress in interpersonal skills, there still are indications that his self-control needs more work."

This man entered prison as a violent gang delinquent who is, in fact, more violent than most violent gang delinquents because he explodes with indignation at the very slightest provocation. The highlight (or lowlight) of the man's prison career replicates his community violence in that he summons members of his gang—including a violent gang leader—when he feels that an officer has affronted him by asking him to take off his gang uniform, and he stages a scene from West Side Story with the officer as target. He also demonstratively explodes and lashes out at everything in sight (including himself) on another occasion when he feels his rights have been violated, and he threatens to avenge his honor, in standard gang fashion, against erstwhile colleagues who he feels have betrayed him.

The man is plausibly transformed when he transfers his loyalty from his peer group to his new wife, and he becomes seriously involved in prison programs, though residues of his volatility remain. In other words, the man has not changed his personality. However, whereas in the past he has engaged in assaultive acts in defense of honor, he now seeks to exert self-control in subservience to his new principles and allegiances.

The Gladiator Syndrome

The clearest nexus between violence and esteem exists when a person prides himself in his violence proficiency and welcomes opportunities that he feels others afford him to engage in aggression that he can justify. In resolving interpersonal problems, the person may react because he sees himself challenged to a duel; he may also resort to violence to impress others with his physical potency.

An example (which is a third success story) is that of an adolescent incarcerated for participation in a robbery while on probation for an earlier robbery. His prison involvements include a great deal of horseplay, a large number of fights, and conflicts with correction officers, though his record somewhat improves in the last months of his sentence.

The man's history suggests that he has a long-term propensity for promoting confrontations. His relatives report that he "constantly picks fights with his siblings" and had been suspended from school "for fighting." At prison intake, he complains that more sophisticated inmates are "bullying him." He is consequently assigned to a company of vulnerable inmates, which he deeply resents, asserting that "he does not like being in a division with homosexuals." He underlines this position by breaking his sink with his bed rails, proclaiming that "if he wasn't moved to 'anywhere' he was going to break his toilet next." When compliance with this request does not follow, the inmate writes to the prison's superintendent threatening that

> if you don't transfer me I'm going to fuck up somebody and break their legs and their back, so I'd appreciate it if you can please transfer me . . . This is a pig division. I hope you know that . . . I don't like this division, so transfer me.

The inmate's communication unsurprisingly does not produce the desired result, so he continues to manifest his disgruntlement, mostly targeted at custodial interventions and those responsible for them. In a typical sequence, the inmate exhorts other inmates in his unit to engage in loud conversation, and when instructed to be quiet he threatens to fight the correction officers. This interaction produces a major disciplinary report, which increases the inmate's displeasure, and 2 hours later he is charged as follows:

> While an officer was releasing you from your cell for keeplock exercise you approached the officer with your right fist clenched and verbally indicated you wanted to fight the officer. At this time you attempted to strike the officer in the face with your fist. In response the officer deflected your blow and physically restrained you while forcing you into your cell . . . Once in your cell you armed yourself with a pen and commenced to attack [another officer]. In response he closed your cell door before you could make contact and stab him.

The inmate spends much time in segregation, where he writes letters to the superintendent of the prison alleging that he is "going crazy" and being starved. The superintendent and other prison staff members suggest that he be transferred. The transfer request is not honored, though, and the inmate becomes involved in a confrontation with a fellow inmate who lays claim to a chair in which the inmate has been sitting. In the course of this argument, the inmate chases his opponent with a board and hits him in the back of the neck, claiming, in justification, proprietary rights to the chair under dispute.

As it happens, the chair incident marks a turning point in the man's history, and thereafter his custodial record improves. He becomes voluntarily involved in group counseling and receives good evaluations from work supervisors. The institution rescinds its transfer requests, and the inmate spends 3 months without disciplinary involvements before he is released.

This man has been a gladiator who stands ready to do combat at the drop of a pin, and he defines fighting as something you do when someone has impugned your honor, challenged you, downgraded you, or subjected you to an affront. The man never feels that he is outclassed, as evidenced by the fact that he tackles correction officers in pugilistic encounters as readily as he does an inmate who dares to lay claim to his chair.

Given the man's outlook, it is doubly humiliating to him to confess that he is being helplessly victimized as he enters prison and to receive a living assignment that stigmatizes him as weak. The intense experience of wounded pride fills the man with rage, but the reaction is short term, and in any event he soon solves the problem by earning a reputation as prison troublemaker. The story ends happily when this campaign subsides. As the inmate settles down, he responds to regular and intensive group counseling and to work assignments he finds congenial, showing maturation, including a tempering of his tendency to fly off the handle when he feels himself aggrieved.

Countering Aspersions

Frequently, the link between esteem and aggression has to do with low rather than high self-esteem, or at least with self-esteem that is laced with doubts, questions, or misgivings. These self-doubts make esteem issues explosive because the person feels that others may disapprove of him, and he becomes upset when he senses evidence of disapproval. In other words, the person easily feels slighted, degraded, or disrespected, which provokes him to expressions of outrage.

This pattern of oversensitivity to affront is illustrated by a man who committed a burglary while on probation for a mugging. His prison problems include fights and assaults, threats against officers, weapons charges, fire settings, and miscellaneous violations such as "refused to return his spoon with his tray," "tampered with his radiator," "had a large amount of garbage in his toilet," "refused to move ahead to keep up with his line in the mess hall," and "failed to obtain a new I.D. card after changing his appearance."

In preparing a presentence report following the man's first conviction, his probation officer writes that "he seems to be held back due to obvious feelings of inadequacy, due to his limited skills and ability to speak English." The next presentence report records:

> He asked his probation officer for help about his drinking problem and was referred to an alcoholism program . . . Probation records verify that the defendant did attend the program . . . He appears to be an inadequate individual who has a great deal of difficulty coping with life.

Several months after the man arrives in prison, he gains visibility by reacting with self-destructive asperity when officers do not expeditiously attend to his wants. He enters the infirmary one morning, for example, suffering from effects of smoke inhalation because he has set his mattress on fire, and presents hand injuries sustained while he "ripped a wooden clothes rack from the wall of his room." He explains to the nurse that "he had informed officers that his ear hurt, and felt it necessary to underline that he 'needed attention for my ear.'" Ten days later the inmate returns with scratches on his forearms, having "cut his arms with a broken lightbulb." The next day the inmate sports innumerable abrasions after "an unsuccessful attempt to assault correction officers."

Later, a progress report notes that the inmate is "currently in special housing serving 200 days . . . for arson, destruction of state property, health and safety hazard, refusing orders, and loud and boisterous conduct. He appears to be in conflict with authority figures." In this report it is also noted that "although there was no indication of psychiatric problems initially, his recent behavior seems to indicate a need for psychiatric help."

In the next prison to which the man is transferred, he files a suit in which he avers that officers "kicked and punched me without provocation . . . smashed my head in against the floor and beat me . . . I vomited blood for approximately two weeks. I suffered bruises and scars over my body, and intense physical and emotional pain." Shortly thereafter, he has a fight in which he "resisted officers who were attempting to restrain him." He explains that he "was extremely angry and did not intentionally break away from the officers or disregard their orders."

The inmate is thereafter transferred to a third prison, where another inmate has to be protected from his attentions. This other inmate "has been threatened by the inmate who has attempted to get inside his cell, to rape him." Six months later the man finally graduates from prison, but his parole has to be rescinded because he "used cocaine, failed to participate in Alcoholics Anonymous meetings, and failed to participate in a residential drug program."

In confinement, the man starts out defining himself as a person in need of and entitled to services. He ends up victimizing vulnerable inmates, but victimizing others is not the man's principal mode of aggression. He is mostly aroused by those whom he thinks have somehow injured his pride, and his reaction includes angry resentment at not being attended to when he feels he needs something, such as attention to a cyst in his ear.

As far as the man is concerned, his exploding is justifiable because he has asked for something (which is demeaning) and has had his request ignored (which is even more demeaning), but the childlike and tantrumlike quality of his demonstrations, including his display of inflicted injuries, raise some possibility in the minds of custodial staff that he may be emotionally disturbed. Because the man regards his explosions as righteous reactions to provocation, he himself dismisses them and centers on the consequences, which he defines as "being beaten up without provocation." This stance (and the man's habit of sullenly disregarding instructions he finds uncongenial) create a communication problem between himself and the prison system.

It is conceivable that the man's limited command of English is somehow related to the fact that he feels the need for physical demonstrations to make himself understood. However, it is equally probable that the man's preferred mode of response when he feels slighted is to express his indignation physically because a verbal response does not adequately communicate the magnitude of the injury he feels.

Disciplinary committees send the man to prison psychiatrists after tantrums, but teachers have already referred him for assistance at age 9 under similar circumstances. Throughout, the man's perspective has disquieting continuity. He says of his early fights that they were products of his "temper." What "temper" means in the man's scheme is that he feels compelled to manifest unrestrained, impulsive aggressivity in the face of perceived injury—which he calls "disrespect."

Preempting Unpopularity

Repeated ratification of low self-esteem produces a related pattern, which is particularly troublesome because it is self-confirming. What the pattern expresses is the expectation of future rejection based on experiences of past rejections. The person reacts to protect what is left of his self-esteem, rejecting anticipated rejectors by treating them with hostility, and he thereby provokes the precise reaction he expects, that is, rejection. The dubious achievement is a worldview in which the reaction of others to one's behavior documents the assumptions that underlie it.

This complex pattern is illustrated in the extended saga of an inmate whose prison transgressions range from minor to major. Minor violations include such things as taking extra cake or an extra pillow, being unclean, being out of place, and arguing. Major violations involve serious fights, harassment of employees, and "promotion of contraband."

The man as a child had suffered severe neglect and abuse, and he had been institutionalized in a variety of settings, from which he habitually absconded. The man's educational career had been similarly unrewarding. Reportedly,

> His school problems included hollering, banging the desk, biting, spitting, and hitting. His teacher resorted to spanking him for every offense, and it was learned that

she had tied him in his chair earlier in the year (first grade). School problems carried over into the foster home where his behavior had been good.

Following a term in a children's home, the inmate was transferred to a state hospital, where he was diagnosed as a sociopath and discharged. He was also evicted from the next institution, which reported that he "started a fire, exposed himself to female staff, showed poor peer interaction and staff rapport, and his academic behavior [had] dropped."

Problems continue after the man is arrested. According to the presentence report,

> The defendant's behavior in the jail has been terrible. He has had conflict with the other prisoners, threw an ashtray at the t.v., and flushed a magazine down the toilet, plugging the drain. He continued to flush the toilet, flooded the cell block, caused water damage to the first floor ceiling . . . The defendant has also set a number of fires in his cell.

A prison sentence follows a review of other options, which at this stage prove nonexistent. In sentencing the inmate, the judge comments:

> Your case does give me some misgivings because a lot of your trouble stems from your unfortunate family background. However . . . the mere fact that you haven't been blessed with parents that really care about you is not going to be your crutch throughout the rest of your life to excuse your criminal conduct . . . At some point while you are still young you are going to have to learn that you're going to have to conform regardless of your background. Therefore, it is the sentence of the court that you be sentenced to [prison] . . . How long you are there will largely be governed by your own conduct. If you go with a chip on your shoulder with the idea of giving them a hard time you are going to receive that back from the authorities. A great measure of your future is going to be determined by your own compliance.

The inmate's "compliance" proves less than desired. Within weeks after the man enters the system, an entry reads:

> He was trying to bum a cigarette and when told by the officer to go to his cell became verbally abusive. He remained angry, so he told his social worker if he didn't get out of here in two weeks he would get out in a pine box.

Three days later the inmate tells the staff that "he was subjected to sodomy and is fearful for his life" and remains apprehensive for the next several days, pleading for a transfer out of the institution. A mental health entry within this period reads:

> Inmate referred to psychiatrist this date . . . caused some disturbance during the night. He makes too many demands on officers and remains bitter and contentious and complains "he takes too much stuff from everybody," indicating a persecution complex. It is his impression he needs to get out of this atmosphere. In the hospital he was kept isolated and says that does not bother him. Stated, "They are trying to subject me to homosexuality," and that about four or five hundred inmates are against him. It seems he is absolutely unrealistic and as a result it is my impression we are dealing with a schizophrenic individual, paranoid type.

The inmate is medicated and sent to a therapeutic milieu, where he is classified as a management problem. A sample entry reads:

> Inmate, after being placed in keeplock for a misbehavior report, became agitated and abusive. He continued to bang on the door and threaten officers and staff. The duty doctor was notified [and] ordered [a tranquilizing injection]. She supervised the injection given by the duty R.N. Inmate was first asked if he would take the injection and he repeatedly refused. Doctors stated the injection

must be given. Myself and officer wrestled inmate to the bed. R.N. on duty gave the first injection. While attempting to give the second injection inmate kicked the nurse in the right knee. Because of the agitated state of this inmate we withdrew from room to prevent further injury to inmate or staff.

Back in the reception center, intake classification staff point out that "obviously what we are dealing with here is not a boy but a byproduct of trauma . . . One cannot be surprised by his current maladjustment." The inmate, however, does not evoke sympathy among other staff. Officers characterize him as "very loud, disrespectful, and indiscrete" and complain that "he doesn't get along with anyone on the gallery and argues with all his peers."

A psychiatrist sees the inmate at this time, and writes:

It seems that a different tack has to be taken with this youngster, and he cannot be reprimanded each time he does something wrong. This is just a continuation of what has happened in the past where he was abused by the parents and as a result had to be in institutions and foster homes all of his life. As a consequence he is living out his resentfulness against his parents and can become hostile and has had to survive the best way he knew how . . . This young man was brought up from keeplock for "fishing." It seems to me that these are all attention getting devices to annoy people as revenge for maltreatment he received in the past.

Although the psychiatrist recommends that the inmate be given "the love and care which every youngster should have," staff find the prescription hard to implement. Three days after the interview with the psychiatrist, the young inmate starts a fight, and it is noted that "when ordered to stop you instead threw your shoes and clothing to the floor." The following day, three more charges are entered. It is alleged in the morning that the man "did refuse to take medication and instead threatened the R.N. with bodily harm." At noon, you destroyed your bedside table, tore up your sheets, broke a total of nine windows, and destroyed your clothing . . . You did attempt to inflict bodily harm on correction personnel by trying to strike them with a sixteen inch iron pipe when they entered your cell, by throwing a steel table against the cell bars and by throwing a lightbulb at the lieutenant. You also attempted to assault said officers by swinging your fists and kicking with your feet, and also by trying to bite any personnel that you could . . . You stated that after you had been released you would return with a gun and kill as many people as you could.

The next day, the inmate caps his previous day's performance with an incident in which it is recorded that "you did destroy your state mattress and started a fire in your cell, thereby endangering the lives of other residents who were housed in the special housing unit area."

The inmate is thereafter assigned to a youth prison, where he is promptly charged with planning an escape. He confesses that he and an associate had "planned to get knives from the mess hall, sharpen them, and use them to take hostages" and that "they planned to hit the officer over the head, tie him up, and take his keys," but "had no way of getting through the front gate unless the officer had left it open." By way of explanation for such plans, the inmate tells the adjustment committee that "the people here don't give him a break and don't like him" and that "he is going to get out of here one way or another." He follows this threat by cutting his forearm and is seen by a psychiatrist, who reviews his unhappy childhood and concludes that "he became very bitter and hostile towards society and toward everyone. At times this includes himself. [He also] tries very seriously to gain attention from others which he needs very badly." The psychiatrist concludes that the inmate "was happy that he was given some attention, telling this examiner his future plans, explaining to this examiner how he will get rich by milking snakes in Florida when he gets a chance." The psychiatrist suggests that the inmate "should be placed in such a division that he will find some understanding from the

officers, from other employees, and even from other inmates." Instead, the inmate faces a term in the segregation
unit and reacts to the prospect with displeasure:

> The officer in charge of SHU [Special Housing Unit]
> phoned and said that the inmate was screaming, yelling,
> and spitting at the officers in SHU. The writer attempted
> to quiet the inmate but he continued to scream, threat-
> ened to kill me and the officers if his gate was opened.
> As this time the entire SHU was in an uproar, with in-
> mates banging on the walls and gates. When the inmate's
> cell was opened he assumed a karate stance and told me
> to come and get him if I wanted to die.

Four days later, the man is assessed $91.10 "because of
destroying a toilet and sink." The psychiatrist who again sees
the inmate acknowledges that "his adjustment to our institution remains deteriorating" and describes a catch-22 situation in which the inmate's experience with the treatment to
which he is subjected makes him bitter, which makes him
obnoxious, which invites further maltreatment. The psychiatrist writes:

> Wherever he went he is always unwanted and unac-
> cepted because of his deep hostility, his strong desire to
> destroy everything, his unbearable attitude, his imma-
> turity, and his constant and limitless attention seeking
> behavior for his dependency needs. This inmate never
> really tried to receive any sincere help from anyone. I
> don't think he will be ready for some time to accept such
> services.

Institution staff finally succeed in having the inmate transferred elsewhere. Before he departs, his counselor interviews
him in the segregation unit where he is serving a 2-month
sentence and writes that the inmate

> appears to be well accustomed to segregation. He ap-
> pears to be making good use of his time via discovery

learning. He appears to be living a "Count of Monte Cristo" type life ... There is much pathos in this case when one takes a macro-view. There is no doubt that from a micro-view he has been a very trying case for the administration. He rationalizes his being confined to the special housing unit as an attempt to secure protective custody, states that he has experienced racial peer pressure on a continuing basis, feels that he would prefer protective custody for 180 days rather than a return to population, states that he does not want a transfer since these problems would surface elsewhere ... The case still does not appear "hopeless."

In the first report filed on the inmate in the institution to which he is sent, his counselor records:

Resident was received and was immediately placed in the SHU to continue serving a sentence of 60 days. A short time after he was released from our SHU he was again held for a superintendent's proceeding for attempted assault on a group of inmates. He received 21 days SHU for that infraction, although while he was serving this 21 days SHU he was again cited for making and exploding a home-made bomb in the SHU. He was ordered to serve another 21 days in the SHU for this infraction ... His last report was for fighting ... It is doubtful if he will be able to adjust at this institution. However, he is being returned to his program at this time.

When the inmate is released from segregation, he signs himself back in, asserting that he "just cannot get along with his peers." The inmate claims that he needs protective segregation because "his life is being threatened" by other inmates. The segregation unit counselor observes that "his personality complex is offensive to his peers, and for this reason he is a constant target of their abuse. His personal hygiene is abominable—he reeks of filth. Actually he is more to be pitied than punished." A week later the same counselor writes:

We again find [the inmate] in the special housing unit as a result of receiving a threatening letter which he himself instigated by allegedly spitting on other residents and writing obscenities to said residents. Intermittently and continually we have endeavored to plead our case with hopes of transferring this individual to a more suitable facility ... Currently we have the individual again in a structured environment where he can or will gain very little. Once again we are appealing for consideration for his transfer to a more suitable facility from which he can enjoy benefits of population.

The inmate is in fact again transferred, and his new counselor writes in the first report on the inmate:

When he is angry he acts out. If he is frustrated he acts out. If he is thwarted he acts out. This leaves him few alternatives to his behavior except to become involved with authority figures. He appears to have related to me in a parent–child fashion ... He drops into my office regularly. He makes minor requests, asks for reassurance, reassures himself and me that he is doing well and is not getting into trouble. He tests me almost continuously to see if I really care about him. To date he is adjusting reasonably well ... He needs a strong parental figure upon whom he can model himself and someone who will be supportive and help him over the rough spots in his life. He will be seen again next week.

Before the week is up, however, the inmate faces a more serious charge because he has been found in possession of torn strips of bedsheeting, road maps of Manhattan, and a piece of pipe, which suggests that he is hatching plans of escape. The inmate claims that "he was being threatened with homosexual acts in population" and "that the contraband in his cell was for protection." A psychologist attempting to test him for the parole board reports:

[The inmate] had become engaged in angry exchanges with several of the Black inmates who were also in special housing. Apparently he had made several racial slurs. He had antagonized the other inmates. Even during the testing session they were shouting and cursing at him. In addition he himself is a difficult subject. He was constantly testing the limits of the examiner, playing with test materials, even after repeated requests to leave them alone. In general he was forcing the examiner to play the authority role.

The examiner also concludes that

> [The inmate's] need for affection is so extreme that he does not even know where to begin looking for it. Almost all persons, especially authority figures, immediately become invested emotionally as love–hate objects that he has to first move towards, then reject before they reject him. During the testing he was constantly provoking the examiner, yet at the same time coming on as a "cute little boy."

At the institution's request, the inmate is sent to another prison at a higher security level. Here he promptly signs himself into protection, claiming that he has not only encountered an enemy but has also made additional enemies by identifying the man to officers in the presence of other inmates, "so now I know I'm in trouble here for sure."

A few months later the inmate is paroled, but a year later he reappears having been arrested in possession of a stolen truck. Classification analysts send him to a special program, where he serves his sentence. Soon after he arrives at this unit, staff record:

> It would appear that there is some hostility and problems between the other inmates and this inmate ... Shortly after his arrival—indeed in the first several weeks—the inmate was involved in a physical altercation with another inmate, apparently over some discussion ... He keeps many inmates away through the use of poor hygiene and his rather obnoxious way of dealing with people.

The inmate also antagonizes the staff, to whom he conveys the impression that he "somehow is doing us a favor for being here." Staff members report that he "informed one of the correction officers that he would not go to the shop at any cost. Nevertheless, he reported to the shop each day since his assertion." As others before them, the staff conclude that the inmate's "rather obnoxious behavior causes people to reject him, and thus he harbors some hostility toward them. This is occasionally evidenced when he chooses to act out this hostility and thus causes further rejection."

The inmate illustrates the process in a sequence that begins when he is charged with failing to get up for breakfast on two consecutive mornings and is penalized because he has ignored prior admonitions. The same afternoon, "the inmate, after receiving the adjustment committee decision went on a rampage slamming furniture, yelling, cursing, threatening, and then giving me a raised finger, hollering '[blank] you.'" The inmate is transferred to a segregation cell, where he "was pounding the walls and screamed obscenities; however, he quickly settled down." He next appears before the adjustment committee to account for his reactions to the last adjustment committee hearing, and he reacts in turn. The charge reads:

> After your recall before the adjustment committee you became verbally abusive toward officers creating a disturbance in the building, and when told to be quiet you refused to do so. You shut the door to your room and continued to be disruptive until you were removed from the building by the sergeant. You further caused a disturbance by banging the gate.

For a brief period, staff think that they note "marginal progress" and specifically observe that "the inmate has shown an increasing ability to get along with the other inmates and has begun to show improved personal hygiene." There are no improvements in the inmate's "ability to get along" with staff, however. On one occasion, he places a stick and an empty can on his cell gate to be "actuated when his room door was opened" and requests an officer to "open the door, causing the noise maker to create a loud noise." On another occasion, he produces two boxes of books to be inventoried by the staff, and a guard reports:

> While talking to the inmate about where and how he got all the books he started telling [another officer] and myself that we had to do things his way. He kept returning to the desk area harassing [us]. I informed the inmate that the sergeant would be through soon and that he could talk to him about the book problem. He still insisted to argue, whereupon I gave the inmate a direct order to leave the desk area. He responded to the order, but not before defiantly looking at me and spitting on the floor in front of the desk.

The inmate also arranges for a second inmate to write a letter claiming to be a witness in possession of evidence that exonerates the inmate in a case he is preparing for appeal.

These incidents cause the man to be segregated, and he spends 2 months "adjusting well" and catching up on his reading. He then returns to his status as marginal program participant with the announcement that "he would change his behavior 'when I want to change, and right now I don't want to change.'" In line with this philosophy, he "seems to become highly defensive when he is confronted in group," which does not stop him from "cross-examining" inmates whose problems are under discussion.

A transmutation occurs a year before the inmate is released. A staff member writes:

> Apparently the pivotal occurrence in persuading the inmate to improve his adjustment occurred when he received word that his appeal had been denied. At that time he probably had to admit to himself that he was not the penultimate jailhouse lawyer he fancied himself to be. His dream of thumbing his nose at the system by being released on appeal was shattered and he was fi-

nally left with the realization that his only chance for release short of maxing out was to improve his overall institutional adjustment. Concurrent with the improvement in his disciplinary record he has improved his participation in group therapy, on his job assignment, in the shop, in the physical education program, and on the building where he houses.

The parole board notes the improvement but opines that "it is too early to determine whether or not you are sincere in your efforts to change your ways." This injunction impresses the inmate, who makes "a somewhat uninspired effort to maintain an acceptable level of participation in the program." But the level of involvement is not sufficient to convince the unit staff, who characterize the inmate as "your basic pain-in-the-neck, immature individual . . . his continuous aggravating behavior is a person you want to grab and shake some sense into."

The man is paroled but returns to prison within 7 months convicted for involvement in the death of a young child. The crime becomes publicized in the prison population, requiring the inmate to shuttle among protection units in search of sanctuary from indignant fellow inmates. This dependent condition does not deter the inmate from conflicts with staff. On one occasion, he pushes an officer to obtain a set of papers the officer is holding. He is also charged with setting a fire, attempting to smuggle items out of the prison, and manufacturing weapons. Such violations, in combination with the inmate's unpopularity among his peers, cause him to gravitate between disciplinary and protective segregation status.

By this time, there is evidence of remarkable consistency in the man's career, which spans three prison terms over 10 years. The decade starts with the man living in fear after he reports that he has been sodomized by other inmates and ends with unsuccessful efforts to find protection from peers who wish him harm. The decade begins with destructive rampages in response to custodial admonitions and ends with the inmate engaged in continued confrontations with officers and other acts of defiance against the custodial regime. There is also consistency in the cycles that characterize this man's interpersonal transactions, in which his confrontative and challenging moves lead to unpopularity, which cements his bitterness and instructs his demeanor. Added consistency becomes obvious when one adds the man's preincarceration history into the equation, which in his case is unavoidable.

Standing Fast

A third pattern that is based on self-doubt is of a different order but is also compensatory, in the sense that the person overreacts so as to keep his vulnerabilities from being exposed. The pattern is one characterized by rigid positions and intransigent stands that are designed to suggest that the person can never be mistaken in judgment, that he is omniscient, steadfastly principled, and infallible. Although the stance prevents people from discovering imperfections, it offends because it impugns the judgments of others and reduces all negotiation to confrontations.

A case in point is that of a heavyset man who shows an affinity for threatening prison personnel, though he is occasionally also involved in fights with other inmates. The man is a mugger who contends that his robbery was justifiable because his victim was a bum. His prison violations have to do with the fact that when he makes trouble (usually loudly) and is taken to account for his behavior, he invariably explodes. As a result, he is not only in hot water for his original violation but has compounded matters to the point where serious repercussions are inevitable.

The man's first prison violation occurs in the intake facility. In this incident, his living unit has been alerted to stand for a count and the man not only obstructs the procedure but "catches a very nasty attitude" when his transgression is brought to his attention. He is written up and, according to the report, "picked up his locker and smashed it against the door and also threw other things in his cell and said 'I'm going to cut my wrists.'" By the time this demonstration is over, the man's cell windows have been destroyed and his footlocker is twisted and broken, and the best he can do is to request a schedule of reimbursement on the installment plan.

The next incident begins with a scene at the commissary window after the inmate has bought ice cream and has been notified that wooden spoons are not available. To this, he reacts by yelling, "If I can't have a wooden spoon, he better take the [blank] ice cream back." An officer reports that

> I showed him our Out of Stock List which plainly states "we have no wooden spoons for ice cream." He then stated "well, he's going to take back the [blank] ice cream."

This monologue draws a sizable group of spectators, and the officer calls for help and suggests to the inmate that he return to his cell, which the inmate repeatedly refuses to do. He ends up taking off his glasses, explaining to the officer "you're not taking me anywhere," a stance which the inmate later describes as "I did refuse to lock in because I was right." The inmate also subsequently suggests that he could not accept the officer's evidence for the unavailability of spoons because he "can't read script writing." A progress report speculates that the inmate "may have a problem with the staff, or has a problem understanding his current predicament." It also concludes that "the resident has had some difficulty adjusting to an authoritarian environment and needs intensive counseling and direction."

Another prison violation is a replay of the by now standard scenario. On this occasion, the inmate is intercepted in a school hallway with the school's copy of *Life* magazine. A teacher writes, "I politely said to him to please never again take a magazine from my class without permission." The teacher repeats this injunction as he and the inmate reenter the classroom. The inmate thereupon

> started losing control and saying that he didn't give a [blank] about the magazine or me and that he better get

out of my class to prevent any trouble, but he didn't. However, he still kept yelling and using obscene language.

The teacher notifies the inmate that he would be subjected to a disciplinary report. He writes that

> upon hearing the word "keeplock" he started threatening me with physical violence and started to take off his shirt. Some of the students in class tried to calm him down. He then started threatening me that sooner or later he would get me. Immediately I went to get an officer to get him out of class. As the officer entered the inmate was losing complete control. His face was getting red and his talking was incoherent. He kept using profanities and adding the word "homosexual."

This incident not only ends the inmate's academic career in the prison but also leads to a request that he be transferred to another prison from which the inmate is eventually paroled after being involved in a number of additional violations.

The inmate does not appear to know the meaning of the word *retreat*. When he has broken a rule or committed a transgression, he regards any injunction or admonition as a reflection on his manhood and a personal challenge. Resistance, however, is unthinkable because prison staff and those of the criminal justice system outnumber him. He is therefore limited to gestures such as taking off his shirt or his glasses, cursing, threatening, and breaking footlockers.

The only question that is hard to resolve is why this individual cannot accommodate the possibility that robbing people or removing magazines from classrooms are actions that one need not bother to defend after one has been caught red-handed and after the prospect of punishment is inevitable. It is not clear what the man cannot assimilate—whether it is the concept that one can do wrong or the possibility that one might accept a sanction or the notion that anything that one decides to do can be subject to interpellation. The most plausible hypothesis is that once this man has embarked on a course of conduct, he feels that it is unreviewable. He functions like a vehicle with no reverse gear and is refractory to information that casts doubt on premises such as "when one wants money one has a right to steal it" and "when somebody sells me ice cream he must give me a spoon." He feels that whatever he does is right because he does it, that no man ever admits that he could have been mistaken or listens to somebody suggesting that he might be mistaken. He also feels that it is embarrassing to be told that you are wrong, that one loses face by permitting oneself to be told that one is wrong, and that it adds injury to insult when the person who has told you that you are wrong then punishes you because you object to being insulted.

Notes

1. Maslow, A. H. (1954). *Motivation and personality*. New York: Harper. Maslow defines as basic needs "the ultimate human goals or desires or needs" (p. 66). By "ultimate," Maslow means that behavior that subserves such needs cannot be tracked to ulterior or "more basic" motives.
2. Lee, A. M. (1945). Levels of culture as levels of social generalization. *American Sociological Review, 10*, 485–495; Gordon, M. M. (1947). The concept of the subculture and its application. *Social Forces*, 40ff.
3. For a discussion of the contraculture concept, see Yinger, M. (1960). Contraculture and subculture. *American Sociological Review, 25*, 625–635. The classic application to delinquency is Cohen, A. K. (1955). *Delinquent boys*. Glencoe, IL: Free Press.
4. Wolfgang, M. E., & Ferracuti, F. (1967). *The subculture of violence: Towards an integrated theory of criminology*. London: Tavistock.
5. Cohen, A. K. (1976). Prison violence: A sociological perspective. In A. K. Cohen, G. F. Cole, & R. G. Bailey (Eds.), *Prison violence*. Lexington, MA: Heath (Lexington Books).
6. Toch (1992), chapter 7, note 2.
7. Ibid., pp. 146–151.
8. Unfortunately, clinical diagnoses do not distinguish between behavior problems that result from impulse-control deficits and those that are compensatorily addressed to issues of self-esteem. Among "associated features" that the *Diagnostic and Statistical Manual of Mental Disorders*

(4th ed.; American Psychiatric Association, 1994) lists for conduct disorders is "self esteem is usually low, though the individual may present an image of toughness" (p. 87). Compensatory behavior related to problems of self-esteem was eloquently highlighted by the psychoanalyst Alfred Adler. See, for instance, Adler, A. (1927). *The practice and theory of individual psychology*. New York: Harcourt.

Chapter

9

Pursuing Autonomy

As we move from childhood to adulthood, we achieve freedom from parental supervision but discover that we must deal with problems our parents have solved on our behalf. A number of the difficulties that arise in adolescence relate to such tradeoffs and have to do with conflicts around the issue of how fast autonomy can be (or ought to be) achieved. Some adolescents, for example, become oversensitive to perceived circumscriptions and restraints while simultaneously demanding childhood-related privileges, such as unconditional support.[1]

Problems of this kind tend to be evanescent, but they are susceptible to recurrence in settings in which authority is exercised, particularly where those who exercise authority also control resources.[2] The problem of autonomy can also remain alive for some individuals and becomes a chronic concern to them; it particularly remains alive where the issue of autonomy–dependence has never been resolved, such as with people for whom autonomy and support have not been available, for whom autonomy has been prematurely forced, or for whom support has been oversupplied.[3]

Reactions that are evoked by autonomy–dependence concerns are maladaptive if they inspire emotionally charged and inappropriate behavior by people who are supervised by others. Settings in which authority is assertively exercised invite autonomy–dependence concerns, and those who operate such settings must take care to draw distinctions between reactions that are proportionate and appropriate, or disproportionate and inappropriate, to the problems posed by their own management styles and patterns of supervision. Supervisors who run authoritarian settings are particularly not entitled to complain of "childlike" reactions of subordinates or to cite such behavior of their subordinates to justify their authoritarian style of supervision.[4] However, there are settings (such as youth prisons) that contain larger-than-usual numbers of individuals for whom authority–dependence issues have been unresolved and who overreact to many situations in which autonomy or dependence is an issue.

The Prodigal Son Syndrome

A maladaptive pattern that authority figures may at times find congenial (though the congeniality reaches diminishing returns) is when a supervised person becomes overdependent on authority figures. Subordinates who take this stance place authorities in the role of parental figures who are prized as advice-givers, dispensers of services, and arrangers of environments.[5] The stance confers expected obligations, however, which often makes the dependent person annoying. At such junctures, the neurotic quality of dependence becomes more obvious, and even the most nurturant authority figures come to see dependent behavior as a symptom of immaturity or resourcelessness, or of personal irresponsibility. Authority figures may also feel themselves manipulated by people who make consistently peremptory demands.

A case in point is that of an offender sentenced for a burglary whose prison misbehavior is largely nonserious. The man is charged with offenses such as "missed chow because he was in the shower room," "yelling and running around his dorm during count," "disruptive and noisy after warning," and "sleeping in the shop after order not to go to sleep." There is also one disciplinary charge of "attempted suicide by hanging."

The inmate has been in prison before, for another burglary, and starts his term belatedly because he has been hospitalized for a suicide attempt while in jail. He has also been a patient in psychiatric settings. In fact, it is recorded that "this inmate has spent ten out of the last twelve years in institutions," which leads prison staff to conclude that "he has never really functioned on the outside and is severely disabled at this point."

The inmate is characterized as "manipulative." An example of his alleged manipulativeness is that during presentence interviews he "admitted to using drugs (various types) and requested placement in a drug program," while at prison intake he "states that he only used drugs on an experimental basis and was attempting to get placed in a drug program rather than go to jail." The conclusion that is drawn is that the inmate either claims or disclaims problems depending on the benefits such claims or disclaimers can produce. However, it is also concluded that the man could be "subject to considerable abuse by other inmates" and therefore requires staff monitoring and attention.

Several incidents continue casting doubts on the seriousness of the man's mental health problems. On one occasion, he is suspected of "actively tactile hallucinating," but it turns out that he "is suffering from a psychosomatic dermatitis superimposed upon which was an unfortunate incident of a bug crawling on him [which] he reported to a physician." For this incident, the man is treated with tranquilizers. In response to a subsequent complaint that he suffers from insomnia, a nurse suggests to other staff that "we give the inmate a placebo with the positive suggestion that if this placebo is too strong for him it will be changed for one less tiring."

Two days after prison entry, the inmate is, however, hospitalized because he reports "ringing in his ears" and "appears acutely depressed," declaring that "I don't want to live. I can't be with people. My nerves are bad. I can't take it any more." Such statements are taken seriously because the man has undertaken two serious suicide attempts and is therefore possibly suicidal. Though retained in the hospital for 2 months, however, the inmate is discharged with the diagnosis "antisocial personality disorder." A week later he is assigned to a special program, where he spends the remainder of his term. Throughout this period, the man vacillates between defining himself as an individual with problems and one who is mentally healthy. When he is denied temporary release consideration, for instance, based on his "history of mental instability," he writes: "I don't have a mental problem. I went to [the prison hospital] because I felt by me going to the hospital it would be a better atmosphere than prison." A month later he tries to hang himself with shoelaces, but thereafter protests that his suicide gesture was not a genuine attempt, "but that he just wanted to manipulate a relocation."

The inmate's living unit staff report that the inmate is "slovenly dressed, withdrawn, childish, and usually resistant to most efforts to communicate with him, whether it be by staff or fellow inmates." In another report, the staff note that "he continues to look like a street urchin out of a Charles Dickens novel."

Midway through the man's stay, the staff write:

> He constantly sits in his own dream world waiting for time to pass. He shows no interest in anyone else, and by his disheveled appearance and lack of motivation has little interest in doing anything for himself. When confronted in a group he verbalizes his dream world of no problems when he is released. He is one of the more remarkable individuals [we have] encountered when it comes to blocking out the real world and the problems he will have to face ... He does as little as possible to pass the day ... In the community he is the local hermit ... [He] spends the majority of time by himself in his room. Psychologically he appears to be somewhat depressed, but other than that he is nothing more than an extremely unmotivated, unrealistic individual. He ... is probably as naive an individual as you can find.

Shortly before the inmate's release, the staff take a dim view of his readiness for release. They complain that "at five feet, six inches tall and probably 130 pounds dripping wet, he wants to be a professional football player" and conclude that "he does not possess the firmest of grasps upon reality and pursues his dreams probably as a way to avoid having to face the hard work and determination he will need to exhibit in order to remain on the street."

When we speak of people who are "institutionalized," we think of an orientation that ties them to an inmate culture and its values. This man is institutionalized in a different sense. He acts beaten down and incapable of functioning autonomously, and he regards institutional staff as benevolent sources of assistance and support. He also feels that the button one must press to mobilize staff includes producing the appropriate self-definition, which consists of the sort of problem or lack of problem that staff use as a criterion for dispensing services. This orientation is unfortunately overladen with the fact that the inmate feels overwhelmed, despondent, impotent, passive, devoid of hope, and occasionally anxious, which means that he does have a problem, though it is the sort of low-key problem that would qualify him as a classic neurotic if he was middle class. However, in the prison, this problem is not a pressing concern of mental health staff.

The reports that cover the later stages of the man's institutional history suggest that he has evolved a strategy for avoiding anxiety, which consists of avoiding reality without resorting to a complete break. He ambles about the prison, spends long periods in the shower room, associates with others as little as he can, neglects his physical care or appearance, and denies or ignores any current or future problems. Of course he has, in fact, no immediate problems, in the sense that the setting in which he resides permits him (reluctantly) to vegetate, but it is clear that as long as this man maintains his way of adjusting to life, he will assume that he must be permitted a passive and isolated existence, that no demands must be made on him, and that his needs must be provided for.

Conditional Dependence

A pattern that is more extreme than chronic dependence is that of conditional dependence, in which the person's behavior becomes congenial or uncongenial depending on whether he is satisfied or dissatisfied with the quality of services he secures. The pattern is extreme on two counts: First, the person makes it obvious through expressed resentments that he regards dependency bids as demand bids and feels entitled to get what he wants; and second, he redefines benefactors as tyrants when they do not comply with his demands and conform with his expectations. The redefinition illustrates the double-edged nature of the dependence–autonomy issue, which makes people in parental roles both prized and resented.

The attitude changes that are characteristic of this pattern are illustrated by a middle-aged inmate convicted of fraudulent use of stolen credit cards. The man starts his prison career with an incident of self-mutilation, but most of his other violations involve threats, abusive language, harassment, and occasionally assaults.

The inmate has a long, checkered, and precocious career as a delinquent and has served time in youth institutions, jails, state prisons, institutions for defective delinquents, federal prisons, and mental hospitals. He was eventually arrested for spending sprees involving stolen credit cards after raising suspicion because of munificent gratuities added to his restaurant bills.

Following his arrest, the man was found mentally incompetent and was sent to a hospital, then escaped from a second hospital after he was found competent, was again found incompetent, and was finally imprisoned after an unsuccessful insanity plea. He is at this juncture described as "a habitual criminal with extensive under-world involvements." The probation officer also records that "the defendant impresses as having low average intelligence but is clever and manipulative" and he adds that "the defendant can feign insanity at will" and is a "dangerous sociopath," who "during a recent prison interview initially appeared resentful of the intrusion, with his eyes popping frog-like out of his head, ultimately adopting an ingratiating stance."

The inmate succeeds in making an unfavorable personal impression on other professional staff. A psychiatrist described him at age 21 as

> an evasive, tricky, abusive, unreliable type who is verbose, untruthful, irritable, and defiant, with temper tantrums. Psychiatrically he is suspicious, argumentative, hostile, a definite chronic recidivist and alcoholic. He is a seriously disturbed psychopath who shows mental confusion and is markedly aggressive and assaultive. He has a cyclic personality which is severely warped and unstable ... [He is a] highly disturbed, unpredictable psychopath.

A first hospital commitment from the prison occurs at a time when commitment procedures were more relaxed than they are today. The commitment document describes the inmate's problem thus:

> He does not respond to discipline, [is] impulsive, doesn't associate too well with other inmates. He is interested in only getting his own way. He is anti-social ... cries readily, wrings hands. He states, "I need psychiatric help." Has a pathetic look to his face.

After the inmate arrives at the hospital, his mother receives "a printed form in which she was requested to permit the administering of electric shock treatments." The man consequently decides that he is not emotionally disturbed, and his lawyer reports that during interviews "his speech was coherent, his reasoning logical, and his memory was excellent." The lawyer also reports that the inmate "has been at times confined with real lunatics who he says imagine themselves to be persons other than themselves" and records that an outside psychiatrist whom he has hired "advises that a continuance of such treatment could actually make the man insane."

The hospital staff, in reply, defend the appropriateness of the inmate's commitment. The director of the institution writes:

> Shortly following his admission he became very sullen, resentful, argumentative, and litigious. He was under a great deal of tension and stated, "I can hardly control myself." He also expressed delusions of persecution, claiming that the correctional and psychiatric personnel with whom he came in contact were discriminating against him. He was also quite aggressive. During his hospital residence he has shown a great deal of hostility, was antagonistic and uncooperative. It has been necessary to place him in isolation at times. He also has a bad habit of teasing some of the other patients.

The inmate is in fact discharged as recovered, however, though he "continues to express ideas of a paranoid coloring, but not to a psychotic degree." Undaunted, he sets out to become a habitual client of psychiatrists in the prison. On one occasion, he requests that the psychiatrist intercede to ensure that his program assignment be left inviolate. On another occasion, he asks for the type of medication he received at the hospital, alleging that he suffers from "nightmares" and "feels tense and nervous." Later, the inmate arranges assignment to an invalid company. Despite this protective assignment, he also manages to accumulate disciplinary violations. On one occasion, he is charged with

> causing a disturbance by running naked on the flats of the north yard. There were about 1,100 inmates in the yard at the time. Your actions were also observed by employees in the administration building. Your actions could have started a major disturbance in the yard. After you were apprehended by the correction officers you continued to drop your trousers in front of the yard inmates, causing further disturbance.

Before the inmate embarks on his next term of incarceration, he throws a crutch at the judge during his trial (he now uses a crutch or cane) and continues to see a psychiatrist for medication he feels he needs to deal with depression and insomnia. Although he has a physical disability he demonstrates that he retains considerable nuisance value. In one incident,

> the officer observed you having an apparent seizure. When placed in a wheel-chair to be taken to the hospital clinic you stated to the officer, "Stay the fuck off our gallery. Leave me the fuck alone, you son of a bitch." You repeated this several times before being taken from the block . . . Due to the hospital staff being in the process of testing [inmates] for T.B. you were ordered to wait in the bullpen. You refused twice to leave and refused a third time when ordered by the sergeant. You then stated that you would return to the block. When the officer tried to push your wheelchair you grabbed the wheels and refused to move.

In another incident, 1 month later,

> you requested from the officer emergency sick call forms. The forms were incomplete and when asked by the officer to complete them you started yelling, "Tell the officer to get me out of this fuckin' cell." While striking the cell door with your cane, you continued yelling, "Get me out of this cell, you fucking asshole." When informed by the officer that you won't be seen by the medical staff until 9 a.m. you stated, "I know it's not your fault, it's that fucking officer. When I go to the hospital I'm going to hit the fucker with my stick." At approximately 9 a.m. on your way to the hospital you passed the console and said to the officer, "When I get back I'm going to give you a good reason to keeplock me."

Despite handicaps, the inmate has developed a propensity for threatening officers and for cursing them in vivid prose that has become legendary in the prison. He also spends a great deal of time complaining that officers are indolent and do not adequately tend to his needs. He complains that officers assigned to his tier at nighttime are excessively noisy and interfere with his sleep. Staff members conclude that the inmate's "ability to relate with staff appears to be marginal," and a counselor relays the consensus of prison personnel "that the subject behaves like a nasty cantankerous old man."

The prevailing impression that the man is a prisoner and has been imprisoned is not shared by the inmate, who regards closed institutions, in which he has spent most of his life, as multiple-service agencies, and he rates them, as one does a hotel, for the quality of the service. He is a discriminating customer, insists on quality for money, and becomes extremely resentful when service falls short of expectations.

The inmate expects mental health staff to furnish him with mood-modulating medication and placements in low-pressure settings. He expects custodial staff to efficiently supply transportation and logistical support and to cater to his physical requirements. As for his mental condition, his diagnosis and status have changed so frequently and he has played so many roles that he finds it at times easy and at other times confusing to classify himself as ill or well and to act accordingly—particularly because his criterion of whether he is ill or well is the consequence of the status for the social welfare and quality of life it offers at the time.

Defying Authority

A pattern that is familiar to prison authorities (as well as to school officials who deal with largely adolescent populations) is one of defiant resentment directed at people who exercise quasi-parental authority. Those who manifest this pattern are described as "having a chip on their shoulder" and sometimes as "troublemakers" who not only show defiance but also recruit others to resist direction and dictates of authority.

As already indicated, one difficulty in reviewing this pattern lies in the need to distinguish legitimate resentment from illegitimate resentment, because only the latter qualifies as maladaptive in the sense of being disproportionate and over-determined. This especially matters because rebelliousness invites repression, which makes challenges of authority almost by definition self-destructive.

One clue to the maladaptiveness of defiance is the promiscuity and chronicity of the reaction. An illustrative case is that of a man serving a sentence for an armed robbery in which he has stolen a car. His disciplinary record is dense during the early years of his confinement and during a period midway in his sentence. Violations become infrequent later; there are no problematic incidents in the last 7 months of the sentence. All of the incidents involve conflicts with staff, and some have to do with riots, disturbances, or strikes.

At intake, the inmate impresses the interviewers as "a dull individual." He rapidly undergoes two transfers through no fault of his own, but the result is that he is removed from an academic program he feels he needs and is assigned to a job that he does not like. The inmate also ends up at a prison where, "because of his young age and small physical stature, he feels intimidated by other inmates in population." He is thereafter sent to a youth prison but is almost immediately removed from this institution as "unsuitable" and "disruptive." He is then sent back to his first prison, and then to another prison, which he decides he detests. A counselor who sees him for an unscheduled interview reports:

> He immediately began to complain about the facility, his assignment, and his pay, demanding that he be transferred. On two or three previous occasions recently he has made similar complaints . . . In today's interview he complained generally that his desires were not being met, stating that we are treating him "like all the rest of these niggers here." He insisted that he be transferred . . . when the counselor refused this request he became very arrogant and hostile. He stated that I should lock him in segregation before he "comes down on somebody."

The psychologist to whom the inmate is referred after this encounter describes him as "very uncooperative." He writes:

[The inmate] is a contentious person who trusts absolutely no one. He claims everyone is watching him ... He is an extremely angry young man. He is isolated and somewhat paranoid. The prognosis for this man's future is that he will probably explode at a guard or another inmate with very little provocation. He needs psychotherapy, and quite soon.

Two months later, the inmate explodes (as predicted) at his supervisors in his mess hall assignment. An officer involved at the inception of this incident reports:

I asked the inmate to serve the bread to the population. The inmate then said, "go fuck yourself," etc., and stated that he would not serve the bread because "it gives him headaches." At this time a fellow inmate who was serving the butter offered to swap jobs to make the inmate happy. This they did. While watching behind the serving line I observed the inmate giving out large sums of butter (much more than allowed). I told the inmate to give out the proper portion and he again stated, "go fuck yourself," and stated that if I did not like it to serve it myself.

The sergeant supervising the mess hall subsequently reports:

The mess hall officer came to me and told me he wanted the inmate locked up for passing out extra butter on the line and that he had told the officer to go fuck himself. I went to the inmate and asked him what he was doing giving out extra butter and talking to an officer that way. He said, "I told him to get out of my face." I told the inmate he was going to keeplock. He said that he wouldn't accept that, and walked out of the kitchen ... I walked over to the inmate and asked him why he was making it harder on himself. He said he wouldn't accept keeplock, that he wanted to go to the box (the segregation unit), where the men were. He went with no problem. When we got over to the unit he refused to bend over and spread his cheeks. He said it was against his religion.

In the segregation unit, the inmate proclaims that he is going on a hunger strike. He indicates that he "is protesting his treatment here, stating that he 'will not be anybody's slave.'" The inmate then reduces his food intake and "advised that he wished to be transferred out of the facility within five days, stating that he would not be alive beyond that time."

The man is indeed transferred, arriving back at his first prison, and almost immediately becomes involved in a group disturbance. At another inmate's direction, he (and four other men) "threw his lunch tray against the wall and then dumped his garbage back on the gallery floor . . . the inmates complained that the hamburger was cold at the noon meal. It was not."

Ten days later, the man's possessions arrive, and while sorting them he "threatened that if any of his property was missing he would fuck up somebody and he didn't care if they wore green or blue. He also refused to sign a disbursement form and deposition of contraband form for property he is not allowed." After the incident, the inmate demands "immediate transfer" but is not transferred. Instead he remains in the prison for another 8 months, does well in his program assignments, and shows "improved behavioral adjustment."

At his next prison, the inmate also does well at work and has no disciplinary problems of consequence for several months, but at the end of this period is removed from the prison because he has become involved in "an unlawful assembly" as a member of a sect. It is reported:

> This unlawful assembly was preplanned and prearranged by the group, and their spokesman stated verbally that the assembly would be held. This direct confrontation was hoped to trigger off even a larger confrontation between employees and other ethnic factions that had been encouraged to join the affair. Fortunately, other inmates used better judgment and avoided the situation.

After the inmate is relocated, he writes letters from his new location alleging that he is being threatened and discriminated against and that his personal property has been impounded. Despite this campaign, his custodial adjustment continues to improve and he becomes eligible for an assignment to a less secure institution. Here he does well for a year, after which he is removed from his work assignment because he resists supervision. At this juncture, it is noted that "his attitude and behavior has been deteriorating" and that he is "resistant to further work assignments." The standoff ends with the inmate demoted to a maximum-security prison, where he objects to what he characterizes as "my mysterious transfer," and writes letters to state officials claiming that he is being subjected to dehumanization and discrimination, "perhaps because of my nationality, ethics, religious and cultural views of life." He also drafts appeals to the administration of the system requesting transfer to a prison closer to his home so that his wife, who has health problems, can visit him.

In the meantime, the inmate does well in school and in program assignments until he decides that his transfer situation has become an emergency. To address this emergency, he goes on another hunger strike, which affects his performance. In response, he is sent to the prison where he started. In this institution he spends 8 months without a single disciplinary incident and is released on parole.

On occasions when this man is at war with the prison system, the battles he fights consist of escalating confrontations. There are two types of such confrontations. In one scenario, the inmate functions as a loyal member of a religious group whose leaders are committed to protest actions and confrontative tactics. The inmate's other campaign is more personal, and this campaign takes a variety of forms. One type of sequence unfolds when the inmate feels he is in an untenable position and has exhausted the procedural remedies for escaping from it. At such junctures, he vigorously demands action and has evolved the gambit of embarking on a hunger strike as a last resort. The man similarly engages in resistance when he finds the supervision at work assignments overly oppressive. His resistance is passive, though in the early phase of his incarceration he often explodes and then follows up his explosions with other forms of protest to underline his grievance.

The man feels himself singled out and persecuted, which not only is congruent with his religious and political views but also buttresses his sense of self-esteem because it implies that he is a political actor whose identity is taken seriously by a system to whom he has advertised his existence through letters and other forms of protest. He maintains his sanity by campaigning but also by settling down and conforming between acts of protest. His repeated transfers, however, make settling down difficult, and the best he can do is to declare a truce whenever he is placed in a prison where he feels that the social milieu and opportunities conform to his predilections and where social movements do not tempt him to join. Ironically, the institution where the man finally settles down is the first prison in which he starts his stormy and cantankerous career, which raises the remote possibility that he might have adjusted to begin with if he had stayed put.

Rejecting Constraints

People who defy authority illustrate the presence of live concerns about autonomy that in some cases are reminiscent of adolescent crises. Developmentally related concerns become particularly explicit in situations that circumscribe or that involve other people instructing one to comply with demands. The motive in such instances is the premise that one cannot be told what to do and what not to do, and the underlying assumption is that an adult ought to be able to determine his or her own course of conduct. If one's course of conduct has been questioned on a number of occasions, the issue can become compounded, and those who object to this person's behavior are reacted to with increased resentment and bitterness.

An instance of this pattern is the career of a man serving the third of three prison terms for drug-related burglaries. The man commits prison violations which are mostly identical. In each case, he refuses to obey instructions of an officer and punctuates his refusal with complaints, abusive language, and threats that attract attention and thus create the possibility of a more widespread disturbance.

The man first arrives in prison and testifies that "he has been using drugs for seven years, using approximately $30 per day." The man also indicates that he has most recently supported himself "by gambling," which is an occupation he enjoys. The probation officer feels that the man is disarmingly honest in describing himself and "seems to have a hopeless attitude about changing his life."

During his first prison stay, the man has accumulated a succession of violations that have a great deal in common. There are charges such as "inmate has to be woke up at least twice each morning and then he is still the last man off the gallery" and "the inmate stated he did not get up on the street and isn't going to change his ways here." There are also other conflicts with officers, such as "disobeying order to remove pasted pictures from cell wall," and

> the officers told him he wasn't entitled to commissary because he was confined to segregation. The inmate used profanity and threats directed toward the officer. He was told he would also be denied exercise due to his threats.

After one such altercation, the inmate assaults an officer and is transferred to a high-security prison. He is also occasionally referred to psychiatrists by the officers, once because they are concerned about his "acting up and destroying the contents of his cell" and on another occasion because he is pummeling a punching bag, "mumbling a name whenever he hit the bag." During this same period, the inmate becomes involved in an art class, from which he is, however, removed because his behavior is "quite erratic" and because "he was becoming a negative influence on other students."

The inmate does well in other academic programs, though his "custodial adjustment remains marginal," a fact that is repeatedly discussed with the inmate by his counselor. The counselor writes:

The resident admits having difficulties communicating with others and this seems to be at least a partial reason for his difficulties with the officers. Although he has a slight tendency to project responsibility for his actions he is aware of his overreaction to situations and has been willing to explore alternatives to this behavior. He is being seen on an ongoing basis to assist him regarding this.

The inmate returns to prison convicted of two burglaries. One of these was a spur-of-the-moment affair prompted by the fact that the inmate encountered an open door while "on his way to the coffee shop next door to have breakfast." A police officer intercepted the inmate with the stolen merchandise and reports that "when the defendant was arrested he said, 'You got me.'" The second incident is less harmoniously resolved, and the inmate is charged with resisting arrest. According the probation officer:

> [The inmate] states that he was using drugs at the time of this offense, was sick and needed money to buy narcotics. He states that he had been drinking as he could only afford to buy wine. He maintains that when he was apprehended by the arresting officer he was assaulted by the officer. He states that the officer stopped him and asked him what was in the box. He states he responded by telling the officer that it was none of his business. He maintains that at this point the officer shoved him. He states he tried to run but was caught. He states the officer then punched him.

During this sentence, the man's prison history is replicated, and one set of charges reads:

> At 7 a.m. an officer awakened you for a count, at which time you told him he didn't have to wake you up in a nasty manner. At 8 a.m. the officer returned to your cell and found you still in bed. He informed you it was time to get ready for your job assignment which was as a porter. At 8:30 a.m. it was necessary to wake you up again. At 9 a.m. you reported to your work assignment

and stated to the officer, "You don't have to wake me up at 7 a.m. for no count. You are harassing me." When the officers gave you two copies of his Notice of Report you threw them out the door through the crack, and told the officer to "Get the fuck away from my cell." After the officer ordered you keeplocked you started yelling in front of other inmates who were standing around listening, "Go fuck yourself, you bastard." The officer has cautioned you previously about reporting to work at 8 a.m. and not starting work until 9 a.m. . . . At 12:35 p.m. when the officer went to feed you, you told him to stop pointing his finger at you and to stop looking at you like he wanted to hit you. You stated to him, "You want to do something about it, come on in my cell any time. I'll take you on, you punk."

The inmate is again transferred to a more substantial prison where he becomes involved in the art program, although he complains that the supplies are inadequate. His disciplinary behavior improves, and he tells his counselor that his problems in his last prison assignment were due to "a personality conflict with a correction officer," though he "does admit to having a poor temper at times, and in hindsight realizes that he could have handled the situation in a more mature manner." The counselor complains, however, that the inmate "does not believe that drugs will be a problem for him in the future," which the counselor feels indicates "that he is not being realistic."

The counselor's assessment proves correct in that the inmate returns several months later, having committed another burglary. The inmate reports that he had been "trying to support himself by selling his paintings on the sidewalk" and points out that "he specializes in seascapes in oils, and portraits in pastels."

During this sentence, the man's difficulties begin in the reception center. The first report reads, "I counseled the inmate yesterday for sleeping through the 7 a.m. count; today he again slept through my 7 a.m. count." A week later another officer complains that the inmate "was sleeping during the 7 a.m. count again. It seems with all the warnings that

the inmate has received about this problem they are not helping." The next morning a report is filed which reads:

> The inmate slept through the 7 a.m. count. I knocked on
> his door and gave him a special invitation to get up but
> he rolled over and returned to sleep. I have counseled
> him verbally on numerous occasions, and last week
> served him with an infraction slip for this very same of-
> fense. The inmate refused the Notice of Report.

Two hours later, another infraction is filed which reads:

> While serving Notice of Report to the inmate for a pre-
> vious offense, he became very abusive. He threw the no-
> tice back at me and said, "Take this fucking thing, you
> punk mother fucker. You mother fuckers are all punks.
> You better keep me locked in this fucking cell, you punk
> mother fucker. You are all just mother fucking punks."
> The inmate kept babbling over and over these and other
> statements while he kicked and banged on the door of
> his cell. The inmate refused the Notice of Report.

The next day another report is filed which reads:

> While witnessing the sergeant counseling the inmate for
> a previous infraction slip, he became very loud and abu-
> sive, stating, "Leave me in my fucking cell you asshole
> mother fuckers. All I want is to do time in my fucking
> cell." The sergeant ordered the inmate repeatedly to be
> seated and to stay quiet. The inmate insisted on causing
> a disturbance, repeating, "All I want is to be left alone
> in my mother fucking cell. If you pig fuckers would leave
> me alone in my cell you could avoid a lot of trouble for
> yourselves. I was sent to do mother fucking time and I
> want to do it my way in my fucking cell. Can't you stu-
> pid asshole mother fuckers understand, in my cell?" The
> inmate was immediately escorted to the Special Housing
> Unit and accommodated with a locked cell.

A sixth report filed later on the same date reads:

> Upon escorting the above inmate to the Special Housing
> Unit [SHU] he remained loud and abusive, stating, "This

bullshit ain't over yet. This fucking box ain't going to change a mother fucking thing. I still gotta do my time and I do my time the hard way." As we were waiting for the key to the SHU gate, inmates from another complex were on reception. The inmate took advantage of this opportunity and began shouting, "We all gotta do something about this mother fucking joint. Us inmates are gonna start running this joint, you'll see, and any police who fuck with us is gonna get it." I ordered the inmate to cease his inciting behavior, as the other inmates were beginning to pay attention to his remarks. At this point the SHU gate was opened and the inmate was escorted to SHU without further altercation.

A similar chain of events occurs several weeks later and culminates in an explosion directed at the adjustment committee. The report which describes this incident records:

After reading charges to the inmate at the adjustment committee he started yelling at the lieutenant, saying, "I'm not standing and putting my light on for the a.m. count for you and anybody else. I ain't putting up with this fucking shit. This court ain't fair anyway." The lieutenant gave the inmate a direct order to calm down and stop yelling, and also reminded the inmate of his whereabouts. The inmate yelled back at the lieutenant saying, "I don't give a fuck. Put me in SHU." The inmate was then handcuffed and escorted to SHU.

The man ends his prison term with "commendations from his work supervisors," which stress that the man "was very cooperative and did not need to be told to carry out his tasks." During this time, however, the inmate has continued to be a discipline problem and "received numerous tickets for refusing direct orders." The inmate acknowledges that he has a "temper," which makes him resistant to people in uniform who impolitely order him about. Obeying the dictates of his nature, this man reacts with outrage when officers interfere with him, trying to impose their will, and his outrage escalates when the same officers threaten him with sanctions for having expressed his justifiable resentments when imposed upon. The man feels that his cell is his castle and that doing time should mean that you can stay in your cell without interference until you are ready to face the day, and that, it being your cell, no one should have the right to intrude with wakeup calls that you have not placed. He particularly feels that he is not a morning person and that it is unnatural for him to stand up and be counted at the crack of dawn in subservience to some arbitrary rule.

Appeals to prison routine or regulations strike the man as irrelevant. Given this view, he classifies his confrontations with officers as "personality conflicts" or at worst as lapses in communication in which he might hypothetically have reacted more politely, thereby reducing the possibility of escalation. In this connection, however, his fatalistic self-conception enters the equation in the form of the "temper," which he feels adds unnecessary color to his language.

The man, in other words, views himself as floating on the tide of his compelling inclinations—which very much include inclinations he feels are less than admirable—and these lead him to drug use, which leads him to crime, which leads him to prison, which leads him to conflicts with officers who are insufficiently understanding of the way he must do time if he is to be true to himself.

The man tells the probation officer who prepared his first presentence report, "ever since I can remember I didn't want to go to school." He also explains that he is responsible for having been barred from a racetrack where he held an enjoyable job, and explains that he "received an undesirable discharge (from the military) for what he referred to as 'being irresponsible.'" The probation officer quotes the inmate as saying, "something must have gone wrong with me in the early stages of my life . . . I need some type of treatment to overcome my addiction to drugs and to help me along with my inadequacy." The man remains philosophical about his "inadequacy" which means that not only must he live with his deficiencies, but so must other people who deal with him.

Rejecting Sanctions

Few experiences are as reminiscent of unwelcome connotations of childhood as the experience of being punished for transgressions. The issue is not merely that punishment is unwelcome, nor is it the presumption that punishments are mostly unjust. A person may deny his culpability with respect to some of his transgressions as a matter of course, but such denials can occur even where culpability is flagrant, and the denials may be designed as pro-forma gestures to salvage one's pride. The concern is with the principle of being apprehended and taken to account when exercising one's god-given right to do what one wants, which is an adult's presumed prerogative.

A person in our sample who exemplifies this pattern is a young man, imprisoned for mugging a resident in the elevator of a housing project. The man's disciplinary record lists a variety of infractions, but most have to do with nonconformity with prison routine compounded by lying, threats against officers, and defiant behavior, including physical assaults on custodial staff members. Examples of chains of events that are recorded in the disciplinary file include:

> After being told not to go to class, the inmate went anyway. He refused to sit down and refused to leave when told to . . . insisted on returning to the class, and refused orders to sit on the bench and wait for his escort . . . Was belligerent and swore at the officer when the officer was escorting the inmate back to the block from the school. Inmate and officer bumped into each other by accident.

> * * *

> The inmate got belligerent toward the officer, ripped his disposition sheet from the adjustment committee and threw it on the floor and refused to pick it up. He told another inmate he should have punched the officer in the face.

> * * *

> The inmate was loitering in the hallway stopping to talk to other inmates. He was warned about this before.

When given Notice of Report, the inmate said that it wasn't his. The officer had to make a call to confirm the name and number.

The man's record includes incidents in which he had been charged with resisting the police. The last such incident immediately preceded his arrest. In this last incident, the man was charged as follows:

Defendant did refuse to move when told to do so by the police officer. Defendant also became loud, using obscene language at the officer and did by said actions cause a large crowd to gather, which caused public alarm and annoyance. Furthermore the defendant did resist arrest as he pushed, shoved, and attempted to kick police officer and his brother officer. Necessary force had to be used to effect arrest.

Several months before this incident, the man had been convicted of an assault. In this encounter, it was alleged that

while in a public place he did become loud and boisterous, and when requested to disperse by the officer who was in uniform, did refuse to do so, and did punch the officer in the face, causing physical injury.

After his last offense, police officers described him as a "real wise ass." His probation officer characterized him as demonstrating "a disregard for authority figures." He also recorded that the man had been discharged from the school system.

The man arrives at the prison reception center with a group of other inmates with whom he has had "a disagreement" in the jail, as a result of which he has been stabbed. His stay in reception is otherwise uneventful but in the prison to which he is assigned the school librarian refers him to an officer assigned to the school for not having his identification card. The officer reports:

I asked the inmate where his I.D. card was and he said he forgot it. I told him he was going to get a ticket and asked him for his name and number. He turned away from the desk and started walking down the hall without answering me. I called to the inmate twice telling him to come back to the desk but both times he ignored me and kept on walking. I got up from the desk and went down the hall and stopped the inmate. I asked him who he thought he was that he didn't have to do what an officer told him to do. He then said "you can't talk to me like that. I'm not a kid. You should talk to me like a man." I then told the inmate to go back to the desk.

When we got back to the desk I called the chart office and asked for the area sergeant to be sent to the building. While waiting for the sergeant I again asked the inmate for his name and number and he said "I'm not going to give you my name until the sergeant gets here." The inmate started talking louder, saying "they want respect from us, but don't give us any. Treat us like kids instead of men. Give us tickets for nothing and then they want respect." I told the inmate to quiet down and sit down at the desk. The inmate refused to sit down and said to me "I'm going to write you up. If you are going to write me up, I'm going to write you up. If you're going to harass me, I'm going to harass you. I want your name and number. What's your name and number?" I gave the inmate a piece of paper to write down my name and told him that I don't have a number.

Two weeks after this incident, a search of the inmate's locker uncovers a pail containing three gallons of homemade wine, which sends the inmate back to the segregation tier. Here it is charged that

during your confinement in the detention unit you forcibly removed the baseboard molding and began beating the radiators in your room. You then refused to comply with the officer's order to stop doing this. When given a second order you still refused to comply.

One consequence of this incident is that the inmate is placed on restrictions, which he ignores. The driver of a prison bus who takes him on an unauthorized expedition to the gymnasium discovers that he is an illegal migrant and reports:

> When I called back to him he yelled "those [blank] idiots don't know anything." He continued ranting and raving and I finally checked his pass. He had the wrong one and got off the bus saying "you're all assholes and none of you know what you're talking about." When he came back on the bus I asked to see his I.D., he kept walking to the rear of the bus saying "I don't have one." I asked him for his I.D. number, he again replied "I don't have one." After the bus started moving he approached me saying that the correction officers in the gym were harassing him and he was not on any restriction. Upon checking this out I discovered he was lying to me. Throughout the bus trip to his unit he continued to complain that these "police were no good" and "the prison was a White prison." After dropping him off at his housing unit I again asked him to get his I.D. and bring it out to me. I held up the bus and waited for his return, and he never came back out.

The prison's experience with the inmate leads to requests that he be transferred to another prison. The inmate joins in this campaign. An example of his contribution occurs after he has been locked up and demands to be let out of his cell because "he is an epileptic and couldn't stay in the cell because it is too stuffy." When officers insist (after consulting a nurse) that there is no connection between the man's alleged epileptic condition and his conditions of confinement, he embarks on a string of obscenities and threatens to destroy his cell, receives a disciplinary report and tears it up, and "said he put in a transfer to go back upstate three weeks ago and that maybe now 'they'll transfer me so I won't have to deal with suck ass police like you.'"

The man is then sent to a maximum-security facility where he continues his refractory involvements. In the most serious of these incidents, the inmate was arguing with an unknown inmate and refused orders to return to the block. The inmate became insolent and struck the officer in the chest with both his hands, pushing him through the bath house door. The inmate then again struck the officer. He returned to the block where the officer found him carrying a broom and threatening the officer with it. When ordered to place his hands on the cell bars for a pat frisk, the inmate turned and swung his fist striking the officer in the shoulder. Force had to be used to subdue him.

This is by far the most volatile and serious incident in this man's checkered career. It is an exception to the man's usual routine, which involves lying, cursing, and threatening but does not include the sort of physical resistance he displays when he is faced with impending arrest in the community.

In the community, the man feels victimized when the police, representing victims of his own actions (to whose fate he is oblivious), place him under arrest. In the prison, he feels that he ought to be permitted to do whatever he feels like doing in defiance of prison rules. When he is caught transgressing, he feels that his self-exonerating lies should be accepted or that he should be able to walk away from the situation in which his transgression has come to light.

He takes all enforcement acts personally. While officers, including custodial officers, think of their uniforms as relevant to their functions and feel that personal involvement is irrelevant, this man interprets every enforcement act as a very personal putdown in which the enforcer plays an illegitimate paternal role and relegates him to the role of a child, which is an affront to his status as an adult male. The game becomes chronic because the man's disregard for anything except his own inclinations places him at continuous risk, in the sense of inviting recriminations and punishments, which he finds demeaning. He goes through life with his hands in every cookie jar and cannot tolerate the parental stance of those whose job it is to protect the cookies.

There is a cognitive and a motivational component to this orientation. The man cannot understand why police officers do not let him escape and why prison guards do not play along with his lies because these officials should realize that they will otherwise interfere with him, which no one has a right to do. He simultaneously explodes with rage when he discovers that authorities can impose their will on him, which he equates with aspersions on his status as an adult autonomous male whose claims and actions are not subject to review.

Notes

1. The diagnostic category that describes this behavior in children is that of oppositional defiant disorder. Part of the *Diagnostic and Statistical Manual of Mental Disorders* (4th ed. [*DSM–IV*]; American Psychiatric Association, 1994) definition of oppositional defiant disorder reads as follows: "The essential feature is a recurrent pattern of negativistic, defiant, disobedient, and hostile behavior toward authority figures." *DSM–IV* notes that "negativistic and defiant behaviors are expressed by persistent stubbornness, resistance to directions, and unwillingness to compromise, give in, and negotiate with adults or peers . . . Usually individuals with this disorder do not regard themselves as oppositional or defiant, but justify their behavior as a response to unreasonable demands or circumstances" (pp. 91–92). *DSM–IV* points out that "there may be a vicious cycle in which parent and child bring out the worst in each other." No equivalent claim is made for institutional staff.
2. McGregor, D. (1960). *The human side of enterprise*. New York: McGraw-Hill; McGregor, D. (1947). Conditions of effective leadership in industrial organization. In E. L. Hartley & T. M. Newcomb (Eds.), *Readings in social psychology*. New York: Holt; Argyris, C. (1957). *Personality and organization*. New York: Harper & Row.
3. Toch, H. (1992). *Living in prison: The ecology of survival*. Washington, DC: American Psychological Association.
4. McGregor (1960) and Argyris (1957), note 2, supra.
5. Szasz, T. (1961). *The myth of mental illness: Foundations of a theory of personal conduct*. New York: Harper & Row; Szasz, T. (1965). *The ethics of psychoanalysis: The theory and method of autonomous psychotherapy*. New York: Basic Books.

10

Seeking Refuge

To cope effectively, one must first face one's problems and decide what to do about them. Reacting to challenges by running from them is a dereliction of appraisal, which is the first step in coping transactions.[1] It can also be dysfunctional behavior, and in some settings, such as prisons, it can be a transgression of rules that prescribe participation.

One reason why retreat from any life situation is maladaptive is that it leads to further retreat, in that the process of giving up reinforces a sense of failure and lowers self-esteem. This relationship is one that we have elsewhere described as a stress-enhancing cycle, which we have summarized as follows:

1. Past successes and failures in dealing with life situations enhance or reduce a person's capacity to respond to stress and to master stress-related problems.
2. A person's successes and failures reflect the person's level of coping skills and the confidence he or she has in his or her coping skills. The latter variable is one's self-confidence or self-esteem.
3. Successes in coping not only cement one's coping skills but build one's self-esteem.
4. Being disabled by stress reduces one's self-esteem and future capacity to cope.

5. Mastering stress enhances one's self-esteem and future capacity to cope.
6. Limited coping skills and low self-esteem tend to be self-perpetuating; so are successful coping skills and high self-esteem.
7. Interventions that help people cope with stress help to break the failure and low self-esteem cycle.[2]

The dictum that prisons are stressful cannot be overestimated. The most obvious prison stressor is the fact that other prisoners who surround the inmate can pose threats to the inmate if he or she is susceptible to intimidation. This threat is tangible because—in male prisons, at least—fear is equated with "weakness," and weakness earns contempt and invites aggression. Predation is selectively aimed at those who are already intimidated and furthers their maladaptation. It means that men whose self-confidence, resilience, and social skills are most limited are put to the heaviest tests, because they are most heavily subjected to harassment. Given this unfortunate paradox, two results can be expected: (a) Self-defined targets often retreat in anticipation of problems with their peers, or (b) such targets may react clumsily and contribute to escalation of their problems and then retreat.

Although retreat and self-stigmatization are not synonymous, a person's request for sanctuary advertises an inability to handle situations that other people (those who do not require sanctuary) can manage unassisted. The initiative places one in a dependant (almost mendicant) role with respect to providers of protection and also implies a contemptuous (passively resistant) posture vis-à-vis those who value—or demand—participation. The combined effect is that one acquires nuisance value to authorities and becomes an object of disdain to peers who place a premium on personal resilience.

A typical career of a refuge seeker is that of a man who enters prison at age 18, explaining that he has "committed burglaries for money to buy marijuana, which he feels should be legalized." He also claims in exoneration "that his drinking problem served to accelerate his periods of wrongdoing."

During intake classification, the man immediately seeks protection, reporting that two other inmates have threatened to rape him. He is still in protection 3 months later, demanding transfer because he is "in constant fear of attacks and even death" and thinks he would like to become involved in an educational program. He has also mobilized his lawyer, who writes to the prison that "I implore you to do what you can before it is too late." The staff meanwhile report that the inmate "stays in his cell most of the time and has very little to do with those who house in his area." They also record that he "is somewhat slow, and seems naive in his interpersonal interactions. He is also oversensitive about sexual attacks, and these factors only exacerbate the problem."

The inmate is transferred to a lower security prison, but here becomes involved in disciplinary incidents. He is dealt with leniently and offered tranquilizing medication. However, he continues to disrupt prison routine and is sent to another institution, where he is discovered involved in narcotics traffic. He is then transferred to a youth prison, where he signs himself into protection after other inmates steal his possessions and threaten to do him "bodily harm." A similar fate befalls him in his next prison, where he is again solicited for sexual favors and placed in protective custody.

The inmate's security level is downgraded at a medium-security institution to which he is assigned. There, he reports that he feels tense and apprehensive and requests "medication for my nerves through the day." A counselor gives the man a lecture on self-control that appears to raise his self-confidence, and for a while the inmate reports no difficulties. He earns a high school diploma and is assigned to a college program. He also receives a large check in settlement of a civil suit arising from an incident in a county jail in which he was raped, and this check is promptly stolen from him by another inmate. This incident leads to another stay in protective segregation because he has named a fellow inmate as a likely suspect. Thereafter, his disciplinary record is again described as "deteriorating" and "horrendous." Supervisors call him "lazy," and the parole board declines to release him because he has made no effort to become involved in alcohol- or drug-related therapy.

Ultimately, this man is transferred to a regular prison. Here he immediately requests protection because he sees himself surrounded by enemies whom he says he recognizes. In protection, he writes letters to the administration complaining about cockroaches and making unwelcome suggestions about needed improvement of conditions in the unit.

The man is transferred to a second protection company, where he is adjudged "conforming" and "cooperative" and rated as demonstrating "favorable overall adjustment." However, he also becomes an informant in a stabbing incident, thereby adding new names to his roster of enemies. He must again be transferred but is eventually paroled.

The parole board complains about the man's failure to participate in alcohol-treatment programs, and this misgiving proves appropriate because he shortly returns to prison after committing more burglaries, preceded by the wholesale consumption of alcohol. This time, the inmate "acknowledges a need for alcohol abuse counseling" in prison. Classification staff also conclude that he "should be seen as vulnerable."

The man has reacted to difficulties in his life by seeking refuge in intoxication. Many of his activities are designed to support his addiction. The man's stance is otherwise passive, and he exudes an air of helplessness, dreaminess, and nervousness and is therefore a ready-made target in settings in which the criterion of vulnerability is susceptibility to intimidation. The situation lends itself to escalation because the more the inmate is threatened, the more nervous, intimidated, and helpless he becomes. His fate is sealed through an extremely traumatic experience in a jail that leaves him in a perpetual state of fear in which he is primed for panic given the slightest cues of danger. These cues are mostly available where the inmate is quartered with more sophisticated peers. This leaves him free to circulate only in the lowest pressure prison environments. In these environments, however, he gravitates in search of drugs or of associates in the addict culture except for one period when he is temporarily distracted by involvement in educational pursuits.

The man's lackadaisical approach to life and his meandering about in low-security settings force the system to upgrade his security classification, which returns him to settings in which his panic button is easily pressed and where he must seek sanctuary in segregation cells. During moments of panic, the man also feels that it is incumbent on him to identify the objects of his fear, which leaves him with the double stigma of being seen as a victim-prone informer.

The most mystifying feature of the inmate's pattern is the fact that despite the disproportionate pain and suffering he experiences in prisons, he continuously arranges for himself to be reincarcerated. One must suspect that his time perspective is infinitesimally short or that his addiction, his need for chemical anesthesia, is preemptive.

Catch 22

One problem with a retreat strategy is that it requires trade-offs, in that a person who separates himself from sources of danger also relinquishes sources of rewards and satisfactions. Protective settings are circumscribing, in that they restrict a person's movement and may increase the level of supervision to which the person is subjected. While a man is consumed with fear, such penalties may seem inconsequential, but with the passage of time, the circumscriptions he has earned as the price of refuge may acquire unwelcome salience.

Some refuge seekers may also regard certain retreat options as preferable to others, depending on the level of amenities they offer and the extent of the tradeoffs they require. The result of such a calculus may be a mixed pattern of conduct, featuring alternating demands for retreat and release or leading to a commute between sanctuaries that variously meet personal specifications.

A case in point is that of a man who has been repeatedly caught in compromising positions with other inmates. His apparent sexual proclivities also color other offenses such as "had a shirt on that had been modified into a feminine garment" and "contraband—nail polish." The man has also been involved in lapses in punctiliousness, such as "has been continually late for his assignment at the tailor shop since he got the job, which then necessitates an escort to bring him up" and "was not with his company when they returned, and was found in the commissary."

This inmate arrives in prison having accumulated a record of convictions for soliciting and female impersonation, shoplifting, indecent dress, disorderly conduct, and similar offenses: It has also been charged that he "did, with his fists, strike a police officer."

Probation staff note that "his IQ had been measured at 72." They point out that "apparently he supported himself by shoplifting and by being a male prostitute ... dresses in women's clothing and considers himself to be female."

Not surprisingly, the inmate spends much time in protective custody. A typical interview in which he requests protection reads:

> He states that on several occasions he has come back to his cell and found notes on his bed which were unsigned. These notes stated in various forms that if he were caught in the right place he would be, as he put it, "iced." The inmate also states that on one occasion when he was on his bed some unidentified inmate threw scalding water on him.

The man's enemies tend to be individuals whose sexual advances he rejects, and there are many such individuals. He insists, however, over staff protests, on signing himself out of protective segregation despite warnings "that there were several inmates in population who were very protective and jealous of him." Problems of jealousy do in fact arise, including a stabbing involving two rivals for the inmate's affections, and he has to return to protection after one inmate tells him he will kill him since "he was doing 'life' and had nothing to lose."

The man is released to the community, but returns to prison. He arrives having experienced difficulties in jail where "another male inmate attempted to assault him." He "indicates that he is interested in studying beautician courses," but his IQ is now measured at 55, reflecting "a potential within the mental defective range," and staff find that "his attention span is very low." Staff also conclude that "his frequent flirtatious advances toward the general population" suggest that he "needs supervision in a structured environment."

The man is therefore assigned to a program for victim-prone inmates, where his programming goal is listed as "dealing appropriately with sexuality in a prison setting, and academic training." Staff write:

> When this resident arrived he ... was constantly seeking support from correction officers and counselors and other correctional staff ... The resident, although still quite insecure, has lessened his dependence and need for verbal support by correctional personnel. Although there have been gains since his arrival, the resident's overall program functioning could still be considered slightly below average. It is, therefore, felt at this time [that the] resident would best benefit by continued participation.

Despite this recommendation, the inmate is transferred out of the unit and accumulates reports "for everything from fighting to homosexual acts," which leads to the conclusion that he "will be unable to function in the mainstream of population in any facility."

A victim-prone unit comes closest to offering this man some possibilities of short-term adjustment without the need for 23-hour-a-day segregation. Long-term solutions, however, are impeded by the man's insistence on a lifestyle that promotes conflicts. Some of the aspirants for his affections are also predatory individuals who back strongly motivated overtures with threats of force that require the inmate to fight uneven battles or to retreat into settings in which he finds insufficient social stimulation.

Staff—particularly during the man's first sentence—are caught in his dilemma because they are responsible for assuring his physical safety. They thereby incur his displeasure because he finds the sanctuaries that staff offer excessively confining, and therefore punitive. Throughout his career, moreover, experiments that increase his degrees of freedom also increase the problems that he generates. Such problems are not only a product of the man's flirtatiousness but also of the fact that his extracurricular activities are his vocation. The exclusivity of this orientation includes a disregard of such inconsequentials as court appearances and prison schedules, and this is one source of his problems. Another is the fact that the man, who is viewed by many as a sex object, in turn views others as objects and (given his intellectual limitations) does not profit from experiences that suggest, among other things, that he has left the minor leagues of crime and is facing encounters involving prospects of violence.

Sheep's Clothing

A person's resilience or "bargaining position" may vary with the setting in which he operates, which means that a person who can meet the challenges posed by one social setting may find himself disadvantaged in another. A person may also react with one type of coping deficit in one setting and show a different style of maladaptation in another.

A dramatic transformation occurs among some men who act as manipulators or become predators when they are surrounded by people weaker than they are but who see themselves as victims and must seek refuge when their peer group contains people stronger than themselves. Such men act the role of sheep (victims) among wolves (predators) but turn out to be sheep in wolves' clothing, and become wolves in sheep's clothing in other milieus. In each setting, these men resonate to power and exploitation, but the role they play with respect to these themes may vary.

A case in point is that of an intellectually challenged child molester whose prison record consists of many inconsequential violations. The record lists offenses such as "suspicion of fighting," "did not turn in sheets," "refused to go to work," "wore civilian shirt to chow," "attempted to mail out a library book," "sleeping after mess callout," "ironing another inmate's pants," "sleeping in room while restricted from going into the room in the daytime," "did not have I.D. card with him," "refused to leave area of officer's desk," "unclean person," and "failed to attend regular gym class."

In the jail, the man has been "raped homosexually" by other inmates. When he arrives in prison, rumors about his child-molesting offense spread in the population, as a result of which he is severely beaten by fellow inmates and must be placed in protective segregation.

The man is sent to a medium-security institution, where he is struck in the face by an inmate who objects to his crime. He also complains that "I am harassed in the mess hall at all meals. I don't feel safe anywhere now. It will be worse now that I told you who hit me. I need protection." The man is permitted to remain segregated for several weeks and is medicated for depression and anxiety, and when he recovers is assigned to a therapeutic community program. In their first report about the inmate, staff write:

> He began his involvement with individual therapy and recreational therapy. It was readily apparent that he did not possess the necessary coping skills required to make it in prison, especially in light of the nature of his present offense. In addition, because of his borderline mental retardation, his ability to function in the program was initially questionable ... He is quite immature and requires a great deal of attention. In striving for the attention, though, he is often quite ill prepared for some of the heavy stuff that goes along with it.

As an example of the "heavy stuff" referred to in the report, the inmate complains that he is the object of sexual advances and of extortion efforts and that he is being beaten by other inmates, but investigation reveals that

> he has tried to be "slick" by running to several inmates stirring things up and then playing dumb. He has also

been involved in selling and/or exchanging articles with other inmates. While involving himself in these activities he thinks he is pretty sharp. However, more times than not the weight eventually falls back on him. In fact, as a result of his "games" he found himself in a bad position, and since he could no longer handle the pressures that went along with the games he requested protective custody under the guise of being sexually harassed by another inmate in his dorm ... His prognosis is poor, but where else would his behavior be tolerated?

After the inmate has spent a year in the program, staff write that "he has shown virtually no growth, nor has he given any indication that he really comprehends his behavior," although "the members of his therapy group, inmate counselors, and staff have devoted a great deal of time and energy into trying to get him to understand his behavior as it relates to his crime as well as his negative nonproductive behavior while incarcerated." The inmate is described as offering "the minimum degree of participation in order to avoid hassles," but there is a suggestion that the man's nonparticipation may be a blessing, given that "he'll give 'tough guy' responses, making a fool of himself when he participates."

Custodially, the inmate accumulates difficulties as a result of the number of infractions he commits and their redundancy. He is repeatedly charged with entering the rooms of other inmates, though he has been admonished for violations of the same kind. He also occasionally threatens the officers who serve him with reports. In one such sequence, he is charged as follows:

> Following the incident you were advised that you would receive a report of misbehavior as a result, and you then stated to another officer that you were going to take care of the officer who wrote you up. When questioned you said you would catch him unaware and take him off the count. When you appeared before the adjustment committee you admitted the threat and stated at that time that you were making plans on how you were going to do it and that you intended to get these officers.

Program staff write that the inmate "seems to be digging himself further and further into a hole ... It was almost as if he was deliberately putting himself in the jackpot." Staff also write:

> Most of the other men are totally discouraged in their efforts to help this inmate. Nothing seems to sink into his head. This is perhaps because he rarely listens to what is being said, and why should he when he already has very concrete responses to offer?

A recurrent difficulty experienced by this inmate is that he tries to manipulate more sophisticated inmates and that these efforts "usually turn disastrous for him." However, the man mostly appears unaware of his difficulties and in fact "is not concerned about the possible problems he may encounter when returned to general population confinement resulting from his interactions with other inmates, despite the efforts of group members on this topic."

The inmate solves part of his problem by gravitating toward peers who do not outclass him. Program staff describe this pattern in a report filed late in the man's sentence. They write:

> He associates solely with a group of individuals who have similar crimes and are viewed by staff and everyone else for that matter as immature, weak, manipulative and victim-prone to aggressive homosexuals. The constant conflicts within this group of individuals and with those inmates trying to take advantage of them produce the need for frequent interventions by staff to resolve these problems. Usually right in the middle of these conflicts is our subject. Despite being labeled as weak when compared with the majority of inmates, within his group of associates he is seen as the manipulator and orchestrator of many of their conflicts.

The inmate extends his catalytic activities to staff and writes a letter to prison officials complaining about an officer who he alleges has subjected him to a systematic beating. In a report about the inmate, program staff write that he is "mendacious in his relations with fellow inmates and staff." They deduce that he "sees the world as a very frightening place where he must scratch out a survival through any means available to avoid being taken advantage of." Elsewhere they speculate that the man "sees the world as a very frightening place where the strong take advantage of the weak," which means that he will "take advantage of those who are weaker than himself, which is a basic description of his present crime."

The other side of the coin is that the man has accumulated considerable experience as one of the "weak" who are taken advantage of in the community—where he has been beaten by an alcoholic father—and in detention, where he has been raped and assaulted. But the man does not define himself as resourceless, because he does not see himself as weak and therefore does not draw the inferences one would expect from a lifetime of victimization experiences. In fact, the man even turns victimization experiences to advantage by claiming that he is victimized when he is not, so as to arrange for himself to be extricated from delicate interpersonal transactions. Mostly, the man draws the surprising inference that is delineated by his therapists, which is that there must be others weaker than himself whom he can victimize. In this connection the man is mostly wrong, including in his assessment of 7-year-old children who describe his overtures (in considerable detail) to their parents.

The limitations of intellect chronicled for this man prominently center on his failure to digest the debacles he arranges for himself. One example is the disquieting redundancy of his disciplinary violations, which adjustment committees classify as stubborn recalcitrance. Beyond this penchant for redundant self-destructiveness lies the possibility that the man may be unconsciously identifying with the aggressors of this world, whom he sees as the only show in town. The man frustrates would-be therapists who want to uncover the ugliness of his victimization game (very much including child molesting) because he can conceive of no other game and can adduce a lifetime of documentation for his position. His own goal becomes one of making sure that he does not consistently lose the game, which is the only game he knows, and this means that he occasionally must play some other role than that of victim. Unfortunately, he makes a very unconvincing aggressor and a clumsy, inefficient manipulator.

Having One's Bluff Called

Transformations of maladaptive strategies can result where the failure of one strategy requires recourse to another. One such juncture occurs when a stance of defiance or of toughness is tested against reality, and the person who has billed himself as pugnacious or rebellious encounters determined opposition and finds that he must seek refuge to escape it. Where this kind of transformation occurs, one possible inference is that the person's stance has all along been a facade designed to disguise a substratum of insecurity or is a means of overcompensating where the person feels inadequate or afraid.

An example of the pattern is provided by a man who has snatched a woman's purse after punching her in the neck. For this offense, the man spends a short time in prison during which he has fights, threatens, and harasses correction officers and distinguishes himself for the use of loud and obscene language.

At the time he is arrested, the man has been a client of a counseling program and tells his probation officer that the counseling "had been helpful regarding a problem he had with fighting" and "that he had problems in the jail because others wanted to fight and he doesn't."

At prison entry, the man's IQ is registered at 80. Intake analysts write:

> The inmate was basically cooperative and tries very hard to make a favorable impression but appears to be very emotionally immature, easily influenced by others, and shows little motivation to change his lifestyle. He can

display a hostile attitude, desires his own way whenever possible, [and] finds constructive criticism hard to accept.

The man is assigned to a youth prison, where he accumulates misbehavior reports for disobeying orders. In a sample incident, he is charged as follows:

> At approximately 5:10 a.m. you were told several times by a correction officer to stop talking from your gate and remove yourself from the gate. You ignored his orders by constantly talking louder ... You consistently yelled obscenities at the officer ["fuck you, you can't tell me what to do"]—and [proclaimed] that you are not afraid of the officers or the lieutenant.

Institution staff conclude that the inmate's attitude toward authority is that of a juvenile who "will not admit he could be wrong. He is very defiant, blames others for his actions, says he will not change, and is willing to do his time." They test the inmate's resolve by changing his living assignment to "give him a chance to be away from the officers who he claims do not get along with him," but this strategy does not improve the man's deportment.

Eventually the inmate is released from prison and commits two robberies—both involving female pedestrians. He admits that "he obtained his spending money by robbing women" and boasts that he "smoked marijuana as often as he could get the money to buy."

When the man reenters prison, an interviewer notes scratch marks on his left forearm, which he "indicates was an attempt by him to change housing locations while incarcerated at the jail." The low-security prison to which he is sent to start with feels unable to accommodate him because "he is very aggressive, constantly challenging authority, [and] this behavior can't be tolerated in our dormitory setting." In an incident of the kind referred to, the man shouts at another inmate who is taking a shower and then refuses to leave the bathroom, inviting the officer to a sexual encounter. He later writes a letter insisting that his transfer from the prison was unfair because he is not in fact "a ballbuster." The following week, however, staff report that he "had in his possession a fifteen-inch metal rod which was sharpened to a point." While in segregation for this offense, the inmate is again written up for "talking through the window in the keeplock yard," and a search of his cell uncovers "what appeared to be a firebomb" and, 3 days later, "a metal rod approximately 18 inches long with one end sharpened to a point and the handle taped."

Subsequently, the man becomes involved in two fights but requests protective custody after officers have concluded that a weapon and a fire in the inmate's cell "were a setup" engineered by enemies, who by this time have multiplied. The man is therefore transferred to still another prison, where he participates in a behavior modification therapy program. His behavior does improve but he must be protected once again because fellow inmates attack him in the yard, inflicting "facial bruises and lacerations." Thereafter the man is classified as "victim-prone," though he now "gets along well with staff" and is "respectful of rules." The man's disciplinary record, in fact, becomes exemplary, except for an incident in which he is apprehended in sexual contact with another inmate, which is interpreted as illustrative of his susceptibility to victimization.

The man has entered the system taking a stance of adolescent rebelliousness, advertising that he resents circumscriptions of his autonomy. He also does a lot of loud, aggressive, and demonstrative socializing, which occasionally degenerates into fighting given that he wants to project the image of a tough delinquent who can handle himself in conflicts. Unfortunately, building this image includes having weapons, which is probably routine for this man in the community. He also does not project his image convincingly, and his problems with both authority figures and peers soon force him to discontinue the effort to project an image of toughness, particularly in a nonadolescent population in which others see through his facade and discover that he is a very young, very vulnerable, and very inadequate person whose intellectual limitations make him socially inept and consequently susceptible to intimidation. The change in the man's status in this peer hierarchy changes his stance toward staff, whom he now regards as benevolent protectors, and who reciprocate by treating him with solicitude.

Turned Tables

Other transformations occur where predatory propensities boomerang and the bully or predator must seek refuge because his bullying or predation has backfired. A combination of antisocial dispositions and maladroitness may provoke retaliatory reactions. The person may view these repercussions as unprovoked threats and may eventually come to present himself as perennial victim, ignoring all contributions he has made to instigating his fate.

An example of this pattern is a man who serves a prison sentence for a rape. In prison he becomes involved in fights, which include attacks on other inmates with urine, water, and more conventional weapons. He also threatens officers. There are entries such as "threatens officer with obscene names," "threatened officer because he was not allowed to enter auditorium," and "when instructed to remove clothing from bars he threatened me and didn't move anything." In addition, he resists authority in more passive ways and is charged with such actions as "refused to leave kitchen area when told to because he wasn't doing any work at the time," "refused to go to shop," "refused to return to area when ordered by officer," "refused to break when ordered," and "did not lock in properly when returning from school program."

One of the first problems the man encounters in prison is that he meets the husband of one of his rape victims. Authorities reassign him to protect him, placing him in a special program from which he demands to be removed, claiming that he does not need therapy and that the unit "is causing me trouble with the other inmates." The man does not need help, as it happens, in engendering "trouble." One inmate who has a fight with him reports:

> He called me a snitch during the community meeting. Later he opened his pants and told me to suck his dick and he said he was going to fuck my mom. I went up to him by his cube and told him to shut his fucking mouth: "I don't want to hear you say that again." He said, "Come on, punk" and took a swing at me. I ducked and swung back at him. The officer yelled, "Break" and I stopped, and he hit me in the eye.

It is more than obvious that the man goes out of his way to promote such encounters. It is reported at one juncture that:

> during a community meeting he stated to everyone (50 inmates, 8 staff personnel) that he would "cut" anyone and he didn't care who he hurt. The same day he was involved in a fight with an inmate causing physical harm to the inmate. It is suggested that a sharp instrument, possibly a razor blade, was used by him to cause injuries to the other inmate. He stated on numerous occasions that he would do anything to get out of the program, including hurting people.

The man not only attacks other inmates but also promotes incidents with prison personnel. One officer complains:

> I was threatened on the gallery by the inmate. The inmate said, "I'm gonna get you. I'm gonna kill your fag ass. That's a promise." He then stated, "I got all the weapons I need to do it right here in my cell." At this point the inmate quickly flashed a metal object at me. I ordered him to give it to me and he refused ... The inmate's cell was frisked and one metal can crushed and formed into a weapon was removed.

Another officer reports:

> While feeding up the keeplock inmates ... the inmate said to me when I gave him his tray, "Why are you giving me that tray?" I then told him there was no special reason. The inmate then yelled, "Ya, I bet you, fucking

fag." I then told him he just got a misbehavior report. He just said, "Good, give me one, you fucking fag. I'll make sure I get you when I get out of this cell."

The staff of the special program reciprocate the inmate's feelings about his participation in the program. In one report, staff writes:

> Although he is twenty-six years old chronologically he impresses as one to be about twelve years old mentally, which is stretching things. Although there is no hard evidence to prove homosexual tendencies, it has been rumored that he indeed made efforts to overpower weaker members of the community for sexual purposes. This writer has not been able to ascertain any feelings of remorse for past deeds committed by the inmate either while in or out of correctional facilities. The inmate has not benefited from the therapeutic environment nor does it seem likely that he will do so if he were to remain. Since he has been one of the more disruptive participants it is felt that he should be transferred at this time.

The inmate is demoted to the introductory segment of the program, where staff write:

> No matter how many times he is told something it is guaranteed that two days later he will again bring up the same question. The subject has received an inordinate amount of individual attention since being returned to phase one and the results are simply nil ... He is demanding, childish, and aggressive toward weaker inmates. It is the writer's opinion that the subject lacks sufficient capacity to understand the complexities of relating to people or to adjust successfully to different situations ... His former therapist has been directed to submit a transfer. Wherever the subject is transferred he should be kept in a controlled environment.

In his next prison, the man continues to assault other inmates and to threaten staff. In one incident, for example, "the inmate had a choke hold on [another inmate] and they were separated with great difficulty." On another occasion, "the inmate caused a disturbance in the kitchen when told to put back sugar he had stolen from the line, and several times refused to obey an order to go to his cell, all the while verbally abusing and threatening the officer."

The man's counselor writes after a period of time that the inmate "has many enemies here" and a transfer therefore has to be effected. In his next institution, the man formally requests protective custody, claiming that difficulties have developed between himself and a gang to which he has belonged (the Five Per Centers), and that a representative of this group "is trying to establish a reputation" by assassinating him. After the inmate is released from protection, however, an investigation shows that he is threatening other inmates, spreading rumors and initiating strongarming efforts. The investigating sergeant reports:

> [One inmate] stated that the inmate keeps telling other inmates on the gallery that he is a fag and also that [another inmate] is his homo. I also received word from [a third inmate] that the inmate wants commissary for homosexual favors from him or he will stab him . . . He has threatened several inmates and officers [and I] believe he extorts or tries to extort other inmates on a regular basis.

Several days later, the inmate receives an anonymous note which tells him that "you might as well pack your shit up, punk, because you will be leaving tomorrow" and he becomes apprehensive. An officer reports:

> He said he wanted to leave the company and he wanted to leave now. I told him I would call the sergeant. When I left to use the phone, the inmate broke his sink and toilet.

The man is later moved and stages another demonstration, pointing out that "he had told the officers to move him because his cell was flooded."

He is transferred to another prison where he spends time in protection, but he is returned to disciplinary segregation after he becomes involved in a fight in which he takes an officer's baton and swings the baton, striking the officer in the shoulder. Three months later, he is briefly released to the community but comes back to be retained to his maximum expiration date. He promptly demands protection again, claiming that the entire membership of his former gang is pursuing him because "the word got out that he snitched on them." He asserts that "they have been pointing fingers at him and he knows they will be coming after him." He also indicates that "he asked his paint shop teacher to lock him up for refusing program in order to get out of population."

The last entry in the file reports another incident:

> During [my] rounds the inmate asked to speak to a ser-geant. I informed the inmate he could speak to a sergeant when he comes on the unit. Approximately at 7:40 a.m. the inmate started breaking up his cell, throwing his metal locker against the bars and all walls. The inmate also broke the sink off the wall into several pieces.

The disciplinary committee insightfully notes that the inmate "seems to feel his request to see the sergeant did in itself justify his behavior." The committee adds that the inmate "refused to sign his admission of guilt and also refused to sign a disbursement request to cover the cost of the property destroyed by himself."

The fact that the inmate "seems to feel his request to see the sergeant did in itself justify his behavior" is symptomatic of his perspective. The man feels he is entitled to announce that he will use violence and to then deploy violence to get what he wants, especially from people who are susceptible to intimidation, such as women and nonaggressive peers. Ironically, prison staff fit into the vulnerable category because (a) constraints under which they labor make it impossible for them to call the man's public bluff and (b) staff must maintain safe prisons, which means that they must remove individuals who are sources of problems from one prison and transfer them to another. The second fact is particularly germane to this man, because it means that he can extricate himself from difficulties he engenders by staging demonstrations that force staff to get him out of corners while preserving his self-image. He wants to be viewed as an aggressor (which he thinks is manly) rather than as a victim (which he feels is unmanly). The same view permeates the man's homosexual encounters in which, given the fact that he is an intimidator and aggressor, he can argue he is staging demonstrations of manliness, which makes his prison homosexual involvement and his rapes equivalent.

One fly in the ointment is that the man on occasion misdiagnoses his victims or underrates their support and now knows himself, or thinks himself, in danger, an issue to which he is extrasensitive given his familiarity with threat and violence. At junctures such as these, he is not above informing on his enemies and invoking staff as protectors, but he can salve his ego by breaking up his cell when pleas for sanctuary are not promptly attended to. This means that the man can define himself as a practitioner of violence even when he is engaged in ignominious flight or in search of protection.

Violence for this man is a tool that the strong use against the weak to secure compliance. What the man must struggle with is that he himself is susceptible to intimidation. A formula he has evolved is that he can use violence to extricate himself from the threat of violence, which, given his primitive view of the world, means that he is still being effective, meaning that he has done a lot of hollering over his shoulder as he retreats.

Earned Rejection

Deficient social skills can translate into victimization because of the unpopularity a person can garner by subjecting others to inappropriate responses. In patterns of this kind, refuge-seeking is a corollary of aversive impact rather than of an antisocial disposition. The person involved in such a sequence usually is well intentioned and may in fact seek friendship or other positive reactions from peers when he earns their threatening responses. A sad transformation occurs, however, in that the person who has unsuccessfully tried to negotiate a social milieu must then retreat from the setting and seek self-insulation.

An inmate who illustrates this pattern is 17 years old when he arrives in prison, having injured a citizen while escaping the police. At intake into prison, the inmate is described as intellectually and educationally deprived as well as emotionally unstable. The evaluation form records that "he admits attempting suicide several times while at the detention facility, claims he was sodomized there and preferred charges"; officially the man's jail status has been "under close observation with suicidal precautions."

The inmate soon finds himself in protective segregation. It develops, according to a counselor, that

> he made the serious mistake of revealing the good fortune of an accident settlement. His "friends" have offered him their services as body guards and "what have you" for the "nominal" figure of a $100 weekly. When he expressed disinterest and disdain for their extortion, he alleges he was threatened by "his friends" that he "better comply or else."

The classifier records the impression that the inmate "is a dolt. He doesn't know 'come here, from sic em' and has a big mouth and ingratiating personality, all of which is capped by gross immaturity." This assessment leads the counselor to the conclusion that the inmate "can't function in population, and in essence just can't function." Some form of protection is therefore recommended.

It soon develops that the inmate cannot even cope with socially disadvantaged inmates in a protection program. He asks for a transfer, a request which the staff enthusiastically endorse. In the next prison to which he is assigned, he again requests protection, reporting that his fellow inmates began to pressure him for goods. He refused to give in, and so these other inmates began to spread the word that he was a homo and also made threats on his life.

The staff conclude that there have in fact been no attempts at extortion or threats and refuse to put the inmate in protection. Subsequently, however, staff change their minds after the man has a fight in which he attacks a would-be extortionist. He explains to the officers:

The White guys want nothing to do with me. They won't let me on the court or hang out with them because I have let this guy get over on me and I haven't done anything about it.

Unfortunately, the inmate chooses the mess hall for his redemptive fight, which from the staff's point of view is the worst place in the prison for a demonstration match to be staged, because of the presence of three hundred excitable spectators. In the transfer request that follows, staff note that the inmate is an "extremely immature and irresponsible individual who by his actions is capable of causing serious problems between himself and other inmates," and write that the inmate not only cannot manage in general population but "of late cannot interact with the others assigned to the protection company." A later entry shows that the man has been successfully pressured by his fellow inmates, who have expropriated his tape player and other possessions.

There follow a series of incidents that involve correction officers. One officer accuses the inmate of having said that he was "going to cut up if I didn't get a sergeant and bring [him] to observation." The officer charges the inmate as follows:

The officer stated that observation was filled up, and you then grabbed your razor blade and told the officer that you were going to cut up. The officer ordered you to put your razor blade back into your locker. You refused to comply with this order and pulled your razor down your

left arm two or three times. The officer ordered you several times to stop and you refused to comply with the
orders. You then took the razor handle and began digging at the cut attempting to make it bleed.

The inmate has become desperate with his situation and
with the pressures exerted on him. Having failed to secure
escape from his dilemma by injuring his arm, he tries other
measures such as kicking his door, throwing his food on the
floor, and throwing toilet paper into the hallway. He also
wrecks his cell and spits on passing officers, testifying that
"I had to get off the tier because I was being harassed. So
much pressure on me, and my life was threatened."
  The inmate next arrives in another facility where he is in
a rage because he is taken to the hospital, and reacts by attacking a nurse and making a scene. He also complains that
he is harassed by officers.
  This man makes enemies of even relatively weak peers,
and antagonizes staff with a combination of excessive dependency and refusals to comply with the protective measures
they take. He oscillates between demands that he be protected and demands that he be extricated from protective settings. These demands are punctuated by dramatic physical
gestures such as self-injury and destruction of furnishings
because he lacks the ability to make his communications convincing, given his lack of verbal skills and social graces. The
most extreme problem the man has is that he does not show
his anxiety directly but manifests it in either fight or flight
terms. The very offense for which he is in prison consists of
a blind flight from a police encounter. The consequence of
this flight is an example of the corners he gets into both in
prison and in life through clumsy maladaptive behavior,
which leads to the need for equally clumsy retreats.

Stress Avoidance

A special case of refuge seeking is the desire to experience
less social stimulation and to gain relief in isolated settings.

The issue here is not to escape danger but to diminish the travails of ordinary living. The person seeks refuge because he finds social situations overwhelming and confusing to him. The person may also experience fear, but fear is apprehension of people in general rather than of people who are concrete sources of danger.

A man who exemplifies this pattern serves a sentence for burglarizing the business of a former employer. His most serious prison infraction centers on the manufacture of wine, but his most frequent difficulties involve attempts at self-mutilation.

One factor that shortens this inmate's prison term is the fact that he has served as a police informant and supplied "information which has resulted in three misdemeanor convictions and one felony conviction." Otherwise the man has not done well. He has ended his educational career after he "dropped three of his subjects and failed the other two that he was carrying," and his military career has lasted for all of 2 weeks, after which he was discharged as "unable to adapt to military life." He also reports that he "has experimented with various drugs, and has used alcohol, sometimes heavily, and was drinking quite heavily on the night of his offense."

When the man arrives in prison, he quickly incurs charges of self-mutilation, abusive language, and refusing to go to meals. He explains his self-injury attempt by saying that "he was upset by pressure other inmates were giving him." He is consequently transferred to a lower security institution, where a search of his cell yields a large amount of yeast, two eggs, sugar, and assorted containers (a large jar, a pitcher, and a cup) that smell of home brew. The offense is aggravated, in that the inmate has stolen the ingredients for his concoction from the institutional bakery where he is employed. He does not deny this transgression, reporting that "I was making the booze for myself and friends, mostly friends."

The man is then involved in repeated self-destructive acts and is sent to an institution where mental health services are available. He stays for a while in the mental health unit, refuses to enter population, and "after much discussion requested protective custody and wished to remain there until his parole release." These wishes are respected, given the "various suicide attempts whenever he has been placed in the general population," but 2 days later the inmate has "self inflicted lacerations to the abdominal area," which he explains by reporting, "I was depressed so I cut my stomach."

The man has severely limited coping skills and even more limited self-confidence, and he takes what he sees as the path of least resistance, which includes stealing from his employers, informing on his crime partners, dropping out of school, quitting the military as soon as he has joined it, and resorting to chemical anesthesia as a form of escape.

The man is clearly not ready to face the adversities of prison or any other setting and resorts to self-mutilation to signify that he is disinterested in meeting the challenges. Even the lowest pressure settings (including a minimum-security institution and a mental health unit) prove inadequate to the task of cementing the man's self-confidence. He retreats to protective isolation, but even this experience is overwhelming to the man, whose term of incarceration mercifully ends 3 weeks after he declares bankruptcy by lacerating his stomach. His capacity to manage outside the prison, of course, is in equally serious question.

Notes

1. Coping has been defined as a process that is initiated by the appraisal of a problem and ends with an adaptive response; this view—which is sometimes called *transactional*—is the most satisfactorily comprehensive perspective in the stress-adaptation literature. See R. S. Lazarus. (1966). *Psychological stress and the coping process*. New York: McGraw-Hill.

2. H. Toch. (1982). Studying and reducing stress. In R. Johnson & H. Toch (Eds.), *The pains of imprisonment* (p. 37). Beverly Hills, CA: Sage.

Chapter

11

Maintaining Sanity

Few questions are as difficult to resolve as those involved in defining the relationship between maladaptive behavior and mental disorder. Some critics assert that pathology is a concept that clinicians sometimes invoke to describe extreme maladaptiveness. By posing the issue in this way, the critics imply that labeling people as "mentally ill" permits us to highlight behavior that is vexatious or annoying, which provides justification for intrusive interventions. The same critics often argue, however, that diagnoses pinpoint conduct we may wish to exculpate, because the concept of mental illness implies that the behavior can be nonvolitional.[1]

These risks are real, but there are probably comparable risks to *not* invoking diagnoses where one can invoke them, because this can deprive someone of services that are earmarked for people who are diagnosed as disturbed which are frequently unavailable to others. Moreover, where maladaptive conduct is not viewed as disturbed, it is often classed as malevolently intentioned and can be dealt with punitively, as it is by the disciplinary process of the prison.

Maladaptiveness denotes unsuccessful coping and there are obviously many people who cannot cope with life who are not diagnosed as disturbed. Moreover, the facts that are used to arrive at diagnoses—which are called *symptoms*—are variegated, and some have nothing to do with how well the person adjusts to his or her environment. Symptoms not only include behavior patterns, but psychological processes, and even physiological indices. And though diagnoses currently highlight behavioral attributes, the same trend deemphasizes speculations about the dynamics of behavior. The prevailing concern is with increasing the reliability of diagnoses by relying on tangible evidence. We can thus better answer *what* questions, but are less able to deal with questions of *how* and *why*.[2] In other words, the concern that is most crucial in our thinking about maladaptation (what is the person trying to accomplish, and how does he run into trouble?) is not the core concern of diagnosticians.

None of these issues have mattered to us thus far, because we have been dealing with maladaptive patterns that are not predominantly characteristic of people who are diagnosed as disturbed. Where people whose maladaptive behavior we have discussed have also been diagnosed as disturbed, we felt we could describe, and to a certain extent explain, the person's maladaptive behavior without raising the issue of his pathology.

The strategy becomes more difficult when the careers we review are of chronic mental patients who spend long periods in hospitals and whose diagnosed pathology is an obvious and salient fact. In the case of such men, it would be foolish to talk of maladaptive behavior without considering the person's diagnosed mental disorder. By the same token, we must make sure that our descriptions are not redundant, that is, not another way of summarizing the information that is used by diagnosticians.

If our subjects were confined hospital patients, we might have difficulty circumventing redundancy, because patients' behavior in hospitals is inventoried in terms of whether it conforms to or deviates from diagnosed indexes of pathology, and the degree of maladaptiveness is more or less equated with the degree of pathology. Prisons, fortunately, use an independent criterion of adaptiveness, which is that of conformity to the prison and its rules, and this criterion is fairly dispassionately applied to the behavior of disturbed inmates while they live in the prison. This means that we can raise some questions about the maladaptiveness of disturbed inmates that are not redundant, and these have to do with difficulties the person has in negotiating his environment (the prison) as perceived by those who run the environment.

In relation to the issue of mental illness, we assume for better or worse that diagnoses are valid (or mostly valid) and that the people we describe are disturbed during portions of their career. Given this assumption, we can expect that diagnosed disordered individuals will encounter difficulties in relating to their environment that have some connection with their disorder. We can therefore ask, "How does the person, by virtue of the fact that he is arguably disturbed, maladaptively relate to the setting in which he lives (which is the prison), and to the people who surround him (who happen to be inmates and prison staff)?"

Because the prison has specific attributes, our answer to the question "How is the disturbed person's behavior maladaptive?" will not apply in detail elsewhere, such as in street settings where most homeless patients reside. However, there are equivalent questions that can be posed for other living environments to help illuminate different links between mental disturbance and disruptive or maladaptive behavior.

Flight: Escaping Reality

The distinction that stress researchers have drawn between successful coping efforts and fight–flight reactions describes some of the salient difficulties that many disturbed people demonstrate in negotiating the world.[3] This is so because many disturbed people find the world that surrounds them painful, hostile, inhospitable, and strange, or at best irrelevant. They often feel that to the extent to which they respond to external demands and stimuli, these will evoke unpleasant thoughts and feelings or will upset some delicate internal balance on which sanity or survival depends. This sense of being threatened by external stimulation and the panic that perceived threats evoke inspires radical solutions, which include substituting a private, self-generated "reality" for stimuli one seeks to avoid. The result of this stance often appears as a refusal to participate in the "real world" as defined by those who inhabit it. As the disturbed person is then seen by others, he is self-insulating and uncommunicative, insistent on vegetating, and unwilling to care for himself. The picture is incomplete, however, in that the disturbed person may not be entirely dead to the world but may live a fantasy life in which private connotations (often threatening connotations) are assigned to people around him.

An example is provided by an inmate who is serving a long sentence for rape and robbery. In the middle period of this sentence, where a fair number of incidents occur, most have to do with offenses such as failure to wake up, refusing to work, not having a light on for the count, not coming out of the cell, and other acts of omission.

As soon as the man arrives in prison he is committed to the hospital after he has created a disturbance by laughing loudly to himself, being unclean and refusing to shower, becoming withdrawn and preoccupied, and claiming that he does not mind the fact that everybody in the world is against him. Subsequent hospital stays are scattered over the next few years and do not register improvements in his condition.

In the prison the man refuses medication, deals with hallucinations by plugging his ears with chewing gum, claims he is perfectly healthy, and says that he has caused the hospital to be closed up. He also refuses to eat, which requires that he be recommitted. Years later he is still shuttled between prison and hospital, still claims that there is nothing wrong with him, reports that "he stayed so long in the hospital because he wanted to finish the Webster's Encyclopedia," and describes his hallucinations as a matter of his debating with himself.

It is during this period, midway in his stay, that the man develops problems in prisons, where he gets written up for disregarding various rules and regulations, mostly having to do with the fact that he wants to spend his time in his cell, does not want to participate in programs, and wants nothing to do with other aspects of institutional life. An entry reads:

> This counselor is unsure as to whether to treat him as a disciplinary case or as an inmate with an ongoing mental problem. He has been referred to the [mental health] unit, but they appear to be unable to help him at the present time with his condition. In all likelihood he will be assigned to the limited privileges program in the near future and will probably be content to remain in his cell, where he will be less of a problem to the security personnel.

There follow two commitments in quick succession, but a year later we find the inmate examined by the parole board, manifesting psychotic symptoms during the interview. In a commitment document shortly thereafter, the inmate is described as hallucinating, having disregarded his personal appearance, and claiming that he is being poisoned. Psychiatrists regretfully report that "his suspiciousness extends to medication."

Although the man's psychotic disorder had become unavoidably obvious to prison authorities, the inmate tended to see himself as an eccentric scholar who periodically opted to inspect hospital conditions and kept himself from being poisoned by rejecting medication (and occasionally, food) in the prison. The man is largely seen as a disruptive inmate when he is more or less in remission, at which time his disruptiveness consists of demanding that he be left alone with his private ruminations.

The man's disciplinary record represents a period within which he experiences more protracted stays in the prison, and the incidents are almost entirely a product of his effort to insulate himself from his surroundings. In other words, he is being written up by officers for wanting to function as a vegetable in his cell. The extremity of the pattern is inferable from the fact that the man finds it painful to get out of his bed in the morning, turn on the light, and have breakfast. Only the availability of a dark, quiet cell with room service would obviate most of these disciplinary involvements.

Flight–Fight

Although disturbed people may struggle determinedly to maintain a precarious equilibrium by withdrawing from the world, they rarely achieve anything approximating peace of mind. The most dramatic crisis points occur where flight reactions are punctuated by periodic or sporadic explosions, which may include attacks on other people or self-directed injuries. Such behavior is motivated by fear, suspicion, frustration, self-hate, and pent-up tension, and it often includes the conviction that the patient is being persecuted by others in his environment.

An example of the pattern is provided by a young man the majority of whose disciplinary violations involve refusing to do things. Three months after he arrives in prison, there is an entry that reads, "inmate refused to come out of his cell to go to work in the mess hall." The following month the man is repeatedly charged with refusing to turn on his cell light when officers need to see him during the inmate count. Another charge reads, "the inmate refused to come out of his cell for his mandatory shower."

One week begins with the notation that "the inmate refused to come out of his cell to go to mandatory breakfast," which is followed (on the same date) with the entry "the inmate refused to come out of his cell to go to mandatory noon meal." The next day an entry reads "the inmate did not come out of his cell for his shower." There are many charges of a similar kind, such as "the inmate refused to do his work assignment and was found sleeping instead of working," "the inmate appeared very dirty and stunk and refused orders to clean his cell and take a shower," "during the live count [the inmate] refuses to acknowledge the officer," "the inmate was not awake for the morning bell," and lastly, "he refused to attend an adjustment committee panel."

There are other incidents that have a tantrumlike flavor. One entry records that the man "broke his cell chair and threatened to kill anyone who came near him," a second notation describes the inmate "disrupting other inmates making phone calls by swearing and using obscene gestures and slamming down the phone," and a third notation records that "the inmate threw his tray into the inmates' serving line in the mess hall." In a series of related incidents, the inmate attacks people who are connected with serving meals. These include the following:

> An officer observed you throwing your food tray at an unidentified inmate porter.

> * * *

> The inmate threw his ration of meat at the meat server and threw his tray at the mess hall worker.

> * * *

> He attempted to grab the inmate who was delivering food trays, stating that someone was trying to poison him and he was going to kill someone.

There are entries that describe assaults, including one which refers to the inmate attacking a fellow inmate with a saw, one which describes him hitting another inmate with a broom, and a third in which he throws a bucket of water into a neighboring inmate's cell. The man also threatens officers on a number of occasions and once attempts to escape from prison.

The man describes conflicts with fellow inmates as reactions to condescending treatment. After one of the occasions in which he throws trays at mess hall workers, he explains that "he [the worker] was talking to me like a homo so I threw a tray at him. I told him to get out of my face." He similarly explains difficulties with correction officers as resulting from the fact that the officers hold him in low esteem and persecute him. As to his refusals to participate in institutional inventory taking, he provides conflicting explanations. He points out that "he has been sleeping covered up for years" and proclaims that he has no recollection of having been told to keep his head uncovered. He also "claims he can't hear anything while he is sleeping."

Officers conclude that "the inmate appears to like keeplock status so he can lay in his cell," and the inmate in turn informs them that "there is nothing they can do for him as he would never get paroled." This prediction proves accurate. The man is discharged on his conditional release date, fails to make his first report to the parole office, and "two days later was arrested in the process of robbing a bank."

After returning to prison, the man is described as "very uncooperative." He cannot be classified because he "continually refused to cooperate with custodial, medical, and program staff." Later, staff record that "he has received a violation when he refused to comply with facility regulations and delayed the count by not complying with orders to uncover himself in bed." Soon the man is referred to mental health staff who record:

> He admitted to hearing voices which occasionally tell him to do self-destructive things. He indicated that he hears voices rather constantly, but they only bother him periodically.

The inmate is diagnosed as suffering from a schizoaffective disorder, and mental health staff indicate that they "would like him to behave in a nonparanoid manner" and that they aspire to "the goal of having him clean and neat at all times." The inmate is introduced to a regime of therapy as well as medication, and staff report that he "participated actively, deriving a certain amount of insight." Three months later they note:

> At the present time he is working in industry. He has adjusted satisfactorily, getting good reports. He seems to display no bizarre behavior on the gallery. He follows procedures as a clean and well-groomed inmate and has many acquaintances.

The inmate is consequently discharged into the general prison population. There he again becomes enmeshed in disciplinary incidents, including an explosion of rage in which he throws a glass jar at someone whose identity remains unclear, since his aim is poor.

Although this man tries hard to offer explanations for his aberrant behavior, his versions of incidents (except where he admits he is afraid that his food is poisoned) do not account for the redundancy and specialization of his offenses. One infers that his disruptiveness has something to do with efforts he makes to keep very unpleasant and fear-arousing feelings and urges in check. The man does this partly by insulating himself and staying asleep as long as he can while he views those around him with suspicion. His suspicions particularly focus on those who can tamper with his food, though on occasions he regards other people as sources of physical danger or as irritants.

The man's efforts include trying to "shut off" the criminal justice system in the shape of a presentence investigator and the prison intake personnel. He fails, however, and things come to a head when he admits that he experiences hallucinations. Later, a tolerant program seems to help the inmate to regroup, but this program graduates him into a situation for which he appears insufficiently prepared, and the cycle starts afresh.

Fight Patterns

Violence that is associated with emotional problems is particularly alarming to observers because the concerns that motivate it appear idiosyncratic and private and inaccessible to others, and because the violence we observe seems disproportionate to stimuli that provoke it, which makes it hard to predict and to prevent.

Paranoid Aggression

Of the violent explosions that are associated with pathology, the most monothematic are those based on delusions of persecution. A person who engages in such violence lives with the suspicion of others and often feels that he is the target of some pervasive conspiracy. The violence he manifests can be preemptively directed at people he thinks plan to harm him, but it is sometimes intended in self-defense when the person feels imminently endangered or threatened. Real threats, unfortunately, can combine with subjective threats and can add documentation to an evolving perspective that is partly reality-based.

An example of the sort of perspective that informs paranoid violence is that of a man who comes to prison with a stiff sentence after initiating a shootout with the police. The officers shoot back, injuring the man while he fires at the officers without hitting them.

Two years after this man enters prison, he requests to see mental health staff, reporting that he is "rather upset" and that he is "feeling uneasy." Later he has an episode in which the psychologist to whom he is referred writes:

> The report is that he claims officers are talking about him, and he speaks of wanting to submit a writ so that they stop . . . I checked and the officers that he claims are talking about him were not even on duty the days that he claims this incident.

The man subsequently "indicates that the officers have stopped talking about him." He also applies for a furlough and supports his request with endorsements from prison staff. A chaplain, for instance, certifies that "I have come to know him rather well and have observed him at close range. He is a quiet, well-behaved individual . . . I would judge that he has embarked on a sincere quest for rehabilitation." A teacher rates the man's performance as "very high," writes that "his attitudes were excellent," and concludes that he "appeared to me to be quite mature and stable." A correction officer reports that "I have never had any problems with him. He is polite and courteous and always respectful to the officers and inmates." A second officer testifies that "he worked for me as a cell block porter, he appears to me a very quiet and serious person. He worked hard, and most of the time he stayed by himself. I can't remember him giving anyone trouble." Finally, the man's supervisor calls him "an asset to the department to which he is assigned."

The man is nevertheless turned down because of his long sentence and serious offense, and he expresses considerable bitterness. Three months later, he has a second episode of feeling persecuted and is hospitalized after he "threw a glass through the bars at an officer, injuring the officer, cutting his face and eyes." The man explains that he "believes that a bunch of officers is following the inmates and calling him names and teasing him," and he "spoke of everyone's calling him a faggot or homosexual [and] claimed that when he would be in his cell at night, officers would stand in front of his cell talking about him, claiming he was a faggot."

After the man returns from the hospital, he reportedly becomes "rather upset" because he discovers that his work assignment, which he likes, has been given to another inmate. He also feels that he is targeted in other respects, and "makes references to being harassed or hustled unfairly by the administration." He later breaks down, and on this occasion feels threatened by a fellow inmate. A psychologist reports:

> He was referred by the security department because he had a fight. The account I received was that he was overtly paranoid and accused [the other inmate] of various activities and actions, which incidentally [the other inmate] denies ... When I saw him he had passed through his paranoid phase and was quiet, seething with anger and rather upset. He was even angry with me who, at other times, he sees as his friend.

A few days later the inmate promises that "he would try again to get along," socially isolates himself, and "spends considerable time polishing, waxing, and mopping the floor." He is, however, transferred to another prison; by this time the staff and other inmates "see him as crazy."

In his next prison, the inmate's counselor reports that "he shows no initiative and displays very little interest in his work," that he received some disciplinary reports, and that "although these are not serious violations, in conjunction with his work record and attitude they indicate an overall inability to accept the rules and regulations of this facility." A supervisor echoes these complaints, writing:

> [The inmate] doesn't seem to associate with hardly any of his coworkers, and whenever he converses with me it

is to complain about slave wages, poor food in the mess
hall, etc. . . . He is frequently complaining that he doesn't
feel good and would like to return to his cell. Also he is
one of the last men in the shop and one of the first to
line up to leave at the end of the shift.

At this time the man is paroled with a long parole period
hanging over his head (given the length of his sentence) and
becomes involved in a robbery. The robbery nets him some
change and several subway tokens, and a prison sentence
added to his parole period, which in theory implies a term
of imprisonment of several decades. He embarks on this sentence visibly irritable, which affects his prison behavior. In
one incident, an officer who is attached to the prison bathhouse reports:

I called him, telling him to come in and pick up a bag of
laundry. He said in front of approximately 85 inmates,
"You get some of those young boys to carry those bags."
I went out into the corridor and ordered him several
times to get in the laundry and get the last bag. He became loud and boisterous, talking in a belligerent voice.
"You talk to me like a man, not an animal." He made
the statement in front of approximately 85 inmates, [but]
he finally went in and picked up the last bag.

Later, the officer's supervisor reports:

The officer called the inmate to the front of the gallery
to advise him that he was submitting a report on him for
an incident which had occurred in the bathhouse corridor. At this time the inmate reached out and pushed the
officer against the wall and ripped the pocket of his shirt.
The officer grabbed the inmate around the chest to subdue him. [Two other officers] immediately came to the
assistance of the officer. [One] grabbed the inmate by the
arms, [the second] grabbed him by both of his legs and
the inmate was wrestled to the floor face down, was held
there until handcuffs were brought to the area and applied to the inmate's arms. The inmate was then escorted

without further incident to the facility hospital . . . seen by [a psychiatrist] who ordered that he be admitted to the hospital for mental observation.

After the inmate has been examined and is segregated, another serious incident occurs in the segregation housing unit. According to the report:

A correction officer informed his sergeant that the inmate appeared to be depressed and did not take his breakfast. The sergeant went down and talked to the inmate but he would not speak. When the sergeant returned to the officer, the officer informed him that the inmate was going to court tomorrow and would have to go through his personal property to get his legal work, to take with him. The sergeant returned to the inmate's cell and told him he would have to come out of his cell to go through his property for his legal work but [the inmate] would not answer the sergeant. Instead he took a piece of paper and wrote on it that he wanted to see his lawyer at his cell. He was informed by the sergeant that this would not be possible, but that he would see his lawyer when he went to court. He again wrote a note asking where his lawyer was. Seeing the state of depression the inmate was in, the sergeant filed an observation report to the psychiatrist for observation. The sergeant notified a deputy superintendent who recommended the sergeant have a psychologist go to the special housing unit and interview the inmate . . . [The psychologist] left the special housing unit and said she would talk to the psychiatrist about her findings and notify the special housing officers if the inmate would have to be moved to hospital observation. [The psychiatrist determined that the inmate must be moved to the observation tier, and officers were so instructed.] . . . The sergeant went to the inmate's cell and told him he had an interview at the hospital and the inmate ignored him.

The incident ends with the inmate having to be tear gassed and "carried by the arms and legs to the shower area, where he was put under the shower for decontamination." Shortly thereafter, the inmate is hospitalized. Psychiatrists report at this time that he has stopped eating because he believes that prison authorities are adding embalming fluid to his food.

There follow 2 quiescent years with only minor incidents. This period ends when an officer in the mess hall insists that the inmate cannot wear a shirt on which he has written his name in large letters, and the inmate (for whom the monogram has special significance) ignores the officer's request. After the inmate sees the disciplinary panel, the staff charge:

> You did threaten the committee by stating that if you weren't locked up you would take them off the count. You also threatened and harassed the committee by stating no one could take your name away and it didn't make any difference if you did 30 years in your cell or six feet under, and that we could kiss your ass, that you were not going to take any more harassment. You also refused direct orders to stand still and place your hands behind your back.

Three days later the inmate is transferred to a psychiatric observation wing, and 2 weeks later he is hospitalized. A psychiatrist reports:

> There was a definite delusional assumption that everybody in prison was against him, especially the officers who had elected him for harassment, for what reason he did not know. He also recognized in other prisoners his brother, and stated his determination to kill these inmates because of these inmates being against his brother. He also included me in his delusional ideation in stating that I am harassing him in observation and therefore joining the crowd who was after him.

Another lull (lasting some 18 months) follows, after which the inmate again becomes irritable, possibly because the time he has lost as a result of disciplinary proceedings is not restored to him. One officer reports, "the inmate was let out of his cell by mistake and became very belligerent—was not going to return to his cell." On another occasion, "the inmate was screaming and hollering about his cell not being opened. He gave the officer a hard time, using obscene language."

Thereafter the inmate is rehospitalized because, according to the psychiatrist, he refuses ophthalmic treatment, "based on a delusional system with very heavy religious overtones in which he believes he is a direct descendant from Cain [while] everyone else is a descendant from a weak maternal object consisting of dyads and triads." The inmate also at this time has been "screaming and hollering at people passing his cell."

Later the man returns to prison, his disciplinary record again becomes very good, and work supervisors are delighted with his performance in his prison assignment. A psychiatrist who interviews the man for the parole board, however, finds him argumentative:

> [The inmate] was offended by the idea that the interviewer is asked to provide a psychiatric report, and that it may have some influence on the parole decision. He did not think it would be possible for anyone to give an opinion on a matter concerning him, as he felt he knew what had happened.

The psychiatrist concludes that the inmate is "very defensive and suspicious of the system." The parole board releases the inmate, however, stipulating that "a mental hygiene referral and evaluation are mandatory."

The man has experienced a downhill progression in his career. He starts out as a delinquent, who sustains a drug habit by modestly dealing in drugs. At this stage, he demonstrates a modicum of eccentricity (his uniform consists of dark glasses and a peaked hat) but is otherwise unremarkable until he panics following an altercation with a drug dealer who has sold him contaminated drugs, and seeks to evade arrest by shooting police officers, which converts him from an overaged delinquent into a long-term prisoner.

The man embarks on his career as a long-term prison resident by being a model inmate, but a brief and sudden lapse into delusions suggests that at some level he may be having difficulties assimilating the awesome sentence that hangs over his head. He is even more seriously traumatized when his failure to earn a furlough underlines the extremity of his fate, and his problems are compounded when he discovers that he has lost a prized work assignment through transfer to the hospital. This is one of several disappointments that convey to the man the feeling that he is subjected to an inhospitable fate, which (in the process of assigning blame or responsibility) sets the stage for a frame of mind that oscillates between chronic bitterness and episodes of paranoid delusions. In his delusions, the man mostly targets correction officers, but on at least one occasion he focuses on a fellow inmate. Between such episodes, he copes by segregating himself and manifesting his displeasure through a solemn demeanor and the stance of a chronic malcontent.

Through an irony of fate, this man, who already feels that the cards are stacked against him, returns to prison facing an even more substantial sentence on the strength of a robbery that nets him almost nothing, and the irony escapes the man, whose resentment and fear of the future are understandably substantial. These feelings place him in an unreceptive frame of mind when he enters prison, and his attitude contributes to an explosion when he feels himself unjustly disciplined for a demonstration of irritability. When the man is in turn penalized for exploding, he appears traumatized. He retreats into a shell of dazed despondency from which he is forcibly extricated with a dose of tear gas, which precipitates a psychotic episode that requires his hospitalization.

Other psychotic episodes follow and invariably result from conditions of extremity, such as when the man feels himself pushed by unreasonable demands and penalties and when he resists these demands, generally by ignoring them. In the interim, the man presents no problems, though when he is pressed (such as by a psychiatrist who interviews him for the parole board), he makes it obvious that he feels put upon and unfairly treated. If one sets aside his own contribution, it is, in fact, obvious that he has been dealt heavy blows, which means that in his case the line between paranoia and life is evanescent. This is particularly the case with circumstances that immediately precede the onset of his symptoms, which typically include a seemingly arbitrary action by someone in authority, such as an officer who insists on converting a technical violation into a disciplinary charge or a review group who turns him down for furlough on seemingly unjust grounds, followed by punishment for a manifestation of disgruntlement.

Such experiences plausibly translate for the man into the assumption that he is subjected to an overwhelmingly inhospitable fate with no recourse and no escape, which no doubt contributes to his feelings that hostile forces are personally invested in a conspiracy that is directed against him. In other words, beyond whatever susceptibilities the man brings to life situations that predispose him to illness, he encounters catch-22 situations that would validate the message of his tattoo, which reads "born to lose." Feeling persecuted is the closest the man can come to answering the question of why this should be the case.

Tinged Rebelliousness

A different form of violence is of most concern to people in authority (such as prison staff), because it consistently is directed toward them. Given its choice of target, the anti-authority violence of disturbed individuals appears to resemble explosions that are sparked by autonomy–dependence concerns (see above). But the motives that are often at issue are more complex, in that they run deeper and are accompanied by feelings (such as fear), assumptions (such as delusions), and distortions of perception that are products of confusion and obsessions. The behavior, in other words, is "overdetermined," meaning that it reflects private as well as public concerns.

An example of the pattern is provided by a man serving a long sentence for a bank robbery. The man's disciplinary record is unusually checkered. There are arguments and fights, threats and attacks against officers, and a great deal of eccentric behavior, which ranges from "sleeping under his bed in a corner of his cell" to "threw human defecation on walls."

A prison psychologist writes that the man "does not appear psychotic, but is aggressive and resents authority." The man's "resentment to authority" takes unusual turns. An incident report mentions that while on his way to religious services, he "broke formation, took a karate stance, hollered something in a foreign language, and went after a sergeant, striking him a glancing blow on the left side of his jaw." The man later tells a psychiatrist, "I sort of flipped out. I guess I got a little mixed up." Two weeks after this interview, the psychiatrist sees the inmate again and this time reports that "he claims that he is seeing things in his cell and would like to be transferred to another cell." The psychiatrist concludes that "this inmate is a manipulator and quite an antisocial personality who could act out at any time." The next day the inmate starts a fire in his cell, throws water into the hallway, and spits at a fellow inmate when he is escorted out of his cell. He advertises that he "did this only to be moved to another cell area," given that he "was having problems with the inmate in the next cell." Thereafter, he requests to be transferred to another prison and later changes his decision because "I was given a job assignment where there are very few people working." A week later, however, he complains that officers and inmates "for some reason or other are trying to kill me."

Thereafter, the man's deportment improves but his state of mind deteriorates. He writes a letter to the commissioner in which he tells him:

> I wish to inform you of a conspiracy going on in [this institution]. This conspiracy is against me . . . The officers are telling the inmates to try and commit sodomy on me. They are giving the inmates drugs and other forms of alcoholic brews to give me. I have written the superintendent about this matter but apparently he is also part of the conspiracy . . . An officer was letting unauthorized and unofficial inmates come from one block or another offering me drugs . . . Sir, would you please review my

records and have me transferred to another facility as soon as possible?

A week later the man threatens self-immolation and is placed in a psychiatric observation cell. Staff complain that he is "constantly screaming obscenities," and he is sent to the hospital, from which he is discharged after 6 weeks with the diagnosis "schizophrenia, paranoid type, in remission."

After a period of quiescence, the inmate again expresses disgruntlement. In one incident he builds a fire, and in another incident, he "threw a cup of water at an officer" and "attempted to get the other inmates on his gallery to start throwing objects at the officer." The inmate explains after the second incident that the officer has insisted that he return his supper dishes before he had finished his meal.

The inmate is recommitted to the hospital after assaulting correction officers "with no apparent provocation." He remains hospitalized for 3 months, and thereafter spends 2 years in the prison where he assaults other inmates, attacks officers, and incurs charges such as the following:

- Refused to attend class. Wanted to be locked in his cell so he could get out of school.
- Talking aloud, totally incoherent and irrational.
- Threatened an officer for standing on his spot.
- Possible sexual assault on an inmate.
- Refused to go to the adjustment committee meeting.
- Refused to sit down in the movies when told.
- Was under his bed with sheets and mattress pulled down around him so officers could not see him. Refused to come out.
- Refused a strip frisk and made threats.
- Refused to take medication. Threw it at an officer. Tried to hit the officer through the bars.
- Had a fire in his cell and would not help put it out.
- Refused to move from the special housing unit to the mental hygiene unit.
- Under the bed and could not be seen for the count.
- Spit in the face of a nurse and used abusive language.
- Threw spaghetti and meatballs at me . . . gave me no

warning . . . nothing was said between us prior to his throwing the food.

□ Began spitting on transportation officers forcing them to return to place him under sedation. It took a lieutenant, a sergeant, and five correction officers to subdue him so the nurse could administer a shot. This medication did not seem to affect him as when the trip resumed he continued to spit at the transportation correction officers. At a stopover he was allowed to use toilet facilities, kicked a correction supervisor, and had to be restrained by five officers. After arriving kicked a sergeant supervising his being frisked.

□ Put medication in his mouth but refused to open his mouth so the officer could see if he swallowed it.

□ Requested a bowl of soup and then complained that it was too full . . . spilled the soup on the floor and the officer.

□ When the sergeant approached cell told him to "get out of my face" and then spit in the face of the sergeant.

□ Set a blanket on fire in his cell which scorched the wall and the floor.

□ Failed to acknowledge the presence of an officer when he tried to wake him for the live count.

□ Refused orders to take a shower.

□ Was belligerent to the officer when getting his hair cut and would not let the officer take a picture of his changed appearance after getting his hair cut.

□ Threatened the officer in front of the companies, stating, "I'll punch your motherfucking head in and kick your ass all over the jail."

□ Stated to the officers, "I'm an inmate and demand the tobacco." Also, "What are you? A new fucking hack? I'll take those fucking glasses right off your motherfucking face." While being escorted, said, "Why don't you guys suck my fucking cock?" . . . [Later] refused order to strip for a frisk, told a lieutenant, "fuck you. I ain't taking off my clothes." Then turned, raised hands, shoved an officer up against the wall and kicked him in groin area. Then hit [another officer] in the left cheek.

□ Threw his food tray and a number of articles out of his cell at an officer.

In the last incident, the inmate is assigned 6 months of segregation consecutive to accumulated previous segregation time for throwing food and cutlery at officers, demanding that they leave the vicinity of his cell, and offering to kill them. Six days later, he is recommitted to the hospital because he has been responding to paranoid delusions. He returns with the diagnosis "schizophrenia undifferentiated, chronic, in remission" and for the next 7 months commits no disciplinary infractions.

During 5 stormy years in confinement, this man has assaulted a great many people, mostly custodial personnel, upon slight provocation. The man lives in an extreme and chronic state of disgruntlement. The most innocent demand can cause him to explode with demonstrative displeasure, and more substantial demands (such as being moved when he does not want to be moved) produce chain reactions in which he rages and struggles and kicks and spits at anyone within reach.

The man is extremely irritated by authority figures, and his recurrent response to those who irritate him is to angrily attack and curse and threaten them and to struggle. The man also resists changes in his environment and his routines, and this includes demands that he take showers or present himself for mental health interviews. In this sense, the continuous segregation time the man earns meets some of his needs, in that it forces him to stay sequestered in his cell. Even in such settings, however, he frequently explodes with rage in reaction to slight intrusions he finds unforgivably offensive.

Cryptic Outbursts

When people think of violence committed by disturbed individuals, they mostly think of explosions that occur "out of the blue," with no discernible motives, unrelated to the antecedents that we assume occasion violence. The description of such violence is apt but tells us more about what the violence is *not* than what it is. To assess cryptic violence motivation would require that we have access to some of the concerns the disturbed person prefers to keep private or that he cannot communicate. If the person could enlighten us, moreover, his concerns would still make no sense, because we would find that they often include illogical inferences from implausible premises.

The seemingly cryptic outbursts of disturbed individuals are actions that denote double failures, in that they mark junctures at which the pathology that is designed to help the person adapt to a reality with which he cannot deal fails him as well, with the result that he is left feeling guilty, resentful, angry, or panic-stricken. Many of the resulting acts, including outbursts (such as self-injuries or acts of arson) express such feelings, whereas others represent destructive outcomes of ill-fated delusions.

An example of a career of this kind is that of a short, over-weight young man whose prison incidents involve fights with other inmates, though during long stretches of time he is hospitalized. The man has serious mental health problems that become salient as soon as he is jailed, and his trial must be postponed for a year. The first psychiatrist who examines him must interview him in a straightjacket because he has assaulted another inmate who has taken one of his cigarettes without permission. A second psychiatrist has an equally difficult time because the inmate, whom he is trying to interview, is crying and drooling and stiff under the influence of medication. The psychiatrist concludes:

> It is my impression, even allowing for depression on the part of the defendant and side effects of medication, that he is a youth of limited intelligence, and that his intellectual capacity and function probably fall within lower reaches of the dull normal range.

Two weeks later, another psychiatrist finds problems that transcend the effects of limited intelligence. He writes:

> So far so good. Now, however, the patient states what appear to be delusions of grandeur, specifically that he is Jesus Christ . . . His purpose here on earth, he says, is

to "forgive you for your sins. Everybody who prays is praying unto me." He points out the misty background to his Department of Correction photograph and states that this is proof of his identity. Later he says that every time he drinks alcohol "clouds become cloudy." On questioning he states that God does not speak to him directly but through the mouths of others ... On further questioning he states that God intends that he be released on these charges ... Despite repeated confrontations he seems to be persistent in his beliefs.

Later, jail psychiatrists certify that the man is now free of mental disorder and conclude that his principal problem is one of mental retardation. However, they also recommend that if the man is sentenced to prison, psychiatric help should be afforded him. The probation officer who prepares the pre-sentence report writes:

[The] defendant impressed as dull intellectually but possibly not positively retarded. "Limited" might be a better nonclinical word ... It is hard to picture this limited, friendly, slow, passive, eager-to-please defendant in an armed robbery. It is hard to fathom, furthermore, why anyone planning an armed robbery would enlist this ineffectual-seeming individual as a cohort since a successful robbery ought to be an efficient operation and this defendant does not impress as efficient, to say the least. In nontechnical terms, if we may be allowed, he impresses as a somewhat "goofy," so to speak, "mama's boy" who finds some of the simplest points in conversation amusing, possibly inappropriately so.

The probation officer adds that "it is sometimes, in some cases, said that the criminal does not seem to fit the crime. This may perhaps be the case in the present offense with the defendant."

Despite the implication that the man is not a hardened criminal, he is sentenced to prison. When he arrives, he at once complains that he is "picked on" by the other inmates and reports that he "hears voices telling him to kill himself." Intake staff write:

> He indicates that he is constantly harassed by other in-
> mates and feels somewhat insecure. He also indicates
> that at times he has heard female voices suggesting that
> he commit suicide, but he indicates that he does not lis-
> ten and claims he has no intention of committing suicide.

For a while, the inmate's behavior appears slightly bizarre. On one occasion, he gets up in the middle of a meal and traverses the prison, arriving at an exercise yard from which staff persuade him to return.

Two weeks later, the inmate's problems transcend eccentricity. He sets his cell on fire "to get rid of garbage" and has to be removed from the conflagration by force. He insists on pacing his cell in the nude; masturbating and playing with excrement; smearing food on the walls, windows, and the floor; and "placing things in his various orifices." When he is interviewed, the inmate explains that he has "a generator in his body" and complains that there are "two women in his cell—one white and one black—both wanting sex with him."

The inmate is hospitalized on two successive occasions and is discharged suffering from "schizophrenia, disorganized, in remission." The "remission," however, is temporary, and the inmate is transferred from the prison to a civil hospital, from which he is eventually released.

Two months after the man's departure from the civil hospital, he is arrested for a bizarre offense in which he and a large canine attack a young female high school student and steal her purse. The offense is a serious one because the victim has been severely bitten by the man's dog and is badly traumatized by the incident. The man himself is less impressed than his victim, and a probation officer reports:

> He went on to admit guilt and express remorse, stating
> ... "Tell him [the judge] I want to live down South. Can
> I have less time?" The defendant impressed as being
> sorry for his offense but as having less than the fullest
> appreciation of the seriousness of his actions and perhaps
> their consequences to the complainant and the serious-

ness of his own legal predicament. He impressed as a
somewhat limited individual: "Tell the judge I ain't bad"
he said on several occasions, sometimes smiling at what
seemed inappropriate times.

The man is held in psychiatric hospitals until he is adjudged sane enough to be tried and is again sentenced to
prison. The person preparing the presentence report writes
that "the defendant's own statements to us indicate that he
is not afraid of returning to jail and did not impress as being
much bothered by the prospect. The defendant does not seem
able to function, except marginally, at liberty."

Almost as soon as the man enters the prison, he is sent to
a hospital on an emergency commitment, and when he leaves
the hospital is assigned to a residential mental health program. At this point, he is diagnosed as a chronic undifferentiated schizophrenic with borderline intellectual functioning, though there is some confusion about how psychotic the
man is because when he is interviewed he proves "unable to
respond to questions about hallucinations and delusions
since he didn't seem to understand the terminology, and
when asked whether he was hearing voices he said, 'yes,
yours.'" The mental health staff member writes:

> It would appear that his almost complete inability to
> function intellectually makes him a poor candidate for
> survival in open prison population, and I can't offhand
> think of another program that would possibly be more
> appropriate for him to be in, so I guess we are left with
> no choice but to accept him into our program. Our goal
> will be to first of all help him be clean and neat and
> sanitary, to help him find his way around the prison, help
> him establish and follow programs, learn how to eat in
> the mess hall and eventually get him into some mean-
> ingful work . . . and hopefully be able to nurse him ever
> so gradually into population.

Even such minimal goals prove difficult to achieve, and
the inmate is discharged within 2 months, accompanied by
a discharge summary that notes:

> During his stay in the program he remained noncom-
> municative and mute. His only signs of life were in re-
> sponse to questions from correction officers and staff
> members, and he was also observed on several occasions
> to be masturbating openly, particularly in the presence
> of females . . . He was given a shower on two occasions.
> [On a third occasion] corrections officers attempted to
> give him another shower and to clean his cell. During
> that time he assaulted and caused physical injury and
> subsequent hospitalization to three correction officers.

Other incidents replicate the pattern referred to in this
summary. On several occasions, the inmate assaults officers
who interfere with him, such as by insisting that he clean his
cell. The inmate also continues to expose himself, particularly
when female staff members are available as witnesses. In addition to periodically wrecking his cell and strewing garbage
in the vicinity, the inmate starts an occasional fire, and as a
result he spends most of his time in segregation. Here he
receives visits from mental health staff, with whom the inmate refuses to communicate.

At the inception of the man's prison career he is seen as a
limited, victim-prone, childlike individual with some psychotic symptoms. However, he soon blossoms into a full-
fledged mental patient who lives in a fantasy world that
heavily accentuates themes having to do with sex and other
bodily functions. Unfortunately, the man has a tendency to
translate his thoughts, such as they are, into action and as a
result he masturbates, smears excrement on walls, sets fires,
and otherwise becomes difficult to manage, especially since
any ministrations to which he is subjected make him explode
with wounded rage.

The man's intellectual limitations compound the problems
created by his disease, in that they further limit his ability to
perceive and discriminate features of his environment and
make it impossible for him to distinguish, for example, between helpful and hostile acts. His limitations similarly make
it difficult for the man to have residual awareness of the inappropriateness of steps he takes to satisfy his needs, such

as when he importunes prepubescent girls or female correction officers. In other words, although the man's disease probably obliterates the lines between fantasy and reality, the primitiveness of his intellect reduces reality to the sort of world experienced by an infant, and the two problems converge so as to make it impossible for this man to function.

Oscillating

One fact that complicates any effort to understand the link between pathology and maladaptation is that there are seriously disturbed individuals who adjust differently in different settings, or react differently at different stages of their careers. Such people can at times be said to *oscillate* between being disturbed and nondisturbed, and also oscillate between maladaptive and nonmaladaptive behavior.

The sharpness of transitions in some cases is such that it creates difficulties both for the person and for the setting because it becomes impossible to reliably define the person's problems and the responses appropriate to them. The behavioral inconsistency then becomes a pattern of maladaptation that is more salient than the detailed behavior it subsumes.

A case in point is that of an inmate who has served a long sentence for a predatory sex offense. His disciplinary record is dense during a 2-year period in the middle of his sentence and sparse before and after this period. The majority of disciplinary incidents appear eccentric. Some examples of incidents are "running back and forth from shower to shower saying someone stole his clothes," "having his cell door tied with a belt, acting quite disturbed," "refusing to be quiet, climbing on his cell bar," "obscene language to nurses," "aggravating Black inmates, started fight," "yelling in bed for no reason," "stated that bed sheets fell into toilet and flooded his cell floor," "refused to take a bath upon being received," "urinated on floor in his room," "threw contents of tray in toilet," "shouting, demanding that light be left on at night," "spitting on wall," "plugged toilet with clothes," "refused to turn the light on in his cell," and so forth.

The inmate has served a previous prison sentence for an assaultive offense. There are indications that the man at this stage was a respected senior gang delinquent, who exercised a leadership role in his group. He has also had a record of fairly steady employment.

There is only one note at this time that is discordant with the general impression of this offender being a substantial figure of the juvenile underworld. In the detention facility, he has smashed the contents of his cell, "wandered around the halls and claimed he had communicated with God, and further stated that he had been called back from the dead." The person who examined the inmate reports:

> He stated that the experience was real in his own mind, but he would not talk of it to anyone other than the examiner who became his confidant, because he could not prove his story and people would think he was fabricating.

During his first prison stay, the man becomes involved in several altercations. In these, he acts as a leader of inmates of his own ethnic group. In one report it is recorded:

> He was to be placed in segregation for a leveling off period. It is felt that he is trying to establish leadership among the Puerto Rican population and trying to tell other inmates what to do. He had been counseled and advised by the deputy superintendent on a number of occasions about his agitating activities and he has totally disregarded this advice. He is the type that just can't keep his mouth shut and keeps telling others of his ilk what to do, whether it is contrary to rules and regulations or not.

He is described as "a chronic agitator with little or no respect for authority, race conscious, with a persecution complex." Aside from one incident in which he becomes despondent because a female friend "had lost interest in him," there is no indication at this time of psychological difficulties, and the inmate's reputation is that of a disruptive figure who has recorded innumerable infractions in a short prison stay.

About a year into the next prison sentence which the inmate earns, there are indications of a marked change. The first indication is a report that records that the inmate has been observed sharpening a soda can, explaining that "he wants to kill everyone." Shortly thereafter, a physician writes:

> He has been playing with feces but when observed said that everything was fine. A pint of ice cream that he had recently received was upside-down next to the toilet bowl. When questioned about this he merely makes the statement that it had tipped over on him . . . His cell is very disorderly, with everything strewn around, some feces mixed with ice cream on the floor. As soon as the cell is cleaned, he messes it up again . . . States that he wishes to serve out his full term and then sue the State of New York for half a million dollars for false imprisonment. Admits analyzing his feces to extract the paste in order to use this material to blot out images on some of his snapshots. When shown a photo of himself, states that the man was a marine and had died.

Interestingly, this description of disturbed behavior does not satisfy a judge, with the result that the inmate is not committed at that time. He is committed shortly thereafter, however, after "playing with an imaginary rifle in the yard, shooting other inmates and officers from the wall. At the time he was dressed rather peculiarly, not wearing shoes and other garments."

The difficulty seems to be that the inmate is often described as undergoing "drastic personality change." After incidents such as the preceding, he is interviewed by a psychiatrist and "appeared friendly, cooperative, clear, in good contact, and correctly oriented." The inmate is next reported in the dining room, throwing baked potatoes at other inmates, but in a subsequent interview seems level-headed and in possession of his faculties. There are referrals to mental health staff in which correction officers report extremely bizarre behavior, but the inmate is interviewed and classified as nonpsychotic.

He cannot keep this up, however, and concerns arise about his safety. He plays with electric outlets, refuses to eat, and lies covered in a sheet ranting and laughing.

He is no longer a substantial figure in the inmate world. He insists on preaching to nonreceptive audiences about his version of Muslim religion and invites being teased and abused. A report from his work assignment indicates that "coworkers do not want to work with him for fear of his irrational behavior." On one occasion, he "stole pictures from other inmates. These pictures were of the inmates' wives and girlfriends. He was also writing letters to girls of other inmates." A psychologist concludes:

> A number of inmates now know him and have spoken to me about him. Many of these inmates are truly angry with him and as such I think that at this point we should not release him to the population.

Psychotic episodes are resolved without the inmate being committed. One such instance finds him "in a catatonic state, lying on his bed, shaking, in a fetal position," but after substantial doses of medication "his transitory psychotic disorder appears to have subsided. He was in excellent contact, was verbal, was pleasant and back to his old style of high verbal production, and the old con."

A psychologist summarizes the situation as follows:

> We can see now a pattern for his behavior. He slips in and out of psychotic episodes with ease and with regularity. We can expect that this behavior will continue.

During a hospital stay, a psychiatrist classifies the inmate as a dissimulator. Two months later, the inmate is back in the hospital giving religious lectures that include delusional content and hallucinations. He also attacks fellow patients. When the inmate returns to prison, he refuses to take medication and spends his time in observation cells after being referred by correction officers for walking around giving himself religious lectures and looking and smelling filthy.

Various experiments are tried to address the problem. One psychiatrist reports:

> Regardless of everything, this examiner felt that the patient should be placed in a cell block and handled for at least some period of time in order to give him the opportunity to adjust to life situations in this facility. The patient was transferred during the day. The next day the patient was returned to the hospital area because the officers were not able to handle him in the block area.

Soon the inmate finds himself back at the hospital threatening to kill his fellow patients and being restrained. Two months later, he is released from the hospital but in short order he is transferred back to the hospital where staff note that "the inmate . . . presents typical symptomology of paranoid schizophrenia . . . is preoccupied with religion, the Devil and Satan . . . is irrational." In the wards, other patients again react adversely to the man's self-styled missionary work. Staff complains that the inmate

> usually has extreme difficulty keeping the lid on (as it were) his hostile, bitter thoughts toward staff and peers as well as delusional material in the area of religious pursuits. An open ward setting is the least likely environment for him to avoid the aggravation of such paranoid thinking. He would be far more capable of maintaining control in a cell setting where he can withdraw from continual contact with peers when he chooses. But he may also become active in a vocational or educational program once he is confident that he is in control of his feelings.

When the inmate returns to the cell environment that is recommended, it does not seem to produce the predicted effect. He spends his time proclaiming loudly that "people are talking about me." He is again committed, but the hospital sends him back, certifying that this patient, though showing improvement at the present time without the aid of medication, very likely will deteriorate when returned to prison and may require additional assistance from medication ... [and from] mental health workers who can recognize when he is decompensating and can recommend that medication be administered. In the meantime, attempts should be made to involve this inmate in programs.

The predicted oscillations occur. A counselor complains:

He is constantly being transferred back to the hospital due to psychiatric disturbances disallowing any possible programming ... It seems he is being thrown from institution to institution because no responsibility appears to be taking place. He is presently at this facility because in the past he did less damage here than elsewhere.

For a while, the inmate does well, takes his high school examination in Spanish, is praised as an excellent worker, has no disciplinary problems, and appears to make good progress in therapy. But soon he is referred by the security staff because he has become "extremely belligerent without provocation and seemed to be completely out of control with his emotions." Another referral starts, "the above inmate was referred by security due to his 'flaky behavior.'"

The next report originates in the hospital, where the inmate

carries on an endless conversation with no one in particular, keeping most of the hospital patients awake. He is frequently flushing the toilet for no apparent reason. He at times is rational and able to carry on an intelligent conversation, but at other times he becomes belligerent and expresses extreme hostility toward the nurses.

We are now past midway into the inmate's sentence and there are no disciplinary reports of consequence through the next 5 years. The inmate is enrolled in college courses and in typing classes. Reports describe him as highly motivated and conscientious. He does a good deal of reading, has steady family contacts, and in interviews impresses everyone as rationally concerned with the pursuit of achievable goals and as being a mature and hardworking inmate.

All of a sudden, we have a report that the "resident was observed by the counselor this morning laying on the floor counting numbers in the air, talking incoherently." The inmate is committed to the hospital following a subsequent report that he

> has been very concerned about the way this institution is being run, and he is afraid another riot will break out. He doesn't believe in inmates having privileges in the institution. He also complains of someone trying to assassinate an inmate in the yard.

Back in prison, the inmate is observed "throwing jars out of his cell, babbling incoherently" and "complaining of glasses flying by his cell and otherwise in fairly serious condition." A series of commitments follow over a period of 2 years. In one document, the inmate is described as "threatening to kill himself by bumping his head into the cell wall." In another, it is recorded that he "believes he is God and a Son of God. He came to earth to save mankind. He hears voices, but considers them normal."

Eighteen months before the inmate's discharge from prison, there is a progress report which notes that "due to psychiatric problems, the inmate is unable to maintain a program." However, the next report reads "in the last 14 months he has maintained a spotless record." The report also mentions that the inmate is gainfully employed. Six months later, it is recorded that there have been "no additional disciplinary reports since the last summary. He has continued in a positive manner getting along with staff and peers and is expected to continue in this positive manner." It is also reported that "the inmate was recently assigned to handicrafts and expresses his satisfaction with the program." The man at this time has been followed up by mental health staff and is on a steady regimen of medication.

This long and redundant account covers a 13-year period of continuous shuttling between prisons and hospitals. Disciplinary problems are mostly a direct result of the man's illness. There are also periods when the inmate has his illness under control (mostly with the help of medication), where he is an impressive, rational, and socially adept person.

The man's adjustment problems range from a preliminary effort at self-insulation and a pattern of self-neglect to a later stage of volatility, suspiciousness, fear, resentment, and a lot of loud eccentric discourse. Prospects of more serious disciplinary incidents arise when other inmates object to the substance of the man's loud, eccentric discourse and when the inmate develops grudges against fellow patients that have to do with his religious delusions.

We have a prior prison stay in which the inmate is a serious disciplinary problem because of his self-appointed status as an ethnic gang leader. As this time he is regarded as a nuisance but also as an impressive and likable person. He is aggressive only in a subcultural context, which includes the gang-related crime for which he has been convicted. If we ignore one episode of religious delusion in the jail, there is nothing to prepare us for what we encounter over the next 13 years: We start with an impulsive sex-related offense irreconcilable with earlier behavior. We infer problems in the jail because the man has been placed under special guard as a suicide risk. One year into his prison stay, the inmate shows a pattern he will follow for the remainder of his sentence, of periodically breaking down while he struggles as hard as he can to keep afloat. The disciplinary incidents reflect both the struggle and the failures of the struggle. There is a similar origin to the contrasts that perplex and confuse various staff members who see the inmate at one juncture or another: One day he is not only rational but meticulously dressed to the point of being prissy, and the next day finds him disheveled and rambling. It is a pitiful fight, and in the last year of the 13-year confinement, it appears as though the man may have won the battle with the help of medication. It is of course an open question whether he has won the war.

Notes

1. Szasz (1961); see chapter 9, note 5. In its introduction, the *Diagnostic and Statistical Manual of Mental Disorders* (4th ed., *DSM–IV*; American Psychiatric Association, 1994) points out that "it must be admitted that no definition adequately specifies precise boundaries for the concept of 'mental disorder.' The concept of mental disorder, like many other concepts in medicine and science, lacks a consistent operational definition that covers all situations" (p. 21).

2. *DSM–IV* (American Psychiatric Association, 1994) continued to rely on the "important methodological innovations" of *DSM–III* (published in 1980), which included "descriptive theories of etiology" (pp. xvii–xviii). According to the historian Edward Shorter (1997), "DSM-III and its successors [were] designed to lead psychiatry from the swamp of psychoanalysis." (Shorter, S. [1997], *A History of Psychiatry.* New York: John Wiley & Sons, p. 305).

3. Howard and Scott (1965) thus distinguish between *assertive* responses, "in which the organism meets the problem directly and attempts a solution," and *divergent* responses, "in which the organism diverts his energies and resources away from confronting the problem" (p. 147). The most prevalent divergent responses are fight, flight, or doing nothing at all. (Howard, A., & Scott, R. A. [1965], A proposed framework for the analysis of stress in the human organism. *Behavioral Science, 10,* 141–160.)

12

Distribution of Patterns

A s noted, we reviewed 239 prison careers of chronic infractors who showed evidence of psychological difficulties, for whom we had enough data (behavior descriptions)
to justify a review. The representativeness of this sample cannot be assumed, but caution is not required to conclude that
all the inmates we surveyed had serious problems, at least
in the prison.

We classified behavior by assigning one theme to each
prison career. The categories we used most frequently were
Maintaining Sanity (60 inmates) and Gratifying Impulses
(57). Of the inmates whose behavior we placed in the first
category, the largest subset (18 patterns) included both flight
(self-insulating) and fight (impulse bursting-through) reactions. Of pure fight patterns, the most frequent (15 out of 24)
was what we called *cryptic outbursts*, meaning that relationships between external stimuli and aggressive responses
would be difficult to specify, and one could have to class the
inmate's aggressivity as reflecting bizarre or inaccessible motives. The finding is consistent with that of studies in psychiatric settings in which patient assaults are subjected to reviews,[1] and we infer that attention to the *content* of disturbed
or delusional thinking could sometimes help to prevent violence. Another theme we encountered among disturbed in-

291

mates is that of *oscillating* ($n = 10$), which means that there are sharp contrasts over the person's career between *mental wellness* and *mental illness*, reducing the reliability of diagnoses at a given point in time.

Of impulsivity-related behavior, one third (19) proved subsumable under *games turned sour*, which is a compounded problem, because it suggests that a person's primitive approach to satisfying needs has misfired. Maladaptation is also compounded because the person at issue reacts with limited insight (egocentric self-pity and the externalizing of blame) to this discovery of failure. However, the pattern also points at a strategic juncture for intervention, in which the *games* the person impulsively plays have manifestly *turned sour*, providing documentation of failure.

Other prevalent impulse-related patterns were *stress to aggression* (11) and *frustration–aggression* (10). In each case the link between stimulus situations (blocked goals or overstimulation) and responses (angry aggression or helpless aggression) is specifiable, a fact that could assist staff in addressing the person's problem.

The next most invoked pattern heading was that of Seeking Refuge, which we used for 52 inmates. The subcategory most frequently emerging under this heading was *earned rejection* ($n = 13$), which describes a sequence in which ineptness comes homes to roost, which in turn inspires flight. The second pattern was *stress avoidance* ($n = 10$), which reflects personal nonresilience. Also frequent ($n = 8$) was *sheep's clothing*, which depicts personal reactions that vary with setting, transforming the self-styled victim in a socially disadvantaged situation into a source of aggression when the power balance shifts.

Esteem-related patterns emerged for 37 inmates. The predominant theme ($n = 11$) was that of *advertising toughness*, followed by *countering aspersions* ($n = 8$). The first pattern features aggression as a demonstration of worth, and the second describes the propensity to react aggressively to perceived slights or affronts.

Pursuing Autonomy was invoked for fewer (33) inmates, but two themes, *conditional dependence* and *rejecting con-*

straints, appear with frequency (*n* = 12 each). A theme that appears least frequently may be the most surprising. This theme, *defying authority* (*n* = 3), is the disposition most prison staff would expect to find with endemic frequency. The relative infrequency of our usage of the theme may mean that the behavior to which staff refer has more complex dynamics. It may also be the case that *defying authority* in pure form occurs among more routine violators than the problem inmates on whom we centered attention.

As noted, prevalent autonomy patterns are conditional dependence (*n* = 12) and rejecting constraints (*n* = 12). The first pattern describes behaviors ranging from anxious and demanding to surly and rebellious, depending on responses the person receives to requests for attention, service, and nurturance. Rejecting Constraints is impulsivity as well as autonomy-related, in that it describes difficulties in accepting curbs to unrestrained behavior as well as reactions to infringement on independence to which the person feels entitled.

Pattern Relationships

Our goal in selecting the sample of 239 inmates was to pick individuals whose careers reflect "extreme maladaptiveness." We wanted chronic prison offenders, but *particularly* offenders who had psychological or sociopsychological problems, including problems calling for mental health assistance. In reviewing the attributes of the sample, it appears that we accomplished our task. Our sample comprises 10% of the stratified cohort, leaving 90% of inmates we did not review. Of those in the sample, 30% had been hospitalized in the prison and 47% had received other mental health assistance; only 23% had received no mental health services. The corresponding proportions for the other 90% of the stratified cohort are 3%, 33%, and 64% respectively, and the estimated figures for the prison population are 1.5%, 14.2%, and 84.3%.

As for disciplinary infraction rates, the average for our sample was 10.6; that of the rest of the cohort was 6.8; the estimated rate for the population was 4.2. The infraction rate of our disturbed infractors (the 60 inmates classified as Maintaining Sanity) was 7.7. The rates for inmates in our other categories was 12.4, 11.9, 11.1, and 10.7, respectively. Even more impressive is the finding that 22.4% of our sample (compared with 3% of the population) consists of chronic infractors. The proportion is particularly high for impulsives (30.4%) and esteem defenders (35.1%). Autonomy seekers comprise a lower proportion of chronics (12.1%), as do the inmates with mental health problems (11.9%). Disturbed inmates, however, spend time in the prison hospital, which makes them unavailable for infractions.

In this connection, it is relevant that variation generally obtains for mental health status. Eighty percent of the Maintaining Sanity group had been hospitalized in prison during their criterion term; only 8% received no mental health assistance. Two other themes (Seeking Refuge and Pursuing Autonomy) show mental health involvement: 15% of the refuge seekers and 18% of autonomy pursuers had been hospitalized, and 64% in each category had received other mental health assistance. Only the Esteem Enhancing pattern is associated with a low hospitalization rate (3%), although 57% of these inmates had received other mental health services.

Our sample contains half (71 of 143) of the hospitalized inmates in the population for whom records are available; two thirds (48) fall in the Maintaining Sanity category, and the other categories are dispersed through the sample. The hospital patients in our sample, as we expected, have high infraction rates (6.4 compared with 2.5). They also have come to the system at an earlier age (19.7 compared with 23.7), have been first arrested earlier (at 17.3 compared with 20), have served more time (55 months compared with 43.8), and more frequently have prior prison records (47% prior prison compared with 31%). Our group also contains more non-White patients (79%) than the other hospital group (63%).

Over 1 inmate out of 5 (22.7%) in our sample has a record of civil hospitalization; this proportion does not vary by themes. The figure for histories of forensic hospitalization is the same (22.3%) but the proportions vary: in the Maintaining

Sanity group, half (47%) have histories of forensic hospitalization; the proportions in the other group range from 11.5% to 19%.

In other respects, the highlights of our classification-related profiles are the following:

1. *The profile for Gratifying Impulses*: The inmates classified as demonstrating impulsivity have by far the highest disciplinary violation rate (12.4) and show the highest assault rate in the prison (2.6). These inmates enter the system at the earliest age (at 17.5, compared with a population average of 20), have a relatively low average IQ (86.8), and have the lowest proportion of high school graduates (11%).

2. *The profile for Enhancing Esteem*: The inmates classified as esteem defenders have the second highest prison infraction rate (11.9) and assault rate (2.2). This group is youngest at admission to prison (21) and the youngest of our groups; the inmates are also among the youngest (15.4 years) at first arrest. These inmates show a low proportion of mental health problems (40% no service) and the lowest proportion of preprison employment (38%).

3. *The profile for Pursuing Autonomy*: This group is relatively old compared with the above (24.7 years at entry, commensurate with the general population) and at first arrest (17.4 years). The group also has a high proportion of men who have been imprisoned before (42%) and as a group serves long average sentences (44.7 months, compared with an estimated 31.1 months for the population). By contrast, the group shows a high proportion of preprison employment (73%), a low proportion of drug addicts (48.5%), and the highest intelligence level in our sample (85% IQs over 80).

4. *The profile for Refuge Seeking*: Inmates who are classified in this category are among the youngest at first arrest (15.4 years), are disproportionately White (50%), and include the highest proportion of drug addicts (75%). The group also contains a large number of inmates (16.9%) convicted of rape, murder, sodomy, and assault.

5. *The profile for Maintaining Sanity*: Inmates classified in this group are the oldest men in our sample (27.8 at

prison entry) and serve the longest sentences (53.3 months). The group contains the highest proportion of non-White inmates (83%) and a high proportion of re-cidivists (45% with prior prison time). The group also contains the highest proportion of inmates with low measured intelligence (53% of inmates with IQs 80 and under) and a low proportion of addicts (44.1%). Eight of the 60 inmates (13.3%) serve sentences for murder.

The profiles contain differences we expected, and others we did not. Refuge seekers are least surprising, in that victim-prone inmates are often described as White inmates who are less sophisticated than the average inmate and have a history of delinquency and addiction. On the other side of the ledger, we find that our group contains a larger proportion of violent offenders than one would expect. The fact makes more sense once we recall that ours are not "pure" refuge seekers but men who combine aggressivity (at least, in the prison) with refuge seeking.

The impulsivity profile is more plausible, in that it over-represents aggressive, institutionalized men with limited roots in the community who also have other deficits (such as low measured intelligence and lack of education). The esteem-related profile is similar, though the inmates are younger, have fewer mental health problems, show higher intelligence, and have less institutional experience.

The autonomy pattern comes as a surprise if we expect inmates classified as autonomy-oriented to be youthful rebels. We find the group chronologically mature, prison-experienced, established in the community (high preprison employment), and serving long sentences. The group also contains low proportions of men with limited intelligence or a history of addiction. The inmates are not—as are the esteem-defending inmates—young toughs; they resemble older and more established denizens of the prison, whose violation records are low. However, we must recall that the issue for these inmates is not peer relations but staff relations, and it may be that they are "mainline" offenders who are less reconciled than equivalent offenders to the strictures of institutional life.

We have noted that inmates we have classified as disruptively Maintaining Sanity are different from other disturbed inmates and are multiply disadvantaged, in that even allowing for the unreliability of intelligence measures among the disturbed, they demonstrate unusually high levels of cognitive deficits as well as emotional problems. These men also serve draconian sentences, and a large proportion of the men have checkered institutional careers, straddling the criminal justice and mental health systems. Though the disciplinary violation rate of seriously disturbed disruptive inmates is the lowest in our sample, it contrasts with that of other inmate-patients. Moreover, the rate would be higher if we accounted for "time at risk" and allowed for hospital infractions and reclassification of behavior by the prison as illness related.

Note

1. Such information can become available in those psychiatric settings in which staff make an effort to understand the antecedents of patient assaultiveness. See Quinsey (1977), chapter 1, note 7. Also see St. Thomas Psychiatric Hospital. (1976). A program for the management and prevention of disturbed behavior. *Hospital and Community Psychiatry*, 27, 724–727. For a recent review, see Quinsey, E. L. (2000). Institutional violence among the mentally ill. In S. Hodgins (Ed.), *Violence among the mentally ill* (pp. 213–235). Dordrecht, The Netherlands: Kluwer Academic.

    A thought-provoking finding is that of Quinsey and Varney (1977), which is based on a review of 198 patient assaults—mainly against staff. In most incidents, staff reported there was "no reason" for the assault. The patients, however, almost invariably cited what to them were compelling reasons, such as staff provocations (perceived abuse or teasing), orders to do something the patient did not want to do, or staff refusals to honor patient requests. See Quinsey, V. L., & Varney, G. W. (1977). Characteristics of assaults and assaulters in a maximum security psychiatric unit. *Crime and Justice, 5,* 212–220.

13

Success Stories

In tracing the careers of men in our cohort, we pointed out that almost irrespective of time spent in prison, the deportment of most inmates tends to improve over time. In other words, the prisoners' maladaptive behavior decreases; one also assumes the corollary, which is that their adaptive behavior increases.

This observation may strike some as counterintuitive, both with respect to maladaptive behavior and prisons. With respect to maladaptiveness, it makes sense to think in terms of cumulative difficulties, in which first, failure breeds failure, and then punitive responses cement the conduct they are meant to deter. As for prisons, the prevailing notion is that such settings are at best stultifying and at worst counter-rehabilitative, and that they function as "breeding grounds for maladaptive behavior."

Given that the picture is not as it is fondly predicted by prevailing pessimistic postulates, one must explore counter-vailing and more heartening assumptions. Some have to do with the nature of humans, and others have to do with attributes of prison. The former must focus on resilience, maturation, self-correction, and growth; the latter must draw attention to nonpunitive features of the prison at the time we studied it, such as ameliorative provisions and program opportunities.

In preceding chapters, we have described types of maladaptive behavior by male offenders in the prison, which we have illustrated with accounts drawn from relatively checkered inmate dossiers. We had expected these accounts to feature many downhill careers (i.e., patterns of increasing maladaptiveness) but discovered that these patterns are relatively rare, whereas the more encouraging sequence (of decreasing maladaptiveness) occurs with appreciable frequency.

Causes of Improvement

What are some facts in the inmates' histories that account for personal transmutations? Are there clues to the dynamics of change in careers that begin inauspiciously but show promise of reform? To explore such questions, we selected over 40 (out of our 239) case histories, in which cessation or diminution of maladaptiveness had occurred. We grouped these accounts in terms of the processes that we inferred might be at work in producing the changes we observed, and in this chapter we describe these themes under relevant process headings.

Involvement

According to *Webster's Collegiate Dictionary*, the verb "involve" can mean "to engage as a participant" and "to occupy (oneself) absorbingly; especially: to commit (oneself) emotionally." The first phrase describes what others must do to secure the impact denoted by the second and third phrase. In tandem, the phrases suggest a process whereby a person is invited to participate in activity that he or she finds enticing, which in turn produces commitment to the goals of the activity.

Involving a person in adaptive behavior can serve to break a pattern of maladaptive acts by providing an alternative to the "wrong" sort of involvement or by creating meaning and purpose where it has not existed. Both of these paths are familiar to students of criminological literature because their counterparts are implied in theories that discuss alternatives to criminal careers and stress the value of psychological bonds that tie the person to society. Criminologists have defined one such bond as that of involvement in personally satisfying activities.[1]

The dictionary definitions we have cited tell us that reform through involvement must be an active and not a passive process; the strategy of leading the horse to water does not in itself promote involvement, because involvement presupposes participation in *absorbing* activity. If we are concerned with promoting real involvement, we must provide tasks that entice rather than activities that fill time.[2] Our probabilities of success increase when the available activities intersect with the interests of the individuals to be involved, which means that personal predilections must be recognized and accommodated by the task providers. Of course, "engagement" can mean self-engagement, which occurs when the involvement is not planned, that is, when a person is enticed by an enterprise he or she happens to run across, because it is routinely available.

In the prison, one arena in which involvement occurs is in educational programs, and another is in work assignments. In either instance, an inmate can discover that what he is doing is enjoyable, meaningful, or engrossing and that it is worthy of the investment of his time and the expenditure of his energy. The short-term benefit the inmate and the system derive is that of deinvestment of time and energy from maladaptive pursuits, to the extent to which this occurs. Longer term benefits also may occur but presuppose more substantial reorientations of investments and goals.[3]

Involvement is not necessarily a one-step process, nor need involvement entail immediate disengagement from maladaptive pursuits. An example of a long-term mixed pattern is provided by a man who served a long prison sentence for participating in two sadistic robberies. His disciplinary dossier is dense and contains reference to many fights and disturbances in which he has been loud and threatening. The man also manufactures and consumes contraband such as wine and is involved in incidents of vandalism and in belligerent defiance of prison authority.

After his last offense, this man did not impress probation officers though they refer to a tragedy he experienced several years earlier. A probation officer writes:

> Underlying the defendant's problems appears to be a deep sense of bitterness and hostility, in part owing to the unexpected deaths of his parents when he was 13 years old and the defendant's failure to accept or adjust to these circumstances. The defendant has expressed the attitude that life has unfairly dealt him "dirty" and that he intends to respond in kind; apparently unmindful or uncaring of the consequences either for himself or his victims.

The possibility of a link between hurt and anger is illustrated elsewhere in the man's presentence report, in which the probation officer records an unusual conversation:

> The defendant is an only child (verified), although he convincingly gave the names and ages of a fictitious family of seven brothers and sisters who he claimed resided in various foster homes in Boston, Massachusetts. When the defendant was confronted as to the reason for the fabrication he became hostile and angry and stated that "everybody wants to have a family."

The man has been an inmate in a reformatory where he "became interested and participated in sewing and tailoring training, which he enjoyed." He does similarly well in his first prison work assignments in which "he is praised as being an excellent worker who does everything that is expected of him." He is requested by mess hall correction officers who indicate that he is an exceptional worker in their operation. As to custodial adjustment, early reports complain that the inmate "will display frustration and a quick temper," though they also point out that in one fight he "assisted a correction officer in breaking up the altercation." Other staff characterize the inmate as "a very headstrong, demanding individual who has no concept of attempting to heed any constructive criticism that can be afforded him." The inmate is also discontinued from his work assignment because he is suspected of stealing glue, a fact that gains significance from his admission that he has extensively experimented with drugs in the community.

At this time, the inmate is upgraded with the notation that "he has a reputation for bulldozing and intimidating weak inmates" and is assigned to a maximum-security institution. Here he eventually experiences substantial problems. One report, for example, describes a disturbance in the prison yard and notes:

> As the officer was assisting a sergeant who was assaulted you were seen by another officer as you attempted to kick the officer. As the second officer went to assist the first, you attempted to hit him with your fist. You then ran into a crowd of inmates.

The man understandably receives a heavy penalty for this incident and is transferred to another prison. In this institution, "he serves as a sheet shaker in the laundry and he likes this work, [stating] that he intends to seek this type of employment on the street." He is also described as participating in extracurricular committee assignments and as demonstrating "a greatly improved record."

Later the inmate is however apprehended carrying a homemade weapon and is identified as a participant in extortion. This involvement leads to fights, and the man arms himself (again) and is placed in segregation, where he is described as "an arrogant, troublesome individual." Thereafter he participates in vocational and academic training and in group therapy at the urging of the parole board. At this juncture, staff write that "the inmate has been able to maintain a satisfactory rapport with both staff and peers [and] his custodial record has improved a great deal over the last six months."

In light of this improvement the inmate is paroled, with a notation that he be assigned to "a residential drug program if possible."

This man participates both in the legitimate and illegitimate opportunity structures of the prison. These involvements to some extent are independent, and the man appears content in relatively simple, structured work assignments while he is also involved in drug trafficking and extortion in the inmate community. He does, however, make periodic efforts to impress staff and ends up achieving a dramatic turnabout in which he functions violation free and is involved in self-improvement pursuits.

Many of the man's prison violations are corollaries of his underworld activities, and others show ambivalence in his stance toward prison staff and other authority figures. One aspect of the ambivalence is that the man resents staff interference with his peer-related activities such as extortion and drug trafficking. The other aspect of his ambivalence is a paradoxical attachment to those who show him kindness and take an interest in him, which includes officers who supervise him at work. In this sense, the man not only responds to the loss of parental figures, which he has deeply felt, but unlike individuals who are more bitter, he seems able to accept prison staff as parental substitutes and to relate positively to them. This fact explains the contrasting characterizations of the man, some of which originate with staff members to whom he reacts with defiance while others are filed by staff who find that he can be obedient, loyal, and hard working when he forms a dependent attachment.

This inmate's pattern is not one of "pure" involvement. He gains satisfaction from completing simple tasks but also prizes benevolent supervisors, which means that the relationships that surround tasks may matter as much (or more) than the sense of accomplishment he derives from achieving a neatly shaken sheet or deft stitch.

Support

Where the wrong sort of support facilitates the wrong sort of conduct, some argue that change can occur if the polarity of this force can be reversed.[4] A similar argument applies where people engage in clumsy, counterproductive and therefore foredoomed efforts to establish links with others.

An example of the latter pattern is provided by an adolescent confined for burglarizing a home and destroying a car. The young inmate enters the system after school authorities have done a great deal of soul searching about what to do with him. Teachers have noted that "the most outstanding feature of his difficulties in school was his continual clowning to get the attention of his peers." One teacher complained:

> He seems to be totally unable to stop talking. He will stand up in the middle of a class and do something quite distracting, for instance, tell a dirty joke, make an off-color remark to another classmate, etc. Today, in the middle of a lesson, he was playing with a leather bracelet. He unzipped his pants, put the bracelet almost inside and ran around the room saying, "what does this look like?" Since this is a mixed class, I believe this act was a definite offense to the girls in the class.

The inmate initiates his delinquency career by running away from home and wandering about the community. He then enlists a sidekick and goes on a crime spree. He claims that he would welcome assignment to a camp for youthful offenders because "it will be better than staying [home]. I hate it here." He subsequently changes his mind, however, and escapes from the institution, and this escape nets him an indeterminate sentence to prison.

In the prison, he gains visibility by escalating an incident in which he has been asked to pick up a piece of bread he has dropped on the floor. Though he is charged with "riot and disturbance," the incident ends with a confrontation that pits him against an officer and all of the other inmates in the mess hall. Most of the incidents in this early term revolve around conflicts with other inmates and have to do with a propensity to accumulate debts that he cannot repay, requiring his placement in protection at his request. He is finally moved and for a few months does well, but soon has renewed difficulties with his peers, which he resolves by drawing staff attention to himself. According to an incident report:

> The inmate had turned his bed upside-down. His mattress was under the bed, the inmate under the mattress, when found by the officers. He had covered his body with red dye. He claims that inmates are trying to kill him and he wished to be placed in protective custody.

Later, a progress review describes "a disastrous adjustment" and points out that "the reports he receives are for fights, horseplay, disturbances, destruction of state property, refusing orders, refusing to accept programs, and littering. His only defense for himself is 'I'm a criminal.'" The inmate also "claims that he is a magician and . . . believes he could escape from any situation if he wished to." Staff conclude that he "is a borderline psychotic case" and place him under a moderate regime of medication.

The man's self-proclaimed escape artistry proves a liability after he supplies toothed blades to fellow inmates to help them saw through cell bars of their windows. He also engages in more bouts of horseplay, fighting, refusing orders, and nonparticipation in programs. Such incidents earn the man a transfer to a tough prison, where he signs himself into protective custody 10 days before he is paroled.

The inmate is reimprisoned for another burglary after which he has called the police, claiming credit as a helpful citizen. Later he escapes from a holding cell, "walked to the desk and said 'Hi' to the officers seated behind it." In prison, the man makes an excellent impression, His first report records that he "appears to get along well with staff and peers" and "performs duties in an average manner." His second report describes his custodial adjustment as "outstanding" and points out that he is involved in college-level art study and is "an intelligent, interested student" who "accepts and completes assignments with minimal supervision." He has also become an active participant in a drug and alcohol counseling program.

The inmate has indeed undergone change, though he has also succeeded in a lifelong campaign to earn attention. The campaign starts at age 6 with a pathetic effort to obtain the esteem of peers by playing the clown, and he tries to capture a spark of love from his parents by running away, hoping that he will be missed. These efforts boomerang and make the boy an obnoxious burden to adults and an object of ridicule to peers. He reacts to whatever rejection he invites by resorting to fantasy, which results in his classification as mentally ill. He also builds an actual fantasy life, which consists of a one-person gang with whom he steals and drinks. Stealing sustains the boy's private world but also draws attention, and attention is probably the closest he can come to receiving affection.

In prison, fellow inmates associate with the man only around the gambling table. But he is not very good at gambling and becomes enmeshed in conflicts that he cannot handle. He discovers that clowning in the prison translates into disciplinary charges of horseplay and results in conflicts with officers when they tell him to stop clowning and he disregards their instructions. He also discovers that escape fantasies are taken seriously in the prison. The situation improves in an adult prison where there is no audience for the man's performances and where the climate is one that demands sobriety. Concurrently, the inmate has demonstrated an interest and an aptitude in art. He can now evolve a formula for gaining recognition that centers on conformity and achievement, and what he does also yields intrinsic satisfactions, making him less dependent on attention and approval from others.

A similar result is experienced by an inmate with a comparably checkered career, whose counselor reports:

> I have seen some of his art work, which is quite outstanding. He is quite an accomplished artist, has a lot of talent . . . Since being incarcerated he has learned more skills in commercial art . . . In art class the teacher has asked him to be her aide due to his advanced talent . . . He has a lot of talent and can be easily worked with, especially

with some positive reinforcement, encouragement, and attention.

Both of these inmates are supported by civilian staff, who view their artistic output with admiration, which they freely and volubly express. In this way, staff act the part of benevolent parent figures, and each inmate finds a niche as teacher's pet and as grateful counseling client.

Attachment

Closely related to support is change through emotional bonds and obligations, which compete with criminogenic temptations and pressures. This process—of attachment—occurs among many offenders who "mature out" of offending. Gang delinquents, for example, graduate as they find mates and undertake responsibilities. Recidivism statistics also show that family links reduce return rates to crime.[5]

The difference between change through support and change through attachment lies in the effects of relationships. Support is nurturance, which is valued and builds confidence. Attachment comes with norms and obligations, which are prices one must pay to sustain a relationship. Attending to these norms and obligations means that a person cannot attend to other, conflicting norms. "Be dependable," for instance, competes with "be ostentatiously irresponsible."

Attachment not only goes hand in hand with support but can also be combined with other processes, such as involvement. An example is provided by a man whose adult career begins at age 17 when he is identified as a participant in a robbery. At the time of this incident, the man is on juvenile probation, "leading a nomadic existence without any stable home residence." The probation officer writes that "it should be strongly noted that when the defendant was questioned as to how he felt about his involvement in the present offense his response was one of smiling and laughter."

In prison the man proves resistant to programming. A counselor explains:

The inmate states that he does not like the program of school at this facility. According to him the education program is slap at best and he is unable to learn. He says that when one leaves classrooms there are several other inmates that are looking for him and it makes it inordinately difficult for him.

The inmate also complains "that although he writes his family, they do not answer his letters." Subsequently, his contacts with his family markedly improve, and so does his prison adjustment. Initially, teachers complain about his attendance, which is virtually nonexistent, and he is removed from work assignments because of "charges involving abuse of privileges, [being] out of place, abusive language, and threats." Two months later the man has received a visit from his wife and son, his work supervisors are satisfied with his work, and he reportedly makes progress in school. He also qualifies for an honors block program.

The man does so well that he is soon transferred to a lower security institution so that he can take college courses. Here his work reports range from good to excellent. His school performance is rated "satisfactory," but staff also complain:

> Overall there has been a deterioration in this resident's attitude and behavioral adjustment since initially being received at this facility. It appeared at initial interview that he would be a model inmate and that his previous, poor disciplinary record was going to be left behind at [his last prison]. However, his disciplinary record to date does not indicate that he is maturing sufficiently enough to avoid disciplinary reports.

For 18 months, the situation remains relatively unchanged. The inmate does extremely well in his academic work but sporadically commits disciplinary violations. He also continues close contact with his wife, who eventually succeeds in changing his deportment in prison. In a progress report written 6 months after a dramatic change in the man's conduct, staff write:

The inmate's biggest problem in this facility has always been his disciplinary record. While he is not regarded as highly assaultive, he does become confrontative and consequently has subjected himself to numerous reports that could have easily been avoided. He had been counseled about this on many occasions. However, I think the point was finally driven home when his wife called the superintendent of the facility regarding the family reunion [conjugal visiting] program. She seemed very sincere and concerned about her husband. She stated to the superintendent and to this writer that if the inmate was going to continue to subject himself to disciplinary reports, thus curtailing his chances for a more positive program, then she did not see him as being worthwhile to wait for. Apparently the inmate got this message loud and clear. He was called out on an interview by the superintendent and this matter was discussed. After that there has been a marked improvement in his behavioral record.

This situation prevails for another 2 years, until the inmate is released. The change is truly extraordinary because early on, the man has seen himself as tough and ready to deploy violence. The man's self-conception also colored his interactions with staff, with whom he insisted on being dealt with on a level of equity, which meant that his word was as good as any staff member's in an altercation.

There are two chinks in this man's armor, however. One is an intense thirst for education and a propensity for becoming interested and involved in work assignments. This propensity provides the prison system with a strong incentive or reward for use in modifying the man's behavior. It also takes the man into a social setting containing others who are similarly oriented and separates him from his antisocial group of peers. The second chink in the man's armor is his close attachment to his family, who are also concerned about modifying his behavior and are not above using the continuation of the relationship as a lever to inspire compliance. In this connection, the inmate undergoes a crisis, and after the wife's seminal intervention, a counselor even complains that "the inmate has apparently broken up with his wife." However, faced with the realization that he must choose between the world of tough manliness and that of middle-class responsibility, the inmate successfully opts for the later.

Detachment

To the extent to which maladaptiveness ties into attributes of settings in which the person is unable to function, a change of scenery can often be regenerative. For example, prison administrators contend—and our data verify—that young inmates often improve their deportment when transferred to a prison with an older population.[6] Entering an age-heterogeneous environment that "detaches," because it reduces peer pressure, permits increased relaxation and tempers anxiety. The more mature social environment also offers fewer occasions for conflict, and it provides diminished opportunity to play to inmate audiences.

Where a transfer between settings works, this does not mean that setting attributes have been to blame for the person's maladaptiveness. Because the entire relationship between person and setting has been changed, the person's propensities to maladaptiveness are as much at issue as the environment in which they were displayed.

This point is exemplified by the career of a youth who participates in many fights, but who ends his prison sentence with 6 months that are free of violations, a period which coincides with a transfer from a youth institution to a maximum-security prison.

The inmate has been placed in structured settings of various kinds since the age of 4, and his probation officer notes that "his family won't even allow him to reside within their home. He was in fact living in an automobile at the time he committed the present offenses."

The probation staff suggests that the man be placed in an inpatient treatment program for addicts, but he is instead committed to a low-security facility that is structured around a cottage system. His removal from this setting is soon requested. The prison reports:

He has been moved to several different cottages because of a confrontational and outspoken self-presentation with peers and staff and because at each new location the possessions of others soon disappear after his arrival. As a consequence the inmate has been involved in fighting episodes which threaten the security of the facility. At this point in time the inmate is no longer deemed an appropriate placement in a minimum-security facility. His behavior and other needs require a more structured setting.

This summary represents the conclusions of a number of cottage officers. One officer writes:

The above inmate is in my cottage for the second time. Both times he has been nothing but trouble. A short time after arriving in the cottage things start to disappear. The cottage becomes very noisy. He is the type of inmate who cannot get along with anyone. In the short time that he has been here he has only enemies in the cottage—no friends . . . I have been informed today that he is stealing in the cottage. Also I have been told today that he has been provoking another inmate all day, and that tonight's fight is the result.

Another officer provides a similar account:

It has been brought to my attention by two inmates that this inmate has been stealing various and sundry items from them (e.g., soap, shampoo, deodorant) and selling these items to other inmates . . . An inmate stated that he found the inmate in his unattended room on several occasions, whereupon items would turn up missing . . . Since the inmate has a lengthy history of thefts within other cottages and because of the extant potential for a physical confrontation between the inmate and the inmates from whom the inmate has reportedly stolen, I strongly urge that the inmate be removed from this cottage forthwith or perhaps be removed from this facility.

The man is transferred to a secure youth prison after losing 6 months of good time for fighting. In the second institution, he continues to be involved in fights, but these conflicts are of a different order, in that he now generates ethnic confrontations. He rejects drug therapy "because he has serious racial prejudice and therapy groups are mainly ethnic Black and Puerto Rican" and also leaves school "due to peer pressures" after making substantial progress.

The inmate undergoes "grief shock" when he learns that his younger sister has committed suicide. At the same time, he is accorded a heavy penalty (90 days of segregation and 180 days loss of good time) because he has assaulted another inmate with a chair. He keeps being segregated for involvements in fights, which reduces the time he spends in the classroom. At this juncture, in response to strong recommendations from the youth prison administration, he is transferred to a maximum-security prison with an older population, where he spends over 6 months without a single disciplinary incident. The type of setting with which this young man can finally cope combines structure and an older population, so that issues of pecking order and of outgrouping and ingrouping and peer rivalries do not arise, and program involvement becomes the only show in town.

Respite

One way in which settings can differ is in terms of amounts of stimulation they offer. Stimulation levels matter particularly to people who react adversely to boredom (low stimulation) or to confusion (high stimulation). Where a person moves from a setting in which the stimulation levels are higher or lower than he or she can handle, reductions in maladaptive behavior can be expected if the person has reacted with aggression or irritability to stimulus overload or underload. This is the type of change that is reported, for example, with students who are removed from classrooms that overwhelm or underchallenge them.

People settle down in low-stimulation settings because they can relax or regroup in such settings. A reduced level of stimulation can also improve deportment when stimuli are viewed as demands to which the person feels obligated to react.

A case in point is that of a 32-year-old man who has been admitted to medical institutions at age 9, suffering from "childhood schizophrenia." He is later diagnosed as having graduated to "schizophrenia, paranoid-type, severe." The presentence report concludes that "he appears to be in need of a highly structured, secure treatment modality where he can receive the necessary assistance in coping with his various emotional problems." This prescription is intended to fit the prison.

At prison intake, a counselor broaches the possibility of an academic program, which the man rejects, stating, "school is for kids." Test scores show the inmate classifiable "within the borderline range of mental functioning."

Two months later the inmate has been sent to a special program. Program staff find the man resistant. They record:

> He has had at least two writeups since his program began, one of which consists of verbally threatening an officer. On occasions where he has been confronted in therapy he becomes very nasty and aggressive . . . However, in recent weeks, in fairness to the inmate, he has begun to relax more and at least speak civilly to other group members and staff.

Three months thereafter, optimism has faded, and we read:

> This man apparently feels his masculinity is threatened if he backs down in a situation. Thus he has difficulty relating to officers, staff, and inmates and will not retreat even if he knows he is wrong. When not in an angered state he can function in a fairly reasonable manner. However, it appears that when he feels challenged he throws all caution to the wind and impulsively acts.

Three months later, staff expand on their observation, and describe the inmate as follows:

He has a very heavy fixation on the validity of his masculinity and will exhibit anger whenever this is challenged. Unfortunately he also feels that his ability to make his own decisions, be they right or wrong, is part of that masculine expression. As a result when he was recently offered the opportunity to attend school he refused and chose to follow disciplinary-type procedures to prevent his attendance. After several attempts to talk with this man and allow him to get by his false pride it was decided that his need for therapy outweighed his need for education at present, and he was reverted back to a shop program.

Five months later, the unit staff reported that the man "will stubbornly refuse any help, although he acknowledges his need for help." Staff add:

In all, he has accumulated sixteen reports to this date. The bulk of these refer to his refusal to meet program activities such as school, therapy, or work. Also, behaviors such as harassment, refusing order, threats, and verbal abuse have been reported. In interviews both prior to and after these incidents he is able to generate acceptable alternative behaviors, but chooses to act out in a manner that pleases him regardless of the consequence.

In another document, staff point out that even with all his difficulties, prison strikes the man as preferable to the outside world. They write:

The inmate appears very resigned to institutional life and has spoken on the positive aspects of institutional life on several occasions. The outlook of this inmate is quite sad in that he feels that the basic needs met by institutional life offers this as a better lifestyle than perhaps that which he is forced to live in on the street. With this rather low opinion of himself and poor outlook for the future he almost appears resigned to illegal activities until his eventual arrest and return to a facility-type setting.

The staff conclude:

> One cannot help but suspect that he is depressed as a result of these prospects and sees little if any motivation towards change. This overall outlook reflects this man's very low self-esteem and poor self-image. It is this attitude that likely causes him to receive occasional misbehavior reports for very minor incidents which he is fully capable of avoiding. There are times when he feels that others may see this feeling in him. It is suspected that these are the times when he acts out very irrational decision-making type of behavior.

In the following few months, there are fewer misbehavior reports, and the man's relationship with correctional staff and peers are noted as having improved. However, shortly thereafter occurs an incident that appears to have been sparked by the fact that the inmate's peers had complained to correction officers about "foot odors while they were sitting by him in the mess hall, eating." The incident shows the inmate claiming that he has no socks or that socks do not fit him and taking a conscientious objector stance because he makes the assumption that any compromise or retreat is inconceivable.

As a result of such sequences, we find the inmate in disciplinary segregation settings where he is invariably described as "quiet, polite, and cooperative" and as "relaxed and content." Not only is he observed to socialize with other segregated inmates and to participate in recreation with obvious enjoyment, but officers record that "he has admirably refused to involve himself in the various shouting matches and other disruptive behavior that has occurred in this special housing unit recently." When the inmate emerges from segregation, however, he renews his "passive resistance to authority figures which has become more aggressive, in the form of threats." Only when he returns to confinement status, observation reports contend that he "adjusts well to the mundane routine and appears very content."

Staff are aware of this setting-specific pattern. They point out that whenever the inmate is confined to his cell, "it has been noted that he generally has adjusted quite well." Segregation unit officers report:

> He presents no custodial problems and is cooperative and friendly to special housing unit staff. The inmate also tends to sing and talk to himself in his cell, but the latter behavior on inspection seems to be his way of "thinking out loud."

Generally speaking, the policy of the institution has become to leave the inmate on unemployed status in his cell, and as a result the last months of his stay pass without incident.

It appears that if and when the inmate does not feel challenged and he is left to his own devices, few problems arise, but when he is instructed to do something or not to do something, there is a risk that he can see himself having to prove his worth, in which instances he digs in his heels and becomes stubbornly wedded to his predefined stand. When custodial moves have to be escalated, this makes the man feel doubly impotent, which causes him to scold and threaten staff. It turns out that in his case, the ultimate managerial gambit is that of punitive segregation, which places the man in a setting in which he no longer feels overtested and overchallenged, and is therefore more or less at peace.

Sanctuary

One implication of the *need hierarchy* described by the psychologist Abraham Maslow is that safety concerns can monopolize attention and thus keep "higher" goals (esteem or social needs) from being experienced.[7] The process does not distinguish between justified and unjustified safety concerns, nor could it do so, because (a) when the danger people feel is great, they cannot afford to play odds in assessing threats, (b) imagined threats feel just as real as actual danger, and (c) once afraid, people become attuned—and often oversensitive—to danger cues.

Just as danger is to varying degrees in the eyes of the beholder, so is safety. When we speak of sanctuaries, we speak of settings that are subjectively reassuring or that feel safer than other settings. A sanctuary must offer physical security, but it also must contain a relaxed atmosphere and an absence of constraints and pressures that fearful individuals can regard as malevolent or hostile.

In New York prisons, "victim-prone" inmates had been recognized as a special class at the time of our study, and a variety of settings had been designed to respond to the needs of this group. The concern of those who ran such settings was humane but also reintegrative, in the sense that inmates were expected to graduate from the ameliorative settings into the prison population at large.[8] Initially it was hoped that inmates who had reacted maladaptively to fear would behave differently when they felt reassured and able to abandon reactions (preemptive strikes, self-insulation, and so forth) that respond to perceived danger.

An example is provided by one of our mature inmates who had listed many drugs to which he was addicted and identified himself as an alcoholic.

The man had been discharged by the army for a psychiatric disability, and the probation officer who prepared his presentence report wrote:

> With his psychological disorders and his extensive drug abuse and with his wildly exaggerated stories, [he] presented the profile of a man trying desperately to convince this writer that he is completely insane and does not deserve to be in jail but rather undergoing treatment . . . He did impress this writer as suffering from one or several mental disorders . . . He stated over and over in several different ways that everyone was out to get him.

In the prison the inmate signs himself into protection, claiming that other inmates have made sexual overtures to him and have subjected him to extortion attempts. A psychiatrist writes:

> He stated he has not been out of special housing during the eight months he has been incarcerated. When I suggested he could possibly enter into a program at this facility he said he could not because he has enemies . . . What we have here is a very paranoid man who suffers from classical delusions of persecution.

Later it develops that the man in fact does have real enemies whom he has good reason to fear, though he also has imaginary enemies, including the military, various agencies of government, and mental health professionals with whom he has dealt. The man eventually agrees, however, to be placed in a less formal, enriched protective program, where he does well. Staff write:

> Since his arrival here very little inappropriate behavior has been observed. The structure of the environment appears to offer the safety and support as well as activity stimulation needed by him. He has been emotionally stable and has not been threatening legal action. He has utilized appropriate channels for suggesting administrative changes which would be helpful in enhancing the effectiveness of our program. He has demonstrated personal initiative in solving problems, and has been patient and delayed gratification. It may be questionable [however] if he can continue with his positive behavior when released.

At the inception of this inmate's sentence, his codefendant arrives in the prison, spreads the word that the man is "a rat," and seeks to do him harm. This creates a fateful confluence because when this man, who suffers from residues of paranoid schizophrenia, senses danger, he evolves conspiracy schemes to "explain" and counter the threat.

Matters are not improved by the fact that the man becomes aware of the skeptical reactions he evokes in some prison staff members, who thus qualify for inclusion as protagonists in his conspiracy scheme. The problems get even worse when the man is segregated and has little to do beyond embroidering his conspiracies, but as a corollary the problem is solved through assignment to a program that is both safe and supportive and offers opportunities for activity and constructive participation. In this program the man feels reassured, his attention is constructively engaged, and his symptoms subside.

Asylum

One deficit prisons share with community settings is that they offer few conditions short of hospitalization under which disturbed individuals can lead some semblance of a normal life. In such settings tolerance for deviance must be high, but not high enough to reinforce eccentricity. The settings must also assist individuals with chores of daily living and encourage involvement in activities that transcend self-management. Beyond these attributes, such environments must provide medical and psychological services to help disturbed people control their symptoms, which may require occasional transfers into more structured (hospital or quasi-hospital) settings when the need for more comprehensive ministrations arises. To the extent to which asylums of this kind are provided, it is often possible to reduce a person's functional handicaps to the point at which a semblance of normalcy can be achieved, which means that the person can engage in as much adaptive behavior as we can expect from someone who manifests continuing symptoms of pathology.

New York prisons have offered asylum arrangements, and a number of disturbed inmates have benefited from them. One such inmate had been repeatedly written up for being unclean and refusing to take showers and otherwise take care of himself. He also had been written up for refusing to do things such as go to school and go to work, and was occasionally charged with being disruptive, destroying and throwing objects, and once for flooding his cell.

The man received an indeterminate sentence with a maximum term of 15 years. Shortly after he arrives in prison, officers report that he "never participates in any activities nor speaks to anyone. He sometimes paces the floor speaking to himself. He was heard recently asking another inmate to cut his throat." The man explains that "you can't mingle with everybody" and describes his behavior as an attempt to "formulate my thoughts and see if they seem logical." He also explains that he couldn't care less if people observe his soliloquies.

At this time, the man is brought to the attention of mental health staff. Mental health staff find the inmate disheveled and unshaven but willing to answer questions because "he said that if he didn't answer them the White man would put the law onto him again and he might even be killed." The interviewer concludes that the man needs hospitalization, but while this suggestion is considered a month elapses during which he "hears voices telling him not to trust anyone" and engages in conversations with "white and black specters in his cell." At one juncture, it also "appeared as if he were going to throw a cup of human excrement at the officers who were feeding the supper meal on the special housing unit." He is thereupon instructed to move to a cell with a plastic front but refuses. He takes his stand with "both fists clenched, with the point of a pen protruding out of each," challenging the officers to come and get him, which they do, first dousing him with "one small blast of tear gas." The inmate surprisingly reports that he feels great though he "claimed his penis had shrunk," and the next day he is transferred to the hospital where he remains for 6 months.

For the next 18 months, the inmate marginally survives in the prison. He refuses mental health assistance. He does not wash. He talks about "sonic noises" that control him, "insists on being the last in line, and wants no one behind him in the food line," "sits at the table very dirty about himself and stares at the other inmates who are afraid to sit and eat with him," and "goes through garbage, especially cans that people have spit in." Hospitalization occurs again after the inmate throws a food tray at an officer, shouting "feed this to the panthers," punches a second officer in the shoulder, and hits another officer in the face, which leads to a wrestling match. In the hospital the inmate remains for an entire year. He is returned to the prison with a notation that "there is acting-out potential in relation to a paranoid decompensation during which time, if the patient feels he is being attacked, he may become violent."

The inmate thereafter manages in the prison for about 2 years with only sporadic incidents of disorderly conduct but continues to have emotional problems as evidenced by a note he writes to his brother instructing him to kill somebody whom he feels is sending him hostile messages in hallucinations. Prison authorities inform the brother that there are "psychiatrists available to help." Several months later the man's mother visits him, whereupon he "assaulted a correction officer who was standing nearby."

The man is once again committed to the hospital and subsequently assigned to a residential mental health program. He begins to participate in available activities. In school he becomes a "good student" and experiences no problems except for an occasion in which he refused to go to class. He manages to control most of his symptoms, though it is reported that "occasionally he talks about 'machines' controlling people. This is a delusional process he regresses to in times of depression or boredom." The inmate is even released to population, where he manages under mental health supervision, alternately enrolled in a prevocational program and unemployed, with only two minor disciplinary violations in his last year in prison.

This man does surprisingly well considering that his delusional system centers around the assumption that people, including people in uniforms, manifest intentions to kill him. The man's success in part derives from the indulgence of officers who permit him to stay in his cell quietly hallucinating and let him take evasive measures to protect himself, provided these do not include attacking officers and other inmates. The man's most prevalent difficulty arises from his phobia in relation to showers, which includes simulating a shower when he cannot evade it altogether.

The man is permitted to partially control his psychiatric treatment, including his hospital commitments. He is permitted to modulate his exposure to perceived danger, and he survives a decade of imprisonment oscillating along a continuum that ranges from mild apprehension to panics that require hospitalization but that ultimately dissipate under an indulgent regime.

Reassessment

One fact that makes maladaptive behavior fascinating is that it frequently continues despite evidence that it does not "work" or achieves results that are counterproductive. This fact tells us that superficial change strategies—such as reasoning with the maladaptive person and giving him advice —are unlikely to work, because they merely tell the person what is (or should be) obvious to him.

It does not by any means follow, however, that insight is superfluous as a vehicle of change. History is redolent with reforms that are based on reevaluation, and most people's lives, including those of critics of insight-related approaches, contain turning points in which reassessment has led to reformation.

The conclusion to be drawn is not that insight-based change is unachievable on its own but that it is difficult and is best deployed at critical junctures in the lives of clients, when they are susceptible to change because of guilt and other sources of discomfort. Even this requisite does not suffice, however, because insights involve self-critiques that are unflattering and frequently painful. Insight-related approaches must thus include techniques for working through expected defensive reactions.

Prisons have not been havens for insight-centered interventions, given prevailing doubts about the value of offender rehabilitation. Some residues of the insight-related approach persist, however, in the shape of therapeutic communities that have been mostly invoked for substance abusers.[9] One of the people who has benefited from this strategy is a man who had been imprisoned for shoplifting and selling drugs to a police officer.

An attack on a correction officer earns this inmate a heavy penalty, but before it is assigned the custody staff request that a psychiatrist examine the inmate because "he is experiencing anxiety and disorientation." The psychiatrist reports that the inmate is suffering from "an anxiety reaction, situational." A month later the inmate is sent to another prison. Psychiatrists there report:

> [The inmate] was admitted to the psychiatric service on the same day of his transfer to this prison . . . During the first three days of admission, attempts at interviews with the resident were unsuccessful as he looked lost, confused, and bewildered. The delusional picture alternated between marked withdrawal and periods of agitation where he would become hostile, impulsive, and demanding. During these periods of agitation he would scream and yell and would almost continuously bang his fists and feet and sometimes his head against his room's metal door . . . He continues to be confused and incoherent, and the clinical picture has remained essentially the same as above. If anything, he has decompensated further and has become a danger to himself . . . Yesterday he ripped up his bedsheets making long strips, causing the staff to take precautionary steps regarding his suicide attempt. [The inmate] also said to the writer that he "cannot take prison any longer" and that "sooner or later something would happen."

From the hospital, the inmate is sent to a therapeutic community. Here, at first, the inmate "states emphatically he doesn't want to be in the program," and staff write that "he seems to carry the proverbial 'chip on his shoulder,' and this attitude will probably make his adjustment to prison difficult." Later they write about the inmate:

> He has made a rather erratic adjustment to the Program. He gives every indication that he considers himself above and beyond those who are his fellow residents. He has been confronted about this by his peers who perceive this at various times. Moreover, he is quite immature and has a problem properly handling authority. He feels that within this environment he can consider himself an exception to the rules and procedures. This is a former drug user who led a vicarious hedonistic life on the street,

void of any responsibility. In addition, his family, particularly his parents, appear to have shielded him when he got himself into trouble. He admits that this has probably not helped him learn from his past experiences. What this man needs most is to learn some responsibility and acceptance of authority.

Staff's point about parental protectiveness is illustrated at this stage of the man's career by a set of letters from his father to various officials, in which he demands that his son be transferred closer to home. One of the man's disciplinary reports also describes an arrangement he has made with his parents to send packages that (owing to his disciplinary status) he cannot receive to a second inmate for transmittal.

Staff conclude that the inmate "appears to be conveniently continuing his dependence upon his parents" and imply that he refuses to accept strictures of confinement because he considers himself a prodigal son in exile. They complain:

> His participation in therapy has been minimal and he has preoccupied himself in putting forth an image of "an old experienced convict." His lack of experience, attitude, and immaturity all betray the validity of this image to both staff and peers. He therefore maintains very few associates and keeps a low profile in the community . . . He goes on at great length about his own personal discomforts, has been extremely indifferent to the therapy, and has on occasion fallen asleep during the sessions.

A traumatic experience, however, unfreezes the inmate's stance, and staff are able to report:

> Several weeks ago he became the center of the community's attention and was confronted very heavily about having involved himself in some homosexual activity . . . Finally he admitted, be it superficially, that he had been involved in such activity . . . During this process he became much more relaxed, surprisingly, in the community setting and was able to deal at least in one group session in a more positive fashion. He somehow feels

that he has been shortchanged in life and perhaps deserves his just reward. This outlook serves as a justification for all of his immature and acting-out behaviors. He was able at least to acknowledge and perhaps absorb some of this in a recent group session, and has been functioning somewhat better since that time.

The breakthrough appears to have lasting effects, although for a while there is "some reversion." Soon the change that has taken place becomes more substantial, and staff report that the inmate "has been successful at eliminating a great deal of the immature behavior noted in previous reports" and "a great deal of his facade of being a 'tough guy' has been dropped and a rather likable well mannered gentleman remains in place." Six months later the man continues to do well and even receives a commendation for "applying first aid and promptly transporting to the clinic an inmate who attempted suicide," and he is credited with successfully tutoring inmates enrolled in a vocational training program. The inmate is also approved for work release and is eventually assigned to the institution his parents had continuously requested for him.

Several observations are highlighted by those who have become involved with this man. The first impression has to do with a symbiotic relationship the man has with his family, who offer him favored treatment and unconditional protection which he then expects elsewhere. He, therefore, in the words of a counselor, "expects the rewards of life without paying the required price." It is also observed that the man's family keeps him from becoming self-reliant, effective, and self-confident. Another set of observations has to do with the man's mental health, which varies over time. The first stage of the progression is one in which the man falls apart. But when the man makes his anxiety obvious, he discovers that this does not impress prison officials (including a psychiatrist), nor does it mitigate his disciplinary disposition. He manifests his despair by screaming and helplessly pounding on a cell door and threatening to kill himself. Even these extreme reactions, however, do not change his fate, beyond the fact that they earn him a 4-week stay in the prison hospital, a discharge diagnosis of dysthymic disorder, and the label "antisocial personality."

The man's advent in the therapeutic community marks the onset of another stage of his reaction to the prison, in which he makes it obvious that he still expects favored and individualized treatment and that he does not feel that productivity or expenditure of energy can be expected from him. He also expresses disdain for the peasants who surround him and shows that he regards prison authorities as individuals to whom he can lie and whose rules he can defy or circumvent to advance his interests. In this enterprise, the man still enjoys the backing of his parents, who have embarked on a campaign designed to extricate him from his prison assignment and to bring him within commuting distance, which is the same strategy they had deployed to end his military career after 6 months (with a "hardship" discharge) so that he could rejoin the parents who ostensibly felt inconvenienced by his absence.

The strategy this time fails, and the man is left at the mercy of the therapeutic community, but this in and of itself does not unfreeze his stance, and it is not until he is caught red-handed in a homosexual encounter that the stage is set for the last phase of his prison career. This transformation is a success story for the therapeutic community because it is doubtful that any change could have occurred in the absence of combined confrontation and support, which defines the therapeutic community process.

What seemingly occurs is that the man for the first time is forced to examine his outlook and approach to life and the reactions of others to his spoiled-child expectations. He is confronted with the nature and consequence of a destructive dependency on parental support that has kept him from being his own man and has made it unnecessary and therefore undesirable to face responsibility, particularly in his role in the community. Subsequent instances in which the man exercises responsibility (such as in his tutorial capacity) suggest that he has indeed been made more autonomous in the prison—at least in the short run. This paradox must be placed in perspective by recognizing that the liberating impact is not merely due to impersonal limits set by the institution (which show the man at prison intake that the world is no longer unconditionally responsive to his needs) but requires interventions that force the man to examine his assumptions and explore alternative approaches to life.

Deterrence

Webster's Collegiate Dictionary defines "to deter" as "to turn aside, discourage, or prevent from acting (as by fear)." None of the examples we could review suggest that undesired behavior can be routinely deterred in this sense. We see offenders whose maladaptiveness has continued unabated in the face of frequent and often predictably painful repercussions.

In those cases in which deterrence works, it appears to do so by exercising an unfreezing, sobering effect, which causes the person to think twice in situations in which he might otherwise proceed to act. Dispositions may be unaffected— the person may be just as impulsive, or feel just as wounded or indignant—but he does not translate these motives into acts as casually as he may have done before. The impact is short-run, but new habits may become ingrained if they bring rewards and satisfactions.[10]

In prisons, deterrence has been traditionally exercised by the parole board. The board may keep the person imprisoned because of patterns of misbehavior, and they may promise (at least by implication) that improved deportment will lead to expedited freedom.

Among inmates with whom this intervention has worked is a 21-year-old man who serves a sentence for robbing a token booth in a subway system. The inmate proves especially troublesome in that he has evolved a penchant for escalating confrontations with correction officers that begin with refusals to obey instructions.

Typical conflicts start with casual violations followed by angry reactions to the prospect of sanctions. In one incident, for example, the man throws trash in front of his cell and when he is escorted to the disciplinary committee, "stopped about three-quarters of the way down the gallery, squared off with me [the officer], raised his hand in a fighting stance, then stated 'back off me. You better cut me some slack.'" In another incident, the man leaves the area where he is supposed to be after having taken a shower, and when he is instructed to lock in offers to take a swing at officers, jumps into his cell, delivers a string of obscenities, and ends up spitting at an officer. Three hours later he throws a tantrum in his cell, banging furniture with his shoe, and finally plugs his toilet and sink and floods a prison gallery.

In a third incident the man is chased all over the institution by officers, who obviously become increasingly annoyed. In still another incident the man approaches an officer who is packing the belongings of a fellow inmate and wants to know what is going on. When he is told to remove himself, he not only refuses but adds a string of expletives and is again chased through half the facility after having refused to lock in. On a fifth occasion he is ordered to leave an exercise yard and declines because he feels that his time is not up. When he receives a Notice of Report, he throws a cup of liquid through his cell bars at one officer and subsequently threatens to throw something at another officer, which he proceeds to do.

Needless to say, the inmate serves an inordinate amount of time in segregation settings for such incidents. And while he is generating a reputation as a troublesome prisoner with staff, he evidences a comparable capacity to initiate and sustain conflicts with peers. It is the latter involvement that finally comes to a head and forces the inmate to seek assistance, testifying that "it's gotten so that I am afraid to step out of my cell."

Meanwhile the man receives a sound rebuff from the parole board who note that "you have incurred some 50 disciplinary reports, several for assaultive behavior" and point to his "minimum participation" in programs. All of this appears to exercise a sobering effect: In his last 6 months in prison, the inmate not only does not receive a single disciplinary report but also makes what is described as "satisfactory progress in a vocational training assignment."

It appears that when this man feels threatened, he loses control and rants and raves, though his preferred strategy is flight. This unfortunately simply delays the game by one move because at the next juncture, he is cornered and rants and raves to again express his displeasure. This self-defeating pattern seems to be redundant and interminable. Somehow, however, the seriousness of consequences in terms of time served as dictated by the parole board (and the manifest threat of peer retribution) are ultimately impressed on the man, and the unfreezing produces at least temporary reformation.

The point is, of course, that the man acts tough but is not really tough. He talks tough when pointing a gun at a subway attendant but looks less tough when sitting in jail (as he eventually does) bemoaning the absence of his mother; he also finds it easy to hurl obscenities at guards until the behavior affects his parole. The man has a facade that will not stay in place over the long haul, and it is probably this fact that makes deterrence ultimately effective.

Relaxation

Facades can be dropped, and compensatory behavior can be discontinued. However, such changes often cannot be traced to experiences that occasion them, nor can specific influences be credited for transmutations.

On occasion, the concerns that impel a person to maladaptive behavior can dissipate, so that the person becomes freed to behave in nonmaladaptive ways. Defenses the person uses may be *relaxed*, so that he can afford to face life with greater equanimity.

An example of the pattern is a young man who spends over 10 years in prison for a violent crime of passion. At prison reception the inmate is seen by a psychiatrist, who writes:

> He is a rather hostile type, and tried to give the examiner a hard time. He made such remarks as that the undersigned as well as his fellow Americans are all murderers,

having taken over the lands of the Indians, killing them when they attempted to defend their property, etc. If looks could kill, the undersigned would probably not be writing this . . . The inmate projects his own hostility and then sees this hostility that he projects as coming from others to him . . . He is very definitely dangerous.

The inmate is assigned to a maximum-security prison, where he is soon referred to another psychiatrist. This psychiatrist describes the man's self-presentation as follows:

"Pressure is building up in me more and more. I am afraid for my life. It is like a conspiracy." Who is involved? "Everybody in prison." Why are they doing this? "I don't know. This I would like to know from you. I asked already the priest but he couldn't answer this question." . . . Diagnosis: paranoid psychosis.

One and a half years after this juncture, the man is reclassified and assigned to a low-security institution. After spending 3 years in this institution, the inmate is able to report:

I have had but one minor disciplinary report in the last five years. During my long incarceration I obtained my high school equivalency diploma, earned certificates in barbering and woodwork, attended one-on-one psychotherapy for 18 months, attended six months of group therapy and have maintained close relations with my parents, sister, and brother-in-law, who visit me regularly during my confinement.

Before he is released years later, the inmate receives additional therapy and completes other vocational training programs.

This man has been extremely sensitive to negative assessments by others and to the experience of being slighted or rejected. This hypersensitivity is so extreme that it at times takes the form of paranoid delusions and possibly psychotic states. It also involves considerable self-pity.

The inmate makes himself unpopular at this time because he is obnoxious, which confirms his unfavorable opinion of himself. His counterattacks range from confrontative verbal hostility to physical explosions, including at the extreme the crime for which he is sent to prison. The prison experience, however, becomes a success story in that the system has taken the risk of deescalating its custody provisions, permitting involvements that ameliorate the man's sensitivity to negative assessments and affronts, and his explosions of outrage and anger when he feels hurt.

Maturation

In our review of maladaptive career patterns, our principal finding has been that misbehavior tends to diminish over time. It is inviting to assume that age and maturation largely account for this trend. The two variables (age and maturation) are admittedly intertwined. One reason maladaptiveness (such as crime, violence, and prison misbehavior) peaks at early ages is that developmental change takes place that expands one's roster of prosocial and adaptive skills.

Given the pervasiveness of age effects, no single explanation is liable to account for them. Moreover, people can achieve tangible increments of sobriety and equally tangible decrements of playfulness at varying ages and to varying degrees. The move in question can be described in terms of contrasts between antecedent childlike, nonserious, ebullient, and irresponsible behavior and consequent adult, serious, and responsible behavior. This does not imply abruptness, however, in that maturation mostly denotes *gradual* change.

An example of the agonizing ebb and flow of maturation is the career of a young man who enters the system for committing a narcotics violation while on probation for two other offenses. When this man enters prison, the reception unit staff describe his custodial adjustment as "atrocious." They report that during his initial confinement "he received five misbehavior reports, which were for horseplay, having a fishline, two reports for throwing water, and another report for horseplaying." The man is consequently sent to a secure prison, where he alleges he has enemies but "feels no need for protective custody screening at this time." He also allegedly "demonstrates a complete reversal in behavior." His disciplinary record becomes violation free and his teachers report that he "tries hard to learn." Work supervisors, however, describe the man as doing "average to below-average" work and indicate that he is "a bit slow, but functions" and "gets along well with others."

Given the man's (relatively speaking) good performance in prison, staff conclude that he is "a suitable candidate for a lower level of security" and assign him to a camp setting. Here he repeatedly refuses work assignments and is found in possession of "a red balloon filled with a leafy substance," which to no one's surprise is identified as marijuana. The man subsequently contends that "he was set up by one of his roommates" and enlists a fellow inmate who perjures himself on his behalf.

Two months later the inmate is paroled, but within 12 days he is identified as the perpetrator of an offense that makes him eligible for a draconian sentence as a predicate felon. He returns to prison for a long-term stay and turns over a new leaf; he expresses interest in furthering his education, receives no disciplinary reports, and is described as "quiet and reserved in appearance and manner."

When a probation officer describes the man at early prison entry as "streetwise," he depicts the way the man plausibly thinks of himself. The characterization denotes heavy involvement in drug usage and drug trafficking and other minor criminal activities, as well as a substantial network of congenial acquaintances with compatible interests. Such is the life this man leads in the community, and such is the life he leads in the prison when the opportunity affords. The man is not "streetwise," however, if the term denotes sophistication, efficacy, or expertise in negotiating the contingencies that arise in the pursuit of underworld activities. He is caught redhanded selling drugs, presents explanations that are transparently silly, and sells more drugs within days after receiving probation. He similarly essays different (and

334   ACTING OUT: MALADAPTIVE BEHAVIOR IN CONFINEMENT

equally noncredible) versions of an alibi for a prison offense, a strategy which at best is not taken seriously.

Such behavior reflects limited perceptiveness of social reality, such as the assessment of risks he can reasonably take when the police and probation or parole authorities have reason to take an interest in his activities. Another implication, of course, is that there is no point to veracity even if there is zero benefit to mendacity. In other words, one does not admit that one has done something even where the evidence is overwhelming.

None of this, however, makes the man a hopeless cause for life. As time passes and circumstances become irrevocably serious, he appears to know that the game has changed and the time for playfulness, prevarication, and wishful thinking is over. He thus pleads guilty to his last offense, does not persevere in his subcultural games, responds to the best of his ability in vocational and educational settings, and demonstrates sobriety when he finds himself in prison shortly after he has been released. The evidence cautiously suggests that the man's unambiguous induction into the mainline prison world has not only traumatized him sufficiently to ensure improved deportment but may have expedited his progression from slap-happy adolescence to relatively mature adulthood.

Notes

1. Social control theory in criminology is the premier sociological theory of crime causation and desistance (see Hirschi, T. [1969]. *Causes of delinquency*. Berkeley: University of California Press).

   For the best psychological perspective on the dynamics of desistance of criminal behavior, see Maruna, S. (2001). *Making good: How ex-convicts reform and rebuild their lives*. Washington, DC: American Psychological Association.

2. The 1972 "Work of America" Task Force wrote that "work has been used as a form of rehabilitation for centuries—but not always successfully. Apparently, many failures occur because meaningless work has been prescribed. Its very uselessness has lowered the self-esteem of the mental patient, welfare recipient, prisoner, or physically handicapped person. Instead of being the means by which self-confidence

was improved, inadequate work struck a further blow at the pride and self-respect of the person who needed help . . . Work may be the best therapy possible for juvenile delinquents, mental patients, prisoners, drug addicts, and alcoholics but unless job satisfaction is made possible as a part of such therapy, work will only compound their difficulties" (Special Task Force to the Secretary of Health, Education and Welfare. [1973]. *Work in America*. Cambridge, MA: MIT Press, p. 90).

3. Irwin (1970), chapter 7, note 4 discusses self-betterment by inmates as a mode of prison adjustment. Most studies of attitudes toward incarceration have reported that the prime interest of inmates is in program-related activities. See Toch, 1992, chapter 9, note 3; also, Glaser, D. (1964). *The effectiveness of a prison and parole system*. Indianapolis, IN: Bobbs-Merrill.

4. See, for example, Vorrath, H. H., & Brendtro, L. K. (1974). *Positive peer culture*. Chicago: Aldine.

5. Sampson, R. J., & Laub, J. (1993). *Crime in the making: Pathways and turning points through life*. Cambridge, MA: Harvard University Press. Attachment is defined and described by Hirschi (see note 1, this chapter) as a major deterrent to crime.

6. The strategy of using prison environments that contain older inmates to modulate the problems of younger inmates must be pursued with caution, since large numbers of young inmates interfere with the prison adjustment of their elders (Toch, 1992, chapter 9, note 3).

7. Maslow (1954), chapter 8, note 1.

8. In some cases, this goal can be accomplished if an inmate's anxiety gets reduced through the passage of time, but the most plausible way of reintegrating vulnerable inmates into the inmate population is to enhance their repertoire of coping skills. We address this subject in chapter 16.

9. Toch, H. (Ed.). (1980). *Therapeutic communities in corrections*. New York: Praeger. Also see, Wexler, H. (1997). Therapeutic communities in American prisons. In E. Cullen, L. Jones, & R. Woodward (Eds.), *Therapeutic communities for offenders* (pp. 161–180). Chichester, England: John Wiley & Sons.

10. Bandura, A. (1977). *Social learning theory*. Englewood Cliffs, NJ: Prentice Hall.

III

What Have We Learned
and What Must We Do?

14

Some Implications of Our Study

Studies of lives over time tell us more than reviews of lives in cross-section. If we compare individuals with each other, we may learn that some are more resilient and competent than others, but if we view the same individuals over time, we discover that some grow and mature, whereas others do not. In this sense, some evolving personal histories encourage an optimistic view of development, and others document a pessimistic view such as that of risk predictors, who assume that, "once a bum, always a bum."

Longitudinal views of good copers often tend to be misleading because they adjudge nonchange favorably and deplore change. As Jack Block has noted,

> The connotations of words indicating absence of change are generally positive, viz., consistency, stability, constancy, continuity, congruence. The connotations of change are often pejorative, viz., inconsistency, instability, inconstancy, discontinuity, incongruence. The Puritan value of solidity appears to have affected our language so that an unchanging character carries the aura of moral and mental soundness, while a transmogrified person is suspect. Connotatively neutral labels to identify continuity and change are most difficult to find, suggesting

that an implicit value orientation may have influenced the cast of prior developmental research.[1]

Gordon Allport similarly complains that psychology is biased toward static views of development, except when psychologists (or any of us) engage in retrospection. He writes:

> When we ask ourselves about our own course of growth such problems as the following come to mind: the nature of our inborn dispositions, the impress of culture and environment upon us, our emerging self-consciousness, our conscience, our gradually evolving style of expression, our experiences of choice and freedom, our handling of conflicts and anxieties, and finally the formation of our maturer values, interests, and aims.[2]

Among the careers we have reviewed, change is generally to be welcomed and lack of change deplored. This is so because the behavior our subjects engage in is frequently undesirable, both from society's perspective, and—should our subjects take the long view—from their own. We intersect with our offenders at a juncture at which change for the worse is rare and room for improvement is overwhelming.

Such facts account for the strange paradox that in a study such as ours, of nightmarishly depressing careers, two firm conclusions stand out as established. First, the major trend we describe is maturation; second, where chronicity of maladaptation occurs, there are patterning and consistency that permit problem definition and (it is hoped) regenerative efforts.

Maturation

The maturation potential of maladaptive behavior has been implicit in a substantial body of data which show that maladaptation (other than mental illness) achieves high rates early and decays over time. The most extreme patterns of maladaptation (quantitatively speaking) are those that have their inception at the earliest ages and manifest chronicity while they last. This trend is so consistent that the *age variable* has become the most reliable predictor of measures related to crime and delinquency, and youth (age 24 or below) virtually delimits behavior (disruptiveness) that is of concern to us.[3]

Before we consider this modal maladaptive career, we must note some exceptions to the sequence that prove instructive because of the contrast they offer. The most contrasting sequence of changes is that of the "downhill" career, such as that of many alcoholics, in which maladaptation starts late and gets worse as it evolves. Typically, the serious alcoholic invests years in sporadic or dedicated drinking but combines such behavior with a more conventional career. The onset of maladaptation occurs as drinking bouts encroach on the person's main career and interfere with vocational success and family life. Failure in these areas creates stress and poses threats to the person's self-esteem, which invites steady intoxication as an ameliorative response. This response in turn exacerbates disability, until a juncture is reached at which the maladaptive behavior (full-time drinking) interferes with the person's self-care and ultimately endangers his or her survival.

Such cycles produce decrements of skills and capacities and make recovery increasingly difficult. The point is not that alcoholics are older while the maladaptive individuals we describe are mostly young but that the pattern typified by the alcoholic is cumulative. The cumulation is partly a function of age but is more saliently a product of failure that breeds loss of self-confidence as well as decrements in coping skills and capacities. Even more dramatically, the behavior can have disabling consequences, including physical and psychological decay, which make recovery problematic.

Subpopulations can be expected to vary in the admixtures of career patterns they comprise. Groups in which the age range is large, such as the urban homeless, include a melange ranging from dead-end alcoholics to young multisubstance-abusers. Hospital patients are a similarly varied group, ranging from young schizophrenics to old senile patients. Predominantly young adult populations such as prison inmates, however, are apt to overrepresent uphill careers, which offer more promising prognoses.

As we have noted, our data suggest an interaction between age and adaptational effects. Prison misbehavior peaks during early phases of imprisonment, but it mostly does so for younger inmates, and particularly for younger inmates who serve long terms in prison. Young inmates maladapt more frequently but improve with experience in the prison. The longer the imprisonment, the greater the improvement (except for seriously disturbed inmates and "chronics"), but improvement is also greater the greater the inmate's age. This does not mean that age accounts for the change, but neither does prison exposure. The older the inmate, and the longer the exposure, the greater the improvement.

The result is not easy to explain. One option is to think of maladaptiveness as a destructive skill: Just as ordinary genius peaks (in mathematics, say, or music), so may a refined penchant for rambunctiousness or knavery. Precocious entropy is another explanatory formula: It posits that as vital juices (such as testosterone levels that have been blamed for aggressivity) ebb, so does the behavior they energize.[4]

Other explanations have to do with aspects of psychological maturation or development. One such view is that of Wilson and Herrnstein, who write about crime:

> The typical person passing into adulthood shifts from the egocentric and hedonistic focus of childhood to more abstract and principled guidelines to action. Meanwhile, time horizons extend further into the future; the average adult delays gratification more readily than the average child or adolescent. If for no other reasons, with stronger internal constraints against wrongdoing and a greater weight on delayed consequences of behavior, the average adult should more often choose noncrime than those less "mature" in these respects.[5]

Wilson and Herrnstein also provide room for decay of misconduct over time. With respect to offenders who "mature out" at more advanced ages, Wilson and Herrnstein write:

> But they [the offenders] do slow down eventually, per-
> haps as the drives cool off, or the prohibitions or com-
> munity ties finally sink in, or the time horizons finally
> stretch out, or the increasingly severe penalties of the
> criminal justice system for recidivists finally make crime
> insufficiently rewarding. Or, failing all that, simply the
> diminishing capacities of later life make crime too dan-
> gerous or unlikely to succeed, especially where there are
> younger and stronger criminal competitors, or victims
> who will not be cowed.[6]

The developmental view of change leaves scope for the
role of environment, such as that of negative or positive effects of peer influence. The environmental effects may be congruent with maturation (peer influence thus becomes less
negative and more positive with age), but may also slow
down the process of maturation, or speed it up. This fact
explains, for instance, that offenders who have been transferred from youth to adult facilities undergo improvements
of behavior. The advent of a favorable environment can
speed up maturation, but that of an inhospitable environment can retard it.

A differentiated picture of maturation is provided by Jack
Block, who talks of a change process that varies with the
maturity level of the person who undergoes change. With
respect to the "impulse-ridden" child, for example, Block
writes that:

> The teachable child at this ego level may, as a matter of
> repeated contiguities and the simple pragmatism of re-
> inforcement, learn to contain certain of his desires, not
> because they are bad—indeed, the idea of badness does
> not exist—but in order to avoid the anticipated retribu-
> tion. "Better control myself, otherwise someone will hurt
> me" is the control paradigm at this stage.[7]

Block's definition of "impulse-ridden" individuals derives
from a classification (by J. Loevinger) of stages of personality
development.[8] The next stage in Loevinger's taxonomy is the
opportunistic stage, which revolves around uses of power in

egocentric exploitation. The inception of change in this stage, according to Block, has to do with the fact that:

> The exploiter of others is, in a fundamental way, also dependent upon those he exploits. In many interactions, it is a matter of interpretation, doubt, or taste as to which party dominates; certainly, the dominance relations often shift in an ongoing relationship. Confronted with the possibility that his actions for advantage may have adverse consequences, the opportunistic individual may choose to prevent the chance of loss by the chance of gain. He will not pick up on an opportunistic opportunity and will thus appear self-controlled, not because of high considerations of morality, but rather for reasons of situational expedience. "Better control myself, otherwise someone will dominate me" is the control paradigm of this stage.[9]

Block's view suggests that environments can affect the behavior of persons at varying maturity levels in different ways. The process may gain flexibility where the person is immature but chronologically adult. The difference may lie in the imperfect correspondence of childhood stages of maturation to the adult patterns that approximate them. The infant's view of reality can thus be wholly chaotic or impulse-ridden, but corresponding adult perspectives have a richer, more eclectic mix. It may also be that extrinsic outcomes such as those Block alludes to (punishments, power shifts, and so forth) are not the only spurs to change among adults. The changes we have talked about seem to illustrate Bandura's point that

> incentives are not the only, nor necessarily the best, means of cultivating interest ... involvement in activities through goal setting can build intrinsic interest. Proximal subgoals serving valued aspirations are well suited for enlisting the sustained involvement in activities that builds competencies, self-efficacy, and interest where they are lacking.[10]

Finally, change potential may vary with degree of mal-adaptation. All maladaptive people have failed to learn from experience, but many may be able to learn, and others (the chronics) may not—at least, they do not do so unaided. A spontaneously developed capacity for learning from experience helps explain our skewed curves and enables us to think of decreased maladaptiveness as coping.

Adaptation

Past studies have ascribed constructive change in prisoners to "anticipation of release." Our review of changes in incident rates, and some of our other findings (such as the lack of the impact we have noted of parole date assignments), do not support this view. Inmate misbehavior peaks after a preliminary interval and diminishes gradually over time. Aging (maturation) plays a substantial role; the remaining variance has to do with what the dictionary alludes to as "adaptation," defined as "adjustment to environmental conditions" or "modification of an organism ... that makes it more fit for existence under the conditions of its environment."

The environment, in this case, is the prison, and prison adaptation requires that the prisoner become "more fit for existence" in the prison. The literature does not offer the inmate much hope in this regard because it accentuates unbridgeable contrasts between confinement and the free world and implies that prison poses excruciating challenges and affronts to one's identity and self-esteem.[11]

It comes as a surprise, therefore, to note that most prisoners serve fairly trouble-free terms, in the sense that they violate few rules and receive few formal and aversive dispositions. One assumes that these inmates manage to accommodate far-from-ideal conditions by leading compromise existences in which they learn to achieve compromise goals, operating within available constraints. The incarceration experience of these men may be at minimum unpleasant but proves no more overwhelming to them than other constraining situations they have encountered in their lives.

The fact that this picture of compromise does not describe the experience of maladaptive inmates is not a result of imprisonment, which is a constant, but of the way these inmates react to the task of adaptation. Two key maladaptive reactions are particularly relevant: First, the inmates may not appraise constraints as parameters within which one must operate (which is the coping problem to be solved) but seek to ignore, evade, or defy constraints; and second, such fight–flight behavior increases constraints because it invites unwelcome reactions, thereby exacerbating the situation with which these individuals are unable to deal.

Given the possibility of ad infinitum escalation, the peak of the misbehavior curve is the low point of the inmate's career and the dilemma from which he must escape. Because the inmate is confined, this dilemma is exacerbated, because absconding, truancy, drug use, vagrancy, and other means of physically evading life problems are foreclosed.

Inmates do not become resilient, flexible, competent, or achieve insight, perspective, and self-knowledge just because they are in prison. Adaptation for poor copers consists of poor coping, such as hit-or-miss, trial-and-error migrations. The result is less one of adaptation than of mutual accommodation by the inmate and the prison. Settings are tried for size, and some challenges, temptations, and pressures prove more manageable than others. The system helps by transferring maladapters for "fresh starts" and by essaying special, low-pressure experiences in extreme cases. Elsewhere, accidental confluences occur, such as where inmates find punitive settings tolerable or encounter activities or staff members or peers they find congenial or helpful.

The process is unselfconscious and serendipitous, but once we see it and know it, we can understand it, and in theory we can use it. What we have to do is to attend to regenerative consequences where they accrue, to experiences that appear to improve personal functioning. This point has been made by Albert Bandura, who describes unplanned experiences as "chance encounters." Bandura argues:

> Some chance encounters touch people only lightly, others
> leave more lasting effects, and still others branch people

into new trajectories of life. Psychology cannot foretell the occurrence of particular fortuitous intersects, however sophisticated its knowledge of human behavior. The unforseeability and branching power of fortuitous influences makes the specific course of lives neither easily predictable nor easily socially engineerable. Fortuity of influence does not mean that behavior is undetermined. The unforseeability of determinants and the determination of actions, by whatever events happen to occur, are separate matters. Fortuitous influences may be unforseeable, but having occurred, they enter as evident factors in causal chains, in the same way as prearranged ones do. A science of psychology does not have much to say about the occurrence of fortuitous intersects, except that personal proclivities, the settings in which one moves, and the kinds of people who populate those settings make some types of intersects more probable than others. However, psychology can provide the basis for predicting the nature, scope, and strength of the impact these encounters will have on human lives.[12]

Locating Silver Linings

The slightest and most modest respites can serve as cues to what may be possible. In a workshop of mental health and corrections staff, for example, a group reviewed a case they described as follows:

> Our group got what is now a 23 year old inmate, who was incarcerated since he was 17, and prior to that was a youthful offender. He came into the system as a result of an armed robbery; also, an outside charge for arson, for setting fire to an adjacent cell with somebody in it, about a year after he was in the system ... His primary problem is extreme acting out ... He is a real winner at this. He seems to have outlasted the system and he's still going ... He has eight pages of disciplinary actions on his Superintendent's card—threats, self-mutilation by cutting, swallowing, hanging himself. He swallowed pens, toothpaste tubes, bed springs ... and these appear

to be an expression of rage at the system. He hates the system, particularly whenever any kind of disciplinary action occurs—when he's not getting what he wants. His most extreme acts have occurred as a result of discipline.[13]

Are there no ways of breaking this sort of cycle? Our group asked whether the cycle had in fact been broken—however briefly—before it escalated to new lows. The group searched for redeeming clues, and it reported:

[The inmate] has had a couple of good experiences, or initial experiences that were positive, with female therapists and female nurses or some kind of female therapeutic staff. Typically, what he does soon after, is he gets sexually attracted and makes some kind of statement about that. He gets in a love–hate kind of situation. The staff becomes very nervous and pulls away the therapist, and he gets another rejection.

One thing we find is he's rejected a lot. He obviously also rejects by his actions, by the extreme anger that he's acting out. But clearly, attempts at making some kind of positive involvement with him fail each time because he's just too much for anybody that tries to deal with him.

One of the interesting things we found is that when he's doing well—which he has done especially when he's been working—he starts working, he starts relaxing, he doesn't act out as much, and he starts getting depressed.

In these short periods of time he's depressed he has sleep problems, sees a psychiatrist and gets some kind of anti-depressant medication. He continues to do okay for a while under the medication, and then something happens. He immediately starts fighting the system again and then he loses his job—he's off and running again in a very aggressive, angry manner.

From what we can see, he has done okay for periods up to maybe three or four months at various times in five or six years. The interesting thing is that when he is doing well he's not getting any attention from anybody.

There are no reports. One other thing that was pretty obvious is that there's not much of anything anybody can say about him in a positive way. And so one of the things that we're considering is that if it's possible to treat this kind of person effectively, you'd probably have to get the most patient person in the world; beyond that, somebody who would put a lot of effort into encouraging whatever positive features this person has, if in fact he has any. He obviously has escalated his behavior, his impulsive, demanding, attention-seeking behavior to such a degree he's outlasted everybody. He's won, except that he's destroyed himself or is in the process of destroying himself.

The comments of one clinician proved particularly hopeful, because they defused impressions on record that made the inmate appear uniformly refractory:

It takes a great deal of patience to work with him. A good deal of hard lining, a good deal of letting him know respect and that sort of thing. As long as we have a case manager, somebody who can stop in once or twice a week to say "how ya doing"—that's all it took—he was fine. He does these little antics. Like he wrote the President and told him he was going to rub him out ... So that means the Secret Service has to come and visit him every 3 months. So he assures himself of a visitor. I don't find him a particularly offensive guy to deal with, I really don't.

If we profit from such observations, we can accelerate the process of adaptation, which otherwise consists of mystifying fits and starts. It is only when viewed as an understandable pattern of diminution of impasse situations that the problem can be defined. What we can then see is an accommodation of person-to-environment and vice versa, which in retrospect seems mildly surprising and takes the form of entries such as "this person had a horrendous performance record, but has been involved in no incidents over the past six months." No explanation is customarily offered, and the dynamics of change are seemingly unascertainable by observers or the person himself.

The changes we encounter can be described as the modification or discontinuance of the sort of patterns we have reviewed. The person has learned to control temper, face adversity, tolerate infringements, accept instructions, and live and let live. He postures less blatantly, accommodates more, becomes less demanding, and feels less affronted. He is calmer, more serious, less afraid, more confident. Maturation and compromise have converged to achieve more congruence between demands and responses, between challenges and the meeting of challenges.

No doubt, much of such change is superficial, evanescent, and transient. To make it less tenuous, pattern-related interventions are needed that create self-awareness that can lead to self-management. In the absence of such individually tailored experiences, the best we can hope for is that some of the adaptive change we see can survive new (or familiar) challenges in settings to which the person returns after he leaves the prison.

Chronic Maladaptation

The problem of chronic maladapters is more serious and leaves less leeway, but some facts we have discussed give us hope. Chronic maladapters engage in frequent, redundant misbehavior. They create many problems, but they show patterned consistency. This does not mean that they do the same things over and over but that they do different things for the same, or similar, reasons.

We can predict chronicity, as we have shown. We can also, however, distinguish chronics from each other, defining the problem to be addressed in individual cases. Chronics can be disaggregated into subsets of individuals who manifest similar patterns of conduct or misconduct. This not only helps us to make sense of what chronics do but also provides homogeneous target groups for classification purposes. Such classification is a prelude to sensible management and reform and differs from the current wholesale segregation strategy that creates heterogeneous enclaves of individuals who prove unmanageable elsewhere.

Consistency, of course, may be largely in the mind of the beholder, such as ourselves. The psychologist seeks closure, and human messiness (variety of behavior) offends. But behavior is seldom messy on all levels. Conduct is a product of personality, which gives it direction and a measure of unity. Where surface (phenotypic) variety exists, personologists such as Allport have instructed us to look deeper.[14] When we follow such instructions we often find genotypic consistency, which means that subsurface motives underlie disparate surface concerns. Our review has shown that, except for extremely disturbed chronics, many consistencies in maladaptation are already phenotypically available even where we find more consistency by digging deeper. This makes pattern-analytic thinking more accessible to observers of conduct, including the person himself and his peers, whose insight is most needed and critical if change is to occur.

Of course, maladaptive individuals almost invariably deny their problems, which means that they hold external environments (or fate) responsible for their misadventures. Another way of describing this propensity is to speak of "defenses," of reactions to information about oneself that make the person resistant to change.

Much change literature has to do with ways of dealing with defenses. The prevailing wisdom is that defenses should rarely be attacked head-on but that they must be surfaced and redundantly highlighted and discussed. Another way of saying this is that resistances to change must be "worked through."[15] This means that we must make it peremptory— if possible, inviting—for the person to face and examine his defenses and to rehearse their discontinuance. It also means that there are two targets at issue in change—one of defenses and the other of the behavior the defenses defend and of the motives that underlie it. In both cases, we must understand the pattern, the person himself must understand the pattern, and the person must learn to abandon it.

Expanding Our Perspective
of Disruptive Behavior

Maladaptive behavior of the kind we have reviewed is invariably disruptive, in the sense that it is seen as causing problems by those who govern the person's environment. However, disruptiveness cannot be equated with maladaptation, even if it is persistent. In theory, a person can *elect* to disrupt his environment, can do so competently and with the utmost consideration for his fellows, can accept penalties as a price worth paying, and can improve his skill at disruptiveness with accumulated experience. When a person behaves in this way, his keepers can confront him and subject him to sanctions. The game (cops-and-robbers) can be played as an adult game, with professionalism and dignity.

The games we have been concerned with have not been played with professionalism or dignity. They have been played poorly, in unsportsmanlike ways, by people driven to them who lose without profit or grace. This is so because the people we have looked at have not been "disruptive" but "disruptive-plus." This "plus" (or perhaps minus) is difficult to define, except as a deviation from standards of mental health or competence.

Nonmental health (or mental nonhealth) is different in degree from mental illness or mental disorder; the former includes the latter but covers a wider range. Our concern has been with the full gamut of nonmental health, and we see value in being sensitive to deficits in personal competence where they recur. We simultaneously see risks (and few benefits beyond reducing the unemployment rate of mental health personnel) in needlessly pathologizing personal deficits.

The problem is that maladaptiveness "this side" of pathology poses sticky definitional issues and makes it difficult to match clients with services. The matching problem becomes obvious when people are shuttled between service deliverers who (mostly justifiably) feel that they do not fit their definition of who is an appropriate client. It is also exemplified by generic outcasts and by the need to mainstream problem people even where this exacerbates their maladaptation and strains the hospitality of settings (such as classrooms) designed for more adequate copers.

To pathologize a problem at such junctures becomes an understandable response, particularly where pathology-related services are the only show in town. Moreover, other obvious avenues of defining the person as "special" to get him off the streets or out of the hair of settings he contaminates usually involve stigmatizing him as a bad apple. This option strikes service workers and observers in settings other than prison as inhumane, though some clients—given their druthers—prefer to be seen as *bad* rather than as *mad* and find the label less injurious to their self-esteem.[16]

If the person becomes more tangibly disruptive, or disruptive for a sufficiently long time, the options begin to change. The person gradually acquires membership in the category of "notoriously disruptive person," which gives him a definite identity. Once the person is defined as a serious behavior problem, it makes pathology specialists reluctant to deal with him. Though staff in various institutions do have a set of (behavior control) options for dealing with disruptive people, they sense that these options do not *fit* the chronically maladaptive client. Even while they are disciplining or punishing the person, they know at some level that what they do is inappropriate and does not address the real problem.

In fact, those who discipline discover that "the problem" they are addressing can be exacerbated through disciplinary sanctions. Vernon Fox makes this point about maladaptation in prison when he writes:

> [T]he individual offender who builds up a series of misconduct reports within the prison is a seriously disturbed individual with complex mental dynamics ... Yet for this complex individual, the pattern of custodial routine is an original demand for compliance, and subsequent deprivation and punishment reinforce the original demand, which intensifies the problems by imposing more pressures upon already existing pressures without providing any solution to the original problem.[17]

354 ACTING OUT: MALADAPTIVE BEHAVIOR IN CONFINEMENT

The response to maladaptive clients can become more sophisticated when staff live with ambiguity and complexity
by taking a more eclectic approach. Hybrid categories such
as *special education* are created to accommodate multiproblem
individuals and offer the potential of multimodal services
that can address different deficits (behavioral, emotional, educational) of people who combine presenting problems to
varying degrees. The fly in this ointment in practice is that
some attributes are more preemptive than others. Options
become foreclosed, for example, as behavioral problems remove the person from the setting and deprive him of its multiple services.

Behavior preempts, and acting-out behavior does so by inviting punitive responses; it takes people out of circulation
and makes them unavailable for empathic scrutiny. The system's attention, and its response, are drawn to the act rather
than to the person who commits it. Due process in fact demands this approach because if we did not center on what
the person has done, we could adjudge the person guilty
because he has a hypothesized propensity, rather than because of evidence relating to his transgression. We also risk
penalizing the person for past behavior for which he has already been punished or exonerated.

The stance makes legalistic sense but forecloses risk management, which is an inviting avenue for addressing maladaptiveness. An example is that of police officers who accumulate citizen complaints. Due process demands that each
incident in which such an officer becomes involved is separately assessed, with careful inattention to other incidents in
which the officer has been involved. This result is fair in
terms of disciplinary processing but creates blindness to the
evidence that could help us understand the officer's potentially remediable problems. It means that we must disregard
a specifiable pattern of maladaptation where it exists, even if
we could (hypothetically) address the pattern, save the officer's career, avoid grief to future beneficiaries of the officer's
maladroit attentions, and save a municipality costly law suits
and public relations debacles.

Police departments frequently attest to the fact that the

problem, as delineated, is real.[18] Fortunately, there is a com-
binatory solution that addresses the problem, which leaves
due process inviolate but responds to the officer as well as
to his behavior.

Behavior Control and Self-Control

The formula that permits us to address the problem officer's
problem would create a two-tier system. It would presume
that (a) the culpability-oriented disciplinary process can run
its course until it results in a finding and disposition; (b) once
this juncture is reached, the disciplinary process can be supplemented by a second process, which asks different questions, with different goals in mind; (c) the officer who is targeted by the first process can become a participant in the
second process; (d) unlike the first process, the second process could be concerned with understanding why the officer
does what he does and with helping him to behave differently if he elects to behave differently; (e) while the first process centers on the last incident with which the officer has
been charged, the second process would be concerned with
reviewing the gamut of incidents in which the officer has
been involved, searching for patterning and consistency in
these incidents; (f) the first process can be punitive, whereas
the second could have no adverse repercussions; and (g) the
second process, unlike the first, would be concerned with the
officer's future behavior and its inappropriateness.

The reason for alluding to this sequence (to which we shall
return later) is to emphasize the fact that maladaptive behavior problems can be addressed by supplementing or expanding the behavior control process and making it more
constructive and more productive and change-oriented. The
reform emphasis can make disciplining less mindless and
give those who must discipline new options to address problems they feel they are not addressing through punishment
of behavior. According to Vernon Fox, organizations "must
be prepared to understand human behavior, rather than try-

ing to judge the amount of pressure necessary to keep a man in line."[19]

The Role of Mental Health Experts

The option of supplementing behavior control opens new roles for mental health professionals, who often feel that they operate in circumscribed ghettoes. A survey in federal prisons, for example, found that psychologists in the system reported that "they were not being allowed to participate enough in the correctional process," whereas "administrators/managers requested (from psychologists) more involvement in the overall correctional process through consultation, staff training, and general program development."[20]

Clinicians on occasion train nonprofessional colleagues, but training content related to maladaptive behavior can prematurely presuppose that answers to motivational questions exist in consumable form. With respect to maladaptation the clinician does not in reality have ready-made diagnoses or prescriptions he or she can disseminate. To reorganize this fact can expand rather than circumscribe the clinician's role and make it potentially more exciting. One way of defining a new, expanded potential role is as follows:

> The psychologist ... designs learning experiences that are dramatic, realistic, and compatible with relevant theory and data. This ... entails tapping the problem-solving skills of other staff members, which engenders mutual respect and colleagueship. It finally means devising nonclassroom learning experiences, including role-playing, the use of critical incidents, and the deployment of supervised inmate–staff confrontations. Good training may also involve trainees in institutional research exercises that sharpen their information-gathering skills and correct for stereotypes of other staff members and inmates. Such exercises may include some that are clinically relevant, such as interviewing inmates who are under stress or participants in violent confrontations.[21]

   This definition of training borders on what is called consultation, though the latter presupposes a continuing relationship and some sort of collaborative (team) activity:

> Where the therapist cannot treat, he or she can often help
> exercise the function indirectly by helping other staff (or
> the inmate's peers) to diagnose and address inmate prob-
> lems. The psychologist may do so by working with a
> given staff member or peer group, by linking staff
> groups, and by experimenting, where possible, with
> "teaming" of the sort that is popular, in theory at least,
> in hospital settings. A team member is not a ghetto res-
> ident, nor an authority figure, nor a person who "does
> his thing" under different auspices in reshaped groups.
> A team is a functional unit designed to address the
> unique problems posed by a client. The membership in-
> cludes whatever persons (psychiatrist, chaplain, fellow-
> inmates, etc.) seem to be serving the interest of the client.
> Ideally the team also includes the client, who must not
> be an object dissected in absentia in a democratic version
> of a case conference.[22]

   A more complex version of this approach involves staff
teams consulting with other teams who work with acting-out
clients. The Mobile Consultation Team of the Washington Department of Corrections was an innovative experiment along
these lines, which was designed in collaboration with the
University of Washington in Seattle. Team members included
four mental health professionals, two nurses, three program
supervisors, and six experienced, sophisticated corrections
officers. A visiting team of four could be convoked on short
notice to work with prison staff who requested a consultation. The team members had been trained to engage in joint
problem solving with the local staff, after "review of records,
visit to [the prisoner's] living unit, interviews with staff and
[the] inmate, [and] behavioral observation if indicated."[23]
   In-house consultation in a prison system can include external consultation, such as with experts in psychopharma-
cology. In the Washington project, the university on occasion
arranged for specialists whose help was requested by the

team and the local prison staff. The product of consultation visits would be an action plan, or proposal, for intervention. Some of the interventions could be implemented locally, whereas others might entail transfer of the prisoner to a different program or institution.

Transfers among settings can necessitate personal contacts between the sending and receiving facilities to ensure treatment continuity. Continuity of treatment can also be assured where the inmate has been assigned a case manager, which is especially desirable with prisoners who are living exemplars of comorbidity.[24]

Another role for mental health experts is a catalytic role in therapeutic community settings. In this role (which we describe in more detail in chapter 16) the maladaptive offender becomes a key protagonist in the change process. Albert Bandura refers to this process in the following terms:

> If they observe their behavior and the circumstances under which it occurs, they begin to notice recurrent patterns. By analyzing regularities in the co-variation between situations and their thoughts and actions, people can identify the psychologically significant features of their social environment that serve as instigators for them. For those who know how to alter their behavior, the self-insights so gained can set in motion a process of corrective change.
>
> Efforts to unravel the causes of behavior traditionally rely upon incomplete and hazy reconstructions of past events. Systematic self-observation provides a self-diagnostic device for gaining a better sense of what conditions lead one to behave in certain ways. Diagnostic self-monitoring need not be confined simply to observing natural occurrences. Significant determinants can be identified more effectively through personal experimentation. By systematically varying things in their daily lives and recording the accompanying personal changes, people can discover how those factors influence their psychological functioning and sense of well-being ... A science of self can be partly based on systematic self-study.[25]

In chapter 16, we turn to a consideration of how this can occur in the prison.

Women as "Special-Need" Prisoners

Before we confront issues relating to the management of difficult prisoners, we must consider an important category of inmate we had not included in our survey. This category is that of female offenders in prisons, who have been the most widely recognized group that are considered to have "special needs."

A National Institute of Justice publication summarizing program involvements has pointed out that "in recent years, researchers and policymakers have argued that women offenders not only need more services to put them on a par with men, but in many instances require different services as well."[26] This statement would not come as a surprise to most correctional practitioners. The director of the Federal Bureau of Prisons has recorded that "all too often, despite the great dedication of our staff, even employees with years of experience have trouble working effectively with a female population. Well-meaning staff who have been successful in all-male facilities have used their proven skills in facilities for women and have come away bewildered, wondering: Why is this so difficult?"[27]

A study that illuminates the question was conducted by Joycelyn Pollock in the New York State system. Pollock interviewed male and female correction officers who had extensive experience working in both male and female prisons and asked the officers to compare experiences working in the two types of settings. Pollock reported that there was considerable consensus in describing women as emotional (83%), complaining (81%), temperamental (76%), and moody (74%). In interviews, officers tended to characterize women as more prone to be confrontational (argumentative, demanding, querying rules, complaining, and critical) and more demonstratively emotional. The second category (demonstrative) subsumed characterizations of acting-out behavior. Whereas male prisoners were regarded by the staff as more dangerous than female prisoners, women were described as more prone to explosive, tantrumlike behavior. Pollock noted:

> When officers were asked if females "acted out" more than male inmates, an overwhelming majority said they did (85 percent). Acting out is a somewhat undefined term, but the officers seemed to be very clear on the meaning they assigned to the term. The most frequently given descriptions of acting-out behavior by women relate to expressive emotionality. Women were described as frequently having tantrums or outbursts of anger in which they engage in verbal assaults on officers. Of those who perceived women to act out more than men, roughly 60 percent described some episode of untrammeled abuse.[28]

Pollock also reported that

> Women's aggression is seen as more frequently directed towards themselves and other female inmates rather than towards officers. The aggression of men is described in very different terms; it is seen as planned, covert, and more often deadly.[29]

In the chapter that follows, the superintendent of New York's maximum security prison for women discusses and illustrates patterns of acting-out behavior of emotionally disturbed female prisoners.

Notes

1. Block, J. (1971). *Lives through time*. Berkeley, CA: Bancroft Books, p. 12.
2. Allport, G. W. (1955). *Becoming: Basic considerations for a psychology of personality*. New Haven, CT: Yale University Press, p. 23.
3. Wilson and Herrnstein note that "criminal behavior depends as much or more on age than on any other demographic characteristic—sex, social status, race, family configuration, etc.—yet examined by criminologists" (Wilson & Herrnstein, chapter 3, note 5, p. 126). See also Hirschi & Gottfredson, chapter 3, note 4.

4. Moyer, K. E. (1987). *Violence and aggression: A physiological perspective.* New York: Paragon House.
5. Wilson and Herrnstein, chapter 3, note 5, p. 147. For a systematic exposition of a comparable perspective, see Gottfredson, M., & Hirschi, T. (1990). *General theory of crime.* Palo Alto, CA: Stanford University Press.
6. Ibid.
7. Block, note 1, supra, p. 149.
8. Loevinger, J. (1966). The meaning and measurement of ego development. *American Psychologist, 21,* 195–206. For a more general discussion of consistency in personality development, see Loevinger, J., & Knoll, E. (1983). Personality: Stages, traits and self. *Annual Review of Psychology, 34,* 195–222.
9. Block, note 1, supra, pp. 249–250.
10. Bandura, A. (1986). *Social foundations of thought and action: A social cognitive theory.* Englewood Cliffs, NJ: Prentice Hall, p. 248.
11. Sykes, chapter 1, note 17; Goffman, chapter 1, note 22.
12. Bandura, note 10, supra, p. 33.
13. Toch, H. (1983, November). *Coping with noncoping convicts.* Address to the Bellevue Forensic Psychiatry 50th Anniversary Symposium, New York, NY. The transcribed text derives from a Workshop on the Disturbed Disruptive Inmate for the New York State Department of Correctional Services underwritten by the National Institute of Corrections, Federal Bureau of Prisons.
14. Allport, G. W. (1961). *Pattern and growth in personality.* New York: Holt, Rinehart & Winston, pp. 363–364.
15. Lewin, K. (1947). Group decision and social change. In T. M. Newcomb & E. L. Hartley (Eds.), *Readings in social psychology* (pp. 330–344). New York: Holt. The same point, of course, is made by Sigmund Freud. See, for example, Freud, S. (1963). *Therapy and techniques.* New York: Collier Books.
16. Irwin, chapter 7, note 4, pp. 46ff.
17. Fox, chapter 1, note 3, p. 326.
18. Independent Commission on the Los Angeles Police Department. (1991). *Report of the Independent Commission on the Los Angeles Police Department.* Los Angeles: Author.
19. Fox, chapter 1, note 3, p. 326.
20. Powitzky, R. (1978). Reflections of a prison psychologist. *Quarterly Journal of Corrections, 2,* 7–12, p. 9.
21. Toch, H. (1981). The psychological treatment of imprisoned offenders. In J. R. Hays, T. K. Roberts, & K. S. Solway (Eds.), *Violence and the violent individual* (pp. 339–340). New York: Spectrum.
22. Ibid., p. 340.
23. Lovell, D., & Rhodes, L. A. (1997). Mobile consultation: Crossing correctional boundaries to deal with disturbed offenders. *Federal Probation, 61,* 40–45, p. 41.

24. Toch, H. (1995). Case managing multi-problem offenders. *Federal Probation, 59,* 41–47.
25. Bandura, note 10, supra, p. 338.
26. Conly, C. (1998). The women's prison association: Supporting women offenders and their families. *National Institute of Justice Program Focus* (No. NCJ172858, p. 4). Washington, DC: National Institute of Justice.
27. Quinlan, J. M. (1992, Spring). The female offender: A prologue. *Federal Prison Journal, 2,* 3.
28. Pollock, J. M. (1986). *Sex and supervision: Guarding male and female inmates.* New York: Greenwood Press, p. 57.
29. Ibid., p. 82.

15

The Prison Careers of Mentally Ill Women

There is no empirical evidence to indicate whether the patterns of maladaptation described in earlier chapters of this book among male prisoners are similar for women in prison, but we should expect to find some differences. After all, men and women are different in their models of adaptation. Women are frequently described as creatures of relationships. They have been brought up in society to place great emphasis on relationships with others and often define themselves in terms of their relationships—as mothers, daughters, aunts, friends—much more often than men. Evidence of this orientation among women can be readily seen in prisons. Visiting rooms in women's facilities are filled with mothers and sisters, accompanied by the inmates' own children, along with nieces and nephews, whereas visiting rooms in men's facilities are mainly populated by wives or girlfriends with the inmate's children. Women's facilities are likely to have parenting programs and groups discussing surviving child abuse and domestic violence. There is also a lower rate of serious violence within women's prisons. The most problematic women in prison appear to be those who

---

This chapter was contributed by Elaine Lord.

are mentally ill, and they are often extremely difficult to deal with, presenting a myriad array of maladaptive behaviors, all in a short time span. Karen[1] was a case in point. She served 29 months—11 months beyond her minimum sentence. When she arrived at the prison, she had been designated as a minimum-security inmate, but when she was released it was with a maximum-security classification, quite the opposite of the norm. In preparation for her release, she was discharged to a Psychiatric Center so that a specialized discharge plan could be developed for her.

Karen was not seen as appropriate for placement in a prison residential therapeutic community for the mentally ill because she was so loud and disruptive that other participants would suffer. Nonetheless, Karen's stay at the prison was punctuated with frequent admissions to the mental health setting.

In all, Karen accumulated 54 disciplinary hearings, of which 34 were in the most serious category, an average of almost two hearings a month. Of the total, 32 incidents involved violence, with 11 involving assaultive behavior against staff or inmates. Fourteen incidents involved throwing liquids, including urine, and 5 incidents included flooding her cell and the adjoining area by stopping up the toilet. Mixed in with all of this misbehavior were intervening incidents of self-mutilation. Karen had scars all over her body from the cuts she had inflicted on herself. These activities seemed impossible to predict.

Karen had accumulated segregation time that went beyond her actual release date, even if she were to serve every day of her maximum sentence of 36 months. Obviously, the facility had reached a point at which conducting the hearings could have no impact on Karen, and this most probably revealed more about the frustrations of staff than the impact of penalties on Karen's behavior.

The first infraction Karen ever received involved refusing to follow an order given by a staff person; it occurred within 8 days of her June arrival. She was transferred to a medium-security facility, as is routine with the vast majority of inmates. However, in her 5 months at medium status in a facility that was too far away for her out-of-state parents to visit and bring her son, she ran up an incredible disciplinary history of 18 incidents, 13 of which were considered major. Six of the major incidents occurred within 12 days of each other and centered around constant disruption of the unit by yelling, banging, making threats, and assaulting staff. As a result, Karen was returned to the maximum-security facility for mental health evaluation in September. After 3 days, mental health staff decided that Karen was simply manipulating the system, and she was released from observation, placed in cell confinement, and then in another 3 days transferred back to the medium facility.

For the next 3 months, Karen continued to accumulate numerous misbehavior reports, including seven major infractions for persistently disruptive and disturbing incidents. In December, she was once again sent back to the maximum-security facility, but on this occasion to the more secure segregation unit there. A little over a month later, toward the end of January, she assaulted an inmate and threw liquids on her. Nine days later, Karen was moved to the mental health unit for evaluation, and the next day she assaulted a staff person on that unit, which prompted her move back to segregation. There, within days, she threw fluids on two occasions and within a month had a fight with yet another inmate. She was once again sent to the mental health unit for evaluation, where she was moved from an observation cell to the dormitory and then was released back to segregation.

This pattern of disrupting, assaulting, throwing, flooding, fighting, destroying property, and generally creating havoc even while segregated continued unabated. There were intermittent referrals for mental health evaluation, placement in observation, more disruptiveness in the mental health unit, and then release back to segregation. It was a cycle interrupted on only two occasions by stays in the infirmary for self-inflicted cuts. In the last few months of her prison term, Karen was almost entirely out of circulation. She never participated in programs during her incarceration, and in fact she never even completed the intake process. She was not classified as in need of intensive mental health services but rather was defined as emotionally immature and impulsive —a behavior problem.

Karen, who was 23 at the time of her incarceration, was an engaging young White woman who had become involved in the drug scene. She came from an intact family of solid working-class people who resided in a neighboring state and who had custody of her son. Upon reception, she told the interviewers that she had received prior services from mental health programs.

Karen would make her son greeting cards of all sorts, first in simple crayon and marker drawings, and then with delightful collages made of tiny pieces of brightly colored pictures in magazines that the staff would let her spend hours tearing and pasting onto heavy paper. Her son, Shawn, bore an uncanny resemblance to Karen, and she was always showing his picture to anyone making rounds of the disciplinary segregation unit. She would usually come right over to the window in the cell door to greet anyone doing rounds, as many of the women do who are in isolation, and it was unusual to have to call out to her.

One day, not long before her discharge, Karen indicated she was not making cards but rather writing poetry, and she shared a whole sheath of her writing with me. Karen seemed much more subdued than usual. Upon reading the poems, I found it was difficult to respond, so I asked if I could take them with me. I walked back to my office and contacted the mental health staff. In all, there were more than 20 poems. All had similar themes of self-destruction. For example:

> Anger you see
> Will be the death of me.
> I don't know what to do
> I am so mad.
> As I take a razor to my wrist,
> I'll cut and cut in a blazing fit.
> Blood will fly; I won't cry.
> That is the only way to rid the
> Anger in me.

One poem illustrated Karen's total lack of self-esteem. She wrote: "Yes, I believe that God forgives, but as for me, thinking of forgiveness just ain't the same. I've played too many games with my life and the ones I love. I feel like dirt—I've been such a jerk." Finally, several poems voiced what may have been the basis for all of the acting out and depression. One began: "I'm afraid of the virus that causes AIDS. It won't leave me alone. I'm going insane. It crept up on me. There's really nothing to do." And then finally:

> Glass and Razors,
> Things I like.
> Cutting, Cutting,
> Til I get it right.
> Blood will flow,
> Then I'll go
> To a quiet place.
> No more pain.
> In peace, I'll be
> Glass and Razors
> Are like friends to me.

Closed Windows of Opportunity

Prison certainly had not helped Karen and may unwittingly have exacerbated already simmering issues. In retrospect, there may have been missed opportunities to understand Karen, to stop the cycle of self-destruction that seemed to drive her. Her parents did come to visit and might have been brought into some family groups, and might have provided enlightening information. Medical staff could have been more formally invited into case conferencing with regard to Karen. Karen's time was not easy for her, for the staff, or for other inmates. Certainly, her inability to cope with the prison environment, absolute lack of program participation, and excessive disciplinary involvement, especially with infractions of a violent nature, led to a longer stay in prison.

It is in murky cases such as Karen's where disagreements

between corrections staff and mental health professionals can ensue about the nature of mad versus bad. It is also in such cases that mentally ill inmates suffer the most because they are caught between two systems, often spending time in disciplinary segregation, only to do something that is considered so bizarre that they are moved to a mental health unit where they engage in serious violence and are again returned to disciplinary segregation. In these cases, energy and resources are drained and frustration builds. Staff from mental health and corrections need to step back at such points and try to work out compromises in order to serve the inmate; they need to agree to disagree about the inmate's mental health versus disciplinary status. In fact, in these cases, mental health staff often believe that an inmate is seeking to avoid punishment by simulating mental illness or engaging in manipulative self-destructive behavior, whereas corrections staff may conclude that the inmate is absolutely unimpressed by any available corrections penalty for behavior and can take self-injury to such a level as to become an accidental suicide.

The Prevalence of Mental Illness

I have been Superintendent of the Bedford Hills Correctional Facility in New York State for 17 years. During that period of time, I have seen the number of mentally ill women entering the prison system rise precipitously. Where once mental institutions kept patients for long years in back wards, today the burden of providing for mentally ill people who have committed crimes has shifted to the correctional system. It is clear that prisons must adapt by creating more appropriate environments for these inmates—as long as society believes that is where mentally ill inmates should be maintained.

A 1999 U.S. Department of Justice study, published by the Bureau of Justice Statistics and based on 1998 data, underlines this need. The report estimates that approximately 24% of the female inmates in local jails and state prisons are mentally ill. The figure for male inmates is significantly lower at 16%.[2] Twenty-nine percent of White inmates, 20% of Black inmates, and 22% of Hispanic inmates in state prisons for women were identified as mentally ill. Nearly 4 in 10 White female inmates age 24 or younger were identified as mentally ill. Many of these mentally ill inmates are homeless prior to entering prison, and many are addicted to drugs.

By the year 2000, 26% of the incarcerated women in New York State facilities were on the active mental health caseload (for men, the figure was 11% systemwide). Far greater numbers of women than men were prescribed psychotropic medication, a fact that leads mental health staff to surmise that there is a greater level of mental illness among women inmates.[3]

As pointed out elsewhere in this book, mental illness leads to maladaptive behavior in confinement. Prisons function because inmates abide by the rules and follow a prescribed daily routine. Therefore, such significant numbers of women inmates with serious mental health needs not only create difficulties for the involved inmates themselves in terms of doing time but also place a burden on both correctional and mental health staff and sap resources.

Acting Out and Acting In

Self-mutilation is a frequent problem among the mentally ill women in prison, and it comes in an astonishingly wide range of gestures: cutting the skin with razors or other sharp objects like screws, pieces of metal from window ledges, radiators, glass, floor tile, pieces of plastic (including little medication cups), even the foil packet in which a skin cream can be administered in individual doses. Self-mutilation by one mentally ill woman also appears to often precipitate self-mutilation by others, especially friends. And relationships between women, not necessarily of a sexual nature, are often at the root of fights or self-mutilation in women's prisons.

Most women seem to have learned this practice as teenagers in one institution or another and to have brought it with them to adult prisons. Cutting of the arms seems to be the most frequently seen gesture, but legs and the neck are also often cut. Women in prison tend to use stray pieces of metal far more often to inflict self-injury than to assault others. Scars often cover both arms, sometimes up to the armpits. Women have told me that it eases their anxiety, that it makes them feel better after they either "swallow" or "cut." Sometimes, the inmate inserts screws or other small objects under her skin and leaves them there, only to suffer infections. Some inmates burn themselves with cigarettes, and these burns are often only noticed by other women in the shower room. This is a good example of the fact that one can encourage women in the prison community to keep an eye out and be aware of mentally ill fellow inmates in trouble and alert the prison staff when they observe such signs of mutilation, and burning is in fact most often reported by the other inmates who live on the same housing unit.

Some women insert foreign objects into their own abdomen. Some insert foreign objects into surgical wounds, causing the need for yet more surgery and, in the worst cases, colostomies. Swallowing in particular seems to almost be a group activity. If one woman swallows, then there is an increased risk of more swallowing by others. Swallowed objects often have to be retrieved by surgery. However, as the incisions are healing, the inmate begins to insert pens, crayons, combs, and other long objects into the incision, causing serious infections.

It is certainly true that men in prison do self-harm, but it appears to be a significantly more serious and extensive problem in female facilities, whether these facilities house juveniles or adults. It also appears that self-mutilation often began before the disturbed women arrived at the prison. This seems to support the contention of some observers that maladaptive men lash out at others, whereas women harm themselves.[4]

Serial Self-Destruction

At Bedford Hills, there was a facility nurse who was seriously affected by the self-harming pattern of an inmate named Robbie. This nurse was working in the facility's emergency clinic one evening when Robbie was brought to the clinic after swallowing several straight pins. Robbie had a history of swallowing and claimed it was the only thing that helped her deal with anxiety. The nurse got a thermometer, put it in Robbie's mouth, and then turned to reach for the blood pressure cuff. It was then that she heard crunching. When she turned around, she noticed that the thermometer was getting shorter and shorter. She reached for it frantically, but it was too late. "It was only a moment. Just a moment that I was turned away," she told the facility's watch commander. "I can't believe it! Nothing has ever happened to me like this in my career! I'm a good nurse. I'm careful and I care about my patients." Robbie was taken to the outside hospital for ingesting crushed glass and the mercury in the thermometer. She recovered and returned to the facility the next day. However, the nurse, who had only been on the job 1 day, never returned.

Indeed, there were many other occasions when Robbie had been at the outside hospital for swallowing. One officer noticed that whenever Robbie ate a piece of bread, she knew that she had swallowed something and was trying to keep it down, a fact confirmed by Robbie. Just as with cutting, inmates may swallow in groups. Robbie and several of her friends often illustrated this phenomenon. On one occasion, Robbie and two other inmates were sent to the local hospital after they had swallowed safety pins. The three underwent surgery and were recuperating. I remember the discussions among the hospital staff, the mental health staff, and corrections staff about not placing the three inmates in the same room at the hospital to try to avoid further group swallowing.

Robbie was particularly hard on nurses. One afternoon, a hospital nurse entered Robbie's room to change her bandages. She placed her tray on the bedside table and claimed that she was distracted only for a moment, as was the correction officer, by someone calling from the corridor. A moment later, the scissors were missing from the tray; Robbie had swallowed them. Shortly after, Debbie swallowed part of the tubing that was attached to her IV, and though not in the same room, Eileen swallowed a pencil with which she was supposed to fill out her menu. It was as if they had ESP. Robbie was released on parole 5 years later and went to live with her mother—to recuperate from recent surgery to remove pins that were beginning to move around internally. In her last month of life, she called me from a metropolitan hospital to tell me that she was having serious kidney problems because of all of the swallowing that she had done since she was a young teen. Not long after, her kidneys failed; Robbie died within a year of her release at 26 years of age.

Victimization and Acting In

Psychiatrist Judith Herman has devoted significant efforts to studying the impact of traumatic stress, especially repetitive stress. She has focused much attention on the effects of child abuse and domestic violence. Herman notes that there is research suggesting that men and women react differently to trauma. For instance, a study by Carmen, Rieker, and Mills found that men who had been abused as children were more likely to take out their aggression on others, whereas women with similar histories were more likely to be further victimized or harm themselves.[5] Herman believes that suicide attempts and self-mutilation are actions correlated with abuse as a child. A study by Brown and Anderson examined the childhood sexual and physical abuse histories of 900 psychiatric patients and found that suicidal actions were strongly related to histories of abuse.[6]

The same type of relationship may hold when we enter substance abuse into the equation. The issue of drug abuse as self-destructive behavior is critical to any discussion of mentally ill women in prison. Owen notes that a recent study by the National Center on Addiction and Substance Abuse found that "women substance abusers are more prone to intense emotional distress, psychosomatic symptoms, depression, and low self-esteem" than male inmates.[7] It is important to understand the relationship between drug abuse and mental illness because almost all of the increase in recent years of women in U.S. prisons has been related to drug use, and the numbers of women in prison who are substance abusers far outstrips the resources available to provide appropriate programming. Study after study has shown that a woman convicted of a crime is likely to have a substance abuse history. There are few prison programs for women who are mentally ill and chemically dependent, a group that is routinely *dually diagnosed*. There is often an argument about which takes precedence for treatment—the drugs or the mental illness—as if it is the treatment modality that is central instead of the whole person.

Some clinicians have concluded that many women inmates resort to abusing substances on the street to numb their pain and to block out flashbacks caused by victimization.[8] These therapists suggest that talk therapy and safe places are critical to assisting these women but that these environments and resources are often lacking in women's prisons. Too often, drug therapy becomes the most expeditious treatment. Certainly, many stories circulate in prison that illustrate the hypothesized link between trauma and drug abuse. It is not unusual to hear a woman talk about turning to drugs at age 13 so as to be able to block out painful memories. It is also clear that inmates continue to seek drugs within prison, and this complicates the work of psychiatrists in dispensing medication and treating patients. Some inmates admit that when they are locked in their cells at night, they need to be able to sleep; they want to be able to block out the scenes that play through their minds over and over again.

A Proliferation of Problems

The Bedford Hill Correctional Facility, with which I am associated, lies within 40 miles of the New York City metropolitan area and houses approximately 850 inmates, three quarters of whom come from the metropolitan area. Approximately 100 to 150 inmates are in reception status; that is, they are being classified, sorted out, screened for special needs including mental health issues, and identified for placement in the facility that is most suitable for them to serve their time. The average age of inmates at Bedford Hills is 37; more than half of the inmates are Black; 23% are Hispanic, and most of the remainder are White. As can be expected, a substantial number of women inmates placed in a maximum-security facility are serving sentences for violent crimes, with 26% serving sentences for drug crimes. More than half of the women are serving sentences of 6 years or more and already have served an average of 37 months.

Women who are seriously and persistently mentally ill at present must remain at Bedford Hills because that is currently the location of intensive mental health services; such services are prohibitively expensive to duplicate at each female facility, even if staff can be located and hired. Therefore, by virtue of their mental health needs, some medium- or minimum-security inmates now end up remaining at Bedford Hills to serve their sentences, even though those sentences are short and do not require the level of security maintained at Bedford Hills. Slightly more than half of the population under custody at Bedford Hills is on the active rolls of the Office of Mental Health (OMH), the agency that provides a range of mental health services to inmates. Of the total number of women on the mental health caseload, 92% receive medication prescribed by psychiatrists. Almost half of the inmates on the mental health caseload fall within Level 1 and Level 2, the two highest need categories for services.

A survey of the women at Bedford Hills Correctional Facility conducted by the facility's mental health staff found that 22% of the inmates on the OMH caseload were diagnosed with impulse-control disorder; 21% were diagnosed with schizophrenia, and 21% were diagnosed with depressive disorders. An additional 13% of these inmates were diagnosed as psychotic (not otherwise specified), 12% as depressive disorder (not otherwise specified), and 10% as adjustment disorder with depressed mood.

Mental illness has the potential to impact a woman at every stage of a criminal sentence. It can create organizational tangles at the jail level while she awaits trial or a psychological evaluation, or even if she decides to plead guilty; it can make it impossible to conduct intake at her arrival at the prison, thus leading the staff to identify her as different and possibly as difficult; it impacts her performance and even her participation in programs; it may be considered by the Family Court when determining the status of her children; it can be a factor in her ability to abide by the rules and routine of an institution that is styled on military protocols for following orders and establishing routines; and finally, it can affect how she is perceived by the paroling authority or even present her with yet one more hurdle—another psychological evaluation—before she can even be considered for parole.

I remember an earlier time as Superintendent when it was unusual to admit a woman to Bedford Hills who was so seriously mentally ill that the intake process had to be halted; then, it became a monthly occurrence, and finally it became and continues to be a daily part of normal operations. Sometimes, the prison staff receive calls to inform them that a new inmate will be sent by special van because she is such a serious suicide risk that transporting her by corrections bus (the usual mode of transfer) would not provide the level of supervision necessary to protect her from herself. Generally, these are women who have made multiple, and often serious, suicide attempts in the past. On occasion, women are admitted into custody who arrive on a one-on-one suicide watch from the county jail; that is, the inmate was assigned a correction officer on a 24-hour basis to watch over her to ensure that she did not try to harm herself. Such inmates are usually moved as quickly as possible into the facility's mental health observation unit, which is the safest (although the most restrictive) environment at Bedford Hills, and as soon as practicable, inmates may be transferred, still on a one-on-one watch, to the Central New York Psychiatric Center (CNYPC) in the middle area of the state. CNYPC provides inpatient forensic services to inmates within the New York State system.

Women such as these have often seriously self-mutilated on numerous past occasions both in and out of prison and jail, and they may have previous psychiatric outpatient contacts or hospital commitments. Their actions, which may or may not be construed as suicidal by mental health staff, can include cutting their own throat, leg, arm, or wrist; head-banging; inserting foreign objects under the skin or into wounds or surgical sites on the body; overdosing on medication; or swallowing an extraordinary variety of objects including, but not limited to, knitting needles, screws, straight pins, safety pins, pens, pencils, light bulbs, springs, nails, pieces of radiator, screens, uniform name tags, pieces of wall, and chips of paint. These actions, of course, create an incredible drain on medical resources, generate numerous and expensive trips to the local hospital emergency rooms, and can result in expensive admissions to local hospitals, as well as dramatically increase the need for staff coverage at area hospitals or for one-to-one observation purposes.

The head of a local hospital once wrote to me questioning how the hospital could treat a woman for self-harm and then a few weeks later treat her again, in a seemingly never-ending cycle. He inquired if we did not have a rubber room at the facility. The issue with the inmate, April, was that she would self-harm, end up in the hospital, then return to Bedford Hills, be committed to a psychiatric center and then return within a few weeks to begin the cycle all over again. The inmate did not self-harm at the psychiatric facility and would invariably be sent back as stabilized and no longer in need of psychiatric hospitalization. Perhaps her behavior was a result of her aversion to being in prison, but that is not the criterion of commitment.

The degree of mental disturbance found in April is extreme, but she is not an isolated case. On another occasion, the corrections bus bearing new inmates arrived one morning at reception with the usual 40 or so women. Newly arriving women, similar to a military recruit process, are showered, issued a State uniform; fingerprinted, given an I.D. card, taken through a medical screening and exam process (including x-rays and dental screening), and begin a round of initial interviews with various staff, including a mental health interview. On this particular morning, we received a woman who was not cooperating—a relatively rare occurrence. Gina told the counselor that her birthplace was Mars.

When the counselor explained that he was just doing his job and asked her to cooperate so they could both get through the interview (a fact that generally gains inmate cooperation), Gina again answered that she was born on Mars. Mental health staff interviewed Gina and, after spending a brief time with her, concluded that she was indeed convinced that she was from Mars. As a result, Gina was transferred to the CNYPC for some months. Her mental illness had to be dealt with so that she could be inducted into the prison.

Mental Illness and the Prison Experience

Prisons run by routines—deadly dull routines: counting inmates several times a day to be sure that no one has escaped, moving inmates from one area of the facility to another, providing meals and showers, and performing other mundane daily tasks. People in the outside free community sometimes intentionally change their routines to prevent boredom, keep life interesting, meet other challenges, and differentiate one day from another. However, for inmates who are confined for long, long stretches of time, the routine never changes. Prison time is not easy—it is exhausting, humdrum, and monotonous.

Certainly, few if any prisons are set up to deal with inmates who are clearly patients in every sense of the word. Inmates like Gina cannot even engage in rudimentary discussions of their crime or begin participation in substance abuse or other programs that address factors considered by the parole board in the course of their decision making. In Gina's case, it was probably helpful to her in the long run that she clearly had a delusion of being from Mars—no one could dispute that her judgment was impaired and that her mental health needed to be addressed.

When an inmate has overriding psychological problems, time weighs even more heavy. She may simply not be able to count the time or even experience the time as passing. It is difficult if not impossible for someone to participate in an education program when she is so medicated that she falls asleep, when she does not know what day it is, where she is in the school year, or what grade she is supposed to be in. Evidence of a woman's mental illness can contaminate programming, such as education. For example, in one case, an inmate named Dorothy surprised her teacher with a 20-page paper explaining that her dead son was the second coming of Messiah. As a teacher, it becomes difficult to point out the run-on sentences or lack of parallel construction in an English essay by a student that expounds on a history of brutal child abuse and a mother who had a drug abuse problem herself and died of the AIDS infection that resulted.

Not only is the eating and movement routine difficult for women with mental health problems to contend with, but they must also stand in long lines for psychotropic medication, sometimes several times a day, because these medications are tightly controlled. The inmates must take their medication in the presence of a staff member, and they must endure mouth checks to be sure that they have indeed swallowed their medication. The amount of medication needed for these women can overwhelm a facility; controlled substances have a great potential for abuse. Overdoses of medication by inmates who are mentally ill are not uncommon. Considering that a majority of the inmate population has a history of drug abuse, it is a serious challenge to get psychotropic medications dispensed in a timely and safe manner. In fact, facility staff must always be alert to inmates who palm their medication, cheek it, or swallow it only to regurgitate it in order to sell it to someone who does not have a prescription or save it up for an overdose.

Inmates are experts in performing myriad techniques designed to get and keep medication surreptitiously, and some women expend significant efforts to obtain the medication needed to get high. This makes trade in psychotropic medication an entrepreneurial enterprise. Sadly, even over-the-counter medications can be sold to a gullible inmate who does not know any better, who will never get a buzz off the mixture she has traded for food or cigarettes. A prison staff member must always be alert, because medication mixtures can be dangerous to internal organs like the liver or kidneys or even cause death. An inmate may not even know which substances she has ingested.

The Impact of Mentally Ill Women on the Prison Environment

More mentally ill women are primarily served on-site at correctional facilities than are receiving inpatient hospital care (a trend that reflects the use of more community resources and less long-term institutionalization in the outside community). Despite the fact that by 1998 more than 20% of women inmates within all of New York's women's facilities were diagnosed with serious mental health needs, women inmates, who still constituted 7% of the prison population, also comprised about 7% of the inpatient population at the forensic hospital.[9] Although bed-space issues figure into this equation, women appear more amenable to treatment than men: They use mental health services in prisons at a much greater rate and are less reluctant to take the medication prescribed to them than male inmates.[10]

Women are simply more apt to ask for help. Women are also less violent, and when they are violent, injuries are generally less serious. Mentally ill women in prison are a generally less frightening presence to staff and other inmates, both in size and voice, than mentally ill men (not much different than in the outside community). Many more women, therefore, remain in the population of women's prisons rather than being housed in specialized mental health units or psychiatric hospitals.

The risk, however, of keeping mentally ill women in a facility's normal housing and program areas, as most prisons currently do, is that when these women are unable to cope with institutional rules and routines, they become easily caught up in the disciplinary system. In many cases, these women pose significant challenges for staff because the serious violence that does occur in prisons for women is often related to their mental illness. For instance, a review of unusual incidents at Bedford Hills found that the vast majority

(80%) of Unusual Incident Reports involved inmates who were on the active OMH caseload. (Unusual Incident reporting is a procedure for monitoring serious occurrences within various facilities, and it includes only incidents that are not of routine nature and that present a serious threat to the safety or security of a facility.)

One of the most serious assaults that occurred at Bedford Hills involved Shawna, a woman who almost everyone, staff and inmates alike, knew had very serious mental health issues. However, new staff and inmates who did not know Shawna's history did not know how to deal with her and how to recognize danger signals, and they thus were at a far higher risk of getting injured or, in the case of an inmate, getting into trouble. Shawna erroneously believed that the detective who had arrested her was actually the person who had committed the homicide for which she was found guilty. She was concerned that the detective would get into the prison because, in her mind, she was the biggest threat to him: She knew he was really the killer. Shawna believed that as part of his plot to get into the prison, he had implanted lasers in every electrical outlet in the prison, and therefore every electrical cord was a device to extend the laser's capacity. In fact, any object in the facility might contain lasers that would enable him to spy on her and provide him with information about what she was doing. On one occasion, she destroyed an extension cord to protect herself from the lasers; no one could ever figure out how she had so totally shredded the electrical wire and insulation.

Shawna had a prior mental health history in the outside community which often included being paranoid and delusional. When she remained on her medication, she did well, but as with so many mentally ill people, when she felt better she tended not to take her medication. In one of the incidents that resulted, a female officer was seriously injured on a housing unit. Without any provocation, Shawna had picked up a chair and brought it down right over the top of this officer's head. During interviews, it became clear that Shawna believed that the correctional officer was the detective and that he had gotten into the facility; it did not seem to matter that the correction officer was a woman and the detective a man.

In another case in the facility's residential therapeutic community for the chronically mentally ill, an officer who was very well-liked and who was doing her round of the unit corridor was slashed so severely with a razor across her back that her blue uniform shirt was shredded and turned bright red. There was no provocation, no prior incident or warning. The inmate who did the slashing was clearly delusional, and in her mind, was not even in the prison.

Sometimes, it is the inmate herself who can be injured because of her mental illness. The mentally ill prisoner can also injure another inmate. Obviously, one of the dangers of having seriously mentally ill women in prison is that they are a source of violent acts within the inmate community that are very difficult to prevent because they are tied to mental illness; they simply make no sense. Just as the public has difficulty comprehending why a mentally ill person pushes someone off a train platform, so, too, prisoners and correction staff have difficulty comprehending seemingly random acts of violence perpetrated within a prison.

An inmate named Micky achieved particular notoriety in our prison. She was a repeat perpetrator of seemingly random violence who had a childishly simple and innocent way but could also be very dangerous. She truly did not know how strong and big she was. She had a serious history of self-mutilation, and had extensive scars on her arms and legs. She loved to sing and would often just begin to belt out a song; "Moon River" was one of her favorites, and she had a passion for Pop Tarts. However, with the weight and force of her 400-pound body, she could hurt people seriously without meaning to during a tantrum. Micky sometimes resided in general population but usually ended up ping-ponging between the mental health unit and disciplinary segregation.

On a beautifully warm summer day, the area sergeant, a tall but lanky 6-footer, stopped to talk with Micky for a few minutes, sitting on a bench with her outside in the yard. When the sergeant got up to go, explaining that he had many things to do, Micky, in the manner of a child, came up behind him urging him to stay and talk. She gave him a bear hug to prevent him from leaving and picked him up off the ground, breaking two of his ribs. When she realized that she had hurt him, Micky began to cry and could not be consoled.

The Mentally Ill Inmate and Her Peer Group

As noted, inmates who are mentally ill have an impact on their peers as well as on staff. Other inmates quickly learn to be vigilant; some also learn to be supportive and helpful. On many occasions, other inmates are the first to point out that a woman needs assistance in bathing or keeping her clothes or cell clean, and very often they help that less fortunate inmate—living in close quarters makes it in their best interest to do so. The women's prison is their community and their neighborhood. (In fact, neighborhood is a description inmates most commonly use to describe their own living unit, and their cell is their house.) Someone who does not bathe affects everyone else on that unit. Someone who hoards food creates a vermin problem for neighboring inmates. Many female inmates enjoy nurturing others and view an inmate who picks through the garbage as someone in need of guidance and assistance, not much different from a child.

I have mentioned that other inmates often perform the informal, unofficial, but important job of monitoring, and even mentoring, inmates whose behavior may be on the verge of becoming self-destructive rather than simply bizarre. In fact, inmates make many referrals with regard to their peers; they often notice behaviors well before a staff person is aware of them. They stop appropriate staff who are going to their posts, changing shifts, or walking to a meeting to let them know what has occurred.

It is not unusual to have female inmates with severe eating disorders living on general housing units. Frequently, women who are on the same unit are aware of an inmate who may eat in the mess hall but then runs upstairs to her cellblock to vomit up her food. They notice and report inmates who have eating disorders. They are the first to see an inmate who does not eat and who exercises excessively. Women bring such actions either to the attention of mental health staff or to trusted work supervisors with requests that the mental health staff be apprised of the situation. In several cases at Bedford Hills, neighboring inmates have reported how much an inmate ate, whether she regurgitated her food, how much she ran or exercised, and what she voiced about her self-image —not because they were snitches or informants but because they cared. This type of experience, when it does occur, often brings collateral requests for information that all of the women in the prison can use—not much different from education about public health issues in any community.

However, the presence of mentally ill inmates also has a negative impact on the ability of other inmates to do their time. A letter that I received 3 years ago indicates the difficulties that mentally ill inmates can create, particularly in the living units:

> I was attacked by inmate C. She has mental health issues and hears voices. She came into my room the night before and hit me. The following morning on my way to programs, she just attacked me for no reason. The officer saw her hit me three times as I kept my hands down. I don't want to fight, only to finish some medical testing and pass my school exam. Now I'm worried I've gotten into trouble. I'm locked in my cell while security conducts an investigation into this incident. Please help.

Sometimes, it is the mentally ill inmate who becomes a victim of her own delusions. One inmate climbed an interior fence and became entangled in the razor wire at its top. Her breasts were seriously cut. Her only explanation—she wanted to see her boyfriend and she was convinced he was in the building that was on the other side.

The Impact of Victimization Experiences

Histories of traumatic experiences do appear to have a significant impact on women and their disciplinary involvements. An older inmate named Bernice, who had killed her abusive husband of many years, worked as my office cleaner. She often said her husband had made her crazy. After 10 years of never having received a misbehavior report, she was issued a ticket for talking back to a new officer who controlled the lobby where she had to pass each day to and from work. Bernice said she got agitated just going through the lobby; the way the officer pointed his finger at her and ordered her around made her upset. Over the next couple of weeks, it became clear that this officer would point to where he wanted an inmate to go when he unlocked the door, but he said very little. Bernice's husband had similarly pointed when he wanted something and also said very little. Working with her counseling group (but also after receiving yet two more tickets for similar behavior), Bernice finally worked up the courage to explain to the officer what he did that upset her. The next time she came into my office, Bernice was elated. On that morning, the officer had opened the door, placed his hands behind him, and wished her a good morning.

A number of feminist investigators suggest that women experience prison in terms of prior histories of sexual or physical abuse that can impede healing of emotional scars. They point out that the prison creates a setting in which women prisoners see the prison as replicating these experiences, leading to immense feelings of impaired safety and personal boundaries, feelings of powerlessness and immobility, difficulties with trust, and feelings of self-hatred. They suggest that this dynamic creates anger and lack of submission and may precipitate acts of self-inflicted harm to reduce anxiety. When a woman acts out in prison, the prison's usual response of punishment and segregation misses the point of the woman's reaction as a sign of emotional distress rather than challenges to security. These authors discuss aggressive behavior and self-injury by women in prison as both coping strategies and outgrowths of their abusive life histories. They believe that the tendency of the prison to punish maladaptive behaviors is liable to revictimize these women.[11]

Browne and Lichter at Harvard's Injury Control Research Center, citing research in a piece written for the *Encyclopedia of Gender,* conclude that past traumas and histories of violence may be a pathway to prison for many women. Childhood histories—including sexual molestation or severe physical abuse among female victims—create a significant risk for alcohol and drug abuse as teenagers and adults, even when risk factors like alcoholic parents are taken into consideration. Girls from such homes are more at risk of being separated from their families before adulthood, may end up being placed outside of the home, or may run away from one such frightening situation only to find themselves in another equally abusive one. These girls are at increased risk of involvement in drug- or prostitution-related activities and are at greater risk of involvement with abusive or violent partners.[12] These experiences in turn are related not only to increased risks of criminal involvement and incarceration but also to mental illness.

The psychiatrist Terry Kupers suggests, as do many other professionals, that posttraumatic stress disorder (PTSD) may be higher among women in prison because of serious and extensive victimization histories as children and adults. He concludes that many women who are diagnosed as manipulative or borderline personality disorder in prison, are actually suffering from PTSD, and he postulates that because these women are not seen as having a "major" mental illness, they receive few if any significant services.[13]

This issue is only one example of the battle that plays out all too often in prisons between mental health and corrections staff over a small but troublesome portion of the inmate population that poses the issue of "mad" versus "bad." Many of the women with serious behavioral problems are not adjudged by mental health staff to be suffering from major mental disorders and appear to end up in disciplinary segregation units. A fruitful discussion between mental health professionals and corrections staff might include analysis of issues such as what is the pattern of maladaption revealed in the woman's history that makes it difficult or impossible for her to cope, how might the pattern be addressed, and how might new behaviors replace violence toward self and others and serious and episodic disruptiveness.

Notes

1. Real names are not used in this or any other illustrating stories in this chapter to protect the identities of the subjects.
2. Ditton, P. M. (1999, July). *Mental health and treatment of inmates and probationers* (No. NCJ 174463, p. 6). Washington, DC: U.S. Department of Justice, Bureau of Justice Statistics. Retrieved January 27, 2001, from http://www.ojp.usdoj.gov/bjs/pub/ascii/mhtip.txt.
3. The most recent state prison census showed that 22% of prisoners in female-only confinement facilities were receiving psychotropic medications; more than 1 in 4 female prisoners were reported to receive psychotherapy on a regular basis from professional staff (the overall percentage of prisoners in therapy was 13%). (Beck, A. J., & Maruschack, L. M. [2001]. *Mental health treatment in state prisons.* Washington, DC: Bureau of Justice Statistics.)
4. Kupers, T. (1999). *Prison madness: The mental health crisis behind bars and what we must do about it.* San Francisco: Jossey-Bass, pp. 129–131.
5. Herman, J. (1997). *Trauma and recovery: The aftermath of violence—from domestic abuse to political terror.* New York: Basic Books, p. 113.
6. Brown, G. R., & Anderson, B. (1991). Psychiatric morbidity in adult inpatients with childhood histories of sexual and physical abuse. *American Journal of Psychiatry, 148,* 55–61.
7. Owen, B. (1999). Women and imprisonment in the United States: The gendered consequences of the U.S. imprisonment binge. In S. Cook & S. Davies (Eds.), *Harsh punishment: International experiences of women's imprisonment* (pp. 81–98). Boston: Northeastern University Press, p. 91.
8. Kupers, note 4, supra, pp. 131–132.
9. Lauvre, T. (1998, October 8). *CNYPC patient demographic profile: Inpatient and outpatient.* Albany: Central New York Psychiatric Center, Program Evaluation Department, p. 1.
10. See note 3, this chapter.
11. Heney, J., & Kristiansen, M. (1998). An analysis of the impact of prison on women survivors of childhood sexual abuse. In J. Harden & M. Hill (Eds.), *Breaking the rules: Women in prison and feminist therapy* (pp. 29–44). New York: Haworth Press, pp. 32–36. See also Connor, H. (1997). Women's mental health and mental illness in custody: Exploring the gap between the correctional system as it is presented and the correctional system as it is experienced. *Psychiatry and Law, 4,* 45–53, pp. 49–51.
12. Browne, A., & Lichter, E. (in press). Imprisonment in the United States. *Encyclopedia of Gender.*
13. Kupers, note 4, supra, pp. 129–131.

Chapter 1

Building Coping Competence

When observers are asked to describe the sort of setting appropriate for treating maladaptive offenders, they often mention *structure* as a prime requisite. The suggestion at first glance makes a good deal of sense. Structure denotes security or safety, which ranks first among Maslowian basic needs. Structure also denotes dependability and reliability. A structured world is a predictable one, in which one knows what to expect. Structure provides rules and guides for action. An absence of structure spells chaos and confusion.

Youths who habitually act out can be the cumulative products of a formative environment deficient in structure. In psychoanalytic parlance, such an environment results in stunted egos, reducing the individual's capacity to mobilize reality checks to curb his or her expressions of impulsivity. From a learning perspective, an environment that lacks structure is one in which prosocial behavior is not effectively rewarded or reinforced.

If late is better than never, the provision of a structured environment to offenders who act out can be viewed as remedying a deficit. Although one would expect transitional adjustment problems when individuals habituated to an unstructured upbringing are subjected to structure, one would predict that such reactions could dissipate and that the person's behavior would eventually improve.

This expectation unfortunately does not consider the connotations assigned to structure by its beneficiaries. To us, "this person needs structure" carries implications of helpfulness, guidance, and salutary routine. We may recognize that structured environments involve circumscriptions of unfettered autonomy (that they "set limits") but expect our transparently benevolent intent to inspire the acceptance of our beneficent strictures. It may thus come as a surprise that to many of our clients, what we call structure equates with deliberate, punitive regimentation.

The reason for the confusion is that it is often not a confusion. Acting-out behavior tends to be noxious, aversive, and annoying and is reacted to as such. The goal of intervention is to arrange for the discontinuance of this behavior. There is also an understandable desire to convey displeasure and disapproval of the behavior. Any action we take is thus contaminated by our desire to promote the discouragement of unpopular acts. While we may define our interventions as dispassionate or benevolent, what the client senses is, "These people are trying to squelch me, because they find me personally offensive." For some, this translates into an invitation to escalate their misbehavior.

In criminal justice settings, the undesirability of the person's acts (the destructive consequences of his or her acting-out behavior) is invariably in the foreground, and the responses of the system involve sanctioning the person for his or her misbehavior. Where this is not done, questions of appropriateness or equity can be raised. In relation to one program for disruptive inmates, for example, a staff member reports that "the critics question why such [a program] should take those prisoners who have, by definition, behaved so badly when other equally disturbed men who have not caused problems are left in the normal prison system."[1] Interventions designed for maladaptive offenders must therefore appear to take care not to ameliorate conditions of confinement and thus seem to "reward" the transgressing offender.

Because responses to acting-out behavior in confinement must try not to advertise helpfulness or benevolence, *structure* must often mean stricture. Environments in which the maladaptive offenders are placed may offer predictability and routine but more saliently must impose deprivations, circumscriptions, and an impoverished existence. Whatever benefits the attribute of structure may provide usually come to be overshadowed by the punitive regimes of so-called structured environments.

The Supermax Solution

At the time of our original study, the New York prison system contained a number of special settings that were indeed structured but nonpunitive in nature. Such settings were designed for prisoners with mental health problems that manifested themselves in general population. Attributes of the settings included a reduced range of stimulation, a protective ambience, and the enhanced availability of mental health services.

Structured ameliorative settings are not as prevalent in prisons today, and disturbed inmates who act out are far more likely to end up in segregated confinement. Segregation settings are very structured but they are predominantly depriving. Some few disturbed inmates may benefit from such settings but most at best just survive them. A significant number of disturbed segregated prisoners may be adversely affected to varying degrees. For these prisoners, segregation as a treatment modality is iatrogenic.

The problem is aggravated in solitary confinement settings for disruptive prisoners, which have proliferated since our study was conducted. These so-called maxi-maxi units, control units, or supermax units have been shown to have the potential of exacerbating mental illness on a massive scale. This fact is of great concern to progressive prison administrators and mental health experts. It has also sparked considerable litigation.

The controversy relating to the psychological effects of segregation happens to rest on historical precedents. Supermax confinement is a reinvention, and exactly replicates experiments with segregated imprisonment that were conducted 200 years ago. These experiments were largely abandoned at the time in horrified disgust because they drove prisoners insane.

Visitors who came to admire and emulate correctional innovations in the young United States recoiled in distress after seeing the results of these early incarceration experiments. The French legislative consultants de Beaumont and de Toqueville, who advocated many American correctional practices, drew the line when it came to "the evil effect of total solitude" they had been forced to observe in their travels.[2]

Unfortunately, some of the early experiments had been conducted on a substantial scale. A segregation wing that had been established by the New York State legislature contained 80 prisoners—an appreciable number in 1821. de Beaumont and de Toqueville dutifully recorded:

> This trial, from which so happy a result had been anticipated, was fatal to the greater part of the convicts: in order to reform them, they had been submitted to complete isolation; but this absolute solitude, if nothing interrupt it, is beyond the strength of man; it destroys the criminal without intermission and without pity; it does not reform, it kills.
>
> The unfortunates, on whom this experiment was made, fell into a state of depression, so manifest, that their keepers were struck with it; their lives seemed in danger, if they remained longer in this situation; five of them, had already succumbed during a single year; their moral state was not less alarming; one of them had become insane; another, in a fit of despair, had embraced the opportunity when the keeper brought him something, to precipitate himself from his cell, running the almost certain chance of a mortal fall.[3]

It also became clear in short order that supermax confinement did not deter serious offenders from reoffending. De Beaumont and de Toqueville noted that "this system, fatal to the health of the criminals, was likewise inefficient in producing their reform."[4] In New York, the governor had been forced to pardon 21 unhappy survivors of the experiment. Fourteen recidivated and had to be reconfined. These reconvicted inmates returned to ameliorated conditions of incarceration, which afforded opportunities for congregate programming.

De Beaumont and de Toqueville returned to France as sadder but wiser observers. They had resolved that "we shall say nothing more of the defective parts of in the prison system of the United States; if at some future period France shall imitate the penitentiaries of America, the most important thing for her will be to know those which may serve as models."[5]

It is ironic that today we grapple with the very same issue that prominently faced our precursors. In the words of the judge in a recent decisive case involving supermax confinement (*Madrid v. Gomez*, 1995), solitary segregation "may press the outer borders of what most humans can psychologically tolerate."[6] More specifically, the judge in the case found that the conditions in California's first supermax prison (Pelican Bay) "cause mentally ill inmates to seriously deteriorate; other inmates who are otherwise able to psychologically cope with normal prison routines may also begin decompensating in SHU [special housing units]."

It does not help that supermax routines contain features serendipitously designed to play into symptoms of mental illness.[7] This affinity was captured by the Pelican Bay judge when he concluded that segregated confinement was "the mental equivalent of putting an asthmatic in a place with little air to breathe." Supermaxes differ to some degree, but all are repositories of custodial technology. The prisoners in supermax are dealt with by machines orchestrated through computerized consoles. They are communicated with by muffled voices through impermeable partitions, and they are intrusively under surveillance. Supermax residents tend to sleep a great deal (especially where no activities are afforded them), but restful regenerative sleep is never attainable. Prison night merges into day (lights never go out in one's cell), and anticipated interruptions are a constant.

During rare respites from isolation, supermax residents are loaded down with tons of hardware that circumscribes their movement. Refusal to come out of one's cell—which is a common symptom where someone is mentally ill—brings a phalanx of intruders in space suits with chemical weapons or gigantic (and sometimes electrified) shields. Such invaders charge in wedge formation and press their targets against the wall or floor with irresistible force. No experience is better calculated to produce panic and an overwhelming sense of helplessness.

Most supermax regimes feature gradations of "levels" that offer calibrated increments in amenities. The lowest levels in such sequences are completely stripped down. They provide a condition of drastic understimulation, enforced inactivity, and sensory deprivation. This condition is defined as a baseline or starting point for an incentive system, but the core of the experience is unfreezing or crisis-promoting. The fact that it occurs during initiation into the setting is also bound to enhance its adverse effects.

The process whereby inmates are assigned to supermax can in itself be stressful and is often reminiscent of inquisitory tribunals. Ascribed gang membership is a popular criterion for supermax placement. The rationale has to do with gang involvement in drug trafficking, internecine warfare, and forcible recruitment. But individual gang members do not stand accused of such conduct. Instead, they are charged with aggravated gang affiliation, or gang activism.

The "evidence" that is invoked consists of information that the person is a presumptive member of an alleged gang. In Arizona, this information is culled by means of a two-stage sequence, which consists of gang "certification" and "validation" of membership. Validation includes the testimony of uncorroborated informants but also comprises observed association with suspected gang members and "gang tattoos." A profession (confession) of gang membership by the offender is considered desirable but is understandably hard to come by since the advent of supermax confinement.

The parallel with the workings of inquisitory tribunals becomes particularly blatant after the prisoner is indicted as a gang member.

> Once validated, the inmate can either refuse to renounce his membership or renounce his membership and debrief [tell what he knows about the gang].
> Those who refuse to renounce their gang affiliation are sent to the Special Management Unit [super-maximum security] where they will complete the remainder of their sentence. Those who debrief successfully are placed in protective segregation, also in the Special Management Unit, where they will complete the remainder of their sentence. Once released, validated STG [gang] members who return to Arizona's prisons will again be confined in the Special Management Unit. As of October 20, there have been 58 inmates who have been successfully debriefed and 399 inmates who have refused to renounce.[8]

Perception of capricious deprivation and custodial overkill predictably engenders bitterness and alienation. For this reason, supermax prisons may turn out to be crucibles and breeding grounds of violent recidivism. The graduates of such settings (often released directly into the community) may even be time bombs that are waiting to explode. Different settings are obviously needed, to deescalate resentments instead of escalating them.

A Contrasting Type of Scenario

Responses to maladaptive behavior can have all sorts of goals, but even in segregation status a constructive objective can be that of seeking to enhance the person's coping competence, which means trying to increase the appropriateness and sophistication of his or her behavior in everyday situations.[9]

In some cases, efforts to improve coping competence may require removing individuals from situations with which they cannot cope and placing them in less demanding environments that pose fewer challenges to their coping skills.

One can then create a set of graduated demands each person *can* meet, until a hypothetical level of difficulty is reached beyond which development cannot take place. The starting point must of course in theory never be depriving and stressful, as in supermax. The endpoint of the regime must be flexible because one ought not to take the position that there is no room for personal development. The task is one of assessing when a person's level of functioning has become congruent with a more complex set of demands (such as a regular prison environment) with some chance of survival or mastery. Such decisions are judgment calls relating to the person's chances of success and his or her chances of failures.

Other components of a graduated strategy have to do with resources and influences that can be brought into play to help the person to evolve new competencies. The aim here must be to promote discontinuance of dysfunctional behavior and to add to the person's repertoire of coping skills. These undertakings are separable, but attempting the first task without addressing the second invites the person ultimately to regress, because recidivism is often the only response to resourcelessness. The danger of consequences of not evolving new coping strategies is worth underlining because it not only applies to disciplinary approaches but also holds for the deployment of mental health services.

Mental health approaches are concerned with removing disabling symptoms of emotional disturbance.[10] This would mean that the removal of symptoms allows the unfolding of behaviors that have been inhibited by the symptoms and that the emerging "normal" conduct is sufficiently resilient so that new challenges do not invite resurgent symptoms or new symptoms. These conditions, however, are rarely met, and relapses are frequent where ostensibly recovered patients are still nonresilient and mental health systems do not offer gradations of challenging and supportive environments with the necessary rehabilitative services. A standard egregious arrangement is one that "mainlines" hospital patients into the streets or the prison yard on a sink-or-swim basis, with a lifeline consisting of uninviting outpatient services, and no waystations between challenging or stressful conditions and the hospital for those who suffer from incipient difficulties.

The exclusive concern with removing dysfunctional behavior (as opposed to a parallel concern with enhancing coping competence) is of course most characteristic of disciplinary strategies. With regard to the prison, Vernon Fox has complained that "in the majority of adult penal institutions in the United States, psychological and social treatment ceases when the rules are violated, and the offenders are placed in solitary confinement or in other punishment status." Fox points out that there is a "dilemma" in a policy of "withdrawing treatment facilities from those who, by their very behavior, have demonstrated that they need treatment most."[11]

Behavior control may, of course, in some instances constructively affect conduct. But we have recorded innumerable instances in which this strategy has not worked or has proved counterproductive. In such instances, it would be more reasonable to attempt a different approach.

A Participatory Strategy for Change

We assume that the offender can become a participant in a self-reform strategy. This assumption may strike some as naive in relation to people who have demonstrable behavior problems, but Bandura has pointed out that:

> according to the basic tenet of cognitive therapy, to alter how people behave one must alter how they think . . . There is a common misconception that the modality of treatment must match the modality of dysfunction: Behavioral dysfunctions presumably require an action-oriented treatment; emotional distress requires an emotive-oriented treatment; and faulty thinking requires a cognitively oriented treatment. In fact, powerful experiences can effect changes in all modalities of functioning —motor, cognitive, and affective . . . In short, the strength of influences rather than the modality in which they are conveyed is more likely to determine the scope of change.[12]

We start by assuming that understanding behavior patterns in the way we have described them is a process that can be shared with chronic maladaptors, if one can convince them to engage in systematic self-study.[13] We assume that participation in self-study is most apt to be useful in the following:

- where the offender has important experiences to offer the participant group
- where the offender's sharing of his or her experience is an asset rather than a liability
- where behavioral improvements benefit both the person and the setting[14]
- where the person is motivated to concentrate on his or her problem
- where increased understanding is possible
- where the person's self-image is enhanced rather than degraded by self-analysis.

The self-study process presupposes that a person who has experienced a problem can bring these experiences to bear in a way that can contribute to the understanding and resolution of the problem. But how do we get a serious trouble-maker to engage in the trouble's solution?

There are two related initiation problems that we must face. One is how to obtain the involvement of the offender in a process that he or she is bound to find at once unfamiliar, threatening, and demanding. We cannot assume, of course, that one can succeed in every instance, but offering the person an experience that makes him or her an object of interest and concern provides a plausible approach to the issue of motivation. In self-analysis, the subject, his or her own behavior, is of consuming interest. It also helps that the person soon discovers to his or her surprise that he or she is not defined as a target for the punitive or controlling action of others but as providing content from which the person and his or her peers can learn.

A later incentive to participation emerges if and when the program candidates become aware of their own contribution to the difficulties they have encountered. This process is illustrated by John Lochman of Duke University, who has designed a group-centered program for violently disruptive male students. Lochman notes that such youngsters often know that their losses of temper are liabilities. In case the point escapes them, Lochman reinforces it by appealing to their own cherished values: "We tell the boys that if another kid gets them so mad they blow up, then the kid is controlling them," said Dr. Lochman. "We tell them they can win by not getting mad."[15]

A contingent incentive can be mobilized when the person, however tentatively, considers the prospect that he or she can expand his or her repertoire of response options by participating in the program. This element is illustrated by the Duke University program's emphasis on social skills training:

> "We tell the boys that this is a group that will teach them how to better handle situations that get them frustrated or angry," Dr. Lochman said. "We give them new ways to respond: instead of getting angry, for instance, they can try to come back at a kid in a playful way . . . One large problem for these children is that they can't think of a friendly response that preserves their own dignity and self-image."[16]

An intervention for the conventional clients that has shown remarkable results, especially in institutions for young offenders, is Positive Peer Culture, which we have alluded to (see chapter 13).[17] This intervention attempts to reverse the polarities or direction of delinquent group norms. Vorrath and Brendtro, the progenitors of the strategy, point out that offering a problem-solving approach provides an attractive alternative to a control-oriented approach, which the offenders have learned to expect. They present an outline contrasting the two approaches (see Exhibit 16.1).[18]

Vorrath and Brendtro provide examples of what they call *relabeling*, a process that points up the liabilities of personal demonstrations of toughness and exploitive behavior and "makes caring fashionable." They write that "since it is virtually impossible to persuade delinquent males to accept a role they regard as weak and sissified, the group leader must

Exhibit 16.1

A Problem-Solving Versus Control-Oriented Approach

Solving Problems	Controlling Problems
1. Problems are a normal part of every person's life.	1. Problems are abnormalities in people (often viewed as mental illness, immorality, ignorance, or deviant behavior).
2. People with problems are no different from all other people: They sometimes hurt themselves or others.	2. People with problems are different, because they show behavior that is objectionable to society.
3. Acknowledging that one has problems is really a sign of strength.	3. Acknowledging that one has problems is really admitting to an abnormality.
4. It is all right for problems to be shown.	4. It is not good to show problems.
5. When problems arise, those around the person have an opportunity to help him or her understand the problems and to become more considerate of oneself and others.	5. When problems arise, those around the person should try to get him or her to stop showing this troublesome behavior.
6. Problems cease to be a concern when the person no longer needs to hurt himself or herself or others.	6. Problems cease to be a concern when problem behavior can no longer be observed.

present caring as a strong and masculine activity." Thus, "helping behavior is referred to in such terms as strong, mature and powerful, while all hurting behavior may be referred to as weak, immature and inadequate."[19]

The same point is made by Gibbs, Potter, and Goldstein, the originators of a peer-reeducative approach called the Equip Program. The authors point out:

> [T]he youth culture cannot be therapeutic unless the giving and receiving of help are perceived in positive terms.

In the culture of antisocial youths, however, giving and receiving help is often viewed as weak, dumb or sissy. Positive words such as *strong, cool, smart,* and *sophisticated* are explicitly or implicitly applied to antisocial behavior instead . . . correcting this distortion is crucial to the development of a positive culture.[20]

The problem is how to create a group culture for obtaining understanding through mutual trust and sharing. This calls for starting small and building a nucleus of committed participants with peer leadership potential. Once such a culture nucleus is established, initial peer leadership becomes less essential, and the enterprise can gain respectability or at least acceptance.

The beauty of a pattern-analysis procedure is that it not only groups participants in terms of their coping problems but also provides criteria for assessing their regenerative behavior. A pool of potential participants can in theory be identified by whatever nominating strategy is compatible with an institution's needs. But the final selection of group members, as a first step to their participation in the program (let us call it a self-management study center), must be controlled by the program's staff, based on a review of the person's record of maladaptive behavior.

Antecedents of the Proposed Approach

1. *Use of Inmates and Staff.* Some 30 years ago, two of the authors of this book (Toch and Grant) ran a pair of companion studies sponsored by the National Institute of Mental Health (NIMH). The first of these studies, the Offender New Careers Project, was intended to train prison inmates as paraprofessionals who would work, after their release on parole, with California state correctional agencies.[21] The second project included offenders and ex-offenders as individual and group interviewers in a study of recidivistic violence.[22]

   The idea of using ex-offenders to work with correctional staff to bring about change in prison programs was a chancy one at best. Fortunately, the emergence

of Economic Opportunity Act programs allowed ex-
offenders to move to the national scene through reform
efforts that tried to create new roles for the poor in
public service careers. The new careers movement of
the late 1960s and 1970s offered not only offenders but
also other people screened out of legitimate participation in society an opportunity to make meaningful contributions to the solution of problems with which they
had firsthand experience.[23]

Our recidivistic violence study provided another
kind of role. The offenders who participated in this
study made splendid coresearchers, working in partnership with individuals who brought more respectable academic credentials, but less experience, to the
problem.[24] In fact, several of our nonprofessional colleagues in this research could have qualified as subjects
for the study.

It is particularly out of this latter experience, which
included a concern with patterns of prison violence,
that we concluded that pattern analysis is a safe and
sane approach to self-study: safe because it is relatively
nonthreatening to the inmate, sane because it does not
threaten the institution with reorganizations of its operation.

2. *The Peer Review Model.* Following our study of violence,
we moved to the applied problem of trying to reduce
violence between police officers and citizens in a large
urban community.[25] We worked with problem police
officers, men who had been involved in unusually high
numbers of confrontations with citizens, and we set
them the task of developing approaches to the reduction of violent incidents involving the police and citizens. The officers developed a peer review process that
became a part of the police department's ongoing operation. It may be worthwhile to describe this process
because it forms the groundwork for the prison version
we outline below:

In its original form, the review panel consisted of the
following stages:

(1) *The necessity for the panel is documented.* Typically,
the process would be initiated when an officer
reached a threshold number of incidents on an up-

to-date inventory of violent involvements. The number used would not be the number of raw incidents but a refined index in which the active role of the subject had been established. It would exclude situations in which unwilling participation had been secured. It would include instances in which another officer had filed a report despite the subject's active role in bringing violence about.

Other ways of mobilizing the review panel would include requests by supervisors or by the subjects themselves. In such cases, however, the record would have to bear out the officer's eligibility by showing a substantial number of recent involvements.

(2) *A preparatory investigation for the interview is conducted.* Data relating to the subject's performance on the street would be obtained from available secondary sources. These could include interviews with supervisors, reports by peers, and all information on record. The investigation would culminate in a "study group" in which panelists would formulate hypotheses and draft questions that streamlined the panel session to follow.

(3) Then came the interview itself, which could be subdivided into three stages:

(a) *Key incidents are chronologically explored,* including not only actions taken by all individuals involved in the incident but also their perceptions, assumptions, feelings, and motives.

(b) *The summation of these data in the form of common denominators and patterns* is undertaken primarily by the subject, with participation by the panelists. An effort is made to test the plausibility and relevance of the hypothesized patterns by extrapolating them into other involvements.

(c) *The discussion of the pattern* occurs last and includes tracing its contribution to violence. This stage features the exploration of alternative approaches that might be conducive to more constructive solutions.

Note that the inception of our group for problem officers required a reversal of the usual subcultural position that, like offenders, each officer must do his own time. The officers themselves developed the idea for the Peer Review Panel, designed the procedures, identified the problem participants, and conducted the panels. They also drafted proposals for programs concerned with landlord/tenant disputes, domestic discord, communications, and training and assisted in their implementation, again demonstrating that individuals who had been designated as problem cases can develop creative and effective solutions to problems of which they had been a part.

3. *Social Learning.* During the time we were concerned with the resocialization of inmates—in fact, before the inmate studies were begun—we had begun collaborating with Maxwell Jones, a British psychiatrist who had been working with maladapted people in settings that he described as therapeutic communities, in which patients and staff jointly addressed problems of living together as a way of developing increased personal and social competence.[26]

Social learning of the sort discussed by Jones centers on constructive feedback about a person's maladaptive behavior (particularly maladaptive behavior that causes problems in the person's relationships with others), which provides "live" learning content for social learning (therapeutic) groups. It is a short step from this view to envisage a group that did not center on day-to-day feedback relating to single instances of behavior but on the reviews of *patterns* of maladaptive behavior, which can be deduced from a series of incidents in which the person had created difficulties both for himself/herself and for others.

4. *Self-Management and Perceived Control.* We concluded that a pattern-analytic self-study approach has other benefits, some of which have been demonstrated in an emerging multidisciplinary field of study concerned with issues of choice and perceived control. A summary of the research implications of this work states:

It is now known that control and choice, however they are operationalized, almost invariably have good effects. Moreover, this has been shown to be the case for a wide variety of situations and manipulations. For example, both people and animals are happier, healthier, more active, solve problems better, and feel less stress when they are given choice and control . . . We are hard pressed to think of another area of psychology that has provided so many potential benefits for mankind in so short a time.[27]

Studies of dependent populations other than offenders have been summarized by Ellen Langer as follows:

I have been struck by the apparent relationship between the individuals' involvement in whatever task we placed before them and the degree to which they seemed to improve both psychologically and physically. The process of mindful involvement is control.[28]

Langer makes a clear distinction between the outcome of a decision (shared or not) and involvement in the process of decision making. There may well be a positive impact (e.g., a successful self-management strategy) derived from a specific decision process (e.g., an incident pattern analysis) but, whether or not this outcome occurs, there is likely to be enhanced learning from the person's involvement in the mindful decision-making process itself. Langer cites many ingenious studies and experiments to show that these are independent consequences that can contribute to the development of self-management skills.

Therapeutic Community Approaches

The program we shall outline is an example of a therapeutic community approach to maladaptive behavior, in that it envisages a residential setting in which groups of disturbed–disruptive inmates would be encouraged to engage in learning by staff members operating as an interdisciplinary team. As the term *community* suggests, the learning process would be a communal one, involving both staff and the prisoners.

Therapeutic communities for disturbed or disruptive inmates were introduced in England in the early 1960s. A prison called Grendon Underwood, located near London, is the flagship of this approach. It is an experimental psychiatric facility that comprises five therapeutic communities of between 35 and 42 residents. The treatment process centers on small groups with two cotherapists, one of whom is a correction officer. Most of the staff in the prison are uniformed officers.

The residents of Grendon are referred from other prisons, usually by mental health staff and physicians. Forty percent are lifers, and most have had extensive problems of adjustment to confinement. These problems are regarded as grist for social learning. Eric Cullen explains:

> [T]he behaviour . . . is not punished by conventional prison means but turned instead back into the therapeutic process. The prescription "take it to your group" encourages both individual and collective responsibilities to be accountable and to change.[29]

One of the assumptions underlying the Grendon approach is that *ad seriatim* disciplining of inmates reinforces feelings of bitterness and resentment that motivate acting-out behavior. Peter Lewis, who was director of therapy at Grendon, points out:

> [T]he significant therapeutic task for staff is to try to understand the subtle danger of repeating such a destructive interpersonal re-enactment. It is all too easy in everyday interaction for inmate and officer to become engaged in such a non-productive repetition of unhelpful ingrained behaviour.[30]

The point is to avoid playing into expectations that undergird antiauthoritarian and destructive behavior but, instead, to subject such premises to review and analysis. Constructive responses foster a "corrective emotional experience," which can draw attention to the defective emotional experience that frequently had its inception in early years of rejection and inconsistency of care. The presumption is that the disconfirming experience of an environment that includes nonrejecting authority figures "frees the person to experiment with new styles of thought, feeling and behaviours in his psychological journey to personality reformation."[31] To inculcate what is described as "an understanding of interdependence and trust that had previously been lacking," the staff at Grendon "model" constructive resolutions of interpersonal conflicts and problems that involve authority figures.[32]

The treatment modality at Grendon requires that the officers who function as cotherapists learn a great deal about running groups. The professional development of the officers consists of mentoring them as they actually run groups and of engaging in frequent, systematic process reviews of sessions.

Although officers at Grendon are encouraged to read, their supervisors supply clinical and other theoretical constructs when the experiences to which the constructs apply arise in therapeutic encounters. There are also periodic staff meetings across the groups and wings in which techniques are discussed and analyses of therapy sessions take place. Outside courses are made available to all staff, including the officers.

Grendon inmates are expected to review their life stories in the groups, including their criminal involvements, which mostly highlight violent acts. As in most therapeutic communities, there is emphasis on the here and now, and any observed "parallels between current behaviour and prior offending . . . are brought into the therapeutic process."[33]

An end product of therapy at Grendon is the formulation of strategies by the inmate for responding to human encounters so as to avoid future misconduct. This goal is nicely described by Genders and Player, who write:

> What Grendon attempts to do is to empower individuals to take control over that which is within their power: namely, their ability to make choices which alleviate their

own and others' victimization, and to anticipate, and take responsibility for, the consequences of their actions.[34]

Among other prison settings in England that serve disruptive prisoners are so-called special units. One of these is C-Wing at Parkhurst, which provides treatment to former residents of segregation settings, under psychiatric supervision. According to the senior psychologist of the prison,

> [T]he Unit Management Team ... were keen to take prisoners who had displayed disruptive or difficult behavior at a number of different establishments so that the likelihood of their settling into normal prison regimen is limited. In addition, the difficult behavior exhibited by the prisoners was to be uncontrolled or irrational, stemming from their mental abnormality rather than any preconceived rational motivation.[35]

Despite the self-conscious selection of prisoners with discouraging histories, the design of the regime is virtually antithetical to that of supermax confinement. The psychologist notes:

> [T]he inmates are encouraged to spend as much of their time out of their cells mixing with both staff and other prisoners ... [I]t is felt that for improvements to be made inmates should be encouraged to associate with both staff and prisoners, to develop social behavior.[36]

Monitoring each inmate is the responsibility of a personal officer assigned to him at intake, who exercises a combination of counseling and custodial responsibilities.

In England the prevalence of psychosis in prisons has been reduced through transfer of seriously mentally ill inmates to forensic hospitals. Despite this fact, Coid has reported that only 10% of disruptive prisoners in special units were found free of lifetime (Axis I) major mental disorders. He also reported that 20% of the unit residents "were suffering from serious mental illness when first interviewed."[37] As example, he notes:

One man padded the staircases and landings of a unit aimlessly, unable to engage in any meaningful activities whatsoever, and received the maximum recommended levels of several antipsychotic medications. He still regularly pleaded with prison staff to give more. He had wrecked the patients' social club in a special hospital and had promptly been returned to prison.[38]

In summarizing the impressions he gained in his research with special unit residents, Coid describes typical careers of disturbed–disruptive inmates. He writes of such individuals:

[Their] last period of imprisonment was characterised by increasing periods of segregation and movements from one prison to another. Hardened malignancy of attitude had now set in with ingrained, repetitive patterns of behavioural disorder. Repeated punishments within the prison setting and the increasingly negative attitudes of prison staff had further confirmed the process, with many men locked into a vicious spiral of punishment–resentment–retaliation–more punishment, from which neither side seemed able to find a way out. Features of mental illness now remained untreated as for some cases the avenue of psychiatric treatment had become closed to them. For others the behavioural disorder remained unchanged in spite of all attempts at psychiatric treatment.[39]

The Role of Correction Officers in Interdisciplinary Teams

One feature of innovative programs we have highlighted is that they often expand the role of correction officers. Such programs provide officers with noncustodial human-service responsibilities that resemble those of traditional mental health professionals. At the same time, the programs create a collegial relationship among the officers and mental health workers who are attached to the programs. The staff of innovative programs come to function as inclusive interdisciplinary teams. And the emphasis on teaming is one that makes a great deal of sense if we remember that we are dealing with problems that cross disciplinary borders, such as those of disturbed–disruptive offenders.

Observers who are unfamiliar with prisons tend to presuppose that resistance to teaming would be likely to primarily originate with officers who would object to playing "social work" roles. Although correction officers often do express these sentiments—especially at first and when the proposition comes up in public—most officers welcome the opportunity to undertake challenging and interesting work when it is afforded them.

A much more insidious source of resistance is that of some clinicians, who prefer to cast officers in handmaiden roles. A popular presumption in this perspective is that correction officers are culturally predisposed to be rigid, insensitive, and punitive, whereas mental health staff tend to be inmate-centered and benevolent. A competing realization, however, is that the activities of mental health staff cannot be fully discharged without raw information provided by officers or without officers acting as delegated informants and monitors. Prison clinicians are forced to make this concession because they recognize that the officers experience inmates at close quarters 24 hours each day, whereas professional workers see them for short periods during 9-to-5 days in a 5-day work week.

It appears difficult for professional staff to abandon stereotypic conceptions of correctional officers. An article by three prison mental health staff members, for example, asserts that "the correctional culture typically involves regimentation, universally applied rules, implicit authority of security staff, and punitive sanction for violations by inmates," whereas the mental health culture "is characterized by individualized treatment, informed consent, and negotiated compliance."[40] This cultural diagnosis is followed by an ecumenical prescription for collaboration with officers, especially in units for mentally ill prisoners. But unsurprisingly, the function assigned to officers remains purely custodial:

> The officers' authority to provide discipline and apply
> sanctions is an important tool in managing and curbing

the maladaptive behaviors of inmates on the residential treatment unit. Although correctional officers are not therapists, the most therapeutic intervention that officers provide for inmates is often in the form of clear boundaries and consequences.[41]

In the same article by mental health staff, there is a suggestion for cross-training, "exposing clinicians to matters of security and exposing officers to clinical matters."[42] Such training in fact potentially enhances mutual understanding, but it simultaneously cements disciplinary boundaries. Even worse, it can attenuate enlightened professional perspectives by oversensitizing clinicians to custodial premises and risk-related considerations.

Only one item in the essay that ostensibly deals with "collaborative" activities is potentially team-promotive. This item is an allusion to "ad hoc case conferences" focused on "challenging cases."[43] To actually promote teaming, however, case conferences would have to dispense with assigned stereotyped positions; they would have to provide for individual interventions without regard to preexisting role definitions. Case conferences that take place in the context of teaming must allow for open-ended analyses of case materials in conjoint efforts to make sense of behavior patterns and the motives underlying them. And such conferences must ultimately encourage everyone to participate in discussions of interventions that can ameliorate patterns of maladaptation.

The Use of Pattern Analysis in Treatment

In this book, we have argued that different offenders act out in different ways for different reasons. We have suggested that disaggregating maladaptive behavior patterns helps us to understand these patterns and that the understanding can be shared with the problem people who are the objects of our concern.

The treatment modality we have in mind differs from approaches that rely on treatment content that is relatively invariant. We assume that because patterns of maladaptation differ from each other, analyses and prescriptions should vary from client to client, though clients can be grouped in terms of similarities of problems to be addressed.

To emphasize individualized differences in the content of appropriate or desirable treatment does not imply any disrespect for theories that generalize about the motivation and dynamics of violent behavior. Anyone who indulges in speculation about violence (ourselves included) must learn to accommodate the heterogeneity of the behavior to be explained. Far from being atheoretical, a reliance on descriptive typologies is one that facilitates the application of relevant theory by enhancing the goodness of fit between explanation and behavior. And we could argue that where the violent offender himself or herself is invited to review a hypothesized pattern of behavior, that offender becomes a fellow theorist, in the sense of engaging in a "self-diagnosis" about the dynamics of his or her behavior. The differential explanation of the behavior (e.g., I feel enraged when I am frustrated, or I stage demonstrations of toughness for my peers, or I feel easily slighted, and so forth) defines the problem to be addressed through treatment (such as control of anger, response to peer norms, and issues of self-esteem) and the outcome to be achieved.

The learning process includes the discovery and study of the pattern and the definition of the person's own unique goal of treatment. The differential learning process involved differs a great deal from the experience of the learner in a conventional one-size-fits-all didactic program that is based on preconceptions about violence causation and asks the learner to implement a standard set of psychological improvements (anger control, cognitive upgrading, and so forth) for addressing the problem.

A solid example of such a strategy is the pioneering Violence Prevention Program (VPP) instituted by the Prison Service of Canada. The program is described as taking into account the extant literature relating to "thoughts, emotions, and behaviors that have been linked to violent offending." Based on a review of this literature, the program offers a sequence of group experiences ranging from modules that are concerned with anger, impulse control, problem solving, conflict resolution, and the role of instrumental violence to sessions dealing with issues of resistances to change. There are 10 modules comprising 94 sessions delineated in six program manuals.

Outcome measures for VPP participants appropriately have to do with involvements with violence which includes reductions in the rate of prison disciplinary infractions. In a differential treatment model, on the other hand, outcome measures are differential and relate to the problems of the offender defined through pattern analysis. The aim of treatment would be to achieve the documented discontinuance of specific destructive behavior patterns and a rehearsal of constructive alternatives.[44]

The differential conception is applied in Positive Peer Culture groups. Vorrath and Brendtro offer a list of target behaviors to be addressed with individual youthful offenders. In each case, they specify desired outcome behaviors that are pattern related. Several of the patterns resemble those we have described (see Exhibit 16.2).

Vorrath and Brendtro illustrate the fact that in a differential treatment context the desired outcome is one in which the problem behavior we have been addressing appears to have been addressed. This presumes that the person has not only stopped acting out in the way he or she repeatedly has in the past (to the discomfort of other persons), but has learned to respond more appropriately under comparable circumstances. The criterion would not only be the discontinuance of misbehavior but the successful substitution of prosocial or constructive behavior. To verify that this result has been attained, we have a right to arrange "tests" involving situations that the person has heretofore "failed," and that he or she is now expected to successfully resolve. In institutions such as prisons, sometimes such situations must be simulated through role play or other enactment.

Since we are dealing with problem behavior that is reliably manifest in confinement, there is some risk that improvements might not be sustainable when the person is at large.

Exhibit 16.2

Pattern-Related Outcome Behaviors in Positive
Peer Intervention

Authority Problem: Does Not Want to Be Managed by Anyone
  a. Views authority as an enemy camp "out to get him."
  b. Resents anybody's telling him what to do, does not read-
     ily accept advice from either adults or peers.
  c. Can't get along with those in authority, gets into big con-
     frontations with authority figures, often over minor mat-
     ters.
  d. Does not respond well to parental control or supervision.
  e. Tries to outmaneuver authority figures, circumventing or
     manipulating them if possible.
When solved: Shows ability to get along with those in authority,
is able to accept advice and direction from others. Does not try
to take advantage of authority figures even if they can be manipulated.

****

Easily Angered: Is Often Irritated or Provoked or Has Tantrums
  a. Frequently becomes upset or explosive but may try to ex-
     cuse such behavior as naturally "having a bad temper."
  b. Easily frustrated, unable to accept failure or disappoint-
     ments.
  e. Responds to the slightest challenge or provocation, thus
     making other people's problems his own.
  d. So sensitive about himself that he cannot stand criticism
     or disagreement with his ideas.
When solved: Is not easily frustrated. Knows how to control and
channel anger, not letting it control him. Understands the putdown process and has no need to respond to challenges. Can
tolerate criticism or even negative behavior from others.

******

Fronting: Puts On an Act Rather Than Being Real
  a. Needs to appear big in the eyes of others, always needs
     to try to prove himself.
  b. Bluffs and cons people, thinks loudness and slick talk are
     better than reason.
  c. Acts superior, always has to be right, argues, needs to be
     best in everything, resents being beaten.
  d. Clowns or shows off to get attention.
  e. Plays a role to keep from having to show his real feelings
     to others.
When solved: Is comfortable with people and does not have to
keep trying to prove himself. Has no need to act superior, con
people, or play the showoff role. Is not afraid of showing his true
feelings to others.[45]

In predicting the risk the person may pose in the community, we must bank on the consistency of behavior patterns and hope that patterning now works in our favor.

Predictions of reduced risk must be based on interpersonal skills the person has demonstrably acquired, on improvements we have observed in that person's coping capacity, on positive attitudes he or she appears to have been manifesting, and on the capacity this person seems to have developed to monitor and control his or her behavior. Risk prediction has to do with behavior that is observed as the end result of treatment, with the usual caveats related to the possibility that pretreatment behavior patterns could reassert themselves.

This type of pattern-related risk prediction is markedly different from the more fashionable reliance on actuarial instruments, which can even be administered at the inception of treatment. Prediction instruments tend to inventory past or invariant facts, which by definition cannot be changed. Advocates of the actuarial strategy point to correlations that have been found in aggregate studies between static predictors and recidivism rates, and condemn any reliance on treatment outcomes as reflecting a prescientific (or even an antiscientific) perspective. Two observers of forensic release decisions thus complained that "such decisions appear to maintain a *traditional clinical* focus on the assessment and treatment of symptomatic, disordered, or disruptive behavior,"[46] and they wrote that attention to behavioral improvements observed in response to treatment "suggests that the traditional role of symptom management has a predominant *and deleterious* influence on forensic decisions pertaining to the risk of violence."[47] This contention reflects continuing doubts about whether it is possible to rehabilitate some persons who manifest disturbed or disruptive and disturbed behavior.

Dealing With the Impact of Past Experiences With Custodial Treatment

As we have noted, the response to problem behavior in confinement is typically punitive and most often involves protracted segregation. This means that maladaptive prisoners typically arrive in treatment programs with extensive experiences of punitive confinement. Whatever the impact of punishment in individual cases, it must be considered in working with the offender. Especially critical are iatrogenic cycles, in which our punitive responses to aversive behavior have produced pathologically tinged rebelliousness, which has in turn inspired sharply escalated punitiveness. It is also important to accommodate effects of long-term segregation experiences on the offender's outlook and disposition. Allowances have to be made for understandable suspiciousness, and some bridging experiences may have to be provided to lead the person from isolation to involvement.

The Berlinnie Special Unit (BSU) of the Scottish Prison Service served as a model for therapeutic communities for formerly segregated disruptive inmates. One of several unique features of the BSU was the fostering of creative talent among its residents, and Jimmy Boyle, arguably the most violent prisoner in Scotland, became an established sculptor and writer. In his first book, *A Sense of Freedom*, Boyle recalls that after he arrived at the unit he found the experience distressing:

> [T]here was a great amount of hatred in me for all screws, yet some of the unit staff would approach me in a way that was so natural and innocent it made it difficult to tell them to fuck off. Something inside me, in spite of all the pent-up hatred, would tell me there was something genuine within them. I knew I didn't really want to recognise this part of the screws. I preferred to see them all as bastards, this would have been so much easier for me ... [but] they were so unlike the screws that I had known in the past. At nights I would lie in my bed tearing my guts out thinking intensely about this place and what it was all about, and often wishing I were back in solitary.[48]

Boyle confessed:

> [F]inally, I decided that I had to get the fuck out of the place, and so I went to the Governor and told him ...

the only way for me to get any peace of mind was to
... return to the solitary situation, as that was the method
I could handle best.[49]

The experience that Boyle describes is one of incipient unfreezing of his customary frame of reference, which included
accommodation to the punitive confinement settings in
which he had spent much of his time. There was also the
painful challenge of having to relinquish a militant warfare
posture by reciprocating the disarming trust bids of the officers in the unit.

With the proliferation of supermax segregation settings,
which accommodate many of the most maladaptive prisoners, the need to deal with the psychological impact of segregation experiences becomes particularly urgent. In addition
to fostering learning and development, we must try to or-
chestrate climates in which healing and regeneration can occur for graduates of extreme segregation settings. Such regimes require the balancing of structure and permissiveness,
nurturance and support, autonomy and the discipline required for inquiry, self-study, and the promotion of change.

A Self-Management Study Center

The goal of the self-management study center we envisage
would be the creation of a fostering and supportive climate,
in an appropriate setting, for the shared self-study, decision
making, and understanding necessary for the development
of self-management skills.

What do we have a right to expect from such a center?
First, chronic maladapters should develop an understanding
of and a strategy for managing their own patterns of conduct.
Second, the participants should increase their general social
coping competence, including reading, writing, and thinking
skills. Third, not only should participants become more competent, but they should also *feel* more competent. Feelings of
competence can be expected to reduce anxieties, depression,
and defensiveness and allow more freedom to think, under-

stand, and grow. Fourth, beyond the profit derived by individual participants, we can expect contributions to the development of our knowledge about maladaptation, as pattern-analytic schemes are updated and expanded and as management strategies are developed for different kinds of incident patterns and for different kinds of settings. Three kinds of knowledge should evolve: institution-specific understandings and specific how-tos (local wisdom), contributions to general concepts and theories concerning the nature of prison incidents and their management (including but not limited to self-management), and contributions to the psychology of social behavior in general.

A central theme of a self-management center would be the interaction of experience with general (academic) knowledge. Resource documents, reports, relevant articles and books, as well as diaries, files, and chronological accounts of experience could be maintained. General knowledge could be fed into the study of specific incident patterns, as it is appropriate, and into studies of incident-related impact of settings.[50] At the same time, local knowledge accumulated by the center could be used to modify and develop social science principles and theories. This process could allow for interaction between the information derived from the institutional setting and that available elsewhere, including in other institutional settings. Furthermore, such cross-fertilization would fit with current philosophy of science approaches to the limits of theory in specific (local) behavior prediction and control.[51]

Concern with the specific situation in which change is promoted is the essence of action research or participatory research efforts.[52] There is a temptation among participation researchers to define their work as a separate paradigm from "basic" or "objective" research.[53] However, a case can and should be made for a mutually enhancing relationship between action research and general knowledge. In our case, this point not only holds for the information to be obtained about maladaptive behavior but also holds for the knowledge developed concerning the establishment and expansion of the self-management approach.

Operation of the Self-Management Program

The inmates to be recruited as participants could be selected by disciplinary hearing officers or other custody staff,[54] though nominations could originate elsewhere, such as through statistical reviews of incident patterns. Program participation *must be voluntary* on the part of the inmate,[55] but it might involve suspension of disciplinary penalties or administrative confinement (such as supermax placement) as an incentive.

The groups of inmates in the program could be staffed by two-person teams consisting of a mental health staff member and a corrections officer. At later stages, inmates drawn from among program graduates could become third members of the staff team, but full participation in center activities would be required from each inmate member throughout the program.

The program would be carried out in small groups, not to exceed eight members, including staff. These groups could initially focus on reviews of prison disciplinary incidents, in an effort to define individual patterns of maladaptive inmate involvements. The review could then be expanded to include incidents that are not fully described in documents to enhance the pool of data available to the groups. Pattern analysis would be followed by the design and rehearsal of alternative approaches to social encounters, as well as by periodic review and reevaluation of behavioral approaches over a period of months.[56]

There would be eight steps in which the inmates could engage to become full participants in the program:

1. Nomination, volunteering, and selection
2. Orientation, group formation, and preparation
3. Preliminary pattern analysis for each of the three to five inmate participants in the group
4. Role and reverse role-playing of representative incidents by and with each participant
5. Development of an incident prevention strategy for and by each offender

6. Setting of an early (e.g., 10 days) reconvening date to verify application of the behavior strategy in regular prison settings

7. Reconvening for a quality control session (e.g., within 3 months) to review performance and to provide feedback

8. Development of an extended strategy and a quality control procedure for each participant.

On completion of Step 5 (the development of an incident prevention strategy), the offender would become a probationary center participant. The offender would then sign a contract with his or her group specifying his or her and the group's commitments for the operation of the strategy the offender has planned. The importance of this step has been highlighted as follows by Bandura:

> When the enactive part of the treatment is implemented only verbally, corrective courses of action are structured for persons to pursue, but they are left to their own devices to carry them out. It is one thing to prescribe corrective action; it is another thing to get people to carry it out, especially when it involves onerous or threatening aspects. The successes achieved will depend on a number of factors: the extent to which individuals are provided with the cognitive and social skills and the self-beliefs of efficacy required to perform effectively, judicious selection and structuring of performance tasks to disconfirm misbeliefs and to expand competencies, incentives to put behavioral prescriptions into practice, and social supports for personal change ... Conditions conducive to personal change are more reliably achieved by enlisting the aid of significant others in the treatment. In fact, when enactive modes of treatment are well developed, nonprofessionals can serve as well or better than professionals in guiding mastery experiences that promote rapid change.[57]

Graduation to probationary status would symbolize a key move in the offender's participation, commitment, and ownership in the program, because it would put the person on record as intending to fulfill his or her behavioral contract with the support of his or her group. This would be a strong indication that both the person's commitment and the integrity of the culture are plausible. It would also supply a shared set of activities for the group members, because the task of monitoring behavior would provide both the participant and the group members with a means for the quality control of their enterprise.

The specific commitments that are undertaken could be as simple as exercises for reducing acute anxiety or as complicated as the development of a special self-help group for inmates with comparable incident patterns. The rehearsed behavior could include self-control routines, actions which the person derives from role-playing and shared thinking of the group about just what sets him or her off when. These self-management responses to incident cues could be a "timeout" session, a memorized talk to oneself (counting to 10 or its equivalent), contacting a previously identified supportive other, working out, counseling, sharing with peer-inmate counselors, involvement in program development or conflict negotiation or mediation, Alcoholic Anonymous-type procedures such as apologizing and seeking a fresh start in one or more relationships, and scheduled or emergent encounters, including conflict situations. The behavior at issue *must* be tasks the offender understands and in which the offender is willing to engage as part of his or her own self-management.

Two kinds of quality control must be undertaken. One concerns the offender's strategy—what does the offender say he or she will do, by what time, and does he or she get it done? The other concerns the center's development, operation, and effectiveness. Although the latter would require some external observation, a major part of both kinds of quality control could be conducted as team projects by the center's participants.

When any participant moves beyond Step 5, he or she would be expected to engage in other activities of the center, to share in its housekeeping, social structure, and educational activities. There could be a 24-hour-a-day routine of study and the maintenance of living space, including a daily living-learning session for handling interpersonal (staff and staff–inmate) issues.

The center should have its own (reasonably isolated) living and work quarters. Although the availability of bed space is always an institution problem, it is important that there be some potential for expanding center space as the self-study culture expands. The center could start with, say, 10 beds (enough for two study groups) that would be filled in 1 week through the initial selection process. The 10 beds could be expanded to 20 over the next 3 weeks.

If the program is to function as a living unit, expansion beyond 20 beds or so is undesirable. However, a cadre of inmates drawn from one unit could help to form a second unit, which in turn could be expanded to 20. The center could thus end up serving 40 inmates, with further expansion depending on the strength and effectiveness of the culture developed in the center.

Each participant must have a full day's schedule built into his or her self-management strategy. Commitments would include, but would not be limited to, participation in one's own group and in teams concerned with the operation of the living unit and the center (such as concern with the infiltration of gangs or cliques in the center, victim–predator relationships, the use of educational resources, housekeeping organization, and operation).

A typical day in the self-management center for a participant who has reached Stage 5 (i.e., who has developed his or her own incident-prevention strategy) might look like this:

6:00 a.m.–8:00 a.m	Housekeeping and breakfast
8:00 a.m.–10:00 a.m.	Reading/writing tutorial
10:00 a.m.–12:00 p.m	Serve as a member of a pattern-analysis team considering a new potential center participant
12:00 p.m.–1:00 p.m.	Lunch
1:00 p.m.–4:00 p.m.	Work with a project team such as a group developing a scenario for a TV tape showing the operation of the center
4:00 p.m.–6:00 p.m.	Recreation

6:00 p.m.–7:00 p.m.   Dinner

7:00 p.m.–9:00 p.m.   Living/learning session (group discussion of interpersonal problems within the living unit)

9:00 p.m.–10:00 p.m.   Reading and homework

We have noted in chapter 13 that educational experiences can play an important role in reversing chronic patterns of maladaptation. Education—the improvement of reading and writing skills and related knowledge—could be enhanced through tutorial support. Although professional education resources should be available, the self-development cause is best advanced when inmates work with peer (inmate) tutors. There may well be confined professional educators who could merge these roles.

Organizational Development Issues

Inherent in the self-management study center's operation would be the development of resources for its own modification and expansion. The incident pattern analyses done in this study offer an initial group of protocols, provide a classification scheme, and contribute coder experiences in the sharing of perceptions that could assist the staff who serve as founders for such a center.[58] Once started, however, the center must become a valued component of the prison organization rather than an "innovation ghetto" that is grudgingly tolerated, because even success can breed suspicion, distrust, and competitiveness.

A central survival theme of the center could be the promotion of positive behavior, of *helpful participation*, which is the converse of maladaptive behavior. The approach used with inmates can be expanded to consultation arrangements that further the center's relations with the rest of the institution, and particularly with staff who are concerned with behavior-control problems; but eagerness to work with one's host institution must not negate the first priority for an effective center. An internal climate of trust and commitment must be established before the center can demonstrate any real effectiveness and before it is entitled to expand or work with others. Although organizational understanding and support must be established before a center can begin operating at all, officials cannot allow—in the name of helpfulness to the host institution—the premature "dumping" of notorious problem cases into the center before an effective self-management climate is developed. Early and consistent mutual understanding is needed to allow the development and maintenance of a helping relationship among the center, the institution, and the system, while at the same time protecting the center's precariously evolving nucleus culture.

Finally, it is possible to think of a self-management center contributing to the development of an informal resource network involving other self-study and participatory research programs. The availability of computer communication makes such exchanges easier on a day-to-day basis, and the knowledge that one is not alone provides feedback and support that help to build program commitment.

Behavior Self-Management as a Modality

The approach we have delineated illustrates a modality of change that differs from other approaches in that (a) it involves the maladaptive person as *participant* rather than as *client*; (b) it does not require a categorization of the person's problem (such as substance abuse, mental illness, or learning disability) to define the service he or she receives; (c) it provides for gradations of environment in which to *test* developing competence; (d) it mobilizes teams of staff members, including staff primarily concerned with behavioral and mental health problems; (e) it relies on group process and group thinking to buttress staff influence; and (f) it accommodates tailor-made interventions to address individual patterns of maladaptation.

One advantage of a pattern analytic approach to clients who act out is that it circumvents organizational interface problems in service delivery networks that are detrimental to those who fall into definitional penumbras and became members of "garbage pail" categories. An example of such a category is special education, which inherited a melange of behavioral problems by default, despite efforts to define the problem area (learning disability) to which programming is in theory addressed.

Definitions of problems frequently evolve to accommodate available resources, rather than vice versa. For example:

> Children considered emotionally disturbed in Delaware or Utah, where that handicap is liberally defined, could find themselves instantly "cured" by moving to Mississippi or Arkansas, where the definitions are more narrow.[59]

In the prison, epidemiological estimates of mental illness often vary with the availability of mental health services,[60] although we assume that the latter would be measured responses the former. On the other hand, generosity of definition need not always translate into appropriateness of response, particularly when services remain narrow-gauged while clients suffer from wide ranges of problems and deficits. This fact matters for maladaptive people, who almost invariably are multiproblem clients.

We have mentioned that the disruptive effects of personal maladaptation frequently foreclose the examination of the dynamics of maladaptive behavior and prevent responses that can address these dynamics. Where responses do occur, combined helping–punishing strategies are frequently deployed, or the person can find himself or herself shuttled between junctures at which services are rendered and those at which punishment is inflicted.

Substituting the concept of "maladaptive" behavior for the bad/mad, responsible/irresponsible dichotomy reduces the need to undersell either the impact or the motive of conduct. Responses to maladaptive behavior such as those we have suggested attend to behavior impact and can include custody staff as members of treatment teams. Punitive dispositions may at times be suspended, but this fact does not carry exculpatory implications because addressing motivational (*why*) questions means that we must implicitly consider the impact of the behavior (*what* questions) which is to be explained; second, self-studying conduct is impossible without considering its dysfunctional results, including damage done to others; and finally, critical reviews are no less uncomfortable—and sometimes more uncomfortable—than the pay-as-you-go complacency of being punished.

What may matter most, however, is that regenerative enterprises can interdict more personal disruptiveness than punitive approaches. Whereas punishment responds to past harm, it need offer no respite—other than through temporary incapacitation—from future reoffending. Personal reform, however, interrupts maladaptive careers and can thus prevent much harm to the community over long stretches of time.

Notes

1. Evershed, S. (1991). Special unit, C wing, HMP Parkhurst. In K. R. Herbst & J. Gunn (Eds.), *The mentally disordered offender* (pp. 88–95). Oxford, England: Butterworth-Heinemann, p. 95.
2. De Beaumont, G., & de Tocqueville, A. (1833). *On the penitentiary system of the United States, and its application to France* [with an appendix on penal colonies and statistical notes]. Philadelphia: Carey, Lea & Blanchard, p. 6.
3. De Beaumont and de Tocqueville, note 2, supra, p. 5.
4. De Beaumont and de Tocqueville, note 2, supra, p. 5.
5. De Beaumont and de Tocqueville, note 2, supra, p. 15.
6. Madrid v. Gomez, 1955 W.I. 17092 (N.D. Cal 1955). In another recent decision (Ruiz v. Johnson, 1999 WL 14460 [S.D. Tex.]), a court found that administrative segregation arrangements in Texas violated the constitutional rights of emotionally disturbed inmates. The judge wrote: "More than mere deprivation ... these inmates suffer actual psychological harm from their almost total deprivation of human contact, mental stimulus, personal property and human dignity." He wrote of prisoners in need of help who "are instead inappropriately managed merely as miscreants."
7. See T. Kupers, chapter 15, note 4. Also, Haney, C. (1993, Spring). Infamous punishment: The psychological consequences of isolation. *The National Prison Project Journal, 8,* 3–21. See also Haney, C., & Lynch,

M. (1997). Regulating prisons of the future: A psychological analysis of supermax and solitary confinement. *New York Review of Law and Social Change, 23,* 477–570.

8. Palumbo, D., Hepburn, J., Griffin, M., Fischer, D., & Janisch, R. (2000, November). *Taking back the yards: Controlling and managing prison gangs.* Paper presented at annual meeting of the American Society of Criminology, San Francisco.

9. R. Johnson (1996) in *Hard time: Understanding and reforming the prison* (Belmont, CA: Wordsworth) refers to this goal as "facilitating mature coping." By "mature coping" among prisoners, Johnson means:

    (1) Dealing directly with one's problems, using the resources legitimately at one's disposal; (2) refusing to employ deceit or violence other than in self defense; and (3) building mutual and supportive relationships with others. Inmates who cope maturely come to grips with problems in prison living, and they do so without violating the rights of others to be safe in their person and in their property. More generally, they treat others, staff and inmates alike, as fellow human beings who are possessed of dignity and worth. (p. 9)

10. There are some mental health experts who do not share this conventional view. Thomas Szasz (1961) in *The myth of mental illness* (chapter 9, note 5) comes closest to outlining a maladaptation-centered intervention when he writes that he favors abolishing the categories of ill and healthy behavior, and the prerequisite of mental sickness for so-called psychotherapy.

    This implies candid recognition that we "treat" people by psychoanalysis or psychotherapy not because they are "sick" but rather because: (1) They desire this type of assistance; (2) they have problems in living for which they seek mastery through understanding of the kinds of games which they, and those around them, have been in the habit of playing; and (3) we want and are able to participate in their "education" because this is our professional role. (p. 255)

11. Fox, chapter 1, note 3, p. 321.

12. Bandura, chapter 14, note 10, p. 519.

13. This attribute constitutes an advantage when one compares a behavior-career-based typology with one that is derived from responses to a personality inventory, such as the Minnesota Multiphasic Personality Inventory (MMPI). The results of psychometrically derived typologies can be communicated to people thus classified, but the rationale for arriving at classifications cannot be shared and internalized by subjects. Interestingly, however, there are similarities and close parallels between some of the patterns we have outlined in this book and those derived from MMPI item clusters. See Megargee, E. I., & Bonn, M. J. (1979). *Classifying criminal offenders: A new system based on the MMPI.* Beverly Hills, CA: Sage. A major disadvantage of actuarial risk prediction instruments to which we have alluded is not only that scores are difficult to explain but also that the rationale of having one's fate

decided based on static predictors and aggregate data is almost impossible to accept, because it sounds blatantly unfair.

14. With respect to behavior modification in the prison, for example, an
    authoritative monograph points out:

    Because the behavioral professional is often in the position of as-
    sisting in the management of prisoners whose antagonism to authority
    and rebelliousness have been the catalyst for conflict within the insti-
    tution, the distinctions among his multiple functions of therapy, man-
    agement, and rehabilitation can become blurred, and his allegiance
    confused . . . Behavior modification should not be used in an attempt
    to facilitate institutionalization of the inmate or to make him adjust to
    inhumane living conditions. Further, no therapist should accept re-
    quests for treatment that take the form "make him 'behave,'" when
    the intent of the request is to make the person conform to oppressive
    conditions. (Brown, B. S., Wienckowski, L. A., & Stolz, S. S. [1975].
    Behavior modification: Perspective on a current issue. Washington, DC:
    Department of Health, Education and Welfare, National Institute of
    Mental Health, pp. 16–17.)

15. Goleman, D. (1987, April 7). The bully: New research depicts a para-
    noid, lifelong loser. *New York Times.*

16. *Ibidem.* Differences among behavior management strategies may have
    to do with the degree to which the alternative responses to be re-
    hearsed are "discovered" by the subject, or evolve out of group de-
    liberation, or are introduced by an expert change agent.

17. Vorrath and Brendtro, chapter 13, note 4.

18. Vorrath and Brendtro, chapter 13, note 4, p. 24.

19. Vorrath and Brendtro, chapter 13, note 4, p. 30.

20. Gibbs, J. C., Potter, G. B., & Goldstein, A. P. (1995). *The equip program:
    Teaching youth to think and act responsibly through a peer-helping approach.*
    Champaign, IL: Research Press, p. 26.

21. Grant, J. D. (1980). From "living learning" to "learning to live": An
    extension of social therapy. In H. Toch (Ed.), *Therapeutic communities
    in corrections* (pp. 41–49). New York: Praeger.

22. Toch, H. (1992). *Violent men* (chapter 7, note 3).

23. Pearl, A., & Riessman, F. (1965). *New careers for the poor: The nonpro-
    fessional in human service.* New York: Free Press.

24. Toch, H. (1967). The convict as researcher. *Transaction, 9,* 71–75.

25. See Toch, H., & Grant, J. D. (1991). *Police as problem solvers.* New York:
    Plenum.

26. Jones, M. (1953). *The therapeutic community: A new treatment method in
    psychiatry.* New York: Basic Books.

27. Pearlmuter, L. C., & Monty, R. A. (1979). *Choice and perceived control.*
    Hillsdale, NJ: Erlbaum, pp. 367–368.

28. Langer, E. J. (1983). *The psychology of control.* Beverly Hills: Sage,
    p. 293.

29. Cullen, E. (1997). Can a prison be a therapeutic community? The Gren-

don template. In E. Cullen, L. Jones, & R. Woodward (Eds.), *Therapeutic communities for offenders* (pp. 75–99). Chichester, England: Wiley, p. 85.

30. Lewis, P. (1997). Context for change (whilst consigned and confined): A challenge for systematic thinking. In E. Cullen, L. Jones, & R. Woodward (Eds.), *Therapeutic communities for offenders* (pp. 207–222). Chichester, England: Wiley, p. 210.

31. Lewis, note 30, supra, p. 210.

32. Lewis, note 30, supra, p. 213.

33. Cullen, note 29, supra, p. 80.

34. Genders, E., & Player, E. (1995). *Grendon: A study of a therapeutic prison.* Oxford, England: Clarendon, p. 14.

35. Evershed, note 1, supra, p. 90.

36. Evershed, note 1, supra, p. 92.

37. Coid, J. (1991). Psychiatric profiles of difficult/disruptive prisoners. In K. Bottomley & W. Hay (Eds.), *Special units for difficult prisoners* (pp. 44–71). Hull, England: Center of Criminology and Criminal Justice, p. 50.

38. Coid, note 37, supra, pp. 50–51.

39. Coid, note 37, supra, p. 70.

40. Appelbaum, K. L., Hickey, J. M., & Packer, I. (2001). The role of correctional officers in multidisciplinary mental health care in prisons. *Psychiatric Services, 52,* 1343–1347, p. 1344.

41. Appelbaum et al., note 40, supra, p. 1345.

42. Appelbaum et al., note 40, supra, p. 1346.

43. Appelbaum et al., note 40, supra, p. 1347.

44. Yazar, R. (2001, April). The Violence Prevention Program: Intensive correctional treatment. *Corrections Today, 63,* 102–107.

45. Vorrath and Brendtro, chapter 13, note 4, pp. 40–41. The material cited here and note 19 above also appear in Vorrath, H. H., & Brendtro, L. K. (1995). *Positive peer culture* (2nd ed.). New York: Aldine de Gruyter, pp. 17, 32–33.

46. Hilton, N. Z., and Simmons, J. L. (2001). The influence of actuarial risk assessment in clinical judgments and tribunal decisions about mentally disordered offenders in maximum security. *Law and Human Behavior, 25,* 403–408, p. 406.

47. Hilton and Simmons, note 46, supra, p. 403, emphasis added.

48. Boyle, J. (1977). *A sense of freedom.* London: Pan Canongate, p. 237.

49. Boyle, note 48, supra, p. 240.

50. We have suggested elsewhere that the type of research that could directly contribute to reducing prison violence would be a strategy in which "hot spots" and low-violence prison subenvironments are studied with the concerned assistance of staff and inmates who live or work in such settings. See Toch, H. (1978). Social climate and prison violence. *Federal Probation, 42,* 21–25.

51. Manicas, P. T., & Secord, P. F. (1983). Implications for psychology of the new philosophy of science. *American Psychologist, 38,* 399–413.
52. Lewin, K. (1946). Action research and minority problems. In K. Lewin (1948). *Resolving social conflicts: Selected papers in group dynamics.* New York: Harper & Row.
53. Reason, P., & Rowan, J. (Eds.). (1981). *Human inquiry: A sourcebook of new paradigm research.* New York: Wiley.
54. Who does the screening of clients into a program of this kind is strategically and conceptually critical. Frontline staff (custodial officers or teachers) make ideal nominators of candidates because such staff are in the best position to observe behavior and to identify maladapters who have problems that could be addressed. Individuals allotted the responsibility of dispensing disciplinary sanctions are the best sources of referrals because they are in the position of discriminating individuals for whom sanctions are or are not inappropriate. It is also critical that such staff consider the behavior self-management option as supplementary to existing behavior management options and as a tool that they themselves (as opposed to some bureaucratic entity) can invoke. By the same token, the staff members of any program must have flexibility in selecting their candidates from a pool of nominees, so that they can assess the risks to be taken and the appropriateness of their modality to the behavior pattern of their clients. (Risk taking must be especially minimized during the first phases of the program, before its culture is established, but at later junctures risk taking must be rewarded, or staff would tend to "play it safe.")
55. Early experiments using behavior modification for dealing with disciplinary problems invited condemnation by insisting that involuntary assignment of clients was not only appropriate but necessary. (See note 14, supra.)
56. The same sort of sequence has been envisaged in the program design (not implemented) of special handling units established to deal with recalcitrant inmates in Canada. The presumption in the design was that each inmate "would examine his problems with his classification officer, his case manager and possibly with other inmates as identified by the case management team." Based on such problem reviews, the inmate would evolve an individual program plan to "evaluate his own progress whilst staff measure his development." Inmates would deal with their problems "through dyads, group settings and individual counseling sessions." They would belong to seven-member groups and participate in activities "to provide opportunities . . . to demonstrate meaningful behavioral change." Provision was made for "regular reviews, carried out every thirty days." See McReynolds, K., & Vantour, J. (1983). Inmates in special handling units. In M. Jackson (Ed.), *Prisoners of isolation: Solitary confinement in Canada.* Toronto, Ontario, Canada: University of Toronto Press, pp. 152–153.
57. Bandura, chapter 14, note 10, p. 520.

58. It goes without saying that the staff cadre must internalize the program's design and insist on having the required facilities and support. Jackson (note 56, supra) illustrates this fact by describing the operation of special handling units, which degenerated into segregation settings because the content of programs was never instituted.

59. Connell, C., & Mitgang, L. (1987, October 26). Special education has its own problems. *Albany Times Union.*

60. McCarthy, M. (1985). Mentally ill and mentally retarded offenders in corrections: A report of a national survey. In *Source Book on the Mentally Disordered Offender.* Washington, DC: National Institute of Corrections. A number of reviews have noted the unreliability of epidemiological surveys in prisons. Lovell and Jemelka (1998, p. 55), for example, point out that "estimates of the number or percentage of prisoners who are mentally ill have varied widely, depending on how 'mental illness' is defined and the methods used to assess its presence" (Lovell, D. R., & Jemelka, R. [1998]. Coping with mental illness in prison. *Family and Community Health, 21*(3), 54–66). Prevalence estimates of mental illness among detained juveniles sometimes approach 100%. One reason is the fact that the diagnostic lexicon contains labels singularly applicable to juveniles who engage in misbehavior. The category of disruptive behavior disorders is particularly problematic. A diagnosis of conduct disorder can be arrived at using criteria (aggression, destruction of property, theft, and violation of rules) that double as definitions of delinquency; the criteria can also qualify as reasons for institutional placement. And if juveniles then prove troublesome in the institutions in which they are placed (or even in school or at home), they qualify for the diagnosis of oppositional conduct disorder (see chapter 9), which subsumes age-related autonomy reactions and covers garden-variety manifestations of social ineptness. Combinations of conduct disorders were not anticipated in the *Diagnostic and Statistical Manual of Mental Disorders* (*DSM*), but sufficiently off-putting juveniles tend to earn multiple labels.

The largest-scale epidemiological study of youthful residents of detention systems sampled 1829 juveniles in the city of Chicago (Teplin, L. A. [2000, November]. *Psychiatric disorders among juvenile detainees: Patterns of co-morbidity and their implications for services.* Paper presented at the meeting of the American Society of Criminology, San Francisco).

The situation we encounter with surveys of juvenile institutionalized offenders holds to a somewhat lesser degree with adults. A diagnosis of antisocial personality disorder becomes the equivalent of conduct disorder, but where the antisocial personality disorder diagnosis is applied, it is used paradoxically as a means to reduce rather than enhance the availability of treatment.

Index

Absolute time model, 43–45, 47
Abuse, sexual or physical, 384–385
Adaptation, 29n., 345–347
Administrative responses, 112–118
Admission (to prison), 59–60
Adolescents, 201
"Advertising toughness," 173–175
    definition of, 130
    and self-esteem diagnosis, 200n.
    statistics regarding, 292
    taxonomy example of, 136–137
Age (age factors), 53–55
    and adjustment, 335n.
    and career typology, 69–71, 73–75
    and criminal behavior, 360–361n.
    and detachment through transfers, 311–313
    and disciplinary rates, 77n.
    and hospitalized inmates, 96n.
    and infraction rates, 57–61, 63
    and long-term inmates, 79n.
    and maturation, 332, 340–341
    and mental illness, 429n.
    of outpatients, 50n.
    and pathologies, 81–83
    and timing of hospitalizations, 93
    and transfer rates, 114–115
    and types of infractions, 64
Aggression. *See also* Violence
    of female prisoners, 384
    frustration leading to. *See* "Frustration to aggression"
    instrumental, 169n.
    male vs. female, 360
    paranoid. *See* Paranoid aggression
    predatory. *See* Predatory aggression

    stress leading to. *See* "Stress to aggression"
Aggressives, unsocialized, 145–146
Alcoholics, 341
Allport, Gordon, 340
Anderson, B., 372
Anticipatory release phenomenon, 91, 345
Anticipatory resocialization, 62, 78–79n.
Antisocial personality disturbance, 27–28n.
Anxiety, 132, 133, 170n.
Anxious moods, 85, 86
Arizona, 392–393
Aspersions, countering. *See* "Countering aspersions"
Assault arrests
    and career typology, 69, 70
    and disciplinary careers, 73–76
    and infraction rates, 54
    and pathologies, 81, 82
Assaultive behavior, 100, 117, 297n.
Assertive responses, 289n.
Asylum, 320–323
Attachment, 308–311
Authoritarian settings, 202
Authority figures, 131, 202–205
Authority(-ies)
    and autonomy issues, 201
    defiance of, 131, 210–215, 293
    and tinged rebelliousness, 271–275
Autonomy, pursuit of. *See* Pursuit of autonomy
Autonomy—dependence issues, 201–202
Avoidance, stress. *See* Stress avoidance

431

About the Authors

Hans Toch is distinguished professor at the University at Albany of the State University of New York, where he is affiliated with the School of Criminal Justice. He obtained his PhD in social psychology at Princeton University, has taught at Michigan State University and at Harvard University and, in 1996, served as Walker–Ames Professor at the University of Washington, Seattle. Dr. Toch is a Fellow of both the American Psychological Association (APA) and the American Society of Criminology. In 1996, he acted as president of the American Association of Correctional Psychology. He is a recipient of the Hadley Cantril Memorial Award and, in 2001, of the August Vollmer Award of the American Society of Criminology for outstanding contributions to applied criminology.

Dr. Toch's research interests range from mental health problems and the psychology of violence to issues of organizational reform and planned change. He has conducted research on prison systems in Michigan, California, New York State, and Scotland and in several police departments across the United States.

Dr. Toch's books include *Police as Problem Solvers* (with J. Douglas Grant, 1991), *Violent Men* (APA, 1992), *Living in Prison* (APA, 1992), *Mosaic of Despair* (APA, 1992), *The Disturbed Violent Offender* (with Kenneth Adams, APA, 1994), *Police Violence* (with William Geller, 1996), *Corrections: A Humanistic Approach* (1997), and *Crime and Punishment* (with Robert Johnson, 2000).

Kenneth Adams is an associate professor in the school of Public and Environmental Affairs at Indiana University–Purdue University–Indianapolis. He received his PhD in criminal justice from the State University of New York at Albany. He is coauthor, with Hans Toch, of *The Disturbed Violent Offender* (1994) and coeditor of *Incarcerating Criminals* (1998).

Within the context of corrections, he has concentrated his research on special populations and on the prison disciplinary process. More generally, his research has involved program evaluations in a variety of areas, including prison education, juvenile curfews, gun control, and citizen complaints against police.